THE MASTER-KEY TO RICHES ...

Opens the door to sound health.

Opens the door to love and romance.

Opens the door to friendship.

Reveals the method by which every adversity, every failure, every disappointment, every error of judgment, and every past defeat may be transmuted into riches of priceless value.

Lifts humble men to positions of power, fame and fortune.

Turns back the hands of the clock and renews the spirit of youth.

Provides the method by which you may take full and complete possession of your own mind, thus giving you unchallengeable control over the emotions of the heart and the power of thinking.

These are only a few of the exciting rewards offered to you here in THE MASTER-KEY TO RICHES.

THE MASTER-KEY TO RICHES

THE
MASTER-KEY
TO RICHES

by Napoleon Hill

FAWCETT CREST • NEW YORK

A Fawcett Crest Book
Published by Ballantine Books

Revised Edition Copyright © 1965 by Napoleon Hill
Copyright © 1965 by Annie Lou Hill

ISBN 0-449-21350-1

Napoleon Hill will be happy to send readers of this book a personal autographed bookplate made out to the reader's name. Send a stamped, self-addressed envelope to Napoleon Hill, P.O. Drawer 917, Charleston, South Carolina 29402.

Manufactured in the United States of America

First Fawcett Crest Edition: November 1965
First Ballantine Books Edition: July 1982
Thirty-sixth Printing: February 1991

Contents

THE
MASTER-KEY
TO RICHES

"I give this account to the American people and ought not of my own political instincts of the presidency . . ."

"I give and bequeath to the American people the greater part of my vast fortune, which consists of the philosophy of individual achievement, through which all of my riches were accumulated . . ."

Thus began the last will and testament of Andrew Carnegie. It is the prologue of a story which may well mark the most important turning-point in the lives of all who read it.

The story began in the late Fall of 1908, when Andrew Carnegie called me in, paid me the great compliment of respect for my judgment and integrity, and entrusted to me what he said was "the greater portion" of his vast fortune, with the understanding that the legacy was to be presented to the American people.

This story has been written *to notify you of your right to share in this huge estate*, and to inform you of the conditions under which you may richly share it.

These conditions are in no way formidable or limited to the very few. The conditions are well within the reach of any adult of average intelligence. There are no tricks or false hopes, either in connection with the conditions or in this promise.

So that you may know whether or not this offers anything you need or desire, let me tell you specifically what is promised:

¶ A clear description of the formula by which you may have the full benefit of the Master-Key to Riches—a key that should unlock the doors to the solution of all your problems, that will help you to convert your past failures into priceless assets, and lead you to attainment of the Twelve Great Riches, including economic security.

¶ An inventory of the riches left by Andrew Carnegie for distribution to those who are qualified to receive them, together with detailed instructions through which you may acquire and use your full share.

¶ A description of the means by which you may have the full benefit of the education, experience, and technical skills of those whose cooperation you may need for the attainment of your major purposes in life, thus providing a practical means by which you may bridge the disadvantages of an inadequate education and attain the highest goals of life as successfully as may those who are blessed with a formal education.

¶ The privilege of using the philosophy of success which was organized from the life experiences, by trial and error, of hundreds of eminent men.

¶ A definite plan by which anyone who works for wages or a salary may promote himself into a higher income *with the full cooperation and consent of his employer.*

¶ A definite plan through which anyone who works for others may get into a business or profession of his own, with more than average chances of success.

¶ A definite plan through which any businessman may convert his customers into permanent patrons, and through their hearty cooperation, add new customers who will likewise become permanent.

¶ A definite plan by which any salesman of useful merchandise, or of services such as life insurance, may convert his buyers into willing workers who will aid him in finding new clients.

¶ A definite plan through which any employer may make personal friends of his employees, under circumstances which will enable him to make his business more profitable for both himself and his employees.

You have here a clear statement of our promises, and the first condition under which you may benefit by these is that you read this book *twice,* line by line, and *think as you read!*

Let it be known at the outset that when we speak of "riches," we have in mind *all riches*—not merely those represented by bank balances and material things.

We have in mind the riches of liberty and freedom, of which we have more than any other nation. We have in mind the riches of human relationships through which every

American citizen may exercise to the fullest the privilege of personal initiative in whatever direction he chooses. Thus, when we speak of "riches" we have reference to the abundant life which is everywhere available to the people of the United States, and obtainable with a minimum amount of effort.

Meanwhile, let it be understood that we shall offer no suggestions to anyone as to the nature of the riches for which he should aim, nor the amount he should undertake to acquire.

Fortunately, the American life offers an abundance of all forms of riches, sufficient in both quality and quantity to satisfy all reasonable human desires. We sincerely hope that every reader will aim for his share, not only of the things that money can buy, *but of the things money cannot buy!*

We shall not undertake to tell any man how to live his life, but we know, from having observed both the rich and poor of America, that material riches are no guarantee of happiness.

We have never yet found a truly happy person who was not engaged in some form of service by which others were benefited. And we do know many who are wealthy in material things, but have not found happiness.

We mention these observations not to preach, but to quicken those who, because of the great abundance of material riches in America, take them for granted, and who have lost sight of the priceless things of life that are to be acquired only through the intangible riches we have mentioned.

napoleon hill

Chapter One

THE TWELVE RICHES OF LIFE

You have, I believe, that human urge for the better things in life which is the common desire of all people. You desire economic security which money alone can provide. You may desire an outlet for your talents in order that you may have the joy of creating your own riches.

Some seek the easy way to riches, hoping to find it without giving anything in return. That too is a common desire. But it is a desire I shall hope to modify for your benefit, as from experience I have learned that there is no such thing as something for nothing.

There is but one sure way to riches, and that may be attained only by those who have the Master-Key to Riches. This Master-Key is a marvelous device which those who possess it may use to unlock doors to the solutions of their problems.

It opens the door to sound health.

It opens the door to love and romance.

It opens the door to friendship, by revealing the traits of personality and character which make enduring friends.

It reveals the method by which every adversity, every failure, every disappointment, every error of judgment, and every past defeat may be transmuted into riches of priceless value.

It kindles anew the dead hopes of all who possess it, and it reveals the formula by which one may "tune in" and draw upon the great reservoir of Infinite Intelligence.

It lifts humble men to positions of power, fame and fortune.

It turns back the hands of the clock and renews the spirit of youth for those who have grown old too soon.

It provides the method by which you may take full and

complete possession of your own mind, thus giving you unchallengeable control over the emotions of the heart and the power of thinking.

It bridges the deficiencies of those who have inadequate formal schooling, and puts them substantially on the same plane of opportunity that is enjoyed by those who have a better education.

And lastly, it opens the doors, one by one, to the Twelve Great Riches of Life which I shall presently describe.

No man may hear that for which he has not the preparation for hearing. The preparation consists of many things, among them sincerity of purpose, humility of heart, a full recognition of the truth that no man knows everything. I shall speak to you of facts and describe to you many principles, some of which you may never have heard, for they are known only to those who have prepared themselves to accept the Master-Key.

Your Two Selves

Before I describe the Twelve Great Riches, let me reveal to you some of the riches you already possess—riches of which you may not be conscious.

First, I would have you recognize that you are a plural personality, although you may regard yourself as a single personality. You and every other person consist of at least two distinct personalities, and many of you possess more.

There is that self which you recognize when you look into a mirror. That is your physical self. But it is only the house in which your other selves live. In that house there are at least two individuals who are eternally in conflict with each other.

One is a *negative* sort of person who thinks and moves and lives in an atmosphere of doubt and fear and poverty and ill health. This negative self expects failure and is seldom disappointed. It dwells on sorry circumstances of life which you want to reject but seem forced to accept—poverty, greed, superstition, fear, doubt, worry, and physical sickness.

Your "other self" is a *positive* sort of person who thinks in dynamic, affirmative terms of wealth, sound health, love and friendship, personal achievement, creative vision, service to others, and who guides you unerringly to the attainment of these blessings. It is this self alone which is capable of recognizing and appropriating the Twelve Great Riches. It is the only self which is capable of receiving the Master-Key to Riches.

You have many other priceless assets of which you may not be aware, hidden riches you have neither recognized nor used. Among these is what we might call your "vibration center," a sort of radio broadcasting and receiving set of exquisite sensitivity, attuned to your fellow men and the universe around you. This powerful unit projects your thoughts and feelings and receives unending swarms of messages of great importance to your success in living. It is a tireless two-way communication system of infinite capacity.

Your radio station operates automatically and continuously, when you are asleep just as when you are awake. And it is under the control at all times of one or the other of your two major personalities—the negative personality or the positive personality.

When your negative personality is in control, your sensitive receivers register only the negative messages of countless negative personalities. Quite naturally, this leads to "what's the use?" and "I haven't got a chance" thinking; perhaps not formulated in just those words, but discouraging, if not deadly, to faith in yourself and the use of your energies to achieve what you desire. Negative messages received when your negative personality is in control of your receiving station, if accepted and used as a guide, invariably lead to circumstances of life that are the very opposite of what you would choose.

But when your positive personality is in control, it directs to your "action center" only those stimulating, high-energy, optimistic, "I can do it" messages which you can translate into physical equivalents of prosperity, sound health, love, hope, faith, peace of mind and happiness—the values of life for which you and all other normal persons are searching.

The Greatest Gift

I wish to give you the Master-Key by which you may attain these and many other riches. Among other things, the Key places every individual radio station under the control of one's "other self," your positive personality.

I shall reveal to you the means by which you may share the blessings of the Master-Key, but the responsibility of sharing must become your own. Every close observer must have recognized that all individual successes which endure *have had their beginning through the beneficent influence of some other individual,* through some form of sharing.

I wish to share with you the knowledge by which you may acquire riches—*all riches*—through the expression of *your own personal initiative!*

That is the greatest of all gifts!

And it is the only kind of gift that anyone who is blessed with the advantages of a great nation like ours should expect. For here we have every form of potential riches available to mankind. We have them in great abundance.

I assume that you too wish to become rich.

I sought the path to riches the hard way before I learned that there is a short and dependable path I could have followed had I been guided as I hope to guide you.

First, let us be prepared to recognize riches when they come within our reach. Some believe that riches consist in money alone! But enduring riches, in the broader sense, consist of many other values than those of material things, and I may add that without these other intangible values the possession of money will not bring the happiness which some believe it will provide.

When I speak of "riches" I have in mind the greater riches whose possessors have made life pay off on their own terms—the terms of full and complete happiness. I call these the Twelve Riches of Life. And I sincerely wish to share them with all who are prepared to receive them.

1. A Positive Mental Attitude:

All riches, of whatever nature, begin as a state of mind; and let us remember that a state of mind is the one and only thing over which any person has complete, unchallenged right of control.

It is highly significant that the Creator provided man with control over nothing except the power to shape his own thoughts and the privilege of fitting them to any pattern of his choice.

Mental attitude is important because it converts the brain into the equivalent of an electro-magnet which attracts the counterpart of one's dominating thoughts, aims and purposes. It also attracts the counterpart of one's fears, worries and doubts.

A *positive mental attitude* (PMA) is the starting point of all riches, whether they be riches of a material nature or intangible riches.

It attracts the riches of true friendship, and the riches one finds in the hope of future achievement.

It provides the riches one may find in Nature's handiwork, as it exists in the moonlit nights, in the stars that float in the heavens, in the beautiful landscapes and in distant horizons.

And the riches to be found in the labor of one's choice, where expression may be given to the highest plane of man's soul.

And the riches of harmony in home relationships, where all members of the family work together in a spirit of friendly cooperation.

And the riches of sound physical health, which is the treasure of those who have learned to balance work with play, worship with love, and who have learned the wisdom of eating to live rather than of living to eat.

And the riches of freedom from fear.

And the riches of enthusiasm, both active and passive.

And the riches of song and laughter, both of which indicate states of mind.

And the riches of self-discipline, through which one may have the joy of knowing that the mind can and will serve any desired end if one will take possession and command it through definiteness of purpose.

And the riches of play, through which one may lay aside all of the burdens of life and become as a little child again.

And the riches of discovery of one's "other self"—that self which knows no such reality as permanent failure.

And the riches of faith in Infinite Intelligence, of which every individual mind is a minute projection.

And the riches of meditation, the connecting link by which anyone may draw upon the great universal supply of Infinite Intelligence at will.

Yes, these and all other riches begin with a positive mental attitude. Therefore, it is but little cause for wonder that a positive mental attitude takes the first place in the list of the Twelve Riches.

2. Sound Physical Health:

Sound health begins with a "health consciousness" produced by a mind which thinks in terms of health and not in terms of illness, plus temperance of habits in eating and properly balanced physical activities.

3. Harmony In Human Relationships:

Harmony with others begins with one's self, for it is true, as Shakespeare said, there are benefits available to those who comply with his admonition, "To thine own self be true, and it must follow, as the night the day, thou canst not then be false to any man."

4. Freedom From Fear:

No man who fears anything is a free man! Fear is a harbinger of evil, and wherever it appears one may find a cause which must be eliminated before he may become rich in the fuller sense.

The seven basic fears which appear most often in the minds of men are:

The fear of *poverty*.
The fear of *criticism*.
The fear of *ill health*.
The fear of *loss of love*.
The fear of the *loss of liberty*.
The fear of *old age*.
The fear of *death*.

5. The Hope of Achievement:

The greatest of all forms of happiness comes as the result of hope of achievement of some yet unattained desire. Poor beyond description is the person who cannot look to the future with hope that he will become the person he would like to be, or with the belief that he will attain the objective he has failed to reach in the past.

6. The Capacity For Faith:

Faith is the connecting link between the conscious mind of man and the great universal reservoir of Infinite Intelligence. It is the fertile soil of the garden of the human mind wherein may be produced all of the riches of life. It is the "eternal elixir" which gives creative power and action to the impulses of thought.

Faith is the basis of all so-called miracles, and of many mysteries which cannot be explained by logic or science.

Faith is the spiritual "chemical" which, when it is mixed with prayer, gives one direct and immediate connection with Infinite Intelligence.

Faith is the power which transmutes the ordinary energies of thought into their spiritual equivalent. And it is the only power through which the Cosmic Force of Infinite Intelligence may be appropriated to the uses of man.

7. Willingness to Share One's Blessings:

He who has not learned the blessed art of sharing has not learned the true path of happiness, for happiness comes only by sharing. And let it be forever remembered that all riches may be embellished and multiplied by the simple process of sharing them where they may serve others. And let it be also remembered that the space one occupies in the hearts of his fellowmen is determined precisely by the service he renders through some form of sharing his blessings.

Riches which are not shared, whether they be material riches or the intangibles, wither and die like the rose on a severed stem, for it is one of Nature's first laws that inaction and disuse lead to decay and death, and this law applies to the material possessions of men just as it applies to the living cells of every physical body.

8. A Labor Of Love:

There can be no richer man than he who has found a labor of love and who is busily engaged in performing it, for labor is the highest form of human expression of desire. Labor is the liaison between the demand and the supply of all human needs, the forerunner of all human progress, the medium by which the imagination of man is given the wings of action. And all labor of love is sanctified because it brings the joy of self-expression to him who performs it.

9. An Open Mind On All Subjects:

Tolerance, which is among the higher attributes of culture, is expressed only by the person who holds an open mind on all subjects at all times. And it is only the man with an open mind who becomes truly educated and who is thus prepared to avail himself of the greater riches of life.

10. Self-discipline:

The man who is not the master of himself may never become the master of anything. He who is the master of self may become the master of his own earthly destiny, the "master of his fate, the captain of his soul." And the highest form of self-discipline consists in the expression of humility of the heart when one has attained great riches or has been overtaken by that which is commonly called "success."

11. The Capacity To Understand People:

The man who is rich in the understanding of people always recognizes that all people are fundamentally alike, in that they have evolved from the same stem; that all human activities are inspired by one or more of the nine basic motives of life, viz:

The emotion of *love*
The emotion of *sex*
The desire for *material gain*
The desire for *self-preservation*
The desire for *freedom of body and mind*
The desire for *self-expression*
The desire for perpetuation of *life after death*
The emotion of *anger*
The emotion of *fear*

And the man who would understand others must first understand himself.

The capacity to understand others eliminates many of the common causes of friction among men. It is the foundation of all friendship. It is the basis of all harmony and cooperation among men. It is the fundamental of major importance in all leadership which calls for friendly cooperation. And some believe that it is an approach of major importance to the understanding of the Creator of all things.

12. Economic Security:

The last, though not least in importance, is the tangible portion of the "Twelve Riches."

Economic security is not attained by the possession of money alone. It is attained by the service one renders, for useful service may be converted into all forms of human needs, with or without the use of money.

A millionaire businessman has economic security, not because he controls a vast fortune of money, but for the better reason that he provides profitable employment for men and women, and through them, goods or services of great value to large numbers of people. The service he renders has attracted the money he controls, and it is in this manner that all enduring economic security must be attained.

Presently I shall acquaint you with the principles by which money and all other forms of riches may be obtained, but first you must be prepared to make application of these principles. Your mind must be conditioned for the acceptance of riches just as the soil of the earth must be prepared for the planting of seeds.

When one is ready for a thing it is sure to appear!

This does not mean that the things one may need will appear without a cause, for there is a vast difference between one's *"needs"* and one's *readiness* to receive. To miss this distinction is to miss the major benefits which I shall endeavor to convey.

So be patient and let me lead you into *readiness* to receive the riches which you desire. I shall have to lead *my way!*

My way will seem strange to you at first, but you should not become discouraged on this account, for all new ideas seem strange. If you doubt that my way is practical, take courage from the fact that it has brought me riches in abundance.

Human progress always has been slow because people are reluctant to accept new ideas.

When Samuel Morse announced his system for communication by telegraph the world scoffed at him. His system was unorthodox. It was new, therefore it was subject to suspicion and doubt.

And the world scoffed at Marconi when he announced the perfection of an improvement over Morse's system; a system of communication by wireless.

Thomas A. Edison came in for ridicule when he announced his perfection of the incandescent electric light bulb, and the first auto-maker met with the same experience when he offered the world a self-propelled vehicle to take the place of the horse and buggy.

When Wilbur and Orville Wright announced the flight of a practical flying machine the world was so little impressed that newspaper men refused to witness a demonstration of the machine.

Then came the discovery of the modern radio, one of the "miracles" of human ingenuity which was destined to make the whole world akin. The "unprepared" minds accepted it as a toy to amuse children but nothing more.

I mention these facts as a reminder to you, who are seeking riches by a new way, that you be not discouraged because of the newness of the way. Follow through with me, appropriate my philosophy and be assured that it will work for you as it has worked for me.

By serving as your guide to riches I shall receive my compensation for my efforts in exact proportion to the benefits you receive. The eternal law of compensation insures this. My compensation may not come directly from you who appropriate my philosophy, but come it will in one form or another, for it is a part of the great Cosmic Plan that no useful service shall be rendered by anyone without a just compensation. "Do the thing," said Emerson, "and you shall have the power."

Aside from the consideration of what I shall receive for my endeavor to serve you, there is the question of an obligation which I owe the world in return for the blessings it has bestowed upon me. I did not acquire my riches without the aid of many others. I have observed that all who acquire enduring riches have ascended the ladder of opulence with two outstretched hands; one extended upward to receive the help of others who have reached the peak, and the other extended downward to aid those who are still climbing.

And here let me admonish you who are on the path to

riches that you too must proceed with outstretched hands, to give and to receive aid, for it is a well known fact that no man may attain enduring success or acquire enduring riches without aiding others who are seeking these desirable ends. To *get* one must first *give!*

I have brought this message in order that I may *give!*

And now that we know what are the real riches of life I shall reveal to you the next step which you must take in the process of "conditioning" your mind to receive riches.

I have acknowledged that my riches came through the aid of others.

Some of these have been men well known to all who will hear my story. The men who have served as leaders in preparing the way for the rest of us, under that which we call *"The American way of life."*

Some have been strangers whose names you will not recognize.

Among these *strangers* are eight of my friends who have done most for me in preparing my mind for the acceptance of riches. I call them the Eight Princes. They serve me when I am awake and they serve me while I sleep.

Although I have never met the Princes face to face, as I have met the others who have aided me, they have stood watch over my riches; they have protected me against fear and envy and greed and doubt and indecision and procrastination. They have inspired me to move on my own personal initiative, have kept my imagination active, and have given me definiteness of purpose and the faith to insure its fulfillment.

They have been the real "conditioners" of my mind, the builders of my *positive mental attitude!*

And now may I commend them to you so that they may render you a similar service?

Chapter Two

THE EIGHT PRINCES

You may call the Princes by another name if you choose. Mentors, perhaps. Or Principles. Or Counselors. Or Guardians of Good Spirit.

By whatever name, the Princes serve me through a technique that is simple and adaptable.

Every night, as the last order of the day's activities, the Princes and I have a round-table session. The major purpose is to permit me to express, and thus reinforce, my gratitude for the service they have rendered me during the day.

The conference proceeds precisely as if the Princes existed in the flesh. It is a time for meditation, review, and thanksgiving, with contact made through the power of thought.

Here you may receive your first test of your capacity to "condition" your mind for the acceptance of riches. When the shock comes, just remember what happened when Morse, and Marconi, and Edison, and the Wright Brothers first announced their perfection of new and better ways of rendering service. It will help you to stand up under the shock.

And now let us go into a session with the Princes:

GRATITUDE!

"Today has been beautiful.

"It has provided me with health of body and mind.

"It has given me food and clothing.

"It has brought me another day of opportunity to be of service to others.

"It has given me peace of mind and freedom from all fear.

"For these blessings I am grateful to you, my Princes of

27

Guidance. I am grateful to all of you collectively for having unraveled the tangled skein of my past life, thereby freeing my mind, my body and my soul from all causes and effects of both fear and strife.

"*Prince of Material Prosperity,* I am grateful to you for having kept my mind attuned to the consciousness of opulence and plenty, and free from the fear of poverty and want.

"*Prince of Sound Physical Health,* I am grateful to you for having attuned my mind to the consciousness of sound health, thereby providing the means by which every cell of my body and every physical organ is being adequately supplied with an inflow of cosmic energy sufficient unto its needs, and providing a direct contact with Infinite Intelligence which is sufficient for the distribution and application of this energy where it is required.

"*Prince of Peace of Mind,* I am grateful to you for having kept my mind free from all inhibitions and self-imposed limitations, thereby providing my body and my mind with complete rest.

"*Prince of Hope,* I am grateful to you for the fulfillment of today's desires, and for your promise of fulfillment of tomorrow's aims.

"*Prince of Faith,* I am grateful to you for the guidance which you have given me; for your having inspired me to do that which has been helpful to me, and for turning me back from doing that which had it been done would have proven harmful to me. You have given power to my thoughts, momentum to my deeds, and the wisdom which has enabled me to understand the laws of Nature, and the judgment to enable me to adapt myself to them in a spirit of harmony.

"*Prince of Love,* I am grateful to you for having inspired me to share my riches with all whom I have contacted this day; for having shown me that only that which I give away can I retain as my own. And I am grateful too for the consciousness of love with which you have endowed me, for it has made life sweet and all my relationships with others pleasant.

"*Prince of Romance,* I am grateful to you for having inspired me with the spirit of youth despite the passing of the years.

"*Prince of Overall Wisdom,* my eternal gratitude to you for having transmuted into an enduring asset of priceless value all of my past failures, defeats, errors of judgment and of deed, all fears, mistakes, disappointments and adversities of every nature; the asset consisting of my willingness and ability to inspire others to take possession of their own minds and to use their mind-power for the attainment of the riches of life, thus providing me with the privilege of sharing all of my blessings with those who are ready to receive them, and thereby enriching and multiplying my own blessings by the scope of their benefit to others.

"My gratitude to you also for revealing to me the truth that no human experience need become a liability; that all experiences may be transmuted into useful service; that the power of thought is the only power over which I have complete control; that the power of thought may be translated into happiness at will; that there are no limitations to my power of thought save only those which I set up in my own mind."

My greatest asset consists in my good fortune in having recognized the existence of the Eight Princes, for it is they who conditioned my mind to receive the benefits of the Twelve Riches.

It is the habit of daily communication with the Princes which insures me the endurance of these riches, let the circumstances of life be whatever they may.

The Princes serve as the medium through which I keep my mind fixed upon *the things I desire* and off the things I do not desire!

They serve as a dependable fetish, a rosary of power, through which I may draw at will upon the powers of thought, with "each hour a pearl, each pearl a blessing."

They provide me with continuous immunity against all forms of negative mental attitude; thus they destroy both the seed of negative thought and the germination of that seed in the soil of my mind.

They help me to keep my mind fixed upon my major purpose in life, and to give the fullest expression to the attainment of that purpose.

They keep me at peace with myself, at peace with the world, and in harmony with my own conscience.

They aid me in closing the doors of my mind to all unpleasant thoughts of past failures and defeats. Nay, they aid me in converting all of my past liabilities into assets of priceless value.

The Princes have revealed to me the existence of that "other self" which thinks, moves, plans, desires and acts by the impetus of a power which recognizes no such reality as an impossibility.

And they have proved, times without number, that every adversity carries with it the seed of an equivalent benefit. So, when adversity overtakes me, as it overtakes everyone, I am not awed by it, but I begin immediately to search for that "seed of an equivalent benefit" and to germinate it into a full blown flower of opportunity.

The Princes have given me mastery over my most formidable adversary, myself. They have shown me what is good for my body and soul, and they have led me inevitably to the source and supply of all good.

They have taught me the truth that happiness consists not in the possession of things, but in the privilege of self-expression through the use of material things.

And they have taught me that it is more blessed to render useful service than to accept the service of others.

Observe that I ask for nothing from the Princes, but I devote the entire ceremony to an expression of gratitude for the riches they have already bestowed upon me.

The Princes know of my needs and supply them!

Yes, they supply all of my needs in over-abundance.

The Princes have taught me to think in terms of that which I can *give* and to forget about that which I desire to *get* in return. Thus they have taught me the proper approach to the *impersonal way of life:* that way of life which reveals to one the powers which come from within, and which may be drawn upon at will for the solution of all personal problems and for the attainment of all necessary material things.

They have taught me to be still and to listen from within!

They have given me the *faith* to enable me to override my reason and to accept guidance from within, with full confidence that the small still voice which speaks from within is superior to my own powers of reason.

My Creed of Life was inspired by the Princes.

Let me share it with you, so that you may adopt it as your Creed.

A Happy Man's Creed

I have found happiness by helping others to find it.

I have sound physical health because I live temperately in all things, and eat only the foods which Nature requires for body maintenance.

I am free from fear in all of its forms.

I hate no man, envy no man, but love all mankind.

I am engaged in a labor of love with which I mix play generously. Therefore I never grow tired.

I give thanks daily, not for more riches, but for wisdom with which to recognize, embrace and properly use the great abundance of riches I now have at my command.

I speak no name save only to honor it.

I ask no favors of anyone except the privilege of sharing my riches with all who will receive them.

I am on good terms with my conscience. Therefore it guides me correctly in all that I do.

I have no enemies because I injure no man for any cause, but I benefit all with whom I come into contact by teaching them the way to enduring riches.

I have more material wealth than I need because I am free from greed and covet only the material things I can use while I live.

I own a great estate which is not taxable because it exists mainly in my own mind in intangible riches which cannot be assessed or appropriated except by those who adopt my way of life. I created this vast estate by observing Nature's laws and adapting my habits to conform therewith.

Workings of the Master-Key

Now let us get on with our story by a description of the philosophy one must adopt in order to acquire the Twelve Riches. I have described a method of preparing the mind to receive riches. But this is only the beginning of the story. I have yet to explain how one may take possession of riches and make the fullest use of them.

The story goes back more than half a century, and has its beginning in the life of Andrew Carnegie, a great philanthropist who was a typical product of the American system.

Mr. Carnegie acquired the Twelve Riches, the financial portion of which was so vast that he did not live long enough to enable him to give it away, so he passed much of it on to men who are still engaged in using it for the benefit of mankind.

He was also blessed with the services of the Eight Princes. The Prince of Overall Wisdom served him so well that he was inspired not only to give away all his material riches, but to provide the people with a complete philosophy of life through which they too might acquire riches.

That philosophy consists of seventeen principles which conform in every respect to the pattern of the Constitution of the United States and the American system of free enterprise.

Mr. Carnegie explained his reason for having inspired the organization of a philosophy of individual achievement when he said:

"I acquired my money through the efforts of other people, and I shall give it back to the people as fast as I can find ways to do so *without inspiring the desire for something for nothing*. But the major portion of my riches consists in the knowledge with which I acquired both the tangible and the intangible portions of it. Therefore, it is my wish that this knowledge be organized into a philosophy and made available to every person who seeks an opportunity for self-determination under the American form of economics."

It is the philosophy which you must adopt and apply if you hope to accept the riches I desire to share with you.

Before I describe the principles of this philosophy I wish to give a brief history of what it has already accomplished for other men throughout more than half the world.

It has been translated into four of the leading Indian dialects and has been made available to more than 2,000,000 people of India.

It has been translated into the Portuguese language for the benefit of the people of Brazil, where it has served more than 1,500,000 people.

It has been published in a special edition for distribution

throughout the great British Empire, where it has served more than 2,000,000 people.

It has benefitted one or more people in practically every city, town and village in the United States, numbering in all an estimated 20,000,000 people.

And it may well become the means of bringing about a better spirit of friendly cooperation between all the peoples of the world, since it is founded on no creed or brand, but consists of the fundamentals of all enduring success, and all constructive human achievements in every field of human endeavor.

It *supports all religions* yet it is a part of none!

It is so universal in its nature that it leads men inevitably to success in all occupations.

But more important to you than all of this evidence, the philosophy is so simple that you may start, right where you stand, to put it to work for you.

So, we come now to the description of the secrets of the Master-Key to all riches!

The seventeen principles will serve as a dependable road-map leading directly to the source of all riches, whether they be intangible or material riches. Follow the map and you cannot miss the way, but be prepared to comply with all of the instructions and to assume all of the responsibilities that go with the possession of great riches. And above all, remember that enduring riches must be shared with others; that there is a price one must pay for everything he acquires.

The Master-Key will not be revealed through any one of these seventeen principles, for its secret consists in the combination of all of them.

These principles represent seventeen doors through which one must pass to reach the inner chamber wherein is locked the source of all riches. The Master-Key will unlock the door to that chamber, and it will be in your hands when you have prepared yourself to accept it. Your preparation will consist of the assimilation and the application of the first five of these seventeen principles which I shall now describe at length.

Chapter Three

DEFINITENESS OF PURPOSE

It is impressive to recognize that all of the great leaders, in all walks of life and during all periods of history, have attained their leadership by the application of their abilities behind a *definite major purpose.*

It is no less impressive to observe that those who are classified as failures have no such purpose, but go around and around, like a ship without a rudder, coming back always empty-handed, to their starting point.

Some of these "failures" begin with a definite major purpose but they desert that purpose the moment they are overtaken by temporary defeat or strenuous opposition. They give up and quit, not knowing that there is a philosophy of success which is as dependable and as definite as the rules of mathematics, and never suspecting that temporary defeat is but a testing ground which may prove a blessing in disguise if it is not accepted as final.

It is one of the great tragedies of civilization that ninety-eight out of every one hundred persons go all the way through life without coming within sight of anything that even approximates definiteness of a major purpose!

Mr. Carnegie's first test, which he applied to all of his associate workers who were under consideration for promotion to supervisory positions, was that of determining to what extent they were willing to *go the extra mile.* His second test was to determine whether or not they had their minds fixed upon a definite goal, including the necessary preparation for the attainment of that goal.

"When I asked Mr. Carnegie for my first promotion," said Charles M. Schwab, "he grinned broadly and replied, '*if you have your heart fixed on what you want there is nothing I can do to stop you from getting it.*'"

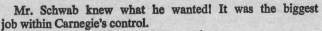

Mr. Schwab knew what he wanted! It was the biggest job within Carnegie's control.

And Mr. Carnegie helped him to get it.

One of the strange facts concerning men who move with definiteness of purpose is the readiness with which the world steps aside that they may pass, even coming to their aid in carrying out their aims.

A Philosophy is Born

The story behind the organization of this philosophy is one with dramatic connotations in connection with the importance that Andrew Carnegie placed upon definiteness of purpose.

He had developed his great steel industry and accumulated a huge fortune in money when he turned his interest to the use and the disposition of his fortune. Having recognized that the better portion of his riches consisted in the knowledge with which he had accumulated material riches and in his understanding of human relationships, his major aim in life became that of inspiring someone to organize a philosophy that would convey this knowledge to all who might desire it.

He was then well along in years and he recognized that the job called for the services of a young man who had the time and the inclination to spend twenty years or more in research into the causes of individual achievement.

When I met Mr. Carnegie by mere chance (having come to interview him for the story of his achievements for a magazine) he had already interviewed more than two hundred and fifty men whom he suspected might have such ability. He was accustomed to probing into the characters of men with keen insight and must have wondered if I might have the qualities for which he had long been searching, for he set up an ingenious plan to make a test.

He began by relating the story of his achievements. Then he began to suggest that the world needed a practical philosophy of individual achievement which would permit the humblest worker to accumulate riches in whatever amount and form he might desire.

For three days and nights he elaborated upon his idea,

describing how one might go about the organization of such a philosophy. When the story was finished Mr. Carnegie was ready to apply his test, to determine whether or not he had found the man who could be depended upon to carry his idea through to completion.

"You now have my idea of a new philosophy," said he, "and I wish to ask you a question in connection with it which I want you to answer by a simple 'yes' or 'no'. The question is this:

"If I give you the opportunity to organize the world's first philosophy of individual achievement, and introduce you to men who can and will collaborate with you in the work of organization, do you wish the opportunity, and will you follow through with it to completion if it is given to you?"

I cleared my throat, stammered for a few seconds, then replied in a brief but fateful sentence.

"Yes," I exclaimed, "I will not only undertake the job, but I will finish it!"

That was definite! It was the one thing Mr. Carnegie was searching for—*definiteness of purpose*.

Many years later I learned that Mr. Carnegie had held a stop-watch in his hand when he asked that question, and had allowed exactly sixty seconds for an answer. If the answer had required more time the opportunity would have been withheld. The answer had actually required twenty-nine seconds.

And the reason for the timing was explained by Mr. Carnegie.

"It has been my experience," said he, "that a man who cannot reach a decision promptly, once he has all of the necessary facts for decision at hand, cannot be depended upon to carry through any decision he may make. I have also discovered that men who reach decisions promptly usually have the capacity to move with definiteness of purpose in other circumstances."

The first hurdle of the test had been covered with flying colors, but there was still another that followed.

"Very well," said Carnegie, "you have one of the two important qualities that will be needed by the man who organizes the philosophy I have described. Now I shall learn whether or not you have the second.

"If I give you the opportunity to organize the philosophy are you willing to devote twenty years of your time to research into the causes of success and failure, without pay, earning your own living as you go along?"

That question was a shock, for I had naturally suspected that I would be subsidized from Mr. Carnegie's huge fortune.

However, I recovered quickly from the shock by asking Mr. Carnegie why he was unwilling to provide the money for so important an assignment.

"It is not unwillingness to supply the money," Mr. Carnegie replied, "but it is my desire to know if you have in you a natural capacity for willingness to *go the extra mile* by rendering service before trying to collect pay for it."

Then he went on to explain that the more successful men in all walks of life were, and had always been, men who followed the habit of rendering more service than that for which they were paid. He also called attention to the fact that subsidies of money, whether they be made to individuals or to groups of individuals, often do more injury than good.

And he reminded me that I had been given an opportunity which had been withheld from more than two hundred and fifty other men, some of whom were much older and more experienced than I, and finished by saying:

"If you make the most of the opportunity I have offered you it is conceivable that you may develop it into riches so fabulous in nature as to dwarf my material wealth by comparison, for that opportunity provides the way for you to penetrate the keenest minds of this nation, to profit by the experiences of our greatest American leaders of industry, and it might well enable you to project your influence for good throughout the civilized world, thereby enriching those who are not yet born."

The opportunity was embraced!

I had received my first lesson on definiteness of purpose and a willingness to *go the extra mile*.

Twenty years later, almost to the day, the philosophy, which Mr. Carnegie had designated as being the better portion of his riches, was completed and presented to the world in an eight volume edition.

"And what of the man who spent twenty years of time without pay?" some ask. "What compensation has been received for this labor?"

A complete answer to this question would be impossible, for the man himself does not know the total value of the benefits received. Moreover, some of these benefits are so flexible in nature that they will continue to aid him the remainder of his life.

But, for the satisfaction of those who measure riches in material values alone, it can be stated that one book, the result of the knowledge gained from the application of the principle of *going the extra mile*, has already yielded an estimated profit of upward of $3,000,000.00. *The actual time spent in writing the book was four months.*

Definiteness of purpose and the habit of *going the extra mile* constitute a force which staggers the imagination of even the most imaginative of people, although these are but two of the seventeen principles of individual achievement.

These two principles have been here associated for but one purpose. That is to indicate how the principles of this philosophy are blended together like the links of a chain, and how this combination of principles leads to the development of stupendous power which cannot be attained by the application singly of any one of them.

The Power of Definite Purpose

We come now to the analysis of the power of definiteness of purpose and psychological principles from which the power is derived.

First premise:
The starting point of all individual achievement is the adoption of a definite purpose and a definite plan for its attainment.

Second premise:
All achievement is the result of a motive or combination of motives, of which there are nine basic motives which govern all voluntary actions. (These motives have been previously described in Chapter One).

Third premise:
Any dominating idea, plan or purpose held in the mind, through repetition of thought, and emotionalized with a burning desire for its realization, is taken over by the subcon-

scious section of the mind and acted upon, and it is thus
carried through to its logical climax by whatever natural
means may be available.

Fourth premise:
Any dominating desire, plan or purpose held in the conscious mind and backed by absolute faith in its realization,
is taken over and acted upon immediately by the subconscious section of the mind, *and there is no known record
of this kind of a desire having ever been without fulfillment.*

Fifth premise:
The power of thought is the only thing over which any
person has complete, unquestionable control—a fact so
astounding that it connotes a close relationship between the
mind of man and the Universal Mind of Infinite Intelligence,
the connecting link between the two being *Faith.*

Sixth premise:
The subconscious portion of the mind is the doorway to
Infinite Intelligence, and it responds to one's demands in
exact proportion to the quality of one's *Faith!* The sub-
conscious mind may be reached through faith and given
instructions as though it were a person or a complete entity
unto itself.

Seventh premise:
A definite purpose, backed by absolute faith, is a form
of wisdom, and wisdom in action produces positive results.

The Major Advantages of Definiteness of Purpose

Definiteness of purpose develops self-reliance, personal
initiative, imagination, enthusiasm, self-discipline and concentration of effort, and all of these are prerequisites for the
attainment of material success.

It induces one to budget his time and to plan all his day-
to-day endeavors so they lead toward the attainment of his
Major Purpose in life.

It makes one more alert in the recognition of opportunities

related to the object of one's *Major Purpose,* and it inspires the necessary courage to act upon those opportunities when they appear.

It inspires the co-operation of other people.

It prepares the way for the full exercise of that state of mind known as *Faith, by making the mind positive* and freeing it from the limitations of fear and doubt and indecision.

It provides one with a *success consciousness,* without which no one may attain enduring success in any calling.

It overcomes the destructive habit of procrastination.

Lastly, it leads directly to the development and the continuous maintenance of the first of the Twelve Riches, a *positive mental attitude.*

These are the major characteristics of *Definiteness of Purpose,* although it has many other qualities and usages, and it is directly related to each of the Twelve Riches because they are attainable only by singleness of purpose.

Compare the principle of definiteness of purpose with the Twelve Riches, one at a time, and observe how essential it is for the attainment of each.

Then take inventory of the men of outstanding achievement which this country has produced, and observe how each of them has emphasized some major purpose as the object of his endeavors.

Thomas A. Edison devoted his efforts entirely to scientific inventions.

Andrew Carnegie specialized in the manufacture and sale of steel.

F. W. Woolworth centered his attention upon the operation of Five and Ten Cent Stores.

Philip D. Armour's specialty was that of meat packing and distribution.

James J. Hill concentrated on the building and maintenance of a great Transcontinental Railway System.

Alexander Graham Bell majored in scientific research in connection with the development of the modern telephone.

Marshall Field operated the world's greatest retail store.

Cyrus H. K. Curtis devoted his entire life to the development and publication of the *Saturday Evening Post.*

Jefferson, Washington, Lincoln, Patrick Henry and Thomas Paine devoted the better portion of their lives and their fortunes to a prolonged fight for the freedom of all people.

Men with singleness of purpose, each and every one!

And the list might be multiplied until it contained the name of every great American leader who has contributed to the establishment of the American way of life as we of today know and benefit by it.

How to Acquire a Definite Major Purpose

The procedure in the development of a Definite Major Purpose is simple, but important, viz:

(a) Write out a complete, clear and definite statement of your *Major Purpose in Life*, sign it and commit it to memory.

Then repeat it orally at least once every day, more often if practicable. Repeat it over and over, thus placing back of your purpose all of your faith in Infinite Intelligence.

(b) Write out a clear, definite plan by which you intend to begin the attainment of the object of your *Definite Major Purpose*. In this plan state the maximum time allowed for the attainment of your purpose, and *describe precisely what you intend to give in return for the realization of your purpose*, remembering that there is no such reality as something for nothing, and that everything has a price which must be paid in advance in one form or another.

(c) Make your plan flexible enough to permit changes at any time you are inspired to do so. Remember that Infinite Intelligence, which operates in every atom of matter and in every living or inanimate thing, may present you with a plan far superior to any you can create. Therefore be ready at all times to recognize and adopt any superior plan that may be presented to your mind.

(d) Keep your *Major Purpose* and your plans for attaining it strictly to yourself except insofar as you will receive additional instructions for carrying out your plan, in the description of the *Master Mind Principle*, which follows.

Do not make the mistake of assuming that because you may not understand these instructions the principles here described are not sound. Follow the instructions to the letter; follow them in good faith, and remember that by so doing you are duplicating the procedure of many of the greatest leaders this nation has ever produced.

The instructions call for no effort that you may not easily put forth.

They make no demands upon time or ability with which the average person may not comply.

And they are completely in harmony with the philosophy of all true religions.

Decide *now* what you desire from life and what you have to give in return. Decide *where* you are going and *how* you are to get there. Then make a start from where you *now* stand. Make the start with whatever means of attaining your goal that may be at hand. And you will discover that to the extent you make use of these, other and better means will reveal themselves to you.

That has been the experience of all men whom the world has recognized as successes. Most of them started with humble beginnings with little more to aid them than a *passionate desire to attain a definite goal.*

There is enduring magic in such a desire!

And lastly, remember:

> "The Moving Finger writes; and, having writ,
> Moves on: nor all thy Piety nor Wit
> Shall lure it back to cancel half a Line,
> Nor all thy Tears wash out a Word of it."

Yesterday has gone forever! Tomorrow will never arrive, but Today is yesterday's Tomorrow within your reach. What are you doing with it?

Presently I shall reveal to you a principle which is the keystone to the arch of all great achievements; the principle which has been responsible for our great American way of life; our system of free enterprise; our riches and our freedom. But first let us make sure that *you know what it is that you desire of life.*

Ideas that Lead to Success Begin as Definiteness of Purpose

It is a well known fact that ideas are the only assets which have no fixed values. It is equally well known that ideas are the beginning of all achievements.

Ideas form the foundation of all fortunes, the starting point of all inventions. They have mastered the air above us and the waters of the oceans around us; they have enabled us to harness and use the invisible energies of the universe.

All ideas begin as the result of Definiteness of Purpose.

The phonograph was nothing but an abstract idea until Edison organized it through definiteness of purpose, and submitted it to the subconscious portion of his brain where it was projected into the great reservoir of Infinite Intelligence, from which a workable plan was flashed back to him. And this workable plan he translated into a machine which worked.

The philosophy of individual achievement began as an idea in the mind of Andrew Carnegie. He backed his idea with definiteness of purpose, and now the philosophy is available for the benefit of millions of people throughout the civilized world.

Moreover, his idea has more than an average chance of becoming one of the great leavening forces of the world, for it is now being used by an ever increasing multitude of people as a means of guiding them through a world of frenzied hysteria.

The great North American continent known as the "New World" was discovered and brought under the influence of civilization as the result of an idea which was born in the mind of an humble sailor and backed by definiteness of purpose. And the time is at hand when that idea, born more than four hundred years ago, may lift our nation to a position where it will become the most enlightened frontier of civilization.

Any idea that is held in the mind, emphasized, feared or reverenced, begins at once to clothe itself in the most convenient and appropriate physical form that is available.

That which men believe, talk about, and fear, whether it be good or bad, has a very definite way of making its appearance in one form or another. Let those who are struggling to free themselves from the limitations of poverty and misery not forget this great truth, for it applies to an individual just as it does to a nation of people.

Self-suggestion, the Connecting Link

Let us now turn our attention to the working principle through which thoughts, ideas, plans, hopes, and purposes which are placed in the conscious mind find their way into the subconscious section of the mind, where they are picked up and carried out to their logical conclusion, through a law of nature which I shall describe later.

To recognize this principle and understand it is to recognize also the reason why Definiteness of Purpose is the beginning of all achievements.

Transfer of thought from the conscious to the subconscious section of the mind may be hastened by the simple process of "stepping up" or stimulating the vibrations of thought through faith, fear, or any other highly intensified emotion, such as enthusiasm, a burning desire based on definiteness of purpose.

Thoughts backed by faith have precedence over all others in the matter of definiteness and speed with which they are handed over to the subconscious section of the mind and are acted upon. The speed with which the power of faith works has given rise to the belief held by many that certain phenomena are the result of "miracles".

Psychologists and scientists recognize no such phenomenon as a miracle, claiming as they do that everything which happens is the result of a definite cause, albeit a cause which cannot be explained. Be that as it may, it is a known fact that the person who is capable of freeing his mind from all self-imposed limitations, through the mental attitude known as faith, generally finds the solution to all of his problems, regardless of their nature.

Psychologists recognize also that Infinite Intelligence, while it is not claimed to be an automatic solver of riddles, nevertheless carries out to a logical conclusion any clearly defined idea, aim, purpose or desire that is submitted to the subconscious section of the mind in a mental attitude of perfect faith.

However, Infinite Intelligence never attempts to modify, change or otherwise alter any thought that is submitted to it, and it has never been known to act upon a mere wish or indefinite idea, thought or purpose. Get this truth well grounded in your mind and you will find yourself in possession of sufficient power to solve your daily problems with much less effort than most people devote to worrying over their problems.

So-called "hunches" often are signals indicating that Infinite Intelligence is endeavoring to reach and influence the conscious section of the mind, but you will observe that they usually come in response to some idea, plan, purpose or desire, or some fear that has been handed over to the subconscious section of the mind.

All "hunches" should be treated civilly and examined carefully, as they often convey, either in whole or in part, information of the utmost value to the individual who receives them. These "hunches" often make their appearance many hours, days or weeks after the thought which inspires them has reached the reservoir of Infinite Intelligence. Meanwhile, the individual often has forgotten the original thought which inspired them.

This is a deep, profound subject about which even the wisest of men know very little. It becomes a self-revealing subject only upon meditation and thought.

Understand the principle of mind operation here described and you will have a dependable clue as to why meditation sometimes brings that which one desires, while at other times it brings that which one does not wish.

This type of mental attitude is attained only by preparation and self-discipline attained through a formula I shall describe later.

It is one of the most profound truths of the world that the affairs of men, whether they are circumstances of mass thought or of individual thought, shape themselves to fit the exact pattern of those thoughts.

Successful men become successful only because they acquire the habit of thinking in terms of success.

Definiteness of purpose can, and it should, so completely occupy the mind *that one has no time or space in the mind for thoughts of failure.*

Another profound truth consists in the fact that the individual who has been defeated and who recognizes himself as a failure may, by reversing the position of the "sails" of his mind, convert the winds of adversity into a power of equal volume which will carry him onward to success, just as,

"One ship sails east, the other west,
    Impelled by the self same blow,
It's the set of the sails and not the gales,
    That bids them where to go."

To some who pride themselves on being what the world calls "cool-headed, practical business men," this analysis of the principle of Definiteness of Purpose may appear to be abstract or impractical.

There is a power greater than the power of conscious thought, and often it is not perceptible to the finite mind of man. Acceptance of this truth is essential for the successful culmination of any definite purpose based upon the desire for great achievements.

The great philosophers of all ages, from Plato and Socrates on down to Emerson and the moderns, and the great statesmen of our times, from George Washington down to Abraham Lincoln, are known to have turned to the "inner self" in times of great emergency.

We offer no apology for our belief that no great and enduring success has ever been achieved, or ever will be achieved, except by those who recognize and use the spiritual powers of the Infinite, as they may be sensed and drawn upon through their "inner selves."

Every circumstance of every man's life is the result of a definite cause, whether it is a circumstance that brings failure or one that brings success.

And most of the circumstances of every man's life are the result of causes over which he has or may have control.

This obvious truth gives importance of the first magnitude to the principle of Definiteness of Purpose. If the circumstances of a man's life are not what he desires, he may change them by changing his mental attitude and forming new and more desirable thought habits.

How Definiteness of Purpose Leads to Success

Of all the great American industrialists who have contributed to the development of our industrial system, none was more spectacular than the late Walter Chrysler.

His story should give hope to every young American who

aspires to the attainment of fame or fortune, and it serves as evidence of the power one may gain by moving with Definiteness of Purpose.

Chrysler began as a mechanic in a railroad shop in Salt Lake City, Utah. From his savings he had accumulated a little more than $4,000, which he intended to use as a fund to set himself up in business.

Looking around diligently he decided that the automobile business was a coming industry, so he determined to go into that field.

His entry into the business was both dramatic and novel.

His first move was one that shocked his friends and astounded his relatives, for it consisted in his investing *all of his savings* in an automobile. When the car arrived in Salt Lake City he gave his friends still another shock by proceeding to take it apart, piece by piece, until the parts were scattered all over the shop.

Then he began to put the parts together again.

He repeated this operation so often that some of his friends thought he had lost his mind. That was because they did not understand his purpose. They saw what he was doing with the automobile, and it looked aimless and without purpose, but what they did not see was the plan which was taking form in Walter Chrysler's mind.

He was making his mind "automobile conscious!" Saturating it with Definiteness of Purpose! He was observing carefully every detail of the car. When he was through with his job of tearing down his automobile and rebuilding it, he knew all of its good points and all of its weak ones.

From that experience he began to design automobiles embodying all of the good points of the car he had bought and omitting all of its weaknesses. He did his job so thoroughly that when the Chrysler automobiles began to reach the market they became the sensation of the entire automobile industry.

His rise to fame and fortune was both rapid and definite, because he knew where he was going before he started, and he prepared himself with painstaking accuracy for the journey.

Observe these men who move with Definiteness of Purpose wherever you find them, and you will be impressed by the ease with which they attract the friendly co-operation of others, break down resistance and get that which they seek.

Analyze Walter Chrysler accurately and observe how definitely he acquired the Twelve Riches of life and made the most of them.

He began by developing the greatest of all the riches, a *positive mental attitude*.

That provided him with a fertile field in which to plant and germinate the seed of his Definite Major Purpose, the building of fine motor cars.

Then, one by one, he acquired other riches: sound physical health, harmony in human relationships, freedom from fear, hope of achievement, the capacity for faith, willingness to share his blessings, a labor of love, an open mind on all subjects, self-discipline, the capacity to understand people, and last, financial security.

One of the strangest facts concerning the success of Walter Chrysler consists in the simplicity with which he attained it. He had no appreciable amount of working capital with which to begin. His education was a limited one. He had no wealthy backers to set him up in business.

But he did have a practical idea and enough personal initiative to begin, right where he stood, to develop it. Everything he needed to translate his Definite Major Purpose into reality seemed almost miraculously placed in his hands as fast as he was ready for it—a circumstance which is not uncommon to men who move with definiteness of purpose.

A $2,000,000 Purpose

Shortly after *Think and Grow Rich* (a one-volume interpretation of a portion of the Andrew Carnegie philosophy of individual achievement) was published, the publisher began to receive telegraphic orders for the book from book stores in and near Des Moines, Iowa.

The orders called for immediate shipment of the book by express. The cause of the sudden demand for the book was a mystery until several weeks later, when the publisher received a letter from Edward P. Chase, a life insurance salesman representing the Sun Life Assurance Company, in which he said:

"I am writing to express my grateful appreciation of your book, *Think and Grow Rich*. I followed its advice to the letter. As a result I received an idea which resulted in the sale of a two million dollar life insurance policy. The largest single sale of its kind ever made in Des Moines."

The key sentence in Mr. Chase's letter is in the second sentence: "I followed its advice to the letter."

He moved on that idea with Definiteness of Purpose, and it helped him to earn more money in one hour than most life insurance men earn in five years of continuous effort.

In one brief sentence Mr. Chase told the entire story of a business transaction which lifted him out of the category of ordinary life insurance salesmen and made him a member of the coveted Million Dollar Round Table.

When he went out to sell a two million dollar life insurance policy he took with him a form of Definiteness of Purpose that was supported by faith. He did not merely read the book, as perhaps several million other men had done, and then lay it aside in an attitude of cynicism or doubt, with the thought that the principles it described might work for others but not for him.

He read it with an open mind, in a spirit of expectancy, recognized the power of the ideas it contained, appropriated those ideas, and moved on them with definiteness of purpose.

Somewhere in the book Mr. Chase's mind established contact with the mind of the author, and that contact quickened his own mind so definitely and intensely that an idea was born. The idea was to sell a life insurance policy larger than any he had ever thought of selling. The sale of that policy became his immediate Definite Major Purpose in life. He moved on that purpose without hesitation or delay, and behold! His objective was attained in less than an hour.

The man who is motivated by definiteness of purpose and moves on that purpose with the spiritual forces of his being, may challenge the man of indecision at the post and pass him at the grandstand. It makes no difference whether he is selling life insurance or digging ditches.

A definite, potent idea, when it is fresh in one's mind, may so change the biochemistry of that mind that it takes on the spiritual qualities which recognize no such reality as failure or defeat.

The major weakness of most men is that they recognize the obstacles they must surmount without recognizing the spiritual power at their command by which those obstacles may be removed at will.

The Road to Mastery

Riches—the real riches of life—increase in exact proportion to the scope and extent of the benefit they bring to those with whom they are shared. I know this to be true for I have grown rich by sharing. I have never benefitted anyone in any manner whatsoever without having received in return, from one source or another, ten times as much benefit as I have contributed to others.

One of the greatest of all truths which have been revealed to me is the fact that the surest way to solve one's personal problems is to find someone with a greater problem and help him to solve it, through some method of application of the habit of Going the Extra Mile.

This is a simple formula, but it has charm and magic, and it never fails to work.

However, you cannot appropriate the formula by the mere acceptance of my testimony as to its soundness. You must adopt it and apply it in your own way. You will then need no testimony as to its soundness.

You will find that many opportunities surround you.

By helping others to find the path *you will find it for yourselves!*

You might begin by organizing a Fellowship Club among your own neighbors or fellow workers, casting yourself for the role of leader and teacher of the group.

Here you will learn another great truth, namely, that the best way to appropriate the principles of the philosophy of individual achievement is by teaching it to others. When a man begins to teach anything he begins also to learn more about that which he is teaching.

You are now a student of this philosophy, but you can become a master of it by teaching it to others. Thus your compensation will be assured you in advance.

If you are a worker in industry here is your big opportunity to find yourself by helping others to adjust their relationships in peace and harmony. For soundness it has never been excelled, for it has been fully verified by the experiences of men in every walk of life.

Labor does not need agitators, but it does need *peace-*

makers. It also needs a sound philosophy for the guidance of its following—a philosophy that benefits both the management and the workers. To this end the principles of this philosophy are perfectly suited.

The labor leader who guides his followers by this philosophy will have the *confidence of his followers and the fullest cooperation of their employers*. Is that not obvious? Is it not sufficient promise of reward to justify the adoption of this philosophy?

A labor organization conducted by the principles of this philosophy would benefit everyone whom it affected. Friction would be supplanted by harmony in human relationships. Agitators and exploiters of labor would be automatically eliminated. The funds of the labor organization could be used for the education of its members and not for political intrigues.

And there would be more profits for distribution as wages—*profits which the management of industry would prefer to give to their workers instead of being forced to use them as a defense fund against the destructive efforts of agitators*.

There is a need for a Fellowship Club in every industry. In the larger industries there is room for many such clubs.

The membership should consist of both the workers and the management, for here is a common meeting ground based upon principles on which everyone could agree. And agreement here would mean agreement at the workbench or the lathe.

I have emphasized this particular field of opportunity because I recognize that the chaos existing in the relationship between the management of industry and the workers constitutes *the number one economic problem of this nation*.

If you have not already adopted a Definite Major Purpose in life here is an opportunity for you to do so. You can start right where you are, by helping to teach this philosophy to those who are in need of it.

The time has come when it is not only beneficial to the individual to help his neighbor to solve his personal problems, *but it is imperative that each of us do so as a means of self-preservation*.

If your neighbor's house were on fire you would volunteer to help him put out the fire, even if you were not on friendly terms with him, for common sense would convince you that this would be the means of saving your own house.

In recommending harmony between the management of industry and the workers, I am not thinking of the interests of management alone, for I recognize that if this harmony does not prevail there soon will be *neither management nor workers as we know them today*.

On the other hand, the man with a sound philosophy of life will find himself surrounded with an abundance of opportunities such as did not exist a decade ago.

The man who tries to get ahead without a Definite Major Purpose will meet with difficulties far greater than the average man can master.

The more lucrative opportunities of the world of today and tomorrow will go to those who prepare themselves for leadership in their chosen calling.

And leadership in any field of endeavor requires a foundation of sound philosophy. The days of the "hit and miss" leadership are gone forever. Skill and technique and human understanding will be required in the changed world we are now approaching.

The foremen and supervisors in industry must take on new responsibilities in the future. They must not only be skilled in the mechanics of their jobs, which is so essential for efficient production, but they must be skilled as well in the production of harmony among the workers for whom they are responsible.

The youngsters of today will become the leaders of our society tomorrow. What are we going to do about them? This is a problem of the first magnitude, and the major portion of the burden of solving it will fall upon the shoulders of the teachers in the public schools.

I mention these obvious facts as evidence that the future holds forth opportunities for useful service such as we have never known before; opportunities born of necessity in a world which has changed so rapidly that some fail to recognize the scope and the nature of the changes which have taken place.

Take inventory, you who are without a Definite Major Purpose, to find out where you fit in this changed world; prepare yourselves for your new opportunities and make the most of them.

Self-chosen Goals

If I had the privilege of so doing I could no doubt choose for you a Definite Major Purpose suited in every way to your qualifications and needs, and I might create for you a simple plan by which you could attain the object of that purpose; but I can serve you more profitably by teaching you how to do this for yourself.

Somewhere along the way the idea for which you are searching will reveal itself to you. That has been the experience of most of the students of this philosophy. When the idea comes you will recognize it, for it should come with such force that you cannot escape it. You may be sure of that provided you are sincerely searching for it.

One of the imponderable features of this philosophy is that it inspires the creation of new ideas, reveals the presence of opportunities for self-advancement which had been previously overlooked, and inspires one to move on his own personal initiative in embracing and making the most of such opportunities.

This feature of the philosophy is not the result of chance. It was designed to produce a specific effect, since it is obvious that an opportunity which a man creates for himself, or an idea with which he may be inspired through his own thought, is more beneficial than any he may borrow from others, for the very procedure by which a man creates useful ideas leads him unerringly to the discovery of the source from which he may acquire additional ideas when he needs them.

While it is of great benefit to a man to have access to a source from which he may receive the inspiration necessary to create his own ideas, and self-reliance is an asset of priceless value, there may come a time when he will need to draw upon the resources of other minds. And that time is sure to come to those who aspire to leadership in the higher brackets of personal achievement.

Presently I shall reveal to you the means by which personal power may be attained, through the consolidation of many minds directed to the achievement of definite ends.

It was by this same means that Andrew Carnegie ushered

in the great steel age and gave America its greatest industry, although he had no capital with which to begin, and very little education.

And it was by this means that Thomas A. Edison became the greatest inventor of all times, although he had no personal knowledge of physics, mathematics, chemistry, electronics or many other scientific subjects, all of which were essential in his work as an inventor.

It should give you hope to know that lack of education, lack of working capital, and lack of technical skill need not discourage you from establishing, as your major goal in life, any purpose you may choose, for this philosophy provides a way by which any goal within reason may be attained by any man of average ability.

The one thing it cannot do for you is to choose your goal for you!

But, once you have established your own goal, this philosophy can guide you unerringly to its attainment. That is a promise without qualifications.

We cannot tell you what to desire, or how much success to hope for, but we can and we shall reveal to you the formula by which successes may be attained.

Your major responsibility right now is to find out what you desire in life, where you are going, and what you will do when you get there. This is one responsibility which no one but you can assume, and it is a responsibility ninety-eight out of every hundred people never assume. *That is the major reason why only two out of every hundred people can be rated as successful.*

The Power of Burning Desire

Success begins through Definiteness of Purpose!

If this fact has seemed to be over-emphasized it is because of the common trait of procrastination which influences ninety-eight out of every hundred people to go all the way through life without choosing a Definite Major Purpose.

Singleness of purpose is a priceless asset—priceless because so few possess it.

Yet it is an asset which one may appropriate on a second's notice.

Make up your mind what you desire of life, decide to get just that, without substitutes, and lo! you will have taken possession of one of the most priceless of all assets available to human beings.

But your desire must be no mere wish or hope!

It must be a *burning desire*, and it must become so definitely an obsessional desire that you are willing to pay whatever price its attainment may cost. The price may be much or it may be little, but you must condition your mind to pay it, regardless of what the cost may be.

The moment you choose your Definite Major Purpose in life you will observe a strange circumstance, consisting in the fact that ways and means of attaining that purpose will begin immediately to reveal themselves to you.

Opportunities you had not expected will be placed in your way.

The cooperation of others will become available to you, and friends will appear as if by a stroke of magic. Your fears and doubts will begin to disappear and self-reliance will take their place.

This may seem, to the uninitiated, a fantastic promise, but not so to the man who has done away with indecision and has chosen a definite goal in life. I speak not from the observation of other men alone, but from my own personal experience. I have transformed myself from a dismal failure to a successful man, and I have therefore earned the right to give you this assurance of what you may expect if you follow the road-map provided by this philosophy.

When you come to that inspiring moment when you choose your Definite Major Purpose, do not become discouraged if relatives or friends who are nearest you call you a "dreamer."

Just remember that the dreamers have been the forerunners of all human progress.

So, let no one discourage you from dreaming, but make sure you back your dreams with action based on Definiteness of Purpose. Your chances for success are as great as have been those of anyone who has preceded you. In many ways your chances are greater, for you now have access to the knowledge of the principles of individual achievement which millions of successful men of the past had to acquire the long and hard way.

He Knew What He Wanted

Lloyd Collier was born on a farm near Whiteville, North Carolina, in a family whose financial circumstances limited his chances of getting a formal education and forced him to begin at an early age to make his own way.

While he was still in his early teens he was stricken by a malady which paralyzed his body from his waist downward, a condition which would have justified him in sitting on a street corner with a tin cup and a pack of pencils.

Some business men in Whiteville raised a small fund and sent Lloyd to a school where he learned watch repairing. On his return he set up a work bench in the back of a small retail store, in rent-free space, and began to ply his trade as a watchmaker.

Despite his affliction, he never lost his self-confidence nor his cheerful disposition, two traits of personality that soon gained for him many friends and all the work he could do.

Lloyd came under the influence of the book *Think and Grow Rich*. It made such a profound impression upon him that he went to work in earnest to apply the famous Andrew Carnegie success formula described in the book.

His first step was that of writing out his *definite major aim*. He committed this to memory and repeated it many times daily. Substantially, it provided for him to own the finest jewelry store in Whiteville, marry the prettiest girl in the city, own the finest home and rear and educate a happy family of children.

Quite an order for a man without the use of his legs, starting from scratch and without operating capital.

But he made it! He attained every objective set down in his definite major aim. Moreover, he did it while he was still young enough to have a long road ahead of him for enjoying his well-earned blessings.

He gets around in a wheel chair and drives his own specially built car, getting in and out of it without help. His jewelry store is managed by trusted employees, with his wife in charge of the books. If you visited his store he would greet you enthusiastically from his wheel chair as you entered. And you would have the definite feeling that you were in the presence of a man whose physical affliction was by no means a handicap.

Lloyd Collier has adopted a habit which men with lesser physical afflictions than his might well copy. Each day he expresses a prayer of gratitude for the blessings he enjoys despite his physical handicap and each day he so lives and relates himself to his fellowmen that he does not seek pity. Instead, he seeks an opportunity to share some of his blessings with those who are more unfortunate than he, believing as he does that only by sharing them may he enrich and multiply his own blessings.

In Lloyd Collier we recognize the major difference between a man on a street corner, with a cup and a bunch of pencils, and a man who has made himself independent financially and has found peace of mind. The difference is mainly one of mental attitude. Lloyd discovered PMA (positive mental attitude) and through it found his way to everything he sought.

Any time you begin to feel sorry for yourself, or let NMA (negative mental attitude) get you down, take a trip to Whiteville, North Carolina, visit Lloyd Collier for a few hours, and you will come away with PMA written all over you.

Wise men share most of their riches generously. They share their confidences sparingly, and take great care not to misplace them. And when they talk of their aims and plans they generally do it by *action* rather than by words.

Wise men listen much and speak with caution, for they know that a man may always be in the way of learning something of value when he is listening, while he may learn nothing when he is speaking, unless it be the folly of *talking too much!*

There is always an appropriate time for one to speak and an appropriate time for one to remain silent. Wise men, when in doubt as to whether to speak or remain silent, give themselves the benefit of the doubt by keeping quiet.

Exchange of thought, through intercourse of speech, is one of the more important means by which men gather useful knowledge, create plans for the attainment of their Definite Major Purpose and find ways and means of carrying out these plans. And the "round table" discussions are an outstanding feature among men in the higher brackets of achievement. But these are far different from the idle discussions in which some men open their minds to anyone who wishes to enter.

Presently I shall reveal to you a safe method by which you may exchange thoughts with other men, with a reasonable assurance that you will *get* as much as you *give*, or more. By this method you may not only speak freely of your most cherished plans, but it will be profitable for you to so do.

I shall reveal to you an important intersection at which you may leave the by-path you are following on your way to success, and get on the main highway! The way will be clearly marked so that you shall not miss it.

This intersection of which I speak is the point at which men in the higher brackets of achievement come to a parting of the ways with many of their former associates and confidants, and join company with men who are prepared to give them a lift on their journey to riches.

Chapter Four

THE HABIT OF GOING THE EXTRA MILE

An important principle of success in all walks of life and in all occupations is a willingness to *Go the Extra Mile;* which means the rendering of more and better service than that for which one is paid, and giving it in a *positive mental attitude.*

Search wherever you will for a single sound argument against this principle, and you will not find it; nor will you find a single instance of enduring success which was not attained in part by its application.

The principle is not the creation of man. It is a part of Nature's handiwork, for it is obvious that every living creature below the intelligence of man is forced to apply the principle in order to survive.

Man may disregard the principle if he chooses, but he cannot do so and at the same time enjoy the fruits of enduring success.

Observe how Nature applies this principle in the production of food that grows from the soil, where the farmer is forced to *go the extra mile* by clearing the land, plowing it, and planting the seed at the right time of the year, for none of which he receives any pay in advance.

But, observe that if he does his work in harmony with Nature's laws, and performs the necessary amount of labor, Nature takes over the job where the farmer's labor ends, germinates the seed he plants and develops it into a crop of food.

And, observe thoughtfully this significant fact: For every grain of wheat or corn he plants in the soil, Nature yields him perhaps a hundred grains, thus enabling him to benefit by the law of *increasing returns.*

Nature *goes the extra mile* by producing enough of

59

everything for her needs, together with a surplus for emergencies and waste; for example, the fruit on the trees, the bloom from which the fruit is grown, frogs in the pond and fish in the seas.

Nature *goes the extra mile* by producing enough of every living thing to insure the perpetuation of the species, allowing for emergencies of every kind. If this were not true the species of all living things would soon vanish.

Some believe that the beasts of the jungle and the birds of the air live without labor, but thoughtful men know that this is not true. It is true that Nature provides the sources of supply of food for every living thing, but every creature must labor before it may partake of that food.

Thus we see that Nature discourages the habit which some men have acquired of trying to get something for nothing.

The advantages of the habit of *going the extra mile* are definite and understandable. Let us examine some of them and be convinced:

The habit brings the individual to the *favorable attention* of those who can and will provide opportunities for self-advancement.

It tends to make one indispensable, in many different human relationships, and it therefore enables him to command more than average compensation for personal services.

It leads to mental growth and to physical skill and perfection in many forms of endeavor, thereby adding to one's earning capacity.

It protects one against the loss of employment when employment is scarce, and places him in a position to command the choicest of jobs.

It enables one to profit by the law of contrast, since *the majority of people do not practice the habit*.

It leads to the development of a positive, pleasing mental attitude, which is essential for enduring success.

It tends to develop a keen, alert imagination because it is a habit which inspires one continuously to seek new and better ways of rendering service.

It develops the important quality of personal initiative.

It develops self-reliance and courage.

It serves to build the confidence of others in one's integrity.

It aids in the mastery of the destructive habit of procrastination.

It develops definiteness of purpose, insuring one against the common habit of aimlessness.

Give More, Get More

There is still another, and a greater reason for following the habit of *going the extra mile. It gives one the only logical reason for asking for increased compensation.*

If a man performs no more service than that for which he is being paid, then obviously he is receiving all the pay to which he is entitled.

He must render as much service as that for which he is being paid, in order to hold his job, or to maintain his source of income, regardless of how he earns it.

But he has the privilege always of rendering an overplus of service as a means of accumulating a reserve credit of goodwill, and to provide a just reason for demanding more pay, a better position, or both.

Every position based upon a salary or wages provides one with an opportunity to advance himself by the application of this principle, and it is important to note that the American system of free enterprise is operated on the basis of providing every worker in industry with a proper incentive to apply the principle.

Any practice or philosophy which deprives a man of the privilege of *going the extra mile* is unsound and doomed to failure, for it is obvious that this principle is the stepping-stone of major importance by which an individual may receive compensation for extraordinary skill, experience and education; and it is the one principle which provides the way of self-determination, regardless of what occupation, profession or calling the individual may be engaged in.

In America, anyone may earn a living without the habit of *going the extra mile*. And many do just that, but economic security and the luxuries available under the great American way of life are available only to the individual who makes this principle a part of his philosophy of life and lives by it as a matter of daily habit.

Every known rule of logic and common sense forces one

to accept this as true. And even a cursory analysis of men in the higher brackets of success will prove that it is true.

The leaders of the American system are adamant in their demands that every worker be protected in his right to adopt and apply the principle of *going the extra mile,* for they recognize from their own experience that the future leadership in industry is dependent upon men who are willing to follow this principle.

It is a well known fact that Andrew Carnegie developed more successful leaders of industry than has any other great American industrialist. Most of them came up from the ranks of ordinary day laborers, and many of them accumulated personal fortunes of vast amounts, more than they could have acquired without the guidance of Mr. Carnegie.

The first test that Mr. Carnegie applied to any worker whom he desired to promote was that of determining to what extent the worker was willing to *go the extra mile.*

It was this test that led him to the discovery of Charles M. Schwab. When Mr. Schwab first came to Mr. Carnegie's attention he was working as a day laborer in one of the steel master's plants. Close observation revealed that Mr. Schwab always performed more and better service than that for which he was paid. Moreover, he performed it in a pleasing mental attitude which made him popular among his fellow workers.

He was promoted from one job to another until at long last he was made president of the great United States Steel Corporation, at a salary of $75,000 a year!

Not through all the ingenuity of man, or all the schemes that men resort to in order to get something for nothing, could Charles M. Schwab, the day laborer, have earned as much as $75,000 during his entire lifetime if he had not willingly adopted and followed the habit of *going the extra mile.*

On some occasions Mr. Carnegie not only paid Mr. Schwab's salary, which was generous enough, but he gave him as much as $1,000,000 as a bonus in addition to his regular salary.

When Mr. Carnegie was asked why he gave Mr. Schwab a bonus so much greater than his salary, he replied in words that every worker, regardless of his job or wages, might well ponder. "I gave him his salary for the work he actually performed," said Mr. Carnegie, "and the bonus for his willingness to *go the extra mile,* thus setting a fine example for his fellow workers."

Think of that! A salary of $75,000 a year, paid to a man who started as a day laborer, and a bonus of more than ten times that amount for a good disposition expressed by a willingness to do more than he was paid for.

Verily it pays to *go the extra mile,* for every time an individual does so he places someone else under obligation to him.

No one is compelled to follow the habit of *going the extra mile,* and seldom is anyone ever requested to render more service than that for which he is paid. Therefore, if the habit is followed it must be adopted on one's own initiative.

But, the Constitution of the United States guarantees every man this privilege, and the American system provides rewards and bonuses for those who follow this habit, and makes it impossible for a man to adopt the habit without receiving appropriate compensation.

The compensation may come in many different forms. Increased pay is a certainty. Voluntary promotions are inevitable. Favorable working conditions and pleasant human relationships are sure. And these lead to economic security which a man may attain on his own merits.

There is still another benefit to be gained by the man who follows the habit of *going the extra mile: It keeps him on good terms with his own conscience and serves as a stimulant to his own soul!* Therefore it is a builder of sound character which has no equal in any other human habit.

You who have young boys and girls growing into adulthood might well remember this for their sake! Teach a child the benefits of rendering more service and better service than that which is customary, and you will have made contributions of character to that child which will serve him or her all through life.

The philosophy of Andrew Carnegie is essentially a philosophy of economics. But it is more than that! It is also a philosophy of ethics in human relationships. It leads to harmony and understanding and sympathy for the weak and the unfortunate. It teaches one how to become his brother's keeper, and at the same time rewards him for so doing.

The habit of *going the extra mile* is only one of the seventeen principles of the philosophy recommended to those who are seeking riches, but let us consider how directly it is related to each of the Twelve Riches.

First, this habit is inseparably related to the development of the most important of the Twelve Riches, a *Positive Mental Attitude*. When a man becomes the master of his own emotions, and learns the blessed art of self-expression through useful service to others, he has gone far toward the development of a positive mental attitude.

With a positive mental attitude as a builder of the proper thought-pattern, the remainder of the Twelve Riches fall into that pattern as naturally as night follows day, and as inevitably. Recognize this truth and you will understand why the habit of *going the extra mile* provides benefits far beyond the mere accumulation of material riches. You will understand also why this principle has been given first place in the philosophy of individual achievement.

Too Good a Man to Lose

Let us now observe that the admonition to render more service and better service than that for which one is paid, is paradoxical because *it is impossible for anyone to render such service without receiving appropriate compensation*. The compensation may come in many forms and from many different sources, some of them strange and unexpected sources, but come it will.

The worker who renders this type of service may not always receive appropriate compensation from the person to whom he renders the service, but this habit will attract to him many opportunities for self-advancement, among them new and more favorable sources of employment. Thus his pay will come to him indirectly.

Ralph Waldo Emerson had this truth in mind when he said (in his essay on Compensation), "If you serve an ungrateful master, serve him the more. Put God in your debt. Every stroke shall be repaid. The longer the payment is withholden, the better for you; *for compound interest on compound interest is the rate and usage of this exchequer.*"

Speaking once more in terms that seem paradoxical, be reminded that the most profitable time a man devotes to labor is that for which he receives no direct or immediate financial compensation. For it must be remembered that there are two forms of compensation available to the man who works for wages. One is the wages he receives in money. *The other is the skill he attains from his experiences;* a form of compensation which often exceeds monetary remuneration, for skill and experience are the worker's most important stock in trade through which he may promote himself to higher pay and greater responsibilities.

The attitude of the man who follows the habit of *going the extra mile* is this: *He recognizes the truth that he is receiving pay* for schooling himself for a better position and greater pay!

This is an asset of which no worker can be cheated, no matter how selfish or greedy his immediate employer may be. It is the "compound interest on compound interest" which Emerson mentioned.

It was this very asset which enabled Charles M. Schwab to climb, step by step, from the lowly beginning as a day laborer to the highest position his employer had to offer; and it was this asset as well which brought Mr. Schwab a bonus of more than ten times the amount of his salary.

The million dollar bonus which Mr. Schwab received was his payoff for having put his best efforts into every job he performed—a circumstance, let us remember, which he controlled *entirely*. And it was a circumstance that could not have happened if he had not followed the habit of *going the extra mile.*

Mr. Carnegie had but little, if anything, to do with the circumstance. It was entirely out of his hands. Let us be generous by assuming that Mr. Carnegie paid off because he knew Mr. Schwab had earned the additional pay which had not been promised him. But the actual fact may be that he paid off rather than lose so valuable a man.

And here let us note that the man who follows the habit of *going the extra mile* thereby places the purchaser of his services under a double obligation to pay a just compensation; one being an obligation based upon his sense of fairness, the other based on *his sense of fear of losing a valuable man.*

Thus we see that no matter how we view the principle of *going the extra mile*, we come always to the same answer, that it pays "compound interest on compound interest" to all who follow the habit.

And we understand, too, what a great industrial leader had in mind when he said: *"Personally I am not so much interested in a forty hours per week minimum work law as I am in finding how I can crowd forty hours into a single day."*

The man who made that statement has an abundance of the Twelve Riches, and he freely admits that he attained his riches mainly by working his way up from a lowly beginning, applying the habit of *going the extra mile* every step of the way.

It was this same man who said, "If I were compelled to risk my chances of success upon but one of the seventeen principles of achievement, I would, without hesitancy, stake everything on the principle of *going the extra mile."*

Fortunately, however, he was not obligated to make this choice, for the seventeen principles of individual achievement are related to each other like the links of a chain. Therefore they blend into a medium of great power through co-ordination of their use. The omission of any one of these principles would weaken that power, just as the removal of a single link would weaken the chain.

The power of the seventeen principles consists not in the principles, but in their *application and use!* When the principles are applied they change the "chemistry" of the mind from a negative to a positive mental attitude. It is this *positive mental attitude* which attracts success by leading one to the attainment of the Twelve Riches.

Each of these principles represents, through its use, a definite, positive quality of the mind, and every circumstance that draws upon the power of thought calls for the use of some combination of the principles.

The seventeen principles may be likened to the twenty-six letters of the alphabet through the combinations of which all human thought may be expressed. The individual letters of the alphabet convey little or no meaning, but when they are combined into words they may express any thought one can conceive.

The seventeen principles are the "alphabet" of individual achievement, through which all talents may be expressed in their highest and most beneficial form. Hence they provide the means by which one may attain the great Master-Key to Riches.

Chapter Five

LOVE, THE TRUE EMANCIPATOR OF MANKIND!

Love is man's greatest experience. It brings one into communication with Infinite Intelligence.

When it is blended with the emotions of sex and romance it may lead one to the higher mountain-peaks of individual achievement through *creative vision*.

The emotions of love, sex and romance are the three sides of the eternal triangle of achievement known as genius. Nature creates geniuses through no other media.

Love is an outward expression of the spiritual nature of man.

Sex is purely biological, but it supplies the springs of action in all creative effort, from the humblest creature that crawls to the most profound of all creations, man.

When love and sex are combined with the spirit of romance the world may well rejoice, for these are the potentials of the great leaders who are the profound thinkers of the world.

Love makes all mankind akin!

It clears out selfishness, greed, jealousy, and envy, and makes right royal kings of the humblest of men. True greatness will never be found where love does not abide.

The love of which I speak must not be confused with the emotions of sex, for love in its highest and purest expression is a combination of the eternal triangle, *yet it is greater than any one of its three component parts*.

The love to which I refer is the "elan vital"—the lifegiving factor—the spring of action—of all the creative endeavors which have lifted mankind to his present state of refinement and culture.

It is the one factor which draws a clear line of demarcation between man and all of the creatures of the earth below him. It is the one factor which determines for every man the amount of space he shall occupy in the hearts of his fellowmen.

Love is the solid foundation upon which the first of the Twelve Riches may be builded, *a positive mental attitude*, and let us take heed that no man may ever become truly rich without it.

Love is the warp and the woof of all the remaining eleven riches. It embellishes all riches and gives them the quality of endurance, evidence of which may be revealed by cursory observation of all who have acquired material riches but have not acquired love.

The *habit* of *going the extra mile* leads to the attainment of that spirit of love, for there can be no greater expression of love than love which is demonstrated through service that is rendered unselfishly for the benefit of others.

Emerson had the vision of the kind of love to which I refer when he said: *"Those who are capable of humility, of justice, of love, of aspiration, are already on the platform that commands the sciences and arts, speech and poetry, action and grace.* For whoso dwells in this mortal beatitude does already anticipate those special powers which men prize so highly. . . .

"The magnanimous know very well that they who give time, or money, or shelter, to the stranger—so it be done for love, and not for ostentation—do, as it were, put God under obligation to them, so perfect are the compensations of the universe. In some way the time they seem to lose, is redeemed, and the pains they take, remunerate themselves. These men fan the flame of human love and raise the standard of civic virtue among mankind."

The great minds of every age have recognized love as the eternal elixir that binds the heart-wounds of mankind and makes men their brothers' keepers. One of the greatest minds this nation ever produced expressed his views on love in a classic that shall live as long as time endures. He said:

"Love is the only bow on life's dark cloud.

"It is the morning and the evening star.

"It shines upon the babe, and sheds its radiance on the quiet tomb.

"It is the mother of art, inspirer of poet, patriot and philosopher.

"It is the air and light of every heart—builder of every home, kindler of every fire on every hearth.

"It was the first to dream of immortality.

"It fills the world with melody—for music is the voice of love.

"Love is the magician, the enchanted, that changes worthless things to joy, and makes right royal kings and queens of common clay.

"It is the perfume of that wondrous flower, the heart, and without that sacred passion, that divine swoon, we are less than beasts; but with it, earth is heaven and we are gods.

"Love is transfiguration. It ennobles, purifies and glorifies. . . . Love is a revelation, a creation. From love the world borrows its beauty and the heavens their glory. Justice, self-denial, charity and pity are the children of love. . . . Without love all glory fades, the noble falls from life, art dies, music loses meaning and becomes mere motions of the air, and virtue ceases to exist."

If a man is truly great he will love all mankind!

He will love the good and the bad among all humanity. The good he will love with *pride* and *admiration* and *joy.* The bad he will love with *pity* and *sorrow,* for he will know, if he be truly great, that both good and bad qualities in men often are but the results of circumstances over which they have, because of their ignorance, little control.

If a man be truly great he will be compassionate, sympathetic and tolerant. When he is compelled to pass judgment upon others he will temper justice with tender mercy, throwing himself always on the side of the weak, the uninformed and the poverty-stricken.

Thus he will not only *go the extra mile* in a true spirit of Fellowship, but he will go *willingly and graciously.* And if the second mile be not enough he will go the third and the fourth, and as many additional miles as may be necessary.

Some Who Have Benefited by the Habit of Going the Extra Mile

No one ever does anything voluntarily without a motive. Let us see if we can reveal a sound motive that will justify the habit of *going the extra mile* by observing a few who have been inspired by it.

Many years ago an elderly lady was strolling through a Pittsburgh Department Store, obviously killing time. She passed counter after counter without anyone paying any attention to her. All of the clerks had spotted her as an idle "looker" who had no intention of buying. They made it a point of looking in another direction when she stopped at their counters.

What *costly business* this neglect turned out to be!

Finally the lady came to a counter that was attended by a young clerk who bowed politely and asked if he might serve her.

"No," she replied, "I am just killing time, waiting for the rain to stop so I can go home."

"Very well, Madam," the young man smiled, "may I bring out a chair for you?" And he brought it without waiting for her answer. After the rain slacked the young man took the old lady by the arm, escorted her to the street and bade her good-bye. As she left she asked him for his card.

Several months later the owner of the store received a letter, asking that this young man be sent to Scotland to take an order for the furnishings of a home. The owner of the store wrote back that he was sorry, but the young man did not work in the house furnishings department. However, he explained that he would be glad to send an "experienced man" to do the job.

Back came a reply that no one would do except this particular young man. The letters were signed by Andrew Carnegie, and the "house" he wanted furnished was Skibo Castle in Scotland. The elderly lady was Mr. Carnegie's mother. The young man was sent to Scotland. He received an order for several hundred thousand dollars worth of household furnishings, and with it a partnership in the store. He later became the owner of a half interest in the store.

Verily it pays to *go the extra mile*.

Some years ago the editor of *The Golden Rule Magazine* was invited to deliver a speech at the Palmer School in Davenport, Iowa. He accepted the invitation on his regular fee basis, which was $100 and traveling expenses.

While the editor was at the college he picked up enough editorial material for several stories for his magazine. After he had delivered the speech and was ready to return to Chicago he was told to turn in his expense account and receive his check.

He refused to accept any money for either his address or his expenses, explaining that he had already been paid adequately by the material he had procured for his magazine. He took the train back to Chicago feeling well repaid for his trip.

The following week he began to receive from Davenport many subscriptions to his magazine. By the end of the week he had received over $6,000.00 in cash subscriptions. Then followed a letter from Dr. Palmer explaining that the subscriptions had come from his students, who had been told of the editor's refusal to accept money which he had been promised and which he had earned.

During the following two years the students and the graduates of the Palmer School sent in more than $50,000 in subscriptions to *The Golden Rule Magazine*. The story was so impressive that it was written up in a magazine that had a circulation throughout the English-speaking world, and the subscriptions came from many different countries.

Thus, by rendering $100 worth of service without collecting, the editor had started the law of increasing returns to work in his behalf, and it yielded him a return of over 500 times his investment. The habit of *going the extra mile* is no pipe-dream. It pays, and pays handsomely!

Moreover, it never forgets! Like the other types of investments, the habit of *going the extra mile* often yields dividends throughout one's lifetime.

Let us look at what happened when one neglected an opportunity to *go the extra mile*. Late one rainy afternoon an automobile "salesman" sat at his desk in a New York show room which displayed expensive automobiles. The door opened and in walked a man jauntily swinging a cane.

The "salesman" looked up from the reading of the afternoon paper, took a swift glance at the newcomer, and immediately spotted him as another of those Broadway "window shoppers" who do nothing but waste one's valuable time. He went ahead with his newspaper, not taking the trouble to rise from his chair.

The man with the cane walked through the show room, looking first at one car and then another. Finally he walked over to where the "salesman" was sitting, teetered on his cane, and nonchalantly asked the price of three different automobiles on the floor. Without looking up from his newspaper, the "salesman" gave the prices and went on with his reading.

The man with the cane walked back over to the three automobiles at which he had been looking, kicked the tires of each one, then returned to the busy man at the desk and said, "Well, I hardly know whether I shall take this one, that one, the other one over there; or whether I shall buy all three."

The busy man at the desk responded with a sort of smirky, wiseacre smile, as much as to say, "Just as I thought!"

Then the man with the cane said, "Oh, I guess I will buy one of them. Send that one with the yellow wheels up to my house tomorrow. And, by the way, how much did you say it was?"

He took out his check book, wrote out a check, handed it to the "salesman," and walked out. When the "salesman" saw the name on the check, he turned fourteen different shades of pink and almost swooned from heart failure. The man who signed the check was Harry Payne Whitney, and the "salesman" knew that if he had only taken the time to get up from his chair he might have sold all three automobiles without any effort.

Withholding anything short of the best service of which one is capable is costly business—a fact which many have learned too late.

The right of personal initiative is not worth much to the fellow who is too indifferent or too lazy to exercise it. Many people are in this class without recognizing the reason they never accumulate riches.

Over forty years ago a young salesman in a hardware store observed that the store had a lot of odds and ends which were out of date and not selling. Having time on his hands, he rigged up a special table in the middle of the store. He loaded it with some of this unsalable merchandise, marking it at the bargain price of a dime an article. To his surprise and that of the owner of the store, the gadgets sold like hot cakes.

Out of that experience grew the great F. W. Woolworth Five and Ten Cent chain store system. The young man who stumbled upon the idea by *going the extra mile* was Frank W. Woolworth. That idea yielded him a fortune estimated at more than $50,000,000. Moreover, the same idea made several other persons rich, and applications of the idea are at the heart of many of the more profitable merchandising systems in America.

No one told young Woolworth to exercise his right to personal initiative. No one paid him for doing so; yet his action led to ever-increasing returns for his efforts. Once he put the idea into practice, increasing returns nearly ran him down.

There is something about this habit of doing more than one is paid for which works in one's behalf even while he sleeps. Once it begins to work, it piles up riches so fast that it seems like queer magic which, like Aladdin's Lamp, draws to one's aid an army of genii which come laden with bags of gold.

Some thirty years ago Charles M. Schwab's private railroad car was switched onto the siding at his steel plant in Pennsylvania. It was a cold, frosty morning. As he alighted from the car he was met by a young man with a stenographer's notebook in his hands who hurriedly explained that he was a stenographer in the general office of the steel company, and that he had come down to meet the car to see if Mr. Schwab needed any letters written, or any telegrams sent.

"Who asked you to meet me?" Mr. Schwab queried. "No one," the young man replied. "I saw the telegram coming through announcing your arrival, so I came down to meet you, hoping I might be of some service."

Think of that! He came down *hoping* he might be able to find something to do for which he was not paid. And he came on his own initiative without being told.

Mr. Schwab thanked him politely for his thoughtfulness, but said he had no need for a stenographer at the moment. After carefully noting the young man's name, he sent the lad back to his work.

That night, when the private car was hitched to the night train for its return to New York City it carried the young stenographer. He had been assigned, at Mr. Schwab's request, for service in New York as one of the steel magnate's assistants. The lad's name was Williams. He remained in Mr. Schwab's services for several years, during which opportunity after opportunity for promotion came to him unsolicited.

It is peculiar how opportunities have a way of trailing

the people who make it their business to *go the extra mile*, but they do very definitely. Finally an opportunity came to young Williams which he could not ignore. He was made president and a large stockholder in one of the largest drug concerns in the United States—a job which yielded him a fortune far greater than his needs.

This incident is clear evidence of what can happen, and of what has been happening all down through the years under the American way of life.

The habit of *going the extra mile* is one that does not confine its rewards to wage earners. It works as well for an employer as it does for an employee, as one merchant whom we knew quite well gratefully testified.

His name was Arthur Nash. His business was merchant tailoring. Some years ago Mr. Nash found his business just one step ahead of the sheriff. Conditions over which he seemed to have no control had brought him to the brink of financial ruin.

One of his most serious handicaps was that his employees had caught his spirit of defeatism and they expressed it in their work by slowing down and becoming disgruntled. His situation became desperate. Something had to be done, and it had to be done quickly if he were to continue in business.

Out of sheer desperation he called his employees together and told them the condition. While he was speaking, an idea occurred to him. He said he had been reading a story in *The Golden Rule Magazine* which told how its editor had *gone the extra mile* by rendering service for which he refused to accept pay, only to be voluntarily rewarded with more than $6,000 worth of subscriptions to his magazine.

He wound up by suggesting that if he and all of his employees caught that spirit and began to *go the extra mile* they might save the business.

He promised his employees that if they would join with him in an experiment he would endeavor to carry on the business, with the understanding that everyone would forget wages, forget working hours, pitch in and do his best, and take chances on receiving pay for work. If the business could be made to pay every employee would receive back wages with a bonus thrown in for good measure.

The employees liked the idea and agreed to give it a trial.

The next day they began to come in with their meager savings, which they voluntarily loaned to Mr. Nash.

Everyone went to work with a new spirit, and the business began to show signs of new life. Very soon it was back on a paying basis. Then it began to prosper as it had never prospered before.

Ten years later the business had made Mr. Nash rich. The employees were more prosperous than they had ever been, and everyone was happy.

Arthur Nash passed on, but today the business continues as one of the more successful merchant tailoring businesses of America.

The employees took over the business when Mr. Nash laid it down. Ask any one of them what he thinks of this business of *going the extra mile,* and you will get the answer!

Moreover, talk with one of the Nash salesmen, wherever you meet one, and observe his spirit of enthusiasm and his self-reliance. When this "extra mile" stimulant once gets into a man's mind, he becomes a different sort of person. The outlook on the world appears different to him, *and he appears different* because he is different.

Here is the appropriate place to remind you of an important thing about the habit of *going the extra mile* by doing more than one is paid for. *It is the strange influence which it has on the man who does it.* The greatest benefit from this habit does not come to those to whom the service is rendered. *It comes to the one who renders the service,* in the form of a changed "mental attitude," which gives him more influence with other people, more self-reliance, greater initiative, more enthusiasm, more vision and definiteness of purpose. All of these are qualities of successful achievement.

"Do the thing and you shall have the power," said Emerson. Ah, yes the *power!* What can a man do in our world without power? But it must be the type of power which attracts other people instead of repelling them. It must be a form of power which gains momentum from the *law of increasing returns,* through the operation of which one's acts and deeds come back to him greatly multiplied.

An Easy Way to Get What You Want

You who work for wages should learn more about this sowing and reaping business. Then you would understand why no man can go on forever sowing the seed of inadequate service and reaping a harvest of full grown pay. You would know that there must come a halt to the habit of demanding a full day's pay for a poor day's work.

And you who do not work for wages, but who wish to get more of the better things of life! Let us have a word with you. Why do you not become wise and start getting what you wish the easy and sure way? Yes, there is an easy and a sure way to promote one's self into whatever he wants from life, and its secret becomes known to every person who makes it his business to *go the extra mile*. The secret can be uncovered in no other manner, *for it is wrapped up in that extra mile*.

The pot of gold at the "end of the rainbow" is not a mere fairy tale! The end of that *extra mile* is the spot where the rainbow ends, and that is where the pot of gold is hidden.

Few people ever catch up with the "end of the rainbow." When one gets to where he thought the rainbow ended he finds it is still far in the distance. The trouble with most of us is that we do not know how to follow rainbows. Those who know the secret know that the end of the rainbow can be reached only by *going the extra mile*.

Late one afternoon, some forty-five years ago, William C. Durant, the founder of General Motors, walked into his bank after banking hours, and asked for some favor which in the ordinary course of business should have been requested during banking hours.

The man who granted the favor was Carol Downes, an under official of the bank. He not only served Mr. Durant with efficiency, but he went the Extra Mile and *added courtesy to the service*. He made Mr. Durant feel that it was a real pleasure to serve him. The incident seemed trivial, and of itself it was of little importance. Unknown to Mr. Downes, this courtesy was destined to have repercussions of a far-reaching nature.

The next day Mr. Durant asked Downes to come to his

office. That visit led to the offer of a position which Downes accepted. He was given a desk in a general office where nearly a hundred other people worked, and he was notified that the office hours were from 8:30 a.m. to 5:30 p.m. His salary to begin with was modest.

At the end of the first day, when the gong rang announcing the close of the day's work, Downes noticed that everyone grabbed his hat and coat and made a rush for the door. He sat still, waiting for the others to leave the office. After they had gone he remained at his desk, pondering in his own mind the cause of the great haste everyone had shown to get away on the very second of quitting time.

Fifteen minutes later Mr. Durant opened the door of his private office, saw Downes still at his desk, and asked Downes whether he understood that he was privileged to stop work at 5:30.

"Oh yes," Downes replied, "but I did not wish to be run over in the rush." Then he asked if he could be of any service to Mr. Durant. He was told he might find a pencil for the motor magnate. He got the pencil, ran it through the pencil sharpener and took it to Mr. Durant. Mr. Durant thanked him and said "good night."

The next day at quitting time Downes remained at his desk again after the "rush" was over. This time he waited with purpose aforethought. In a little while Mr. Durant came out of his private office and asked again if Downes did not understand that 5:30 was the time for closing.

"Yes." Downes smiled. "I understand it is quitting time for the others, but I have heard no one say that I have to leave the office when the day is officially closed, so I chose to remain here with the hope that I might be of some slight service to you."

"What an unusual *hope*," Durant exclaimed. "Where did you get the idea?"

"I got it from the scene I witness here at closing time every day," Downes replied. Mr. Durant grunted some reply which Downes did not hear distinctly and returned to his office.

From then on Downes always remained at his desk after closing time until he saw Mr. Durant leave for the day. He was not paid to remain over time. No one told him to do it. No one promised him anything for remaining, and as far as the casual observer might know, *he was wasting his time.*

Several months later Downes was called into Mr. Durant's office and informed that he had been chosen to go out to a new plant that had been purchased recently to supervise the installation of the plant machinery. Imagine that! A former bank official becoming a machinery expert in a few months.

Without quibbling, Downes accepted the assignment and went on his way. He did not say, "Why, Mr. Durant, I know nothing about the installation of machinery." He did not say, "That's not my job," or "I'm not paid to install machinery." No, he went to work and did what was requested of him. Moreover, he went at the job with a pleasant "mental attitude."

Three months later the job was completed. It was done so well that Mr. Durant called Downes into his office and asked him where he learned about machinery. "Oh," Downes explained, "I never learned, Mr. Durant. I merely looked around, found men who knew how to get the job done, put them to work, and *they did it*."

"Splendid!" Mr. Durant exclaimed. "There are two types of men who are valuable. One is the fellow who can do something and do it well, without complaining that he is being overworked. The other is the fellow who can get other people to do things well, without complaining. You are both types wrapped into one package."

Downes thanked him for the compliment and turned to go.

"Wait a moment," Durant requested. "I forgot to tell you that you are the new manager of the plant you have installed, and your salary to start with is $50,000.00 a year."

The following ten years of association with Mr. Durant was worth between ten and twelve million dollars to Carol Downes. He became an intimate advisor of the motor king and made himself rich as a result.

The main trouble with so many of us is that we see men who have "arrived" and we weigh them in the hour of their triumph without taking the trouble to find out how or why they "arrived."

There is nothing very dramatic about the story of Carol Downes. The incidents mentioned occurred during the day's business, without even a passing notice by the average person who worked along with Downes. And we doubt not that many of these fellow-workers envied him because they believed he had been favored by Mr. Durant, through some sort of pull or luck, or whatever it is that men who do not succeed use as an excuse to explain their own lack of progress.

Well, to be candid, Downes did have an inside "pull" with Mr. Durant!

He created that "pull" on his own initiative.

He created it by *going the extra mile* in a matter as trivial as that of placing a neat point on a pencil when nothing was requested except a plain pencil.

He created it by remaining at his desk "with the hope" that he might be of service to his employer after the "rush" was over at 5:30 each evening.

He created it by using his right of personal initiative by finding men who understood how to install machinery instead of asking Durant where or how to find such men.

Trace down these incidents step by step and you will find that Downes' success was due solely to his own initiative. Moreover, the story consists of a series of little tasks well performed, in the right "mental attitude."

Perhaps there were a hundred other men working for Mr. Durant who could have done as well as Downes, but the trouble with them was that they were searching for the "end of the rainbow" by running away from it in the 5:30 rush each afternoon.

Long years afterward a friend asked Carol Downes how he got his opportunity with Mr. Durant. "Oh," he modestly replied, "I just made it my business to get in his way, so he could see me. When he looked around, wanting some little service, he called on me because I was the only one in sight. *In time he got into the habit of calling on me."*

There you have it! Mr. Durant "got into the habit" of calling on Downes. Moreover, he found that Downes could and would assume responsibilities by *going the extra mile.*

What a pity that all of the American people do not catch something of this spirit of assuming greater responsibilities. What a pity that more of us do not begin speaking more of our "privileges" under the American way of life, and less of the lack of opportunities in America.

Is there a man living in America today who would seriously claim that Carol Downes would have been better off if he had been forced, by law, to join the mad rush and quit his work at 5:30 in the afternoon? If he had done so, he would have received the standard wages for the sort of work he performed, but nothing more. Why should he have received more?

His destiny was in his own hands. It was wrapped up in this one lone privilege which should be the privilege of every American citizen: the right of personal initiative through the exercise of which he made it a habit always to *go the extra mile*. That tells the whole story. There is no other secret to Downes' success. He admits it, and everyone familiar with the circumstances of his promotion from poverty to riches knows it.

There is one thing no one seems to know: Why are there so few men who, like Carol Downes, discover the power implicit in doing more than one is paid for? It has in it the seed of all great achievement. It is the secret of all noteworthy success, and yet it is so little understood that most people look upon it as some clever trick with which employers try to get more work out of their employees.

Just after the end of the Spanish-American War, Elbert Hubbard wrote a story entitled *A Message to Garcia*. He told briefly how President William McKinley commissioned a young soldier by the name of Rowan to carry a message from the United States Government to Garcia, the rebel chieftain, whose exact whereabouts were not known.

The young soldier took the message, made his way through the fastnesses of the Cuban jungle, finally found Garcia, and delivered the note to him. That was all there was to the story—just a private soldier carrying out his orders under difficulties, and getting the job done without coming back with an excuse.

The story fired imaginations and spread all over the world. The simple act of a man doing what he was told, and doing it well, became news of the first magnitude. *A Message to Garcia* was printed in booklet form and the sales reached an all-time high for such publications, amounting to more than ten million copies. This one story made Elbert Hubbard famous, to say nothing of helping to make him rich.

The story was translated into several foreign languages. The Japanese Government had it printed and distributed to every Japanese soldier during the Japanese-Russian war. The Pennsylvania Railroad Company presented a copy of it to each of their thousands of employees. The big life insurance companies of America presented it to their salesmen. Long after Elbert Hubbard went down on the ill-fated Lusitania in 1915, *A Message To Garcia* continued as a best-seller throughout America.

The story was popular because it had in it something of the magic power that belongs to the man who does something, and does it well.

The whole world is clamoring for such men. They are needed and wanted in every walk of life. American industry has always had princely berths for men who can and will assume responsibilities and who get the job done in the right "mental attitude," by *going the extra mile*.

Andrew Carnegie lifted no fewer than forty such men from the lowly station of day laborers to millionaires. He understood the value of men who were willing to *go the extra mile*. Wherever he found such a man, he brought "his find" into the inner circle of his business and gave him an opportunity to earn "all he was worth."

People do things or refrain from doing them because of a motive. The soundest of motives for the habit of *going the extra mile* is the fact that it yields enduring dividends, in ways too numerous to mention, to all who follow the habit.

No one has ever been known to achieve permanent success without doing more than he was paid for. The practice has its counterpart in the laws of nature. It has back of it an impressive array of evidence as to its soundness. It is based on common sense and justice.

The best of all methods of testing the soundness of this principle is that of putting it to work as a part of one's daily habits. Some truths we can learn only through our own experience.

Americans want greater individual shares of the vast resources of this country. That is a healthy desire. The wealth is here in abundance, but let us stop this foolish attempt to get it the wrong way. Let us get our wealth by giving something of value in return for it.

We know the rules by which success is attained. Let us appropriate these rules and use them intelligently, thereby acquiring the personal riches we demand, and adding to the wealth of the nation as well.

The Case of the Greedy Employer

Some will say, "I am already doing more than I am paid for, but my employer is so selfish and greedy he will not recognize the sort of service I am rendering." We all know there are greedy men who desire more service than that for which they are willing to pay.

Selfish employers are like pieces of clay in the hands of a potter. Through their greed they can be induced to reward the man who renders them more service than he is paid to render.

Greedy employers do not wish to lose the services of one who makes a habit of *going the extra mile*. They know the value of such employees. Here, then, is the crow-bar and the fulcrum with which employers can be pried loose from their greed.

Any clever man will know how to use this crow-bar, not by withholding the quality or quantity of service he renders, *but by increasing it!*

The clever salesman of his personal services can manipulate a greedy purchaser of his services as easily as a smart woman can influence the man of her choice. The effective technique is similar to that used by clever women in managing men.

The clever man will make it his business to become indispensable to a greedy employer by doing more work and better work than any other employee. Greedy employers will "give their eye teeth" before parting with such a man. Thus the alleged greed of employers becomes a great asset to the man who follows the habit of *going the extra mile*.

We have seen this technique applied at least a hundred times as a means of manipulating greedy employers through the use of their own weakness. Not once have we seen it fail to work!

On some occasions the greedy employer failed to move as quickly as expected, but that proved to be his hard luck, because his employee attracted the attention of a competitive employer who made a bid for the services of the employee and secured them.

There is no way to cheat the man who follows the habit

of *going the extra mile*. If he does not get proper recognition from one source, it comes voluntarily from some other source—usually when it is least expected. It always comes if a man does more than he is paid for.

The man who *goes the extra mile* and does it in the right kind of "mental attitude" never spends time looking for a job. He does not have to, for the job is always looking for him. Depressions may come and go; business may be good or poor; the country may be at war or at peace; but the man who renders more service and better service than he is paid for *becomes indispensable to someone and thereby insures himself against unemployment.*

High wages and indispensability are twin-sisters. They always have been and always will be!

The man who is smart enough to make himself indispensable is smart enough to keep himself continuously employed, and at wages which not even the most greedy labor leader would ask.

Most men spend their lives searching for the "breaks," waiting for opportunities to overtake them, depending upon "luck" to provide them with their needs, but never come within sight of their goal because they have no definite goal. Therefore they have no *motive* to inspire them to form the habit of *going the extra mile*. They never recognize:

> "The Worldly Hope men set their Hearts upon
> Turns Ashes—or it prospers; and anon,
> Like Snow upon the Desert's dusty face
> Lighting a little Hour or two—is gone."

Their haste becomes waste! For they go round and round, like goldfish in a bowl, coming back always to the place from whence they started; coming back empty-handed and disappointed.

Riches may be attained by appointment only; by the choice of a definite goal and a definite plan for attaining it; also by the selection of a definite starting point from which to take off.

But, let no one make the mistake of assuming that the habit of *going the extra mile* pays off only in terms of material riches. The habit definitely helps one to tap the source of spiritual riches, and to draw upon that source for every human need.

The Revealing Story of Edward Choate

Some men who are smart, and others who are wise, have discovered the way to riches by the deliberate application of the principle of *going the extra mile* for pecuniary gain.

However, those who are truly wise recognize that the greatest pay-off through this principle comes in terms of friendships which endure throughout life, in harmonious human relationships, in a labor of love, in the capacity to understand people, in a willingness to share one's blessings with others, all of which are among the Twelve Riches of life.

Edward Choate is one who has recognized this truth and has found the Master-Key to Riches. His home is in Los Angeles, California, and his business is that of selling life insurance.

At the outset of his career as a life insurance salesman he made a modest living from his efforts, but he broke no records in that field. Through an unfortunate business venture he lost all of his money and found himself at the bottom of the ladder, and was forced to make a new start.

I said "an unfortunate business venture," but perhaps I should have said "a fortunate business venture," for his loss influenced him to stop, look, listen, *think,* and to meditate concerning the fates of men which seem to lift some to high places of achievement but condemn others to temporary defeat or permanent failure.

Through his meditations he became a student of the philosophy of individual achievement. When Mr. Choate reached the lesson on *going the extra mile* he was awakened by a keen sense of understanding he had never before experienced, and he recognized that the loss of material riches may lead one to the source of greater riches, consisting of one's spiritual forces.

With this discovery Mr. Choate began to appropriate, one by one, the Twelve Riches of life, beginning at the head of the list by the development *of positive mental attitude.*

For the time being he ceased to think about the amount of life insurance he might sell, and began to look around for opportunities to be of service to others who were burdened with problems they could not solve.

His first opportunity came when he discovered a young

man out in the deserts of California who had failed in a mining venture and was facing starvation. He took the young man into his home, fed him, encouraged him and kept him in his home until he found a good position for him.

In thus casting himself for the role of the good Samaritan, Mr. Choate had no thought of pecuniary gain, for it was obvious that a poverty-stricken, broken-spirited boy might never become a prospective purchaser of life insurance.

Then other opportunities to help the less fortunate began to reveal themselves so rapidly that it seemed as if Mr. Choate had made of himself a magnet which attracted only those with difficult problems to be solved.

But the appearance was deceiving, for he was only passing through a testing period by which he might demonstrate his sincerity of purpose in helping others. A period, let us not forget, which everyone who applies the principle of *going the extra mile* must experience in one way or another.

Then the scene shifted, and the affairs of Edward Choate began to take a turn he probably had not expected. His life insurance sales began to mount higher and higher, until at last they had reached an all-time high level. And miracle of miracles, one of the largest policies he had ever written up to that time was sold to the employer of the young man of the desert whom he had befriended. The sale was made without Mr. Choate's solicitation.

Other sales began to come his way in the same manner, until he was actually selling more insurance, without any strenuous effort, than he had ever sold previously by the hardest kind of labor.

Moreover, he had tapped a field of life insurance salesmanship in which the policies he sold were of large amounts. Men of great responsibilities and extensive financial affairs began to send for him to counsel them in connection with their life insurance problems.

His business grew until it brought him that goal which is so greatly coveted by all life insurance men—Life Membership in the Million Dollar Round Table. Such a distinction is attained only by those who sell a minimum of a million dollars a year in insurance for three consecutive years.

So, in seeking spiritual riches Edward Choate also found material riches; found them in greater abundance than he had ever anticipated. Six brief years after he had begun to cast himself for the role of the good Samaritan, Mr. Choate wrote more than two million dollars of life insurance during the first four months of the year.

The story of his achievements began to spread throughout the nation. It brought him invitations to speak before life insurance conventions, for other life insurance salesmen desired to know how he had managed to lift himself to so enviable a position in that profession.

He told them! And quite contrary to the usual practice among men who have attained success in the upper brackets of achievement, he revealed the humility of heart by which he is inspired, frankly admitting that his achievements were the result of the application of the philosophy of others.

The average man who is successful has a tendency to try to convey the impression that his success is due to his own smartness or wisdom, but very seldom does he frankly give credit to his benefactors.

What a pity there are not more Edward Choates in the world!

For it is obvious to all who think accurately that no man ever attains a high degree of enduring success without the friendly co-operation of others; nor does any man ever attain enduring success without helping others.

Edward Choate is as rich in material values as he needs to be. He is far richer in spiritual values, for he has discovered, appropriated and made intelligent use of all of the Twelve Riches of Life, of which money is the last *and the least in importance.*

Chapter Six

THE MASTER MIND

Definition: *An alliance of two or more minds blended in a spirit of perfect harmony* and co-operating for the attainment of a definite purpose.

Note well the definition of this principle, for it carries a meaning which provides the key to the attainment of great personal power.

The Master Mind principle is the basis of all great achievements, the foundation stone of major importance in all human progress, whether it be individual progress or collective progress.

The key to its power may be found in the word "harmony!"

Without that element, collective effort may constitute co-operation, but it will lack the power which harmony provides through co-ordination of effort.

The tenets of major importance in connection with the Master Mind principle are these:

Premise 1:

The Master Mind principle is the medium through which one may procure the full benefit of the *experience, training, education, specialized knowledge* and *native ability* of others, just as completely as if their minds were one's own.

Premise 2:

An alliance of two or more minds, in a spirit of *perfect harmony* for the attainment of a definite purpose, stimulates each individual mind with a high degree of inspiration, and may become that state of mind known as Faith! (A slight idea of this stimulation and its power is experienced in the relationship of close friendship and in the relationship of love.)

Premise 3:

Every human brain is both a broadcasting station and a

receiving station for the expression of the vibrations of thought, and the stimulating effect of the Master Mind principle stimulates action of thought, through what is commonly known as telepathy, operating through the sixth sense.

In this manner many business and professional alliances are translated into reality, and seldom has anyone ever attained a high station or enduring power without the application of the Master Mind principle through which he secured the benefit of other minds.

This fact alone is sufficient evidence of the soundness and the importance of the Master Mind principle, and it is a fact which anyone may observe without straining his powers of observation or over-taxing his credulity.

Premise 4:

The Master Mind principle, when actively applied, has the effect of connecting one with the subconscious section of the mind, and the subconscious sections of the minds of his allies—a fact which may explain many of the seemingly miraculous results obtained through the Master Mind.

Premise 5:

The more important human relationships in connection with which one may apply beneficially the Master Mind principle are these:

(a) In marriage
(b) In religion
(c) In connection with one's occupation, profession or calling.

The Master Mind principle made it possible for Thomas A. Edison to become a great inventor despite his lack of education and his lack of knowledge of the sciences with which he had to work—a circumstance which offers hope to all who erroneously believe themselves to be seriously handicapped by the lack of a formal education.

With the aid of the Master Mind principle one may understand the history and the structure of this earth on which we live through the knowledge of skilled geologists.

Through the knowledge and experience of the chemist one may make practical use of chemistry without being a trained chemist.

With the aid of scientists, technicians, physicists and practical mechanics one may become a successful inventor without personal training in any of these fields.

There are two general types of Master Mind alliances, viz:

1. Alliance, for purely social or personal reasons, with one's relatives, religious advisors and friends, where no material gain or objective is sought. *The most important of this type of alliance is that of man and wife.*

2. Alliances for business, professional and economic advancement, consisting of individuals who have a personal motive in connection with the object of the alliance.

Now let us consider some of the more important examples of power that have been attained by the application of the Master Mind.

The American form of government, as it was originally written into the Constitution of the United States, should have first analysis because it is one form of power which vitally affects every citizen of our country, and to a large degree affects the entire world.

Our country is noted for three obvious facts:

1. It is the richest country of the world.
2. It is the most powerful nation of the world.
3. It provides its citizens with more personal freedom than does any other nation.

Riches, freedom and power! What an awe-inspiring combination of realities!

The source of these benefits is not difficult to determine, for it centers in the Constitution of our country and in the American system of free enterprise, these having been so harmoniously coordinated that they have provided the people with both spiritual and economic power, such as the world has never before witnessed.

Our form of government is a stupendous Master Mind alliance made up of the harmonious relationship of all the people of the nation, functioning through fifty separate groups known as states.

The central core of our American Master Mind is easily discernible by breaking down our form of government and examining its component parts, all of which are under the direct control of a majority of the people.

These parts are:

1. The executive branch of our government (maintained by a President)
2. The judiciary branch (maintained by the Supreme Court)
3. The legislative branch (maintained by the two Houses of Congress)

Our Constitution has been so wisely constructed that the power behind all three of these branches of government is held by the people. It is a power of which the people cannot be deprived *except by their own neglect to use it!*

Our political power is expressed through our government.

Our economic power is maintained and expressed through our system of free enterprise.

And the sum total of the power of these two is always in exact ratio to the degree of harmony with which the two are coordinated!

The power thus attained *is the property of all the people!*

It is this power which has provided the people with the highest standard of living that civilization has yet evolved, and which has made our nation truly the richest and the freest and the most powerful nation of the world.

We speak of this power as "The American Way Of Life!"

It was this way of life and our desire to maintain it which brought about the consolidation of our forces, both economic and spiritual, in a war that threatened the destruction of civilization as well as our way of life.

The future of mankind may have been determined by the application of our American Master Mind, for it is obvious that ours was the balance of power which turned the tide of war in favor of freedom for all mankind.

Another illustration of the Master Mind applied to industry may be found in the great American systems of transportation and communications. The men who manage our railroads and our air lines, our telephone and telegraph systems, have established a service which has never been equaled in any other country. Their efficiency and the resultant power consist entirely in their application of the Master Mind principle of harmonious co-ordination of effort.

Still another example of power attained through the Master Mind principle may be found by observing the relationship of our military forces—our Armies, our Navy and our Air Forces. Here, as elsewhere, the keystone to the arch of our power has been *harmonious co-ordination of effort*.

The modern football team is an excellent example of power attained through harmony of effort.

The great American system of chain store merchandising is still another example of economic power attained through the Master Mind principle.

And every successful industry is the result of application

of the Master Mind. The American system of free enterprise in its entirety is a marvelous illustration of economic power produced by friendly, harmonious co-ordination of effort.

The Master Mind principle is not the exclusive property of the rich and the powerful, but it is the means of major importance by which men may attain desirable ends.

The humblest person may benefit from this principle by forming a harmonious alliance with anyone of his choice. The most profound, and perhaps the most beneficial application of this principle that any man may make is the Master Mind alliance in marriage, provided the motive behind that alliance is Love!

This sort of alliance not only co-ordinates the minds of man and wife, but it also blends the spiritual qualities of their souls.

The benefits of such an alliance not only bring joy and happiness to man and wife, but they profoundly bless their children with sound character, and endow them with the fundamentals of a successful life.

You now have an understandable interpretation of the greatest source of personal power known to men—the Master Mind. The responsibility for its right use is yours.

Use it well and you will be blessed with the privilege of occupying great space in the world; space that can be estimated in both geography and in human relationships which are friendly and cooperative.

Do not be afraid to aim high when you establish your goal.

Remember that you live in a land of opportunities where no man is limited in the quality, the quantity or the nature of the riches he may acquire, provided he is willing to give adequate value in return.

Before you fix your goal in life, memorize the following lines and take to heart the lesson they teach:

> "I bargained with Life for a penny,
>   And Life would pay no more,
> However I begged at evening
>   When I counted my scanty store.

> "For Life is a just employer,
>   He gives you what you ask,
> But once you have set the wages,
>   Why, you must bear the task.

> "I worked for a menial's hire,
>   Only to learn, dismayed,
> That any wage I had asked of Life,
>   Life would have *willingly paid*."

Successful men do not bargain with Life for poverty!

They know that there is a power through which Life may be made to pay off on their own terms. They know that this power is available to every man who comes into possession of the Master-Key to Riches. They know the nature of this power and its unlimited scope. They know it by a name of one word; the greatest word in the English language!

This word is known to all men, but the secrets of its power are understood by few.

Chapter Seven

ANALYSIS OF THE MASTER MIND PRINCIPLE

When I was commissioned by Andrew Carnegie to organize the philosophy of individual achievement I asked him to describe the Master Mind principle so it might be appropriated and used by others, for the attainment of their Definite Major Purpose.

"Mr. Carnegie," I requested, "will you define the Master Mind principle as it may be applied through the individual efforts of men and women who are seeking their places in the great American way of life? Describe, if you will, the various forms of application that may be made of this principle by the man of average ability, in his daily efforts to make the most of his opportunities in this country."

And this is Mr. Carnegie's reply:

"The privileges which are available to the American people have back of them a source of great power. But privileges do not spring, mushroom-like, from nothing. They must be created and maintained by the application of power.

"The founders of our American form of government, through their foresight and wisdom, laid the foundation for all of our American form of liberty, freedom and riches. But, they only laid the foundation. The responsibility of embracing and using this foundation must be assumed by every person who claims any portion of this freedom and wealth.

"I will describe some of the individual uses of the Master Mind principle, as it may be applied in the development of various human relationships which may contribute to the attainment of one's Definite Major Purpose.

"But first I wish to emphasize the fact that the attainment of one's Definite Major Purpose can be carried out only by a series of steps; that every thought one thinks, every

93

transaction in which one engages, in relationship with others, every plan one creates, every mistake one makes, has a vital bearing on his ability to attain his chosen goal.

"The mere choice of a Definite Major Purpose, even though it be written out in clear language and fully fixed in one's mind, will not insure the successful realization of that purpose.

"One's major purpose must be backed up and followed though by continuous effort, *the most important part of which consists in the sort of relationship one maintains with others.*

"With this truth well established in one's mind it will not be difficult for one to understand how necessary it is to be careful in one's choice of associates, especially those with whom one maintains close personal contact in connection with his occupation.

"Here, then, are some of the sources of human relationship, which the man with a Definite Major Purpose must cultivate, organize and use in his progress toward the attainment of his chosen goal:

Occupation

"Outside of the relationship of marriage (which is the most important of all Master Mind relationships) there is no form of relationship as important as that which exists between a man and those with whom he works in his chosen occupation.

"Every man has a tendency to take on the mannerisms, beliefs, mental attitude, political and economic viewpoint, as well as other traits of the more outspoken of the men with whom he associates in his daily work.

"The major tragedy of this tendency lies in the fact that not always is the most outspoken among one's daily associates the soundest thinker; and very often he is a man with a grievance, who takes pleasure in airing the grievance among his fellow workers.

"Also, the most outspoken man often is an individual who has no Definite Major Purpose of his own. Therefore he devotes much of his time endeavoring to belittle the man who has such a purpose.

"Men of sound character, who know exactly what they wish, usually have the wisdom to keep their own counsel, and seldom waste any of their time trying to discourage others. They are so busily engaged in promoting their own purpose that they have no time to waste with anyone or anything which does not contribute in one way or another to their benefit.

"Realizing that one may find in almost every group of associates some person whose influence and cooperation may be helpful, the man of keen discrimination, who has a Definite Major Purpose he desires to attain, will prove his wisdom by forming friendships with those who can be, and who are willing to become, mutually beneficial to him. The others he will tactfully avoid.

"Naturally he will seek his closest alliances with men whom he recognizes possess traits of character, knowledge and personality which may become helpful to him; and of course he will not overlook those holding positions of higher rank than his own, keeping his eye on the day when he may not only equal such men, but excel them, remembering meanwhile the words of Abraham Lincoln, who said: 'I will study and prepare myself, and some day my chance will come.'

"The man with a constructive Definite Major Purpose will never envy his superiors, but he will study their methods and learn to acquire their knowledge. You may accept it as a sound prophecy that the man who spends his time finding fault with his superiors will never become a successful leader on his own account.

"The greatest soldiers are those who can take, and carry out, orders of their superiors in rank. Those who cannot or will not do this, never will become successful leaders in military operations. The same rule is true of any man in other walks of life. If he fails to emulate the man above him, in a spirit of harmony, he will never benefit greatly from his association with that man.

"No fewer than a hundred men have risen from the ranks in my own organization, and have found themselves richer than they need be. They were not promoted because of bad dispositions or the habit of finding fault with those above or those below them, but they promoted themselves by appropriating and making practical use of the experience of everyone with whom they came in contact.

"The man with a Definite Major Purpose will take careful inventory of every person with whom he comes in contact in his daily work, and he will look upon every such person as a possible source of useful knowledge or influence which he may borrow and use in his own promotion.

"If a man looks about him intelligently he will discover that his place of daily labor is literally a school room in which he may acquire the greatest of all educations—that which comes from observation and experience.

"How may one make the most of this sort of schooling? some will ask.

"The answer may be found by studying the nine basic motives which move men to voluntary action. Men lend their experience, their knowledge, and they cooperate with other men, because they have been given a sufficient motive to cause them to desire as much. The man who relates himself to his daily associates in a friendly, cooperative way, with the right sort of mental attitude toward them, stands a better chance of learning from them than does the man who is belligerent, irritable, discourteous or neglectful of the little amenities of courtesy which exist between all cultured people.

"The old saying that 'a man can catch more flies with honey than with salt' might well be remembered by the man who wishes to learn of his daily associates who know more about many things than he does, and whose cooperation he needs and seeks.

Education

"No man's education is ever finished.

"The man whose Definite Major Purpose is of noteworthy proportions must remain always a student, and he must learn from every possible source, especially those sources from which he may acquire specialized knowledge and experience related to his major purpose.

"The public libraries are free. They offer a great array of organized knowledge on every subject. They carry, in every language, the total of man's knowledge on every subject. The successful man with a Definite Major Purpose makes it his business and his responsibility to read books relating to that purpose, and thus acquire important knowledge which comes from the experiences of other men who have gone before him. It has been said that a man cannot consider himself even a kindergarten student of any subject until he has availed himself, as far as reasonably possible, of all the knowledge on that subject which has been preserved for him through the experience of others.

"A man's reading program should be as carefully planned as his daily diet, for that too is food, without which he cannot grow mentally.

"The man who spends all of his spare time reading the funny papers and the sex magazines is not headed toward any great achievement.

"The same may be said of the man who does not include in his daily program some form of reading that provides him with the knowledge which he may use in the attainment of his major purpose. Random reading may be pleasant, but it seldom is helpful in connection with one's occupation.

"Reading, however, is not the only source of education. By a careful choice among his daily associates in his occupation, one may ally himself with men from whom he can acquire a liberal education through ordinary conversation.

"Business and professional clubs offer an opportunity for one to form alliances of great educational benefit, provided the man chooses his clubs and his close associates in those clubs with a definite objective in mind. Through this sort of association many men have formed both business and social acquaintances of great value to them in carrying out the object of their major purpose.

"No man can go through life successfully without the habit of cultivating friends. The word 'contact,' as it is commonly used in relationship to personal acquaintanceship, is an important word. If a man makes it a part of his daily practice to extend his list of personal 'contacts' he will find the habit of great benefit to him in ways that cannot be foretold while he is cultivating those acquaintances, but the time will come when they will be ready and willing to render aid to him if he has done a good job of selling himself.

"As I have stated, a man with a Definite Major Purpose should form the habit of establishing 'contacts' through every source possible, using care of course to choose those sources through which he is most likely to meet people who may be helpful to him.

"The church is among the more desirable sources through which one may meet and cultivate people, because it brings people together under circumstances which inspire the spirit of fellowship among men.

"Every man needs some source through which he can associate with his neighbors under circumstances that will enable him to exchange thoughts with them for the sake of mutual understanding and friendship, quite aside from all considerations of pecuniary gain. The man who shuts himself up in his own shell becomes a confirmed introvert, and soon becomes selfish and narrow in his views on life.

Politics

"It is both the duty and the privilege of an American citizen to interest himself in politics and thereby exercise his right to help place, through his ballot, worthy men and women in public office.

"The political party to which a man belongs is of much less importance than the question of his exercising his privilege of voting. If politics become smeared with dishonest practices there is no one to blame but the people who have it within their power to keep dishonest, unworthy and inefficient people out of office.

"In addition to the privilege of voting and the duty it carries with it, one should not overlook the benefits which may be gained from an active interest in politics, through 'contacts' and alliances with people who may become helpful in the attainment of one's Definite Major Purpose.

"In many occupations, professions and businesses, political influence becomes a definite and important factor in the promotion of one's interests. Business and professional men and women certainly should not neglect the possibility of promoting their interests through active political alliances.

"The alert individual, who understands the necessity of reaching out in every possible direction for friendly allies whom he can use in attaining his major purpose in life, will make the fullest use of his privilege of voting.

"But, the major reason why every American citizen should

take an active interest in politics, and the one which I would emphasize above all others, is the fact that if the better type of citizen fails to exercise his right to vote, politics will disintegrate and become an evil that will destroy this nation.

"The founders of this nation pledged their lives and their fortunes to provide all the people with the privileges of liberty and freedom in the pursuit of their chosen purpose in life. And chief among these privileges is that of helping, by the ballot, to maintain the institution of Government which the founders of this nation established to protect those privileges.

"Everything that is worth having has a definite price.

"You desire personal freedom and individual liberty! Very well, you may protect this right by forming a Master Mind alliance with other honest and patriotic men, and making it your business to elect honest men to public office. And it is no exaggeration to state that this may well be the most important Master Mind alliance that any American citizen can make.

"Your forefathers insured your personal liberty and freedom by their votes. *You should do no less for your offspring and the generations that will follow them!*

"Every honest American citizen has sufficient influence with his neighbors, and his daily associates in connection with his occupation, to enable him to influence at least five other people to exercise their right to vote. If he fails to exercise this influence he may still remain an honest citizen, but he cannot truthfully call himself a *patriotic citizen,* for patriotism has a price consisting in the obligation to exercise it.

Social Alliances

"Here is a fertile, almost unlimited, field for the cultivation of friendly 'contacts.' It is particularly available to the married man whose wife understands the art of making friends through social activities.

"Such a wife can convert her home and her social activities into a priceless asset to her husband, if his occupation is one that requires him to extend his list of friends.

"Many professional men whose professional ethics forbid direct advertising or self-promotion, may make effective use of their social privileges, provided they have wives with a bent for social activities.

"A successful life insurance man sells more than a million dollars a year of insurance, with the aid of his wife, who is a member of several Business Women's Clubs. His wife's part is simple. She entertains her fellow club members in her home from time to time, along with their husbands. In this way her husband becomes acquainted with them under friendly circumstances.

"A lawyer's wife has been credited with helping him to build one of the most lucrative law practices in a middle western city, by the simple process of entertaining, through her social activities, the wives of wealthy business men. The possibilities in this direction are endless.

"One of the major advantages of friendly alliances with people in a variety of walks of life consists in the opportunity such contacts provide for 'round-table' discussions which lead to the accumulation of knowledge one may use in the attainment of his Definite Major Purpose.

"If one's acquaintances are sufficiently numerous and varied, they may become a valuable source of information on a wide range of subjects, thus leading to a form of intellectual intercourse which is essential for the development of flexibility and versatility required in many callings.

"When a group of men get together and enter into a round-table discussion on any subject, this sort of spontaneous expression and interchange of thought enriches the minds of all who participate. Every man needs to reinforce his own ideas and plans with new food for thought, which he can acquire only through frank and sincere discussions with people whose experience and education differ from his own.

"The writer who becomes a 'top-notcher' and remains in that exalted position must add continuously to his own stock of knowledge by appropriating the thoughts and ideas of others, through personal contacts and by reading.

"Any mind that remains brilliant, alert, receptive and flexible must be fed continuously from the storehouse of other minds. If this renewal is neglected the mind will atrophy, the same as will an arm that is taken out of use. This is in accordance with nature's laws. Study nature's plan and you will discover that every living thing, from the smallest insect to the complicated machinery of a human being, grows and remains healthy only by constant use.

"Round-table discussions not only add to one's store of useful knowledge, but they develop and expand the power of the mind. The person who stops studying the day he finishes his formal schooling will never become an educated person, no matter how much knowledge he may acquire while he is going to school.

"Life itself is a great school, and everything that inspires thought is a teacher. The wise man knows this; moreover, he makes it a part of his daily routine to contact other minds, with the object of developing his own mind through the exchange of thoughts.

"We see, therefore, that the Master Mind principle has an unlimited scope of practical use. It is the medium by which the individual may supplement the power of his own mind with the knowledge, experience and mental attitude of other minds.

"As one man so aptly expressed this idea: 'If I give you one of my dollars in return for one of yours, each of us will have no more than he started with; but, if I give you a thought in return for one of your thoughts, each of us will have gained a hundred percent dividend on his investment of time.'

"No form of human relationship is as profitable as that through which men exchange useful thoughts, and it may be surprising but true that one may acquire from the mind of the humblest person ideas of the first magnitude of importance.

"Let me illustrate what I mean, through the story of a preacher who picked from the mind of the janitor of his church an idea that led to the attainment of his Definite Major Purpose.

"The preacher's name was Russell Conwell, and his major purpose was the founding of a college he had long desired to establish. All he needed was the necessary money, a tidy sum of something more than a million dollars.

"One day the Reverend Russell Conwell stopped to chat with the janitor who was busily at work cutting the church lawn. As they stood there talking in light conversation, Reverend Conwell casually remarked that the grass adjoining the churchyard was much greener and better kept than their own lawn, intending his remark as a mild reprimand to the old care-taker.

"With a broad grin on his face the janitor replied: 'Yes, that grass sure does look greener, but that's because we're so used to the grass on this side of the fence.'

"Now there was nothing brilliant about that remark, for it was not intended to be anything more than an alibi for laziness, but it planted in the fertile mind of Russell Conwell the seed of an idea—just a bare, tiny seed of thought, mind you—which led to the solution of his major problem.

"From that humble remark an idea was born for a lecture which the preacher composed and delivered more than four thousand times. He called it 'Acres of Diamonds.' The central idea of the lecture was this: A man need not seek his opportunity in the distance, but he can find it right where he stands, by recognizing the fact that the grass on the other side of the fence is no greener than that where he stands.

"The lecture yielded an income during the life of Russell Conwell of more than six million dollars. It was published in book form and became a best seller throughout the nation for many years thereafter, and it may be obtained to this day. The money was used to found and maintain Temple University of Philadelphia, Pennsylvania, one of the great educational institutions of the country.

"The idea around which that lecture was organized did more than found a university. It enriched the minds of millions of people by influencing them to look for opportunity right where they were. The philosophy of the lecture is as sound today as it was when it first came from the mind of a working man.

"Remember this: Every active brain is a potential source of inspiration from which one may procure an idea, or the mere seed of an idea, of priceless value in the solution of his personal problems, or the attainment of his major purpose in life.

"Sometimes great ideas spring from humble minds, but generally they come from the minds of those closest to the individual, where The Master Mind relationship has been deliberately established and maintained.

"The most profitable idea of my own career came one afternoon when Charlie Schwab and I were walking across a golf course. As we finished our shots on the thirteenth hole, Charlie looked up with a sheepish grin on his face, and said, 'I'm three strokes up on you at this hole, Chief; but I have just thought of an idea that should give you a lot of free time to play golf.'

"Curiosity prompted me to inquire as to the nature of the idea. He gave it to me, in one brief sentence, each word of which was worth, roughly speaking, a million dollars. 'Consolidate all your steel plants,' said he, 'into one big corporation and sell it out to Wall Street bankers.'

"Nothing more was said about the matter during the game, but that evening I began to turn the suggestion over in my mind and think about it. Before I went to sleep that night I had converted the seed of his idea into a definite major purpose. The following week I sent Charlie Schwab to New York City to deliver a speech before a group of Wall Street bankers, among them, J. Pierpont Morgan.

"The sum and substance of the speech was a plan for the organization of the United States Steel Corporation, through which I consolidated all my steel plants and retired from active business, with more money than anyone needs.

"Now let me emphasize one point: Charlie Schwab's idea might never have been born, and I never would have received the benefit of it if I had not made it my business to encourage in my associates the creation of new ideas. This encouragement was provided through a close and continuous Master Mind alliance with the members of my business organization, among whom was Charlie Schwab.

"Contact, let me repeat, is an important word!

"It is much more important if we add to it the word 'harmonious!' Through harmonious relationships with the minds of other men an individual may have the full use of his capacity to create ideas. The man who overlooks this great fact thereby condemns himself eternally to penury and want.

"No man is smart enough to project his influence very far into the world without the friendly cooperation of other men. Drive this thought home in every way you can, for it is sufficient unto itself to open the door to success in the higher brackets of individual achievement.

"Too many people look for success in the distance, far from where they are; and altogether too often they search for it through complicated plans based upon a belief in luck or 'miracles' which they hope may favor them.

"As Russell Conwell so effectively stated the matter in

his lecture, some people seem to think the grass is greener on the other side of the fence from where they stand, and they pass up the 'Acres of Diamonds' in the form of ideas and opportunities which are available to them through the minds of their daily associates.

"I found my 'Acres of Diamonds' right where I stood, while looking into the glow of a hot steel blast furnace. I remember well the first day I began to sell myself the idea of becoming a leader in the great steel industry instead of remaining a helper in another man's 'Acres of Diamonds.'

"At first the thought was not very definite. It was a wish more than it was a definite purpose. But I began to bring it back into my mind and to encourage it to take possession of me, until there came the day when the idea began to drive me instead of my having to drive it.

"That day I began with earnestness to work my own 'Acres of Diamonds,' and I was surprised to learn how quickly a Definite Major Purpose may find a way to translate itself into its physical equivalent.

"The main thing of importance is to know what one wants.

"The next thing of importance is to begin digging for diamonds right where one is, using whatever tools may be at hand, even if they be only the tools of thought. In proportion to the faithful use a man makes of the tools at hand, other and better tools will be placed in his hands when he is ready for them.

"The man who understands the Master Mind principle and makes use of it will find the necessary tools much more quickly than will the fellow who knows nothing of this principle.

"Every mind needs friendly contact with other minds, for the food of expansion and growth. The discriminating person who has a Definite Major Purpose in life chooses, with the greatest of care, the types of minds with whom he associates most intimately, because he recognizes that he will take on a definite portion of the personality of every person with whom he thus associates.

"I wouldn't give much for a man who does not make it his business to seek the company of people who know more than he. A man rises to the level of his superiors or falls to the level of his inferiors, according to the class he emulates through his choice of associates.

"Lastly, there is one other thought which every man who

works for wages or a salary should recognize and respect. It lies in the fact that his job is, and should be, a schooling for a higher station in life, for which he is being paid in two important ways; first, by the wages he receives directly, and secondly, by the experience he gains from his work. And it frequently becomes true that a man's greatest pay consists not in his pay envelope, *but in the experience he gains from his work!*

"This overplus pay a man may gain from his experience depends largely for its value upon the mental attitude in which he relates himself to his associate workers; both those above him and those beneath him. If his attitude is positive and cooperative, and he follows the habit of Going The Extra Mile, his advancement will be both sure and rapid.

"Thus we see that the man who gets ahead not only makes practical use of the principle of the Master Mind, but he also applies the principle of Going The Extra Mile, and the principle of Definiteness of Purpose; the three principles which are inseparably associated with successful men in all walks of life.

Marriage

"Marriage is by far the most important alliance any man ever experiences during his entire life.

"It is important financially, physically, mentally and spiritually, for it is a relationship bound together by all of these.

"The home is the place where most Master Mind alliances should begin, and the man who has chosen his mate wisely will, if he is wise in an economic sense, make his wife the first member of his personal Master Mind group.

"The home alliance should include not only man and wife, but it should include other members of the family if they live in the same household, particularly children.

"The Master Mind principle brings into action the spiritual forces of those who are thus allied for a definite purpose; and spiritual power, while it may seem intangible, is nevertheless the greatest of all powers.

"The married man who is on the right terms with his wife—terms of *complete harmony, understanding, sympathy* and *singleness of purpose* in which each is interested—has a priceless asset in this relationship which may lift him to great heights of personal achievement.

"Inharmony between a man and his wife is unpardonable, no matter what may be the cause. It is unpardonable because it may destroy a man's chances of success, even though he has every attribute necessary for success.

For Wives Only

"And may I here interpolate a suggestion for the benefit of the wives of men?

"The suggestion may, if it is heeded and followed, make just the difference between a lifetime of poverty and misery and a lifetime of opulence and plenty.

"The wife has more influence over her husband than has any other person. That is, she has this superior influence if she has made the most of her relationship to her husband. He chose her in marriage in preference to all other women of his acquaintance, which means that she has his love and his confidence.

"Love heads the list of the nine basic motives of life which inspire all voluntary actions of people. Through the emotion of love the wife may send her husband to his daily labor in a spirit which knows no such reality as failure. But remember that 'nagging,' jealousy, fault-finding and indifference do not feed the emotion of love. They kill it.

"If a wife is wise she will arrange with her husband for a regular Master Mind hour each day; a period during which they will pool all of their mutual interests and discuss them in detail, in a spirit of love and understanding. The periods most suited for this Master Mind talk are those following the morning meal and just before retiring at night.

"And every meal hour should be a period of friendly intercourse between the wife and her husband. They should not be converted into periods of inquisition and fault-finding, but rather should be converted into periods of family worship, during which there will be good cheer, and the discussion of pleasant subjects of mutual interest to the husband and wife.

"More family relationships are wrecked at the family meal

hour than at any other time, for this is the hour which many families devote to settling their family differences of opinion, or to disciplining the children.

"It has been said that a man's stomach is the way to his heart. Therefore the meal hour provides an excellent opportunity for a wife to reach her husband's heart with any idea she desires to plant there. But the approach must be based on love and affection; not upon negative habits of discipline and fault-finding.

"The wife can coax her husband to do many things!

"The wife should take a keen interest in her husband's occupation. She should become familiar with every feature of it, and never overlook an opportunity to express a keen interest in everything that concerns the source from which he earns his livelihood. And above all, she should not be one of those wives who say to their husbands, by inference if not by words, 'You bring home the money and I will spend it, but don't bother me with the details as to how you earn it, for I am not interested in that.'

"If a wife takes that attitude, the time will come when her husband will not be interested as to how much money he brings home, and the time may come when he will not bring it all home!

"I think that wives who are wise will understand just what I mean.

"When a woman marries she becomes the majority stockholder in the firm. If she relates herself to her husband by a true application of the Master Mind principle she will continue, as long as the marriage exists, to vote that stock as she pleases.

"The wife who is wise will manage the firm's business by a carefully prepared budget, taking care not to spend more than the income will allow. Many marriages go on the rocks because the firm runs out of money. And it is no mere axiom to say that when poverty knocks on the front door, love takes to its heels and runs out through the back door. Love, like a beautiful picture, requires the embellishment of an appropriate frame and proper lighting. It requires cultivation and food, just as does the physical body. Love does not thrive on indifference, nagging, fault-finding or domineering by either party.

"Love thrives best where a man and his wife feed it through singleness of purpose. The wife who remembers this may remain forever the most influential person in the life of her husband. The wife who forgets it may see the time when her husband begins to look around for an opportunity 'to trade her in on a newer model,' to use the phraseology of the automobile industry.

"The husband has the responsibility of earning the living, but the wife may have the responsibility of softening the shocks and the resistances which he will meet in connection with his occupation—a responsibility which the wife can discharge by planning a pleasant home-life, through whatever social activities may be fitting to her husband's calling.

"The wife should see to it that the home is the one place where her husband may lay aside his business or occupational cares and enjoy the ecstasies which only the love and affection and understanding of a wife can provide. The wife who follows this policy will be as wise as the sages, and richer—in the ways that count most—than most queens.

"I would also caution a wife against allowing her maternal instinct to supplant her love for her husband, by transferring all of her love and attention to her children. This mistake has wrecked many homes, and it might well wreck any home if the wife neglects to guard against the error so many wives make of switching their love from their husbands to their children.

"A woman's love, if it be the right kind of love, is sufficient in abundance to serve both the children and her husband; and it is a happy wife who sees to it that her love is sufficient to serve her husband and the children generously, without unfair preference in favor of either.

"Where love abounds as the basis of the family Master Mind relationship the family finances will not be likely to give cause for disturbance, for love has a way of surmounting all obstacles, meeting all problems and overcoming all difficulties.

"Family problems may arise, and they do in every family, but love should be the master of them. Keep the light of love shining brightly and everything else will shape itself to the pattern of your most lofty desires.

"I know this counsel is sound as I have followed it in my own family relationship, *and I can truthfully say that it has been responsible for whatever material success I have achieved*."

(Mr. Carnegie's frank admission becomes impressive when

one considers the fact that he accumulated a fortune of more than $500,000,000.00. Mr. Carnegie made a huge fortune, but those who knew of his relationship with his wife know that *Mrs. Carnegie made him!*)

Women Behind the Scene

Taking up the subject of family Master Mind relationships where Andrew Carnegie left it, this seems an appropriate place to call attention to the fact that his experience is by no means an isolated one.

The late Thomas A. Edison freely admitted that Mrs. Edison was the major source of his inspiration. They held their Master Mind meetings daily, usually at the close of Mr. Edison's day's work. And nothing was permitted to interfere with these meetings. Mrs. Edison saw to that, for she recognized the value of her keen interest in all of Mr. Edison's experimental work.

Mr. Edison often worked late into the night, but his homecoming found his wife awaiting him in keen anticipation of hearing him tell of his successes and failures during the day. She was familiar with every experiment he conducted and took an interest in them.

She served as a sort of "sounding board" for Mr. Edison, through whom he had the privilege of looking at his work from the sidelines, and it has been said that she often supplied the missing link to many of his unsolved problems.

If the Master Mind relationship was considered to be of value to men of this caliber, surely it should be regarded as such by men who are struggling to find their places in the world.

The Princes of Love and Romance have played an important role in the lives of all truly great leaders. The story of Robert and Elizabeth Browning is replete with evidence that these unseen entities, which they recognized and respected, were largely responsible for the inspirational literary works of these great poets.

John Wanamaker, the Philadelphia "Merchant Prince," as he was known to thousands of people, gave credit to his wife for his rise from poverty to fame and fortune. Master

Mind meetings were a part of their daily routine, every evening being set aside in part for these meetings—usually just before they retired.

History attributes the rise to military power of Napoleon Bonaparte to the inspirational influence of his first wife, Josephine. Napoleon's military successes began to wane when he allowed his ambition for power to cause him to put Josephine aside, and his defeat and banishment to the lonely island of St. Helena was not far ahead of this act.

It may not be amiss to mention the fact that many a modern-times business "Napoleon" has met with the same kind of defeat for the same reason. Men often maintain their Master Mind relationships with their wives until they attain power, fame and fortune, then "trade them in for newer models," as Andrew Carnegie expressed it.

Charles M. Schwab's story was different. He too gained fame and fortune through his Master Mind alliance with Andrew Carnegie, aided by a similar relationship with his wife, who was an invalid during the major portion of their married life. He did not put her away on that account, but stood loyally by her until her death, because he believed that loyalty is the first requirement of sound character.

Loyalty

While we are on the subject of loyalty, it may not be out of place to suggest that the lack of loyalty among men in business Master Mind relationships is among the more frequent causes of business failure. As long as associates in business maintain the spirit of loyalty between one another, they generally find a way to bridge their defeats and overcome their handicaps.

It has been said that the first trait of character which Andrew Carnegie looked for in the young men whom he raised from the ranks of his workers to highly paid executive positions, was the trait of loyalty. He often said that if a man did not have inherently the quality of loyalty, he did not have the proper foundation for a sound character in other directions.

His methods of testing men for loyalty were both ingenious and multiple in scope. The testings took place before promotions were made and afterward, until such time as there no longer remained any doubt as to a man's loyalty. And it is a tribute to the deep understanding of men which Mr. Carnegie possessed, that he made but few mistakes in judging men of loyalty.

Do not reveal the purpose of your Master Mind alliance to those outside of the alliance, and make sure that the members of your alliance refrain from so doing, because the idle, the scoffers and the envious stand on the sidelines of life, looking for an opportunity to sow the seeds of discouragement in the minds of those who are excelling them. Avoid this pitfall by keeping your plans to yourself, except insofar as they may be revealed by your actions and achievements.

Do not go into your Master Mind meetings with your mind filled with a negative mental attitude. Remember, if you are the leader of your Master Mind group it is your responsibility to keep every member of the alliance aroused to a high degree of interest and enthusiasm. You cannot do this when you are negative. Moreover, men will not follow with enthusiasm the man who shows a tendency toward doubt, indecision or lack of faith in the object of his Definite Major Purpose. Keep your Master Mind allies keyed up to a high degree of enthusiasm by keeping yourself keyed up in the same manner.

Do not neglect to see that each member of your Master Mind alliance receives adequate compensation, in one form or another, in proportion to the contributions each man makes to your success. Remember that no one ever does anything with enthusiasm unless he benefits thereby. Familiarize yourself with the nine basic motives which inspire all voluntary action, and see that each of your Master Mind allies is properly motivated to give you his loyalty, enthusiasm and complete confidence.

If you are related to your Master Mind allies by the motive of desire for financial gain, be sure that you give more than you receive, by adopting and following the principle of Going the Extra Mile. Do this voluntarily, before you are requested to do so, if you wish to make the most of the habit.

Do not place competitors in your Master Mind alliance,

but follow the Rotary Club policy of surrounding yourself with men who have no reason to feel antagonistic toward each other—men who are not in competition with one another.

Do not try to dominate your Master Mind group by force, fear or coercion, but hold your leadership by diplomacy based upon a definite motive for loyalty and cooperation. The day of leadership by force is gone. Do not try to revive it, for it has no place in civilized life.

Do not fail to take every step necessary to create the spirit of fellowship among your Master Mind allies, for friendly teamwork will give you power attainable in no other way.

The most powerful Master Mind alliance in the history of mankind was formed by the United Nations during World War II. Its leaders announced to the whole world that their Definite Major Purpose was based upon the determination to establish human liberty and freedom for all the peoples of the world, *both the victors and the vanquished alike!*

That pronouncement was worth a thousand victories on the fields of battle, for it had the effect of establishing confidence in the minds of people who were affected by the outcome of that war. Without confidence there can be no Master Mind relationship, either in the field of military operations or elsewhere.

Confidence is the basis of all harmonious relationships. Remember this when you organize your Master Mind alliance if you wish that alliance to endure and to serve your interests effectively.

I have now revealed to you the working principle of the greatest of all the sources of personal power among men —the Master Mind.

By the combination of the first four principles of this philosophy—the Habit of Going the Extra Mile, Definiteness of Purpose, the Master Mind, and the one which follows—one may acquire a clue as to the secret of the power which is available through the Master-Key to Riches.

Therefore, it is not out of place for me to warn you to approach the analysis of our next chapter in a state of expectancy, for it may well mark the most important turning-point of your life.

I shall now reveal to you the true approach to a full understanding of a power which has defied analysis by the entire world of science. Moreover, I shall hope to provide you with the formula by which you may appropriate this power and use it for the attainment of your Definite Major Purpose in life.

Chapter Eight

APPLIED FAITH

Faith is a royal visitor which enters only the mind that has been properly prepared for it; the mind that has been set in order through *self-discipline*.

In the fashion of all royalty, Faith commands the best room; nay, the finest suite, in the mental dwelling place.

It will not be shunted into servant's quarters, and it will not associate with envy, greed, superstition, hatred, revenge, vanity, doubt, worry or fear.

Get the full significance of this truth and you will be on the way to an understanding of that mysterious power which has baffled the scientists down through the ages.

Then you will recognize the necessity for *conditioning your mind*, through self-discipline, before expecting Faith to become your permanent guest.

Recalling the words of the sage of Concord, Ralph Waldo Emerson, who said, "In every man there is something wherein I may learn of him, and in that I am his pupil," I shall now introduce a man who has been a great benefactor of mankind, so that you may observe how one goes about the conditioning of his mind for the expression of Faith.

Let him tell his own story:

"During the business depression which began in 1929 I took a post-graduate course in the University of Hard Knocks, the greatest of all schools.

"It was then I discovered a hidden fortune which I possessed, but had not been using.

"I made the discovery one morning when a notice came that my bank had closed its doors, possibly never to be re-opened again, for it was then that I began to take inventory of my intangible, unused assets.

"Come with me while I describe what the inventory re-

114

vealed. Let us begin with the most important item on the list, *unused Faith!*

"When I searched deeply into my own heart I discovered, despite my financial losses, I had an abundance of Faith left in Infinite Intelligence and Faith in my fellowmen.

"With this discovery came another of still greater importance; the discovery that *Faith can accomplish that which not all the money of the world can achieve.*

"When I possessed all the money I needed I made the grievous error of believing money to be a permanent source of power. Now came the astonishing revelation that money, without Faith, is nothing but so much inert matter, *of itself possessed of no power whatsoever.*

"Recognizing, perhaps for the first time in my life, the stupendous power of enduring Faith, I analyzed myself carefully to determine just how much of this form of riches I possessed. The analysis was both surprising and gratifying.

"I began the analysis by taking a walk into the woods. I wished to get away from the crowd, away from the noise of the city, away from the disturbances of civilization and the fears of men, that I might meditate in silence.

"Ah! what gratification there is in that world 'silence'.

"On my journey I picked up an acorn and held it in the palm of my hand. I found it near the roots of the giant oak tree from which it had fallen. I judged the age of the tree to have been so great that it must have been a fair-sized tree when George Washington was but a small boy.

"As I stood there looking at the great tree, and its small embryonic offspring which I held in my hand, I realized that the tree had grown from a small acorn. I also realized that all the men living could not have built such a tree.

"I was conscious of the fact that some form of intangible Intelligence created the acorn from which the tree grew, and caused the acorn to germinate and begin its climb up from the soil of the earth.

"Then I realized that the greatest powers are the intangible powers, and not those which consist in bank balances or material things.

"I picked up a handful of black soil and covered the acorn with it. I held in my hand the *visible portion* of the substance out of which that magnificent tree had grown.

"At the root of the giant oak I plucked a fern. Its leaves were beautifully designed—yes, *designed*—and I realized as

115

I examined the fern that it, too, was created by the same Intelligence which had produced the oak tree.

"I continued my walk in the woods until I came to a running brook of clear, sparkling water. By this time I was tired, so I sat near the brook to rest and listen to its rhythmic music, as it danced on its way back to the sea.

"The experience brought back memories of my youth. I remembered playing by a similar brook. As I sat there listening to the music of the water I became conscious of an unseen being—an Intelligence—which spoke to me from within and told me the enchanting story of the water, and this is the story it told:

" 'Water! Pure sparkling water. The same has been rendering service ever since this planet cooled off and became the home of man, beast and vegetation.

" 'Water! Ah, what a story you could tell if you spoke man's language. You have quenched the thirst of endless millions of earthly wayfarers; fed the flowers; expanded into steam and turned the wheels of man-made machinery, condensing and going back again to your original form. You have cleaned the sewers, washed the pavements, rendered countless services to man and beast, returning always to your source in the seas, there to become purified and start your journey of service once again.

" 'When you move you travel in one direction only, toward the seas from whence you came. You are forever going and coming, but you always seem to be happy at your labor.

" 'Water! Clean, pure, sparkling substance. No matter how much dirty work you perform, you cleanse yourself at the end of your labor.

" 'You cannot be created, nor can you be destroyed. You are akin to all life. Without your beneficence no form of life on this earth would exist!'

"And the water of the brook went rippling, laughing, on its way back to the sea.

"The story of water ended, but I had heard a great sermon; I had been close to the greatest of all forms of Intelligence. I felt evidence of that same Intelligence which had created the great oak tree from a tiny acorn; the Intelligence which had fashioned the leaves of the fern with mechanical and esthetic skill such as no man could duplicate.

"The shadows of the trees were becoming longer; the day was coming to a close.

"As the sun slowly descended beyond the western horizon I realized that it, too, had played a part in that marvelous sermon which I had heard.

"Without the beneficent aid of the sun there could have been no conversion of the acorn into an oak tree. Without the sun's help the sparkling water of the flowing brook would have remained eternally imprisoned in the oceans, and life on this earth could never have existed.

"These thoughts gave a beautiful climax to the sermon I had heard; thoughts of the romantic affinity existing between the sun and the water and all life on this earth, beside which all other forms of romance seemed unimportant.

"I picked up a small white pebble which had been neatly polished by the waters of the running brook. As I held it in my hand I received, from within, a still more impressive sermon. The Intelligence which conveyed that sermon to my mind seemed to say:

" 'Behold, mortal, a miracle which you hold in your hand.

" 'I am only a tiny pebble of stone, yet I am, in reality, a small universe in which there is everything that may be found in the more expanded portion of the universe which you see out there among the stars.

" 'I appear to be dead and motionless, but the appearance is deceiving. I am made of molecules. Inside my molecules are myriads of atoms, each a small universe unto itself. Inside the atoms are countless numbers of electrons which move at an inconceivable rate of speed.

" 'I am not a dead mass of stone, but an organized group of units of ceaseless energy.

" 'I appear to be a solid mass, but the appearance is an illusion, for my electrons are separated one from another by a distance greater than their mass.

" 'Study me carefully, O humble earthly wayfarer, and remember that the great powers of the universe are the intangibles; that the values of life are those which cannot be added by bank balances.'

"The thought conveyed by that climax was so illuminating that it held me spell-bound, for I recognized that I held in my hand an infinitesimal portion of the energy which keeps the sun, the stars and the earth, on which we live for a brief period, in their respective places in relation to one another.

"Meditation revealed to me the beautiful reality that there is law and order, even in the small confines of a tiny pebble of stone. I recognized that within the mass of that tiny pebble the romance and the reality of nature were combined. I recognized that within that small pebble fact transcended fancy.

"Never before had I felt so keenly the significance of the evidence of natural law and order and purpose which reveal themselves in everything the human mind can perceive. Never before had I felt myself so near the source of my Faith in Infinite Intelligence.

"It was a beautiful experience, out there in the midst of Mother Nature's family of trees and running brooks, where the very calmness of the surroundings bade my weary soul be quiet and rest awhile, so that I might look, feel and listen while Infinite Intelligence unfolded to me the story of its reality.

"Never, in all my life, had I previously been so overwhelmingly conscious of the real evidence of Infinite Intelligence, or of the source of my Faith.

"I lingered in this newly found paradise until the Evening Star began to twinkle; then reluctantly I retraced my footsteps back to the city, there to mingle once again with those who are driven, like galley slaves, by the inexorable rules of civilization, in a mad scramble to gather up material things they do not need.

"I am now back in my study, with my books and my typewriter, on which I am recording the story of my experience. But I am swept by a feeling of loneliness and a longing to be out there by the side of that friendly brook where, only a few hours ago, I had bathed my soul in the satisfying realities of Infinite Intelligence.

"I know that my Faith in Infinite Intelligence is real and enduring. It is not a blind Faith; it is one based on close examination of the handiwork of Infinite Intelligence, and as such has been expressed in the orderliness of the universe.

"I had been looking in the wrong direction for the source of my Faith. I had been seeking it in the deeds of men, in human relationships, in bank balances and material things.

"I found it in a tiny acorn, a giant oak tree, a small pebble or stone, the leaves of a simple fern and the soil of the earth; in the friendly sun which warms the earth and gives motion to the waters; in the Evening Star; in the silence and calm of the great outdoors.

"And I am moved to suggest that Infinite Intelligence reveals itself through silence more readily than through the boisterousness of men's struggles, in their mad rush to accumulate material things.

"My bank account vanished, my bank collapsed, but I was richer than most millionaires, because I had discovered a direct approach to Faith. With this power behind me I can accumulate other bank balances sufficient for my needs.

"Nay, I am richer than are most millionaires, because I depend upon a source of inspired power which reveals itself to me from within, while many of the more wealthy find it necessary to turn to bank balances and the stock ticker for stimulation and power.

"*My source of power is as free as the air I breathe,* and as *limitless!* To avail myself of it I have only to turn on my Faith, and this I have in abundance.

"Thus, once again I learned the truth that every adversity carries with it the seed of an equivalent benefit. My adversity cost me my bank balance. It paid off through the revelation of the means to all riches!"

Enduring Sources of Faith

Stated in his own words, you have the story of a man who has discovered how to condition his mind for the expression of Faith.

And what a dramatic story it is! *Dramatic because of its simplicity.*

Here is a man who found a sound basis for an enduring Faith; not in bank balances or material riches, but in the seed of an oak tree, the leaves of a fern, a small pebble, and a running brook; things which everyone may observe and appreciate.

But his observation of these simple things led him to recognize that the greatest powers are intangible powers which are revealed through the simple things around us.

I have related this man's story as I wished to emphasize the manner in which one may clear his mind, even in the midst of chaos and insurmountable difficulties, and prepare it for the expression of Faith.

The most important fact which this story reveals is this:

When the mind has been cleared of a *negative mental attitude* the power of Faith moves in and begins to take possession!

Surely no student of this philosophy will be unfortunate enough to miss this important observation.

Let us turn now to an analysis of Faith, although we must approach the subject with full recognition that Faith is a power which has defied analysis by the entire scientific world.

Faith has been given fourth place in this philosophy because it comes near to representing the "fourth dimension," although it is presented here for its relationship to personal achievement.

Faith is a state of mind which might properly be called the "mainspring of the soul" through which one's aims, desires and purposes may be translated into their physical or financial equivalent.

Previously we observed that great power may be attained by the application of (1) the habit of Going the Extra Mile, (2) Definiteness of Purpose, and (3) the Master Mind. But that power is feeble in comparison with that which is available through the combined application of these principles with the state of mind known as Faith.

We have already observed that *capacity for faith* is one of the Twelve Riches. Let us now recognize the means by which this "capacity" may be filled with that strange power which has been the main bulwark of civilization, the chief cause of all human progress, the guiding spirit of all constructive human endeavor.

Let us remember, at the outset of this analysis, that Faith is a state of mind which may be enjoyed only by those who have learned the art of taking *full and complete control* of their minds! This is the one and only prerogative over which an individual has been given complete control.

Faith expresses its powers only through the mind that has been prepared for it. But the way of preparation is known and may be attained by all who desire to find it.

The Fundamentals of Faith are These:

(a) Definiteness of Purpose supported by personal initiative or *action*.

(b) The habit of *going the extra mile* in all human relationships.

(c) A Master Mind alliance with one or more people who radiate courage based on Faith, and who are suited spiritually and mentally to one's needs in carrying out a given purpose.

(d) A positive mind, free from all negatives, such as fear, envy, greed, hatred, jealousy and superstition. (A positive mental attitude is the first and the most important of the Twelve Riches.)

(e) Recognition of the truth that every adversity carries with it the seed of an equivalent benefit; *that temporary defeat is not failure* until it has been accepted as such.

(f) The habit of affirming one's Definite Major Purpose in life, in a ceremony of meditation, at least once daily.

(g) Recognition of the existence of Infinite Intelligence which gives orderliness to the universe; that all individuals are minute expressions of this Intelligence, and as such the individual mind has no limitations except those which are accepted and set up by the individual in his own mind.

(h) A careful inventory (in retrospect) of one's past defeats and adversities, which will reveal the truth that all such experiences carry the seed of an equivalent benefit.

(i) Self-respect expressed through harmony with one's own conscience.

(j) Recognition of the oneness of all mankind.

These are the fundamentals of major importance which prepare the mind for the expression of Faith. Their application calls for no degree of superiority, but application does call for intelligence and *a keen thirst for truth and justice*.

Faith fraternizes only with the mind that is positive!

It is the *"elan vital"* that gives power, inspiration and action to a positive mind. It is the power that causes a positive mind to act as an "electro-magnet," attracting to it the exact physical counterpart of the thought it expresses.

Faith gives resourcefulness to the mind, enabling the mind to make "grist of all that comes to its mill." It recognizes favorable opportunities, in every circumstance of one's life, whereby one may attain the object of Faith, *going so far as to provide the means by which failure and defeat may be converted into success of equivalent dimensions*.

Faith enables man to penetrate deeply into the secrets of Nature and to understand Nature's language as it is expressed in all natural laws.

From this sort of revelation have come all the great inventions that serve mankind, and a better understanding of the way to human freedom through harmony in human relationships.

Faith makes it possible to achieve that which man can *conceive* and *believe!*

Thomas A. Edison *believed* he could perfect a practical incandescent electric lamp, and despite the fact that he failed more than 10,000 times that Faith carried him to the discovery of the secret for which he was searching.

Signor Marconi *believed* the energy of the ether could be made to carry the vibrations of sound without the use of wires. His Faith carried him through endless failures until at long last he was rewarded by triumph.

Christopher Columbus *believed* the earth was round; that he would find land in an uncharted ocean if he sailed on. Despite the rebellious protests of his *unbelieving* sailors he sailed on and on until he was rewarded for his Faith.

Helen Keller *believed* she would learn to speak, although she had lost the power of speech, her hearing, and her eyesight as well. Her Faith restored her speech and provided her with the equivalent of hearing, through the sense of touch, thus proving that Faith can and will find a way to the realization of human desires.

If you would have Faith, keep your mind on that which you desire. And remember that there is no such reality as a "blanket" faith, for faith is the outward demonstration of definiteness of purpose.

Faith is guidance from within! The guiding force is Infinite Intelligence directed to definite ends. It will not bring that which one desires, but it will guide one to the attainment of the object of desire.

How to Demonstrate the Power of Faith

(a) Know what you want and determine what you have to give in return for it.

(b) When you affirm the objects of your desires, through prayer, inspire your imagination to see yourself already in possession of them, and act precisely as if you were in the physical possession thereof. (Remember, the possession of anything first takes place mentally, in the mind.)

(c) Keep the mind open at all times for *guidance from within*, and when you are inspired by "hunches" to modify your plans or to move on a new plan, move without hesitancy or doubt.

(d) When overtaken by temporary defeat, as you may be overtaken many times, remember that man's Faith is tested in many ways, and your defeat may be only one of your "testing periods." Therefore, accept defeat as an inspiration to greater effort and carry on with *belief* that you will succeed.

(e) Any negative state of mind will destroy the capacity for Faith and result in a negative climax of any affirmation you may express. Your state of mind is everything; therefore take possession of your mind and clear it completely of all unwanted interlopers that are unfriendly to Faith, and keep it cleared, no matter what may be the cost in effort.

(f) Learn to give expression to your power of Faith by writing out a clear description of your Definite Major Purpose in life and using it as the basis of your daily meditation.

(g) Associate with your Definite Major Purpose as many as possible of the nine basic motives, described in Chapter One.

(h) Write out a list of all the benefits and advantages you expect to derive from the attainment of the object of your Definite Major Purpose and call these into your mind many times daily, thereby making your mind "success conscious." (This is commonly called auto-suggestion.)

(i) Associate yourself, as far as possible, with people who are in sympathy with your Definite Major Purpose; people who are in harmony with you, and inspire them to encourage you in every way possible.

(j) Let not a single day pass without making at least one definite move toward the attainment of your Definite Major Purpose. Remember, "Faith without works is dead."

(k) Choose some prosperous person of self-reliance and courage as your "pace-maker," and make up your mind not only to keep up with that person, but to excel him. Do this silently, without mentioning your plan to anyone. (Boastfulness will be fatal to your success, as Faith has nothing in common with vanity or self-love.)

(l) Surround yourself with books, pictures, wall mottoes and other suggestive reminders of self-reliance founded upon Faith as it has been demonstrated by other people, thus building around yourself an atmosphere of prosperity and achievement. This habit will be fruitful of stupendous results.

(m) Adopt a policy of never evading or running away from unpleasant circumstances, but recognize such circumstances and build a counter-fire against them right where they overtake you. You will discover that recognition of such circumstances, without fear of their consequence, is nine-tenths of the battle in mastering them.

(n) Recognize the truth that everything worth having has a definite price. The price of Faith, among other things, is eternal vigilance in carrying out these simple instructions. Your watchword must be *persistence!*

These are the steps that lead to the development and the maintenance of a *positive mental attitude,* the only one in which Faith will abide. They are steps that lead to riches of both mind and spirit as well as riches of the purse. Fill your mind with this kind of mental food.

These are the steps by which the mind may be prepared for the highest expressions of the soul.

Faith in Action

Feed your mind on such mental food and it will be easy for you to adopt the habit of *going the extra mile.*

It will be easy for you to keep your mind attuned to

that which you desire, with assurance that it shall become yours.

"The key to every man," said Emerson, "is his thought."

That is true. Every man today is the result of his thoughts of yesterday!

James J. Hill sat with his hand on a telegraph key, waiting for an "open line." But he was not idle. His imagination was at work, building a great Transcontinental Railway System through which he hoped to tap the vast resources of the undeveloped western portion of the United States.

He had no money. He had no influential friends. He had no record of great achievement to give him prestige. But he did have Faith, that irresistible power that recognizes no such reality as "impossible."

He reduced his Definite Major Purpose to writing, omitting no detail.

On a map of the United States he sketched the course of his proposed railroad.

He slept with that map under his pillow. He carried it with him wherever he went. He fed his mind on his desire for the fulfillment of his "dream" until he made that dream a reality.

The morning after the great Chicago fire had laid waste the business portion of the city, Marshall Field came down to the site where, the day before, his retail store stood.

All around him were groups of other merchants whose stores had also been destroyed. He listened in on their conversations and learned that they had given up hope and many of them had already decided to move on further West and start over again.

Calling the nearest groups to him Mr. Field said:

"Gentlemen, you may do as you please, but as for me I intend to stay right here. Over there where you see the smoking remains of what was once my store I shall build the world's greatest retail store."

The store that Mr. Field built on Faith still stands on that spot, in Chicago.

These men and others like them have been the pioneers who produced our great American way of life.

They gave us our system of railroads and our system of communications.

They gave us the talking pictures; the talking machines; the airplanes; the skyscrapers skeletoned with steel; the automobile; the improved highways; the household electrical appliances; the electric power installations; the x-ray; the banking and investment institutions; the great life insurance companies; yes, and more important than all these, they prepared the way, through their Faith, for the freedom each and every one of us enjoys as an American citizen.

Human progress is no matter of accident or luck!

But it is the result of *applied faith,* expressed by men who have conditioned their minds, through the seventeen principles of this philosophy, for the expression of Faith.

The space that every man occupies in the world is measured by the Faith he expresses in connection with his aims and purposes.

Let us remember this, we who aspire to enjoy freedom and riches.

Let us remember, too, that Faith fixes no limitations of freedom or riches, but it guides every man to the realization of his desires whether they be great or small, according to his expression of it.

And though Faith is the one power which defies the scientists to analyze it, the procedure by which it may be applied is simple and within the understanding of the humblest, thus it is the common property of all mankind.

All that is known of this procedure has been simply stated in this chapter, and not a single step of it is beyond the reach of the humblest person.

Faith begins with *definiteness of purpose* functioning in a mind that has been prepared for it by the development of a *positive mental attitude.* It attains its greatest scope of power by *physical action* directed toward the attainment of a definite purpose.

All voluntary physical action is inspired by one or more of the nine basic motives. It is not difficult for one to develop Faith in connection with the pursuit of one's desires.

Let a man be motivated by *love* and see how quickly this emotion is given wings for action through Faith. And action in pursuit of the objective of that love quickly follows. The action becomes a labor of love, which is one of the Twelve Riches.

Let a man set his heart upon the accumulation of material riches and see how quickly his every effort becomes a labor of love. The hours of the day are not long enough for his needs, and though he labors long he finds that fatigue is softened by the joy of *self-expression*, which is another of the Twelve Riches.

Thus, one by one the resistances of life fade into nothingness for the man who has prepared his mind for self-expression through Faith. Success becomes inevitable. Joy crowns his every effort. He has no time or inclination for hatred. *Harmony in human relationships* comes naturally to him. His *hope of achievement* is high and continuous, for he sees himself already in possession of the object of his definite purpose. Intolerance has been supplanted by an *open mind*.

And *self-discipline* becomes as natural as the eating of food. He *understands people* because he loves them, and because of this love he is willing to *share his blessings*. Of *fear he knows nothing*, for all his fears have been driven away by his Faith. The Twelve Riches have become his own!

Faith is an expression of gratitude for man's relationship to his Creator. Fear is an acknowledgment of the influences of evil and it connotes a lack of *belief* in the Creator.

The greatest of life's riches consist in the understanding of the four principles which I have mentioned. These principles are known as the "Big Four" of this philosophy, because they are the warp and the woof and the major foundation-stones of the Master-Key to the power of thought and the inner secrets of the soul.

Use this Master-Key wisely and you shall be free!

Some to Whom the Master-Key Has Been Revealed

In a one-room log cabin, in Kentucky, a small boy was lying on the hearth, learning to write, using the back of a wooden shovel as a slate, and a piece of charcoal as a pencil.

A kindly woman stood over him, encouraging him to keep on trying. The woman was his mother! The boy grew into manhood without having shown any promise of greatness.

He took up the study of law and tried to make a living at that profession, but his success was meager.

He tried store-keeping, but the sheriff soon caught up with him.

He entered the army, but he made no noteworthy record

there. Everything to which he turned his hand seemed to wither and disappear into nothingness.

Then a great love came into his life. It ended with the death of the woman he loved, but the sorrow over that death reached deeply into the man's soul and there it made contact with the *secret power* that comes from within.

He seized that power and began to put it to work. It made him President of the United States. It wiped out the curse of slavery in America. And it saved the Union from dissolution in the time of a great national emergency.

The Great Emancipator is now a citizen of the universe, but the spirit of this great soul—a spirit that was set free by the secret power from within his own mind—goes marching on.

So, this power that comes to men from within knows no social caste! It is as available to the poor and the humble as it is to the rich and the powerful. It need not be passed on from one person to another. It is possessed by all who think. It cannot be put into effect for you by any one except yourself. It must be acquired from within, and it is free to all who will appropriate it.

What strange fear is it that gets into the minds of men and short-circuits their approach to this secret power from within, and when it is recognized and used lifts men to great heights of achievement? How and why do the vast majority of the people of the world become the victims of a hypnotic rhythm which destroys their capacity to use the secret power of their own minds? How can this rhythm be broken?

"How may one tap that secret power that comes from within?" some will wish to ask! Let us see how others have drawn upon it.

A young clergyman by the name of Frank Gunsaulus had long desired to build a new type of college. He knew exactly what he wanted, but the hitch came in the fact that it required a million dollars in cash.

He made up his mind to get the million dollars! Definiteness of decision, based upon definiteness of purpose, constituted the first step of his plan.

Then he wrote a sermon entitled "What I Would Do With a Million Dollars!" and announced in the newspapers that he would preach on that subject the following Sunday morning.

At the end of the sermon a strange man whom the young preacher had never seen before arose, walked down to the pulpit, extended his hand and said, "I like your sermon, and you may come down to my office tomorrow morning and I will give you the million dollars you desire."

The man was Philip D. Armour, the packing-house founder of Armour & Company. His gift was the beginning of the Armour School of Technology, one of the great schools of the country.

This is the sum and the substance of what happened. What went on in the mind of the young preacher, that enabled him to contact the secret power that is available through the mind of man, is something with which we can only conjecture, but the modus operandi by which that power was stimulated was *applied Faith!*

Shortly after birth Helen Keller was stricken by a physical affliction which deprived her of sight, hearing and speech. With two of the more important of the five physical senses stilled forever she faced life under difficulties such as most people never know throughout their lives.

With the aid of a kindly woman who recognized the existence of that secret power which comes from within, Helen Keller began to contact that power and use it. In her own words, she gives a definite clue as to one of the conditions under which the power may be revealed.

"Faith," said Miss Keller, "rightly understood, is *active* not *passive!* Passive faith is no more a force than sight is in an eye that does not look or search out. Active faith knows no fear. It denies that God has betrayed His creatures and given the world over to darkness. It denies despair. Reinforced with faith, the weakest mortal is mightier than disaster."

Faith, *backed by action*, was the instrument with which Miss Keller bridged her affliction so that she was restored to a useful life.

A Source of Secret Power

Go back through the pages of history and you will observe that the story of civilization's unfoldment leads inevitably to the works of men and women who opened the door to that secret power from within, with *applied faith* as the master-key! Observe, too, that great achievements always are born of hardship and struggle and barriers which seem insurmountable; obstacles which yield to nothing but *an indomitable will backed by an abiding faith!*

And here, in one short phrase—*indomitable will backed by an abiding faith*—you have the approach of major importance that leads to the discovery of the door of the mind, behind which the secret power from within is hidden!

Men who penetrate that secret power and apply it in the solution of personal problems sometimes are called "dreamers!" But, observe that they back their dreams with action.

When Henry J. Kaiser was building the great Hoover Dam, in Nevada, he sublet a portion of his grading work to Robert G. LeTourneau. Everything moved smoothly for the first few weeks and it looked as if everyone was going to make a lot of money.

Then, as often happens in the lives of men, the streak of good fortune played out when the equipment struck a deep layer of hard granite which was not supposed to exist.

LeTourneau went right ahead with his contract, hoping that the layer of hard stone would not be too thick, giving the job everything he had until he ran out of money.

Meanwhile he had tested the depth of the stone with deep drilling and discovered that it was too much for him, so he reluctantly admitted that he was temporarily defeated.

His friends begged him to go through bankruptcy so he could make a new start in some other field of business.

"No," he exclaimed, "I lost my money in dirt and I will make it back from dirt, and when I do I will pay off every cent I owe."

In that brief sentence LeTourneau expressed about everything worthy of mention that any success philosophy can provide. He expressed definiteness of purpose and faith in his ability to translate that purpose into victory despite his defeat.

"In my hour of greatest distress," said LeTourneau, "I found my greatest asset in the form of a new partner. I took this partner into business with me. I did the muscle work and my partner told me how to do it. His name is God."

His partner sent him into strange places to find the means with which to make a new start. With his wife's curtain rods and some pieces of discarded automobile parts he built his first dirt scraper, with the badly used motor serving to supply the power. The thing worked but it was not large enough to justify its use, so LeTourneau scratched through an automobile "graveyard" until he found better parts and built a second machine. This one did much better than the first but it was still far short of being suitable for commercial use.

"What shall I do now, partner?" LeTourneau asked of the senior member of his firm. And he got the answer swiftly. "Borrow the money you need and build a real machine with new materials."

LeTourneau did just that. From that moment on he began to ride the success beam onward to fame and fortune. He had found that "seed of an equivalent benefit" that came with his loss in Nevada, and he germinated it into the full-blown flower of success.

First, he built a plant in Peoria, Illinois, where his dirt removing equipment was produced in quantity. Next he built a similar plant in Toccoa, Georgia. Not satisfied he built another large plant in Vicksburg, Mississippi, and later another in Longview, Texas.

I was associated with Mr. LeTourneau for eighteen months, mainly for the purpose of finding out at first hand what made him "tick." I was willing to accept Mr. LeTourneau's claim that his success was due to his partnership with God, but I wanted to learn *how and when* the great industrialist contacted his senior partner.

One night when LeTourneau and I were returning to Toccoa from a speaking engagement in LeTourneau's private plane, the secret he had been seeking was revealed. Shortly after the plane took off LeTourneau flopped himself on a couch and in a few minutes he was sound asleep and snoring. In about thirty minutes he raised himself up on his elbow, took a little book from his pocket and wrote several lines in it. Meanwhile he was looking out into space instead of in the notebook.

This happened three different times before the plane reached Toccoa. After the plane landed I asked LeTourneau if he remembered making notes in his notebook.

"Why no!" exclaimed LeTourneau. "Did I make notes?"

He pulled the book from his pocket, looked at it a few seconds, then said, "There it is! There it is! I have been

131

waiting for this for more than a month. There it is! The very information I had to have before I could go ahead."

We got into a car and drove directly to LeTourneau's home. Not a word was spoken on the way.

Regardless of what one may think of Mr. LeTourneau's claim of partnership with the Creator, two facts stand out boldly and they cannot be brushed aside because of what anyone believes or does not believe.

First, he failed in business and lost all of his money under circumstances which might have discouraged the average person from trying the same line of work again.

Secondly, he made a comeback, and despite his almost total lack of formal education he became one of the very rich and successful industrialists of America.

As to *how and when* LeTourneau contacted his senior partner, I got the answer I was seeking. The contact was made through LeTourneau's subconscious mind, where he had carefully etched a clear picture of what he wanted and backed it with absolute *faith* that he would get it in due time.

There is nothing new about the system. And it may be applied by anyone who makes use of definiteness of purpose and applied faith as intensely as LeTourneau did.

One of the strange features of "faith, rightly understood," is that it generally appears because of some emergency which forces men to look beyond the power of ordinary thought for the solution of their problems.

It is during these emergencies that we draw upon that secret power from within which knows no resistance strong enough to defeat it. Such emergencies, for example, as that faced by the fifty-six men who gave birth to this nation when they signed their names to the Declaration of Independence.

That was "active faith, rightly understood!" for each man who signed that document knew that it might become his own death-warrant! Fortunately it became a license to liberty for all mankind claiming its protection, and it may well prove yet to be a license to liberty for the entire world.

The benefits of the document were proportionate to the risk assumed by those who signed it. The signers pledged their lives, their fortunes and their rights to liberty, the greatest privileges of a civilized people, and they made the pledge without mental reservations.

A Test of Faith

Here, then, is the suggestion of a test by which men may measure their capacity for *active faith!* To be effective it must be based on a willingness to risk whatever the circumstances demand; liberty, material fortune, and life itself. Faith without risk is a passive faith which, as Helen Keller stated, "is no more a force than sight is in an eye that does not look or search out."

And let us examine the records of some of the great leaders who came after the signers of the Declaration of Independence, for theirs was also an active faith.

They, too, discovered that secret power that comes from within, drew upon it, applied it and converted a vast wilderness into the "cradle of democracy."

Such men as James J. Hill, who pushed back the frontiers of the West and brought the Atlantic and Pacific Oceans into easy access of the people, through a great transcontinental railroad system.

And Lee De Forest, who perfected the mechanical means by which the boundless force of the ether has been harnessed and made to serve as a means of instantaneous communication between the peoples of the world, through the radio.

And Thomas A. Edison, who pushed civilization ahead by thousands of years, with the perfection of the incandescent electric lamp, the talking machine, the moving picture and scores of other useful inventions which lighten the burdens of mankind and add to his pleasure and education.

These, and others of their type, were men of *active faith!* We sometimes call them "geniuses," but they disclaimed the right to the honor because they recognized that their achievements came as the result of that secret power from within which is available to everyone who will embrace it and use it.

We all know of the achievements of these great leaders; we know the rules of their leadership; we recognize the nature and the scope of the blessings their labors have conferred upon the people of this nation, and we have preserved for the people the philosophy of individual achievement through which these men helped to make this the world's richest and freest country.

But, unfortunately, not all of us recognize the handicaps under which they worked, the obstacles they had to overcome, and the spirit of *active faith* in which they carried on their work.

Of this we may be sure, however: *Their achievements were in exact proportion to the emergencies they had to overcome!*

They met with opposition from those who were destined to benefit most by their struggles; people who, because of the lack of *active faith*, always view with skepticism and doubt that which is new and unfamiliar.

The emergencies of life often bring men to the crossroads, where they are forced to choose their direction, one road being marked Faith and another Fear!

What is it that causes the vast majority to take the Fear road? The choice hinges upon one's *mental attitude!*

The man who takes the Faith road is the man who has conditioned his mind to believe; conditioned it a little at a time, by prompt and courageous decisions in the details of his daily experiences. The man who takes the Fear road does so because he has neglected to condition his mind to be positive.

In Washington, a man sits in a wheel chair with a tin cup and a bunch of pencils in his hands, gaining a meager living by begging. The *excuse* for his begging is that he lost the use of his legs, through infantile paralysis. His brain has not been affected. He is otherwise strong and healthy. But, his choice led him to accept the Fear road when the dreaded disease overtook him, and his mind atrophies through disuse.

In another part of the same city was another man who was afflicted with the same handicap. He, too, had lost the use of his legs, but his reaction to his loss was far different. When he came to the cross-roads at which he was forced to make a choice he took the Faith road, and it led straight to the White House and the highest position within the gift of the American people.

That which he lost through incapacity of his limbs, he gained in the use of his brain and his will, and it is a matter of record that his physical affliction did in no way hinder him from being one of the most active men who ever occupied the position of President.

The difference in the stations of these two men was very great! But, let no one be deceived as to the cause of this difference, for it is entirely a difference of *mental attitudes*. One man chose Fear as his guide. The other chose Faith.

And, when you come right down to the circumstances which lift some men to high stations in life and condemn others to penury and want, the likelihood is that their widely separated positions reflect their respective mental attitudes. The high man chooses the high road of Faith, the low man chooses the low road of Fear, and education, experience, and personal skill are matters of secondary importance.

When Thomas A. Edison's teacher sent him home from school, at the end of the first three months, with a note to his parents saying he had an "addled" mind and could not be taught, he had the best of excuses for becoming an outcast, a do-nothing, a nobody, and that is precisely what he proceeded to become for a time. He did odd jobs, sold newspapers, tinkered with gadgets and chemicals until he became what is commonly known as a "jack of all trades" and not very good at any.

Then something took place in the mind of Thomas A. Edison that was destined to make his name immortal. Through some strange process which he never fully disclosed to the world, he discovered that secret power from within, took possession of it, organized it and lo! instead of being a man with an "addled" brain he became the outstanding genius of invention.

And now, wherever we see an electric light, or hear a phonograph, or see a moving picture we should be reminded that we are observing the product of that secret power from within which is as available to us as it was to the great Edison. Moreover, we should feel sorely ashamed if, by neglect or indifference, we are making no appropriate use of this great power.

The Power Within

One of the strange features of this secret power from within is that it aids men in procuring whatever they set their hearts upon, which is but another way of saying it translates into reality one's dominating thoughts.

In the little town of Tyler, Texas, a boy still in his 'teens walked into a grocery store where some loafers were sitting by a stove. One of the men looked at the youth, grinned broadly and said, "Say, Sonny, what are you going to be when you are a man?"

"I'll tell you what I'm going to be," the boy answered. "I'm going to be the best lawyer in the world—that's what I'm going to be if you wish to know."

The loafers yelled with laughter! The boy picked up his groceries and quietly walked out of the store.

Later, when the loafers laughed, it was in a different vein, for that boy had become a recognized authority in the legal world and his skill at law was so great that he was earning more than the President of the United States.

His name was Martin W. Littleton. He, too, discovered the secret power within his own mind and that power enabled him to set his own price on his services and get it.

As far as knowledge of the law is concerned there are thousands of lawyers who perhaps are as skilled at law as Martin W. Littleton, but few of them are making more than a living from their profession because they have not discovered there is something that brings success in the legal profession which is not taught in law schools.

The illustration might be extended to cover every profession and all human endeavor. In every calling there are a few who rise to the top while all around them are others who never get beyond mediocrity.

Those who succeed usually are called "lucky." To be sure they are lucky! But, learn the facts and you will discover that their "luck" consists of that secret power from within, which they have applied through a *positive mental attitude;* a determination to follow the road of Faith instead of the road of Fear and self-limitation.

The power that comes from within recognizes no such reality as permanent barriers.

It converts defeat into a challenge to greater effort.

It removes self-imposed limitations such as fear and doubt.

And, above all else, let us remember that it makes no black marks against any man's record which he cannot erase.

If approached through the power from within, every day brings forth a newly-born opportunity for individual achievement which need not in any way whatsoever be burdened by the failures of yesterday.

It favors no race or creed, and it is bound by no sort of arbitrary consistency compelling man to remain in poverty because he was born in poverty.

The power from within is the one medium through which the effects of Cosmic Habitforce may be changed from a negative to a positive application, instantaneously.

It recognizes no precedent, follows no hard and fast rules, and makes royal kings of the humblest of men at will—their will!

It offers the one and only grand highway to personal freedom and liberty.

It restores health where all else fails, in open defiance of all the rules of modern medical science.

It heals the wounds of sorrow and disappointment regardless of their cause.

It transcends all human experience, all education, all knowledge available to mankind.

And its only fixed price is that of an unyielding faith!—an active applied faith!

It was the inspiration of the poet who wrote:

> "Isn't it strange that princes and kings
>   And clowns that caper in saw-dust rings;
>   And common folks, like you and me,
>   All are builders for eternity.
>
> "To each is given a book of rules,
>   A block of stone and a bag of tools;
>   And each must shape ere time has flown,
>   A stumbling block or a stepping stone."

Search until you find the point of approach to that secret power from within, and when you find it you will have discovered your true self—that "other self" which makes use of every experience of life.

Then, whether you build a better mouse trap, or write a better book, or preach a better sermon, the world will make a beaten path to your door, recognize you and adequately reward you, no matter who you are or what may have been the nature and scope of your failures of the past.

What if you have failed in the past?

So, at one time, did every man we recognize as a towering success. They all met with failure in one way or another, but they didn't call it by that name; they called it *"temporary defeat."*

With the aid of the light that shines from within, all truly great men have recognized temporary defeat for exactly what it is—*a challenge to greater effort backed by greater faith!*

Anyone can quit when the going is hard!

Anyone can feel sorry for himself when temporary defeat overtakes him, but self-coddling was no part of the character of the men whom the world has recognized as great.

The approach to that power from within cannot be made by self-pity. It cannot be made through fear and timidity. It cannot be made through envy and hatred. It cannot be made through avarice and greed.

No; your "other self" pays no heed to any of these negatives! It manifests itself only through the mind that has been swept clean of all negative mental attitudes. *It thrives in the mind that is guided by faith!*

Up From Failure

Lee Braxton, of Whiteville, North Carolina, admits that he became acquainted with poverty early in life, and by hard struggle he managed to get through the sixth grade in school.

He was the tenth child in a family of twelve, and he was forced to begin at a very early age to shift for himself. His father was a village blacksmith. He shined shoes, delivered groceries, sold newspapers, worked in a hosiery mill, washed automobiles, served as a mechanic's helper, and worked his way up to become shop foreman.

He fought hard for every inch of ground he covered until at long last he married, owned a home of his own, and had an income sufficient to provide a modest living for himself and his family.

Then misfortune struck him hard. His income was shut off and his home was advertised for sale to satisfy a mortgage. He lost everything he owned except the most important of his assets—his will to make a new start and his faith in his ability to convert his misfortune into an advantage.

He began at once to look for that "seed of an equivalent

benefit" which came with his temporary defeat, and he found it in *Think and Grow Rich.* Someone gave him a copy of this book. Before he had finished reading it through his mental attitude began to change from negative to positive. By the time he finished it he had formed a plan for a comeback and he began immediately to put it into operation.

Through the pages of this book Lee Braxton was introduced to the most important person living—his "other self." That self which he had not known previously. The self that recognized temporary defeat, but failure, never!

From the day of this discovery of his real self everything Lee Braxton touched turned into gold or something finer than gold. He organized the First National Bank of Whiteville and became its first president. Then he promoted and built Whiteville's finest hotel, a modern structure that would be a credit to any city. He organized a company for the financing of automobiles, and a company to sell and distribute automobile parts as well as an automobile sales agency. Then he organized and promoted a retail musical instruments store, and built and paid for one of the finest homes in Whiteville.

The people of Whiteville elected him as mayor of the city and it was said that there was scarcely a single business or profession in the city which had not recognized some form of benefit from his influence and business operations.

His Ship of Fortune was sailing so smoothly that he made up his mind to accumulate as much money as he needed and retire from business by the time he reached the age of fifty. He made it at the age of forty-four, sold out all of his business interests and began contributing his services, free of charge, to a well-known evangelist, in the capacity of radio and television manager. In a very short time he had this evangelist's daily program going on hundreds of radio and television stations in almost every portion of the United States.

Despite his generous praise of *Think and Grow Rich,* it seems but fair to mention that Lee Braxton had the essentials of success before he ever read the book, just as you and every reader of this story have all of the essentials for success of any proportion and nature you desire.

The book took his mind away from his misfortune and gave it an opportunity to reveal to Lee the hidden riches he possessed in the power of his own mind. A power which can be transmuted into any material thing one desires. The book informed Lee Braxton of this irresistible force that dwelled within his brain. He recognized the existence of that power, embraced it and directed it to ends of his own choice.

And that is about all there is to any success story.

When PMA (positive mental attitude) takes over, success is just around the corner and defeat is nothing more than an experience with which one may motivate himself for greater effort. Lee Braxton learned this truth and profited by it. And because he did something about what he learned he placed himself in a position where he could truthfully say "there is no material thing under the sun which I desire that I cannot acquire."

He made Life pay off on his own terms, engaged in the sort of work he liked best and found peace of mind.

It is not a new philosophy of achievement that the world needs!

But it is a re-dedication of the old and tried principles which lead unerringly to the discovery of that power from within which "moves mountains."

The power that has brought forth great leaders in every walk of life and in every generation is still available. Men of vision and faith, who have pushed back the frontiers of ignorance and superstition and fear, have given the world all that we know as civilization.

The power is clothed in no mystery and it performs no miracles, but it works through the daily deeds of men, and reflects itself in every form of service rendered for the benefit of mankind.

It is called by myriad names, but its nature never changes, no matter by what name it is known.

It works through but one medium, and that is the mind.

It expresses itself in thoughts, ideas, plans and purposes of men, and the grandest thing to be said about it is that *it is as free as the air we breathe and as abundant as the scope and space of the universe.*

Chapter Nine

THE LAW OF COSMIC HABITFORCE

*Habit is a cable; we weave a thread of it
every day, and at last we cannot break it.*
— *Horace Mann.*

So, we come now to the analysis of the greatest of all of
Nature's laws, the law of Cosmic Habitforce!

Briefly described, the law of Cosmic Habitforce is Nature's method of giving fixation to all habits so that they
may carry on automatically once they have been set into
motion—the habits of men the same as the habits of the
universe.

Every man is where he is and what he is because of his
established habits of thoughts and deeds. The purpose of
this entire philosophy is to aid the individual in the formation of the kind of habits that will transfer him from where
he is to where he wishes to be in life.

Every scientist, and many laymen, know that Nature
maintains a perfect balance between all the elements of matter and energy throughout the universe; that the entire universe is operated through an inexorable system of orderliness
and habits which never vary, and cannot be altered by any
form of human endeavor; that the five known realities of
the universe are (1) Time, (2) Space, (3) Energy, (4) Matter, and (5) Intelligence, which shapes the other known realities into orderliness and system based upon *fixed habits*.

These are Nature's building-blocks with which she creates
a grain of sand or the largest stars that float through space,
and every other thing known to man, or that the mind of
man can conceive.

These are the known realities, but not every one has

taken the time or the interest to ascertain the fact that Cosmic Habitforce is the particular application of Energy with which Nature maintains the relationship between the atoms of matter, the stars and the planets in their ceaseless motion onward toward some unknown destiny, the seasons of the year, night and day, sickness and health, life and death. Cosmic Habitforce is the medium through which all habits and all human relationships are maintained in varying degrees of permanence, and the medium through which thought is translated into its physical equivalent in response to the desires and purposes of individuals.

But these are truths capable of proof, and one may count that hour sacred during which he discovers the unescapable truth that man is only an instrument through which higher powers than his own are projecting themselves. This entire philosophy is designed to lead one to this important discovery, and to enable him to make use of the knowledge it reveals, *by placing himself in harmony with the unseen forces of the universe which may carry him inevitably into the success side of the great River of Life.*

The hour of this discovery should bring him within easy reach of the Master-Key to all Riches!

Cosmic Habitforce is Nature's Comptroller through which all other natural laws are co-ordinated, organized and operated through orderliness and system. Therefore it is the greatest of all natural laws.

We see the stars and the planets move with such precision that the astronomers can predetermine their exact location and their relationship to one another scores of years hence.

We see the seasons of the year come and go with a clock-like regularity.

We know that an oak tree grows from an acorn, and a pine tree grows from the seed of its ancestor; that an acorn never makes a mistake and produces a pine tree, nor does a pine seed produce an oak tree. We know that nothing is ever produced that does not have its antecedents in something similar which preceded it, that the nature and the purpose of one's thoughts produce fruits after their kind, just as surely as fire produces smoke.

Cosmic Habitforce is the medium by which every living thing is forced to take on and become a part of the environmental influences in which it lives and moves. Thus it is clearly evident that success attracts more success, and failure attracts more failure—a truth that has long been known to men, although but few have understood the reason for this strange phenomenon.

It is known that the person who has been a failure may become a most outstanding success by close association with those who think and act in terms of success, but not every one knows that this is true because the law of Cosmic Habitforce transmits the "success consciousness" from the mind of the successful man to the mind of the unsuccessful one who is closely related to him in the daily affairs of life.

Whenever any two minds contact each other there is born of that contact a third mind patterned after *the stronger* of the two. Most successful men recognize this truth and frankly admit that their success began with their close association with some person whose positive mental attitude they either consciously or unconsciously appropriated.

Cosmic Habitforce is silent, unseen and unperceived through any of the five physical senses. That is why it has not been more widely recognized, for most men do not attempt to understand the intangible forces of Nature, nor do they interest themselves in abstract principles. However, these intangibles and abstractions represent the real powers of the universe, and they are the real basis of everything that is tangible and concrete, the source from which tangibility and concreteness are derived.

Understand the working principle of Cosmic Habitforce and you will have no difficulty in interpreting Emerson's essay on Compensation, for he was rubbing elbows with the law of Cosmic Habitforce when he wrote this famous essay.

And Sir Isaac Newton likewise came near to the complete recognition of this law when he made his discovery of the law of gravitation. Had he gone but a brief distance beyond where his discovery ended he might have helped to reveal the same law which holds our little earth in space and relates it systematically to all other planets in both Time and Space; the same law that relates human beings to each other and relates every individual to himself through his *thought habits*.

The term "Habitforce" is self-explanatory. It is a force which works through established habits. And every living thing below the intelligence of man lives, reproduces itself and fulfills its earthly mission in direct response to the power of Cosmic Habitforce through what we call "instinct."

Man alone has been given the privilege of choice in connection with his living habits, and these he may fix by the patterns of his thoughts—the one and only privilege over which any individual has been given complete right of control.

Man may think in terms of self-imposed limitations of fear and doubt and envy and greed and poverty, and Cosmic Habitforce will translate these thoughts into their material equivalent. Or he may think in terms of opulence and plenty, and this same law will translate his thoughts into their physical counterpart.

In this manner may one control his earthly destiny to an astounding degree—simply by exercising his privilege of shaping his own thoughts. But once these thoughts have been shaped into definite patterns they are taken over by the law of Cosmic Habitforce and are made into permanent habits, and they remain as such unless and until they have been supplanted by *different and stronger* thought patterns.

Now we come to the consideration of one of the most profound of all truths; the fact that most men who attain the higher brackets of success seldom do so until they have undergone some tragedy or emergency which reached deeply into their souls and reduced them to that circumstance of life which men call "failure."

The reason for this strange phenomenon is readily recognized by those who understand the law of Cosmic Habitforce, for it consists in the fact that these disasters and tragedies of life serve to break up the established habits of man—habits which have led him eventually to the inevitable results of failure—and thus break the grip of Cosmic Habitforce and allow him to formulate new and better habits.

The War Within The Self

Wars grow out of maladjustments in the relationships of men! These maladjustments are the results of the negative thoughts of men which have grown until they assume *mass proportions*. The spirit of any nation is but the sum total of the dominating thought-habits of its people.

And the same is true of individuals, for here too the spirit of the individual is determined by his dominating thought habits. Most individuals are at war, in one way or another, throughout their lives. They are at war with their own conflicting thoughts and emotions. They are at war in their family relationships and in their occupational and social relationships.

Recognize this truth and you will understand the real power and the benefits which are available to those who live by the Golden Rule, for this great rule *will save you from the conflicts of personal warfare.*

Recognize it and you will understand also the real purpose and benefits of a Definite Major Purpose, for once that purpose has been fixed in the consciousness, by one's thought habits, it will be taken over by Cosmic Habitforce and carried out to its logical conclusion, *by whatever practical means that may be available.*

Cosmic Habitforce does not suggest to an individual what he shall desire, or whether his thought habits shall be positive or negative, but it does act upon all his thought habits by crystallizing them into varying degrees of permanency and translating them into their physical equivalent, through inspired motivation to action.

It not only fixes the thought-habits of individuals, but it fixes also the thought-habits of groups and masses of people, according to the pattern established by the preponderance of their individual dominating thoughts.

The same rule applies to the individual who thinks and talks of disease. At first he is regarded as a hypochondriac —one who suffers with imaginary illness—but when the habit is maintained the disease thus manifested, or one very closely akin to it, generally makes its appearance. Cosmic Habitforce attends to this! For it is true that any thought held in the mind through repetition begins immediately to translate itself into its physical equivalent, by every practical means that may be available.

It is a sad commentary on the intelligence of people to observe that more than three-fourths of the people who have the full benefits of a great country such as ours, should go all the way through life in poverty and want, but the reason for this is not difficult to understand if one recognizes the working principle of Cosmic Habitforce.

Poverty is the direct result of a "poverty consciousness"

which results from thinking in terms of poverty, fearing poverty, and talking of poverty.

If you desire opulence, give orders to your subconscious mind to produce opulence, thus developing a "prosperity consciousness," and see how quickly your economic condition will improve.

First comes the "consciousness" of that which you desire; then follows the physical or mental manifestation of your desires. The "consciousness" is your responsibility. It is something you must create by your daily thoughts, or by meditation if you prefer to make known your desires in that manner. In this manner one may ally himself with no less a power than that of the Creator of all things.

"I have come to the conclusion," said a great philosopher, "that the acceptance of poverty, or the acceptance of ill health, is an open confession of the lack of Faith."

We do a lot of proclaiming of Faith, but our actions belie our words. Faith is a state of mind that may become permanent only by actions. Belief alone is not sufficient, for as the great philosopher has said, "Faith without works is dead."

The law of Cosmic Habitforce is Nature's own creation. It is the one universal principle through which order and system and harmony are carried out in the entire operation of the universe, from the largest star that hangs in the heavens to the smallest atoms of matter.

It is a power that is equally available to the weak and the strong, the rich and the poor, the sick and the well. It provides the solution to all human problems.

The major purpose of the seventeen principles of this philosophy is that of aiding the individual to adapt himself to the power of Cosmic Habitforce by self-discipline in connection with the formation of his habits of thought.

17 Elements of the Master-Key

Let us turn now to a brief review of these principles, so that we may understand their relationship to Cosmic Habitforce. Let us observe how these principles are so related that they blend together and form the Master-Key which unlocks the doors to the solution of all problems.

The analysis begins with the first principle of the philosophy:

(a) THE HABIT OF GOING THE EXTRA MILE.

This principle is given first position because it aids in conditioning the mind for the rendering of useful service. And this conditioning prepares the way for the second principle—

(b) DEFINITENESS OF PURPOSE.

With the aid of this principle one may give organized direction to the principle of Going The Extra Mile, and make sure that it leads in the direction of his major purpose and becomes cumulative in its effects. These two principles alone will take anyone very far up the ladder of achievement, but those who are aiming for the higher goals of life will need much help on the way, and this help is available through the application of the third principle—

(c) THE MASTER MIND.

Through the application of this principle one begins to experience a new and a greater sense of power which is not available to the individual mind, as it bridges one's personal deficiencies and provides him, when necessary, with any portion of *the combined knowledge of mankind* which has been accumulated down through the ages. But this sense of power will not be complete until one acquires the art of receiving guidance through the fourth principle—

(d) APPLIED FAITH.

Here the individual begins to tune in on the powers of Infinite Intelligence, which is a benefit that is available only to the person who has conditioned his mind to receive it. Here the individual begins to take full possession of his own mind by mastering all fears, worries and doubts, by recognizing his oneness with the source of all power.

These four principles have been rightly called the "Big Four" because they are capable of providing more power than the average man needs to carry him to great heights of personal achievement. But they are adequate only for the very few who have other needed qualities of success, such as those which are provided by the fifth principle.

(e) PLEASING PERSONALITY.

A pleasing personality enables a man to sell himself and his ideas to other men. Hence it is an essential for all who desire to become the guiding influence in a Master Mind alliance. But observe carefully how definitely the four preceding principles tend to give one a pleasing personality.

These five principles are capable of providing one with stupendous personal power, but not enough power to insure him against defeat, for defeat is a circumstance that every man meets many times throughout his lifetime; hence the necessity of understanding and applying the sixth principle—

(f) HABIT OF LEARNING FROM DEFEAT.

Notice that this principle begins with the word "habit," which means that it must be accepted and applied as a matter of habit, under all the circumstances of defeat. In this principle may be found hope sufficient to inspire a man to make a fresh start when his plans go astray, as go astray they must at one time or another.

Observe how greatly the source of personal power has increased through the application of these six principles. The individual has found out where he is going in life; he has acquired the friendly cooperation of all whose services are needed to help him reach his goal; he has made himself pleasing, thereby insuring for himself the continued cooperation of others; he has acquired the art of drawing upon the source of Infinite Intelligence and of expressing that power through applied faith; and he has learned to make stepping stones of the stumbling blocks of personal defeat. Despite all of these advantages, however, the man whose Definite Major Purpose leads in the direction of the higher brackets of personal achievement will come many times to the point in his career when he will need the benefits of the seventh principle—

(g) CREATIVE VISION.

This principle enables one to look into the future and to judge it by a comparison with the past, and to build new and better plans for attaining his hopes and aims through the workshop of his imagination. And here, for the first time perhaps, a man may discover his sixth sense and begin to draw upon it for the knowledge which is not available through the organized sources of human experience and accumulated knowledge. But, in order to make sure that he puts this benefit to practical use he must embrace and apply the eighth principle—

(h) PERSONAL INITIATIVE.

This is the principle that starts action and keeps it moving toward definite ends. It insures one against the destructive habits of procrastination, indifference and laziness. An approximation of the importance of this principle may be had by recognizing that it is the "habit-producer" in connection with the seven preceding principles, for it is obvious that the application of no principle may become a *habit* except by the application of personal initiative. The importance of this principle may be further evaluated by recognition of the fact that it is the sole means by which a man may exercise full and complete control over the only thing that the Creator has given him to control, *the power of his own thoughts.*

Thoughts do not organize and direct themselves. They need guidance, inspiration and aid which can be given only by one's personal initiative.

But personal initiative is sometimes misdirected. Therefore it needs the supplemental guidance that is available through the ninth principle—

(i) ACCURATE THINKING.

Accurate thinking not only insures one against the misdirection of personal initiative, but it also insures one against errors of judgment, guess-work and premature decisions. It also protects one against the influence of his own *undependable emotions* by modifying them through the power of reason commonly known as the "head."

Here the individual who has mastered these nine principles will find himself in possession of tremendous power, but personal power may be, and often it is, a dangerous power if it is not controlled and directed through the application of the tenth principle—

(j) SELF-DISCIPLINE.

Self-discipline cannot be had for the mere asking, nor can it be acquired quickly. It is the product of carefully established and carefully maintained habits which in many instances can be acquired only by many years of painstaking effort. So we have come to the point at which the power of the will must be brought into action, *for self-discipline is solely a product of the will.*

Numberless men have risen to great power by the application of the preceding nine principles, only to meet with disaster, or they carry others to defeat by their lack of self-discipline in the use of their power.

This principle, when mastered and applied, gives one complete control over his greatest enemy, himself!

Self-discipline must begin with the application of the eleventh principle—

(k) CONCENTRATION OF ENDEAVOR.

The power of concentration is also a product of the will. It is so closely related to self-discipline that the two have been called the "twin-brothers" of this philosophy. Concentration saves one from the dissipation of his energies, and aids him in keeping his mind focused upon the object of his Definite Major Purpose until it has been taken over by the sub-conscious section of the mind and there made ready for translation into its physical equivalent, through the law of Cosmic Habitforce. It is the camera's eye of the imagination through which the detailed outline of one's aims and purposes are recorded in the sub-conscious section of the mind; hence it is indispensable.

Now look again, and see how greatly one's personal power has grown by the application of these eleven principles. But even these are not sufficient for every circumstance of life, for there are times when one must have the friendly co-operation of many people, such as customers in business, or clients in a profession, or votes in an election to public office, all of which may be had through the application of the twelfth principle—

(l) CO-OPERATION.

Co-operation differs from the Master Mind principle in that it is a human relationship that is needed, and may be had, without a definite alliance with others, based upon a complete fusion of the minds for the attainment of a definite purpose.

Without the co-operation of others one cannot attain success in the higher brackets of personal achievement, for co-operation is the means of major value by which one may extend the space he occupies in the minds of others, which is sometimes known as "good-will". Friendly co-operation brings the merchant's customers back as repeat purchasers of his wares, and insures a continuance of patronage from the clients of the professional man. Hence it is a principle that belongs definitely in the philosophy of successful men, regardless of the occupation they may follow.

Co-operation is attained more freely and willingly by the application of the thirteenth principle—

(m) ENTHUSIASM.

Enthusiasm is a contagious state of mind which not only aids one in gaining the co-operation of others, but more important than this, it inspires the individual to draw upon and use the power of his own imagination. It inspires action also in the expression of personal initiative, and leads to the habit of concentration of endeavor. Moreover, it is one of the qualities of major importance of a pleasing personality, and it makes easy the application of the principle of Going The Extra Mile. In addition to all these benefits, enthusiasm gives force and conviction to the spoken word.

Enthusiasm is the product of *motive*, but it is difficult of maintenance without the aid of the fourteenth principle—

(n) THE HABIT OF HEALTH.

Sound physical health provides a suitable housing place for the operation of the mind; hence it is an essential for enduring success, assuming that the word "success" shall embrace all of the requirements for happiness.

Here again the word "habit" comes into prominence, for sound health begins with a "health consciousness" that can be developed only by the right habits of living, sustained through self-discipline.

Sound health provides the basis for enthusiasm, and enthusiasm encourages sound health; so the two are like the hen and the egg; no one can determine which came into existence first, but everyone knows that both are essential for the production of either. Health and enthusiasm are like that. Both are essential for human progress and happiness.

Now take inventory again and count up the gains in power which the individual has attained by the application of these fourteen principles. It has reached proportions so stupendous that it staggers the imagination. Yet it is not sufficient to insure one against failure; therefore we shall have to add the fifteenth principle—

(o) BUDGETING TIME AND MONEY.

Oh! what a headache one gets at the mention of saving of time and the conservation of money. Nearly everyone wishes to spend both time and money freely, but budget and conserve them, never! However, independence and freedom of body and mind, the two great desires of all mankind, cannot become enduring realities without the self-discipline of a strict budgeting system. Hence this principle is of necessity an important essential of the philosophy of individual achievement.

Now we are reaching the ultimate in the attainment of personal power. We have learned the sources of power and how we may tap them and apply them at will to any desired end; and that power is so great that nothing can resist it save only the fact that the individual may unwisely apply it to his own destruction and the destruction of others. Hence, to guide one in the right use of power it is necessary to add the sixteenth principle—

(p) THE GOLDEN RULE *APPLIED*.

Observe the emphasis on the word "applied." Belief in the soundness of the Golden Rule is not enough. To be of enduring benefit, and in order that it may serve as a safe guide in the use of personal power, it must be applied as a matter of habit, in all human relationships.

Quite an order, this! But the benefits which are available through the application of this profound rule of human relationship are worthy of the efforts necessary to develop it into a habit. The penalties for failure to live by this rule are too numerous for description in detail.

Now we have attained the ultimate in personal power, and we have provided ourselves with the necessary insurance against its misuse. What we need from here on out is the means by which this power may be made permanent during our entire lifetime. We shall climax this philosophy, therefore, with the only known principle by which we may attain this desired end—the seventeenth and last principle of this philosophy—

(q) COSMIC HABITFORCE.

Cosmic Habitforce is the principle by which all habits are fixed and made permanent in varying degrees. As stated, it is the controlling principle of this entire philosophy, into which the preceding sixteen principles blend and become a part. And it is the controlling principle of all natural laws of the universe. It is the principle that gives the *fixation of habit* in the application of the preceding principles of this philosophy. Thus it is the controlling factor in conditioning the individual mind for the development and the expression of the "prosperity consciousness" which is so essential in the attainment of personal success.

Mere understanding of the sixteen preceding principles will not lead anyone to the attainment of personal power. The principles must be understood and applied as a matter of strict habit, and habit is the sole work of the law of Cosmic Habitforce.

Cosmic Habitforce is synonymous with the great River of Life to which frequent references have been made previously, for it consists of a negative and a positive potentiality, as do all forms of energy.

The negative application is called "hypnotic rhythm" because it has a hypnotic effect on everything that it contacts. We may see its effects, in one way or another, on every human being.

It is the sole means by which the "poverty consciousness" becomes fixed as a *habit!*

It is the builder of all established *habits* of fear, and envy, and greed, and revenge, and of desire for something for nothing.

It fixes the *habits* of hopelessness and indifference.

And it is the builder of the *habit* of hypochondria, through which millions of people suffer all through their lives with imaginary illness.

It is also the builder of the "failure consciousness" which undermines the self-confidence of millions of people.

In brief, it fixes *all negative habits*, regardless of their nature or effects. Thus it is the "failure" side of the great River of Life.

The "success" side of the River—the positive side—fixes all constructive habits, such as the habit of Definiteness of Purpose, the habit of Going The Extra Mile, the habit of applying the Golden Rule in human relationships, and all the other habits which one must develop and apply in order to get the benefits of the sixteen preceding principles of this philosophy.

Enforcement of Habits

Now let us examine this word "habit"!

Webster's dictionary gives the word many definitions, among them: "Habit implies a settled disposition or tendency *due to repetition;* custom suggests the fact of repetition rather than the tendency to repeat; usage (applying only to a considerable body of people) adds the implication of long acceptation or standing; both custom and usage often suggest authority; as, we do many things mechanically from force of habit."

Webster's definition runs on into considerable additional detail, but no part of it comes within sight of describing the law that fixes all habits; this omission being due no doubt to the fact that the law of Cosmic Habitforce had not been revealed to the editors of this dictionary. But we observe one significant and important word in the Webster definition—the word "repetition." It is important because it describes the means by which any habit is begun.

The habit of Definiteness of Purpose, for example, becomes a habit only by repetition of the thought of that purpose, by bringing the thought into the mind repeatedly; by *repeatedly* submitting the thought to the imagination with a burning desire for its fulfillment, until the imagination creates a practical plan for attaining this desire; by applying the *habit* of Faith in connection with the desire, and doing it so intensely and repeatedly that one may see himself already in possession of the object of his desires, *even before he begins to attain it*.

The building of voluntary positive habits calls for the application of self-discipline, persistence, will-power and Faith, all of which are available to the person who has assimilated the sixteen preceding principles of this philosophy.

Voluntary habit-building is self-discipline in its highest and noblest form of application!

And all voluntary positive habits are the products of will-power directed toward the attainment of definite ends. *They originate with the individual,* not with Cosmic Habitforce. And they must be grounded in the mind through repetition of thoughts and deeds until they are taken over by Cosmic Habitforce and are given fixation, after which they operate automatically.

The word *habit* is an important word in connection with this philosophy of individual achievement, for it represents the real cause of every man's economic, social, professional, occupational and spiritual condition in life. We are where we are and what we are because of our fixed habits. And we may be where we wish to be and what we wish to be only by the development and the maintenance of our *voluntary habits.*

Thus we see that this entire philosophy leads inevitably to an understanding and application of the law of Cosmic Habitforce—the power of fixation of all habits!

The major purpose of each of the sixteen preceding principles of this philosophy is that of aiding the individual in the development of a particular, specialized form of habit that is necessary as a means of enabling him to *take full possession of his own mind!* This too must become a habit!

Mind-power is always actively engaged on one side of the River of Life or the other. The purpose of this philosophy is to enable one to develop and maintain habits of thought and of deed which keep his mind concentrated upon the "success" side of the River. This is the sole burden of the philosophy.

Mastery and assimilation of the philosophy, like every other desirable thing, has a definite price which must be paid before its benefits may be enjoyed. That price, among other things, is eternal vigilance, determination, persistence and the will to make Life pay off on one's own terms instead of accepting substitutes of poverty and misery and disillusionment.

There are two ways of relating one's self to Life.

One is that of playing horse while Life rides. The other is that of becoming the rider while Life plays horse. The choice as to whether one becomes the horse or the rider is the privilege of every person, but this much is certain: if one does not choose to become the rider of Life, he is sure to be forced to become the horse. Life either rides or is ridden. It never stands still.

The "Ego" and Cosmic Habitforce

As a student of this philosophy you are interested in the method by which one may transmute the power of thought into its physical equivalent. And you are interested in learning how to relate yourself to others in a spirit of harmony.

Unfortunately our public schools have been silent on both of these important needs. "Our educational system," said Dr. Henry C. Link, "has concentrated on mental development and has failed to give any understanding of the way emotional and personality habits are acquired or corrected."

His indictment is not without a sound foundation. The public school system has failed in the obligation of which Dr. Link complains, because the law of Cosmic Habitforce was but recently revealed, and even now it has not been recognized by the great mass of educators.

Everyone knows that practically everything we do, from

the time we begin to walk, is the result of habit. Walking and talking are habits. Our manner of eating and drinking is a habit. Our sex activities are the results of habit. Our relationships with others, whether they are positive or negative, are the results of habits, but few people understand why or how we form habits.

Habits are inseparably related to the human ego. Therefore, let us turn to the analysis of this greatly misunderstood subject of the ego. But first let us recognize that the ego is the medium through which faith and all other states of mind operate.

Throughout this philosophy great emphasis has been placed upon the distinction between passive faith and active faith. The ego is the medium of expression of all action. Therefore we must know something of its nature and possibilities in order that we may make the best use of it. We must learn how to stimulate the ego to action and how to control and guide it to the attainment of definite ends.

Above all, we must disabuse our minds of the popular error of believing the ego to be only a medium for expression of vanity. The word "ego" is of Latin origin, and it means "I". But it also connotes a driving force which may be organized and made to serve as the medium for translating desire into faith, through action.

The Misunderstood Power of the Ego

The word ego has reference to all the factors of one's personality!

Therefore it is obvious that the ego is subject to development, guidance and control through voluntary habits—habits which we deliberately and with purpose aforethought develop.

A great philosopher who devoted his entire life to the study of the human body and the mind, provided us with a practical foundation for the study of the ego when he stated:

"Your body, whether living or dead, is a collection of millions of little energies that can never die.

"These energies are separate and individual; at times they act in some degree of harmony.

"The human body is a drifting mechanism of life, capable

but not accustomed to control the forces within, except as habit, will, cultivation or special excitement (through the emotion) may marshal these forces to the accomplishment of some important end.

"We are satisfied from many experiments that this power of marshalling and using these energies can be, in every person, cultivated to a high degree.

"The air, sunlight, food and water you take, are agents of a force which comes from the sky and earth. You idly float upon the tide of circumstances to make up your day's life, and the opportunities of being something better than you are drift beyond your reach and pass away.

"Humanity is hemmed in by so many influences that, from time immemorial, no real effort has been made to gain control of the impulses that run loose in the world. It has been, and still is, easier to let things go as they will rather than exert the will to direct them.

"But the dividing line between success and failure is found at the stage where aimless drifting ceases. (Where Definiteness of Purpose begins.)

"We are all creatures of emotions, passions, circumstances and accident. What the mind will be, what the heart will be, what the body will be, are problems which are shaped to the drift of life, even when special attention is given to any of them.

"If you will sit down and think for a while, *you will be surprised to know how much of your life has been mere drift*.

"Look at any created life, and see its efforts to express itself. The tree sends its branches toward the sunlight, struggles through its leaves to inhale air; and even underground sends forth its roots in search of water and the minerals it needs for food. This you call inanimate life; but it represents a force that comes from some source and operates for some purpose.

"There is no place on the globe where energy is not found.

"The air is so loaded with it that in the cold north the sky shines in boreal rays; and wherever the frigid temperature yields to the warmth, the electric conditions may alarm man. Water is but a liquid union of gases, and is charged with electrical, mechanical and chemical energies, any one of which is capable of doing great service and great damage to man.

"Even ice, in its coldest phase, has energy, for it is not subdued, nor even still; its force has broken mountain rocks into fragments. This energy about us we are drinking in water, eating in food and breathing in air. Not a chemical molecule is free from it; not an atom can exist without it. We are a combination of individual energies."

Man consists of two forces, one tangible, in the form of his physical body, with its myriad individual cells numbering billions, each of which is endowed with intelligence and energy; and the other intangible, in the form of an ego—the organized dictator of the body which may control man's thoughts and deeds.

Science teaches us the tangible portion of a man weighing one hundred and sixty pounds is composed of about seventeen chemical elements, all of which are known. They are:

95 pounds of oxygen.
38 pounds of carbon.
15 pounds of hydrogen.
4 pounds of nitrogen.
4½ pounds of calcium.
6 ounces of chlorine.
4 ounces of sulphur.
3½ ounces of potassium.
3 ounces of sodium.
¼ ounce of iron.
2½ ounces of fluorine.
2 ounces of magnesium.
1½ ounces of silicon.
Small traces of arsenic, iodine and aluminum.

These tangible parts of man are worth only a few cents commercially and may be purchased in any modern chemical plant.

Add to these chemical elements a well developed and properly organized and controlled ego, and they may be worth any price the owner sets upon them. The ego is a power which cannot be purchased at any price, but it can be developed and shaped to fit any desired pattern. The development takes place through organized habits which are made permanent by the law of Cosmic Habitforce, which carries out the thought-patterns one develops through controlled thought.

One of the major differences between men who make valuable contributions to mankind and those who merely take up space in the world, is mainly a difference in egos, because the ego is the driving force behind all forms of human action.

Liberty and freedom of body and mind—the two major desires of all people—are available in exact proportion to the development and use one makes of the ego. Every person who has properly related himself to his own ego has both liberty and freedom in whatever proportions he desires.

A man's ego determines the manner in which he relates himself to all other people. More important than this, it determines the policy under which a man relates his own body and mind, wherein is patterned every hope, aim and purpose by which he fixes his destiny in life.

A man's ego is his greatest asset or his greatest liability, according to the way he relates himself to it. The ego is the sum total of one's thought habits which have been fastened upon him through the automatic operation of the law of Cosmic Habitforce.

Every highly successful person possesses a well-developed and highly disciplined ego, but there is a third factor associated with the ego which determines its potency for good or evil—the self-control necessary to enable one to transmute its power into any desired purpose.

"Training" the Ego

The starting point of all individual achievements is some plan by which one's ego can be inspired with a "success consciousness". The person who succeeds must do so by properly developing his own ego, impressing it with the object of his desires, and removing from it all forms of limitation, fear and doubt which lead to the dissipation of the power of the ego.

Auto-suggestion (or self-hypnosis) is the medium by which one may attune his ego to any desired rate of vibration and charge it with the attainment of any desired purpose.

Unless you catch the full significance of the principle of

auto-suggestion you will miss the most important part of this analysis, because the power of the ego is fixed entirely by the application of self-suggestion.

When this self-suggestion attains the status of faith the ego becomes limitless in its power.

The ego is kept alive and active, and it is given power by constant feeding. Like the physical body, the ego cannot and will not subsist without food.

It must be fed with Definiteness of Purpose.

It must be fed with Personal Initiative.

It must be fed with Continuous Action, through well organized plans.

It must be supported with Enthusiasm.

It must be fed by Controlled Attention, directed to a definite end.

It must be controlled and directed through Self-discipline.

And it must be supported with Accurate Thought.

No man can become the master of anything or anyone until he becomes the master of his own ego.

No man can express himself in terms of opulence while most of his thought-power is given over to the maintenance of a "poverty consciousness." Nevertheless, one should not lose sight of the fact that many men of great wealth began in poverty—a fact which suggests that this and all other fears can be conquered and removed from interference with the ego.

In the one word, ego, may be found the composite effects of all the principles of individual achievement described in this philosophy, co-ordinated into one single unit of power which may be directed to any desired end by any individual who is the complete master of his ego.

We are preparing you to accept the fact that the most important power which is available to you—the one power which will determine whether you succeed or fail in your life's ambition—is that which is represented by your own ego.

We are also preparing you to brush aside that time-worn belief which associates the ego with self-love, vanity and vulgarity, and to recognize the truth that the ego is all there is of a man outside of the few cents' worth of chemicals, of which his physical body is composed.

Sex is the great creative force of man. It is definitely associated with and is an important part of one's ego. Both sex and the ego got their bad reputations from the fact that both are subject to destructive as well as constructive application, and both have been abused by the ignorant, from the beginning of the history of mankind.

The egoist who makes himself offensive through the expression of his ego is one who has not discovered how to relate himself to his ego in a manner which gives it constructive use.

Constructive application of the ego is made through the expressions of one's hopes, desires, aims, ambitions and plans, and not by boastfulness or self-love. The motto of the person who has his ego under control is, "Deeds, not words."

The desire to be great, to be recognized and to have personal power, is a healthy desire; but an open expression of one's belief in his own greatness is an indication that he has not taken possession of his ego, that he has allowed it to take possession of him; and you may be sure that his proclamations of greatness are but a cloak with which to shield some fear or inferiority complex.

The Ego and Mental Attitude

Understand the real nature of your ego and you will understand the real significance of the Master Mind principle. Moreover, you will recognize that to be of the greatest service to you, the members of your Master Mind alliance must be in complete sympathy with your hopes, aims and purposes; that they must not be in competition with you in any manner whatsoever. They must be willing to subordinate their own desires and personalities entirely for the attainment of your major purpose in life.

They must have confidence in you and your integrity, and they must respect you. They must be willing to accentuate your virtues and make allowances for your faults. They must be willing to permit you to be yourself and live your own life in your own way at all times. Lastly, they must receive from you some form of benefit which will make you as beneficial to them as they are to you.

Failure to observe the last mentioned requirement will bring an end to the power of your Master Mind alliance.

Men relate themselves to one another in whatever capacities they may be associated because of a motive or motives. There can be no permanent human relationship based upon an indefinite or vague motive, or upon no motive at all. Failure to recognize this truth has cost many men the difference between penury and opulence.

The power which takes over the ego and clothes it with the material counterparts of the thoughts which give it shape, is the law of Cosmic Habitforce. This law does not give quality or quantity to the ego; it merely takes what it finds and translates it into its physical equivalent.

The men of great achievement are, and they have always been, those who deliberately feed, shape and control their own egos, leaving no part of the task to luck or chance, or to the varying vicissitudes of life.

Every person may control the shaping of his own ego, but from that point on he has no more to do with what happens than does the farmer have anything to do with what happens to the seed he sows in the soil of the earth. The inexorable law of Cosmic Habitforce causes every living thing to perpetuate itself after its kind, and it translates the picture which a man paints of his ego into its physical equivalent, as definitely as it develops an acorn into an oak tree, and no outside aid whatsoever is required, except time.

From these statements it is obvious that we are not only advocating the deliberate development and control of the ego, but also we are definitely warning that no man can hope to succeed in any calling without such control over his ego.

So that there may be no misunderstanding as to what is meant by the term "a properly developed ego" we shall describe briefly the factors which enter into its development, viz:

First, one must ally himself with one or more persons who will co-ordinate their minds with his in a spirit of perfect harmony for the attainment of a definite purpose, and that alliance must be continuous and active.

Moreover, the alliance must consist of people whose spiritual and mental qualities, education, sex and age are suited for aiding in the attainment of the purpose of the alliance. For example, Andrew Carnegie's Master Mind alliance was made up of more than twenty men, each of whom brought to the alliance some quality of mind, experience, education or knowledge which was directly related to the object of the alliance and not available through any of the other members of the alliance.

Second, having placed himself under the influence of the proper associates, one must adopt some definite plan by which to attain the object of the alliance and proceed to put that plan into action. The plan may be a composite plan created by the joint efforts of all the members of the Master Mind group.

If one plan proves to be unsound or inadequate, it must be supplemented or supplanted by others, until a plan is found which will work. But there must be no change in the purpose of the alliance.

Third, one must remove himself from the range of influence of every person and every circumstance which has even a slight tendency to cause him to feel inferior or incapable of attaining the object of his purpose. Positive egos do not grow in negative environments. On this point there can be no excuse for a compromise, and failure to observe it will prove fatal to the chances of success.

The line must be so clearly drawn between a man and those who exercise any form of negative influence over him that he closes the door tightly against every such person, no matter what previous ties of friendship or obligation or blood relationship may have existed between them.

Fourth, one must close the door tightly against every thought of any past experience or circumstance which tends to make him feel inferior or unhappy. Strong, vital egos cannot be developed by dwelling on thoughts of past unpleasant experiences. Vital egos thrive on the hopes and desires of the yet unattained objectives.

Thoughts are the building-blocks from which the human ego is constructed. Cosmic Habitforce is the cement which binds these blocks together in permanency, through fixed habits. When the job is finished it represents, right down to the smallest detail, the nature of the thoughts which went into the building.

Fifth, one must surround himself with every possible physical means of impressing his mind with the nature and the purpose of the ego he is developing. For example, the author should set up his workshop in a room decorated with pictures and the works of authors in his field whom he most admires. He should fill his book shelves with books related to his own work. He should surround himself with every

163

possible means of conveying to his ego the exact picture of himself which he expects to express, because that picture is the pattern which the law of Cosmic Habitforce will pick up; the picture which it translates into its physical equivalent.

Sixth, the properly developed ego is at all times under the control of the individual. There must be no over-inflation of the ego in the direction of "egomania" by which some men destroy themselves.

Egomania reveals itself by a mad desire to control others by force. Striking examples of such men are Adolph Hitler, Benito Mussolini and the Kaiser.

In the development of the ego, one's motto might well be, "Not too much, not too little, of anything." When men begin to thirst for control over others, or begin to accumulate large sums of money which they cannot or do not use constructively, they are treading upon dangerous grounds. Power of this nature grows of its own accord and soon gets out of control.

Nature has provided man with a safety-valve through which she deflates the ego and relieves the pressure of its influence when an individual goes beyond certain limits in the development of the ego. Emerson called it the law of Compensation, but whatever it is, it operates with inexorable definiteness.

Napoleon Bonaparte began to die, because of his crushed ego, on the day he landed on St. Helena Island.

People who quit work and retire from all forms of activity, after having led active lives, generally atrophy and die soon thereafter. If they live they are usually miserable and unhappy. A healthy ego is one which is always in use and under complete control.

Seventh, the ego is constantly undergoing changes, for better or for worse, because of the nature of one's thought habits. The two factors which force these changes upon one are Time and the law of Cosmic Habitforce.

Time for Growth

Here I desire to bring to your attention the importance of Time as a significant factor in the operation of Cosmic Habitforce. Just as seeds which are planted in the soil of the earth require definite periods of Time for their germination, development and growth, so do ideas, impulses of thought and desires which are planted in the mind require definite periods of Time during which the law of Cosmic Habitforce gives them life and action.

There is no adequate means of describing or pre-determining the exact period of Time which is required for the transformation of a desire into its physical equivalent. The nature of the desire, the circumstances which are related to it, and the intensity of the desire, are all determining factors in connection with the Time required for transformation from the thought stage to the physical stage.

The state of mind known as faith is so favorable for the quick change of desire into its physical equivalent that it has been known to make the change almost instantaneously.

Man matures physically in about twenty years, but mentally—which means the ego—he requires from thirty-five to sixty years for maturity. This fact explains why men seldom begin to accumulate material riches in great abundance, or to attain outstanding records of achievement in other directions, until they are about fifty years of age.

The ego which can inspire a man to acquire and retain great material wealth is of necessity one which has undergone self-discipline, through which he acquires self-confidence, definiteness of purpose, personal initiative, imagination, accuracy of judgment and other qualities, without which no ego has the power to procure and hold wealth in abundance.

These qualities come through the proper *use* of Time. Observe that we did not say they come through the lapse of Time. Through the operation of Cosmic Habitforce every individual's thought habits, whether they are negative or positive, whether of opulence or of poverty, are woven into the pattern of his ego, and there they are given permanent form which determines the nature and the extent of his spiritual and physical status.

The Ego Behind Success

About the beginning of the 1929 economic depression the owner of a small beauty salon turned over a back room in her place of business to an old man who needed a place to sleep. The man had no money, but he did have considerable knowledge of the methods of compounding cosmetics.

The owner of the salon gave him a place to sleep and provided him with an opportunity to pay for his room by compounding the cosmetics she used in her business.

Soon the two entered into a Master Mind alliance which was destined to bring each of them economic independence. First, they entered into a business partnership, with the object of compounding cosmetics to be sold from house to house; the woman providing the money for the raw materials, the man doing the work.

After a few years the Master Mind arrangement between the two had proved so profitable that they decided to make it permanent by marriage, although there was a difference of more than twenty-five years in their ages.

The man had been in the cosmetic business for the better portion of his adult life, but he had never achieved success. The young woman had barely made a living from her beauty salon. The happy combination of the two brought them into possession of a power which neither had known prior to their alliance, and they began to succeed financially.

At the beginning of the depression they were compounding cosmetics in one small room, and selling their products personally from door to door. By the end of the depression, some eight years later, they were compounding their cosmetics in a large factory which they had bought and paid for, and had more than a hundred employees working steadily, and more than four thousand agents selling their products throughout the nation.

During this period they accumulated a fortune of over two million dollars, despite the fact that they were operating during depression years when such luxuries as cosmetics were naturally hard to sell.

They have placed themselves beyond the need for money for the remainder of their lives. Moreover, they have gained financial freedom on precisely the same knowledge and the same opportunities they possessed prior to their Master Mind alliance, when both were poverty-stricken.

We wish the names of these two interesting people could be revealed, but the circumstances of their alliance and the nature of the analysis we shall now present makes this impractical. Nevertheless, we are free to describe what we conceive to be the source of their astounding achievement, viewing every circumstance of their relationship entirely from the viewpoint of an unbiased analyst who is seeking only to present a true picture of the facts.

The motive which brought these two people together in a Master Mind alliance was definitely economic in nature. The woman had previously been married to a man who failed to earn a living for her and who deserted her when her child was an infant. The man also had been previously married.

There was not the slightest indication of the emotion of love as a motive for their marriage. The motive was entirely a mutual desire for economic freedom.

The business and the elaborate home in which the couple live are entirely dominated by the old man, who sincerely believes that he is responsible for both.

Their house is expensively furnished, but no one—not even invited guests—is permitted to take a turn at the piano, or to sit in one of the chairs in the living room, without special invitation from the "lord and master" of the household.

The main dining room is equipped with ornate furniture, including a long dining table which is suitable for use on "state" occasions, but the family is never permitted to use it on other occasions. They dine in the breakfast room, and nothing may be served at the table at any time except food of the "master's" choice.

A gardener is employed to attend the gardens, but no one is permitted to cut a flower without special invitation from the head of the house.

Such conversations as are carried on by the family are conducted entirely by the head of the house, and no one may intervene, not even to ask a question or to offer a remark, unless he invites it. His wife never speaks unless she is definitely requested to do so, and then her speech is very brief and carefully weighed so as not to irritate her "master."

Their business is incorporated and the man is the president of the company. He has an elaborate office which is furnished with a large hand-carved desk and overstuffed chairs.

On the wall, directly in front of his desk, is an enormous oil painting of himself at which he gazes, sometimes for an hour at a time, with obvious approval.

When he speaks of the business, and particularly of the unusual success it enjoyed during the country's worst business depression, the man takes full credit for all that has been accomplished, and he never mentions his wife's name in connection with the business.

While the wife goes to business daily, she has no office and no desk. She is apt to be found strolling around among the workers, or assisting one of the girls in wrapping packages as nonchalantly as if she were an ordinary paid employee.

The man's name is on every package of merchandise which leaves the factory. It is printed in large letters on every delivery truck they operate, and it appears in large type on every piece of sales literature and in every advertisement they publish. The wife's name is conspicuous by its total absence.

The man believes that he built the business; that he operates it; that it could not operate without him. The truth of the matter is precisely the opposite. His ego built the business, runs it, and the business might continue to run as well or better without his presence as with it, for the very good reason that *his wife developed that ego,* and she could have done the same for any other man under similar circumstances.

Patiently, wisely and with purpose aforethought, this man's wife completely submerged her own personality into that of her husband, and step by step she fed his ego the type of food which removed from it every trace of his former inferiority complex, which was born of a lifetime of deprivation and failure. She hypnotized her husband into believing himself to be a great business tycoon.

Whatever degree of ego this man may have possessed before it came under the influence of a clever woman, had died of starvation. She revived his ego, nurtured it, fed it and developed it into a power of stupendous proportions despite his eccentric nature and his lack of business ability.

In truth every business policy, every business move, and every forward step the business has taken was the result of the wife's ideas, which she so cleverly planted in her husband's mind that he failed to recognize their source. In reality she is the brains of the business, he the mere window dressing; *but the combination is unbeatable,* as evidenced by their astounding financial achievements.

The manner in which this woman completely effaced herself was not only convincing evidence of her complete self-control, but it was evidence of her wisdom, for she probably knew she could not have accomplished the same results alone, or by any other methods than those she adopted.

This woman has very little formal education, and we have no idea how or where she learned enough about the operation of the human mind to inspire her to merge her entire personality with that of her husband for the purpose of developing in him the ego he now has. Perhaps the natural intuition which many women possess was responsible for her successful procedure. Whatever it was, she did a thorough job, and it served the ends she sought by bringing her economic security.

Care and Feeding of the Ego

Here then is evidence that the major difference between poverty and riches is merely the difference between an ego that is dominated by an inferiority complex and one that is dominated by a feeling of superiority. This old man might have died a homeless pauper if a clever woman had not blended her mind with his in such a way as to feed his ego with thoughts of, and belief in, his ability to attain opulence.

This is a conclusion from which there is no escape. Moreover, this case is only one of many that could be cited which prove that the human ego must be fed, organized and directed to definite ends if one is to succeed in any walk of life.

The Key Is in Your Hands

You now have, in the seventeen principles of this philosophy, all that is required to place you in possession of the Master-Key!

You are now in possession of all the practical knowledge which has been used by successful men from the dawn of civilization to the present.

This is a complete philosophy of life—sufficient for every human need. It holds the secret to the solution of all human problems. And it has been presented in terms which the humblest person may understand.

You may not aspire to become internationally famous, but you can and you should aspire to make yourself useful in order that you may occupy as much space in the world as your ego desires.

Every man comes finally to resemble those who make the strongest impression upon his ego. We are all creatures of imitation, and naturally we endeavor to imitate the heroes of our choice. This is a natural and healthful trait.

Fortunate indeed is the man whose hero is a person of great Faith, because hero-worship carries with it something of the nature of the hero one worships.

In conclusion let us summarize what has been said on the subject of the ego by calling attention to the fact that it represents the fertile garden spot of the mind wherein one may develop all the stimuli which inspire active Faith, or by neglecting to do so he may allow this fertile soil to produce a negative crop of fear and doubt and indecision which will lead to failure.

The amount of space you occupy in the world is now a matter of choice with you. The Master-Key To Riches is in your hands. You stand before the last gate which separates you from the success you desire. The gate will not open to you without your demand that it do so. You must use the Master-Key by making the seventeen principles of this philosophy *your own!*

You now have at your command a *complete philosophy* of life that is sufficient for the solution of every individual problem.

It is a philosophy of principles, some combination of which has been responsible for every individual success in every occupation or calling, although many may have used the philosophy successfully without recognizing the seventeen principles by the names we have given them.

No essential factor of successful achievement has been omitted. The philosophy embraces them all and describes them in words and similes that are well within the understanding of a majority of the people.

It is a philosophy of concreteness that touches only rarely the abstractions, and then only when necessary. It is free from academic terms and phrases which all too often serve only to confuse the average person.

The overall purpose of the philosophy is to enable one to get from where he stands to where he wishes to be, *both economically and spiritually;* thus it prepares one to enjoy the abundant life which the Creator intended all people to enjoy.

And it leads to the attainment of "riches" in the broadest and fullest meaning of the word, *including the twelve most important of all riches.*

The world has been greatly enriched by abstract philosophies, from the days of Plato, Socrates, Copernicus, Aristotle and many others of the same profound caliber of thinkers, on down to the days of Ralph Waldo Emerson and William James.

Now the world has a complete, concrete philosophy of individual achievement that provides the individual with the practical means by which he may take possession of his own mind and direct it to the attainment of peace of mind, harmony in human relationships, economic security, and the fuller life known as happiness.

Not as an apology, but to serve as an explanation, I shall call your attention to the fact that throughout this analysis of the seventeen principles we have emphasized the more important of these principles by continuous reference to them. The repetition was not accidental!

It was deliberate and necessary because of the tendency of all mankind to be unimpressed by new ideas or new interpretations of old truths.

Repetition has been necessary also because of the interrelationship of the seventeen principles, being connected as they are like the links of a chain, each one extending into and becoming a part of the principle preceding it and the principle following it.

And lastly, let us recognize that repetition of ideas is one of the basic principles of effective pedagogy and the central core of all effective advertising. Therefore it is not only justified, but it is definitely necessary as a means of human progress.

When you have assimilated this philosophy you will have a better education than the majority of people who graduate from college with the Master of Arts degree. You will be in possession of all the more useful knowledge which has

171

been organized from the experiences of the most successful men this nation has produced, and you will have it in a form which you can understand and apply.

But remember that the responsibility for the proper use of this knowledge will be yours. The mere possession of the knowledge will avail you nothing. Its *use* is what will count!

Chapter Ten

SELF-DISCIPLINE

The man who acquires the ability to take full possession of his own mind may take possession of everything else to which he is justly entitled.

—*Andrew Carnegie.*

We shall now reveal the methods by which one may take possession of his own mind.

We begin with a quotation from a man who proved the truth of his statement by his astounding achievements.

Those who knew him best, who worked with him most closely, say that his most outstanding trait of character consisted in the fact that he took full possession of his own mind at an early age, and never gave up any portion of his right to think his own thoughts.

What an achievement! and what a blessing it would be if every man could truthfully say, "I am the master of my fate; I am the Captain of my soul."

The Creator probably intended it to be so!

If it had been intended otherwise man would not have been limited solely to the right of control over but one power—the power of his own thoughts.

We go all the way through life searching for freedom of body and mind, yet most men never find it! Why? The Creator provided the means by which men may be free, and gave every man access to these means; and also inspired every man with impelling motives for the attainment of freedom.

Why then do men go through life imprisoned in a jail of their own making, when the key to the door is so easily

173

within their reach? The jail of poverty, the jail of ill health, the jail of fear, the jail of ignorance.

The desire for freedom of body and mind is a universal desire among all peoples, but few ever attain it because most men who search for it look everywhere except the one and only source from which it may come—*within their own minds.*

The desire for riches is also a universal desire, but most men never come within sight of the real riches of life because they do not recognize that all riches begin within their own minds.

Men search all their lives for power and fame without attaining either, because they do not recognize that the real source of both is within their own minds.

The mechanism of the mind is a profound system of organized power which can be released only by one means, and that is *by strict self-discipline.*

The mind that is properly disciplined and directed to definite ends is an irresistible power that recognizes no such reality as permanent defeat. It organizes defeat and converts it into victory; makes stepping-stones of stumbling-blocks; hitches its wagon to a star and uses the forces of the universe to carry it within easy grasp of its every desire.

And the man who masters himself through self-discipline never can be mastered by others!

Self-discipline is one of the Twelve Riches, but it is much more; it is an important prerequisite for the attainment of all riches, including freedom of body and mind, power and fame, and all the material things that men call wealth.

It is the sole means by which one may focus the mind upon the objective of a Definite Major Purpose until the law of Cosmic Habitforce takes over the pattern of that purpose and begins to translate it into its material equivalent.

It is the key to the *volitional power of the will* and the *emotions of the heart,* for it is the means by which these two may be mastered and balanced, one against the other, and directed to definite ends in *accurate thinking.*

It is the directing force in the maintenance of a Definite Major Purpose.

It is the source of all persistence and the means by which one may develop the habit of carrying through his plans and purposes.

It is the power with which all thought habits are patterned

and sustained until they are taken over by the law of Cosmic Habitforce and carried out to their logical climax.

It is the means by which one may take *full and complete control of his mind* and direct it to whatever ends he may desire.

It is indispensable in all leadership.

And it is the power through which one may make of his conscience a co-operator and guide instead of a conspirator.

It is the policeman who clears the mind for the expression of Faith, by the mastery of all fears.

It clears the mind for the expression of Imagination and of Creative Vision.

It does away with indecision and doubt.

It helps one to create and to sustain the "prosperity consciousness" that is essential for the accumulation of material riches, and the "health consciousness" necessary for the maintenance of sound physical health.

Also it operates entirely through the functioning system of the mind. Therefore, let us examine this system so that we may understand the factors of which it consists.

The Ten Factors of the "Mechanism" of Thought

The mind operates through ten factors, some of which operate automatically, while others must be directed through voluntary effort. *Self-discipline is the sole means of this direction.*

These ten factors are:

1. INFINITE INTELLIGENCE: The source of all power of thought, which operates automatically, but it may be organized and directed to definite ends through Definiteness of Purpose.

Infinite Intelligence may be likened to a great reservoir of water that overflows continuously, its branches flowing in small streams in many directions, and giving life to all vegetation and all living things. That portion of the stream which gives life to man supplies him also with the power of thought.

The brain of man may be likened to the water spigot, while the water flowing through the spigot represents Infinite Intelligence. The brain does not generate the power

175

of thought; *it merely receives that power from Infinite Intelligence and applies it to whatever ends the individual desires.*

And remember, this privilege of the control and the direction of thought is the only prerogative over which an individual has been given complete control. He may use it to build, or he may use it to destroy. He may give it direction, through Definiteness of Purpose, or he may neglect to do so, as he chooses.

The exercise of this great privilege is attained solely by self-discipline.

2. THE CONSCIOUS MIND: The individual mind functions through two departments. One is known as the conscious section of the mind; the other as the sub-conscious section. It is the opinion of psychologists that these two sections are comparable to an iceberg, the visible portion above the water line representing the conscious section, the invisible portion below the water line representing the sub-conscious section. Therefore it is obvious that the conscious section of the mind—that portion with which we consciously and voluntarily turn on the power of thought—is but a small portion of the whole, consisting of not more than one-fifth of the available mind power.

The sub-conscious section of the mind operates automatically. It carries on all the necessary functions in connection with the building and the maintenance of the physical body; keeps the heart beating to circulate the blood; assimilates the food through a perfect system of chemistry, and delivers the food in liquid form throughout the body; removes worn out cells and replaces them with new cells; removes bacteria which are deleterious to health; creates new physical beings by the blending of the cells of protoplasm (the formative material of animal embryos) contributed by the male and female of living organisms.

These and many other essential functions are performed by the sub-conscious section of the mind, in addition to which *it serves as the connecting link between the conscious mind and Infinite Intelligence.*

It may be likened to the spigot of the conscious mind, through which (by its control through self-discipline) more thought power may be turned on. Or it may be likened to a rich garden spot wherein may be planted and germinated the seed of any desired idea.

The importance of the sub-conscious section of the mind may be estimated by recognition of the fact that it is the only means of *voluntary approach* to Infinite Intelligence. Therefore it is the medium by which all prayers are conveyed and all answers to prayer are received.

It is the medium that translates one's Definite Major Purpose into its material equivalent, *a process which consists entirely in guidance of the individual in the proper use of the natural means of attaining the objects of his desires.*

The sub-conscious section of the mind acts upon all impulses of thought, carrying out to their logical conclusion all thoughts which are definitely shaped by the conscious mind, *but it gives preference to thoughts inspired by emotional feeling,* such as the emotion of fear or the emotion of Faith; hence the necessity for self-discipline as a means of providing the sub-conscious mind with only those thoughts or desires which lead to the attainment of whatever one wishes.

The sub-conscious section of the mind gives preference also to the dominating thoughts of the mind—those thoughts which one creates by the repetition of ideas or desires. This fact explains the importance of adopting a Definite Major Purpose and the necessity of fixing that purpose (through self-discipline) as a dominating thought of the mind.

3. THE FACULTY OF WILL-POWER: The power of the will is the "boss" of all departments of the mind. It has the power to modify, change or balance all thinking habits, and its decisions are final and irrevocable except by itself. It is the power that puts the emotions of the heart under control, and it is subject to direction only by self-discipline. In this connection it may be likened to the Chairman of a Board of Directors whose decisions are final. It takes its orders from the conscious mind, *but recognizes no other authority.*

4. THE FACULTY OF REASON: This is the "presiding judge" of the conscious section of the mind which may pass judgment on all ideas, plans and desires, and it will do so if it is directed by self-discipline. But its decisions can be set aside by the power of the will, or modified by the power of the emotions when the will does not interfere. Let us here take note of the fact that all accurate thinking requires the co-operation of the faculty of reason, *although*

177

it is a requirement which not more than one person in every ten thousand respects. This explains why there are so few accurate thinkers.

Most so-called thinking is the work of the emotions without the guiding influence of self-discipline; without relationship to either the power of the will or the faculty of reason.

5. THE FACULTY OF THE EMOTIONS: This is the source of most of the actions of the mind, the seat of most of the thoughts released by the conscious section of the mind. The emotions are tricky and undependable and may be very dangerous if they are not modified by the faculty of reason under the direction of the faculty of the will.

However, the faculty of the emotions is not to be condemned because of its undependability, for it is the source of all enthusiasm, imagination and Creative Vision, and it may be directed by self-discipline to the development of these essentials of individual achievement. The direction may be given by modification of the emotions through the faculties of the will and the reason.

Accurate thinking is not possible without complete mastery of the emotions.

Mastery is attained by placing the emotions under the control of the will, thus preparing them for direction to whatever ends the will may dictate, modifying them when necessary through the faculty of reason.

The accurate thinker has no opinions and makes no decisions which have not been submitted to, and passed upon by, the faculties of the will and the reason. He uses his emotions to *inspire the creation of ideas through his imagination,* but refines his ideas through his will and reason before their final acceptance.

This is self-discipline of the highest order. The procedure is simple but it is not easy to follow; and it is never followed except by the accurate thinker who moves on his own *personal initiative.*

The more important of the Twelve Riches, such as (1) a positive mental attitude, (2) harmony in human relationships, (3) freedom from fear, (4) the hope of achievement, (5) the capacity for faith, (6) an open mind on all subjects, and (7) sound physical health, *are attainable only by a strict direction and control of all the emotions.* This does not mean that the emotions should be suppressed, but they must be controlled and directed to definite ends.

The emotions may be likened to steam in a boiler, the power of which consists in its release and direction through the mechanism of an engine. Uncontrolled steam has no power, and though it be controlled it must be released through a governor, which is a mechanical device corresponding to self-discipline in connection with the control and release of emotional power.

The emotions which are most important and most dangerous are, (1) the emotion of sex, (2) the emotion of love, and (3) the emotion of fear. *These are the emotions which produce the major portion of all human activities.* The emotions of love and sex are creative. When controlled and directed they inspire one with imagination and creative vision of stupendous proportions. If they are not controlled and directed they may lead one to indulge in destructive follies.

6. THE FACULTY OF IMAGINATION: This is the workshop wherein are shaped and fashioned all desires, ideas, plans and purposes, together with the means of attaining them. Through organized use and self-discipline the imagination may be developed to the status of Creative Vision.

But the faculty of the imagination, like the faculty of the emotions, is tricky and undependable if it is not controlled and directed by self-discipline. Without control it often dissipates the power of thought in useless, impractical and destructive activities which need not be here mentioned in detail. *Uncontrolled imagination is the stuff that day dreams are made of!*

Control of the imagination begins with the adoption of definiteness of purpose based on definite plans. The control is completed by strict habits of self-discipline which give definite direction to the faculty of the emotions, for the power of the emotions is the power that inspires the imagination to action.

7. THE FACULTY OF THE CONSCIENCE: The conscience is the moral guide of the mind, and its major purpose is that of modifying the individual's aims and purposes so that they harmonize with the moral laws of nature and of mankind. The conscience is a twin-brother of the faculty of reason in that it gives discrimination and guidance to the reason when reason is in doubt.

The conscience functions as a co-operative guide only so long as it is respected and followed. If it is neglected, or

179

its mandates are rejected, it finally becomes a conspirator instead of a guide, and often volunteers to justify man's most destructive habits. Thus the dual nature of the conscience makes it necessary for one to direct it through strict self-discipline.

8. THE SIXTH SENSE: This is the "broadcasting station" of the mind through which one automatically sends and receives the vibrations of thought. It is the medium through which all thought impulses known as "hunches" are received. And it is closely related to, or perhaps it may be a part of the sub-conscious section of the mind.

The sixth sense is the medium through which Creative Vision operates. It is the medium through which all basically new ideas are revealed. And it is the major asset of the minds of all men who are recognized as "geniuses."

9. THE MEMORY: This is the "filing cabinet" of the brain, wherein is stored all thought impulses, all experiences and all sensations that reach the brain through the five physical senses. And it may be the "filing cabinet" of all impulses of thought which reach the mind through the sixth sense, although all psychologists do not agree as to this.

The memory is tricky and undependable unless it is organized and directed by self-discipline.

10. THE FIVE PHYSICAL SENSES: These are the physical "arms" of the brain through which it contacts the external world and acquires information therefrom. The physical senses are not reliable, and therefore they need constant self-discipline. Under any kind of intense emotional activity the senses become confused and unreliable.

By the simplest sort of legerdemain the five physical senses may be deceived. And they are deceived daily by the common experiences of life. Under the emotion of fear the physical senses often create monstrous "ghosts" which have no existence except in the faculty of the imagination, and there is no fact of life which they will not and do not exaggerate or distort when fear prevails.

Control of Thought Habits

Thus we have briefly described the ten factors which enter into all mental activities of man. But we have supplied enough information concerning the "mechanism" of the mind to indicate clearly the necessity for self-discipline in their manipulation and use.

Self-discipline is attained by the control of thought habits. And the term "self-discipline" has reference only to the power of thought, because all discipline of self must take place in the mind, although its effects may deal with the functions of the physical body.

You are where you are and what you are because of your habits of thought!

Your thought habits are subject to your control!

They are the only circumstances of your life over which you have complete control, which is the most profound of all the facts of your life because it clearly proves that your Creator recognized the necessity of this great prerogative. Otherwise He would not have made it the sole circumstance over which man has been given exclusive control.

Further evidence of the Creator's desire to give man the unchallengeable right of control over his thought habits has been clearly revealed through the law of Cosmic Habitforce —the medium by which thought habits are fixed and made permanent, so that habits become automatic and operate without the voluntary effort of man.

For the present we are interested only in calling attention to the fact that the Creator of the marvelous mechanism known as a brain ingeniously provided it with a device by which all thought habits are taken over and given automatic expression.

Self-discipline is the principle by which one may voluntarily shape the patterns of thought to harmonize with his aims and purposes.

This privilege carries with it a heavy responsibility because it is the one privilege which determines, more than all others, the position in life which each man shall occupy.

If this privilege is neglected, by one's failure to voluntarily form habits designed to lead to the attainment of definite ends, *then the circumstances of life which are beyond one's control will do the job;* and what an extremely poor job it often becomes!

Every man is a bundle of habits. Some are of his own making while others are involuntary. They are made by his fears and doubts and worries and anxieties and greed and superstition and envy and hatred.

181

Self-discipline is the only means by which one's habits of thought may be controlled and directed until they are taken over and given automatic expression by the law of Cosmic Habitforce. Ponder this thought carefully, for it is the key to your mental, physical and spiritual destiny.

You can make your thought habits to order and they will carry you to the attainment of any desired goal within your reach. Or you can allow the *uncontrollable* circumstances of your life to make your thought habits for you and they will carry you irresistibly into the failure side of the great River of Life.

You can keep your mind trained on that which you desire from Life and get just that! Or you can feed it on thoughts of that which you *do not desire* and it will, as unerringly, bring you just that. *Your thought habits evolve from the food that your mind dwells upon.*

That is as certain as that night follows day!

Awake, arise, and quicken your mind to the attunement of the circumstances of life which your heart craves.

Turn on the full powers of your will and take complete control of your own mind. It is your mind! It was given to you as a servant to carry out your desires. And no one may enter it or influence it in the slightest degree *without your consent and co-operation.* What a profound fact this is!

Remember this when the circumstances over which you appear to have no control begin to move in and aggravate you. Remember it when fear and doubt and worry begin to park themselves in the spare bed-room of your mind. Remember it when the fear of poverty begins to park itself in the space of your mind that should be filled with a "prosperity consciousness."

And remember, too, that this is self-discipline! the one and only method by which anyone may take full possession of his own mind.

You are not a worm made to crawl in the dust of the earth.

If you were you would have been equipped with the physical means by which you would have crawled on your belly instead of walking on your two legs. Your physical body was designed to enable you to stand and to walk and to think your way to the highest attainment which you are capable of conceiving. Why be contented with less? Why should you insult your Creator by indifference or neglect in the use of His most priceless gift—the power of your own mind?

Tap Your Inexhaustible Mind-Power

The potential powers of the human mind are beyond comprehension.

And one of the great mysteries which has endured down through the ages consists in man's neglect to recognize and to use these powers as a means of shaping his own earthly destiny!

The mind has been cleverly provided with a gateway of approach to Infinite Intelligence, through the subconscious section of the mind; and this gateway has been so arranged that it can be opened for voluntary use by preparation through that state of mind known as Faith.

The mind has been provided with a faculty of imagination wherein may be fashioned ways and means of translating hope and purpose into physical realities.

It has been provided with the stimulative capacity of desire and enthusiasm with which one's plans and purposes may be given action.

It has been provided with the power of the will through which both plan and purpose may be sustained indefinitely.

It has been given the capacity for Faith, through which the will and the reasoning faculty may be subdued while the entire machinery of the brain is turned over to the guiding force of Infinite Intelligence; and it has been prepared, through a sixth sense, for direct connection with other minds (under the Master Mind principle) from which it may add to its own power the stimulative forces of other minds which serve so effectively to stimulate the imagination.

It has been given the capacity to reason, through which facts and theories may be combined into hypotheses, ideas and plans.

It has been given the power to project itself into other minds, through what is known as telepathy.

It has been given the power of deduction by which it may foretell the future by analysis of the past. This capacity explains why the philosopher looks backward in order that he may see the future.

It has been provided with the means of selection, modification and control of the nature of its thoughts, thereby giving to man the privilege of building his own character to order, to fit any desired pattern, and the power to determine the kind of thoughts which shall dominate his mind.

It has been provided with a marvelous filing system for receiving, recording and recalling every thought it has expressed, through what is known as a memory, and this marvelous system automatically classifies and files related thoughts in such a manner that the recall of one particular thought leads to the recall of associated thoughts.

It has been provided with the power of emotion through which it can stimulate at will the body for any desired action.

It has been given the power to function secretly and silently, thereby insuring privacy of thought under all circumstances.

It has an unlimited capacity to receive, organize, store and express knowledge on all subjects, in both the fields of physics and metaphysics, the outer world and the *inner world*.

It has the power to aid in the maintenance of sound physical health, and apparently it is the sole source of cure of physical ills, all other sources being merely contributory; and it maintains a perfect repair system for the upkeep of the physical body—a system that works automatically.

It maintains and automatically operates a marvelous system of chemistry through which it converts food into suitable combinations for the maintenance and repair of the body.

It automatically operates the heart through which the blood stream distributes food to every portion of the body and removes all waste material and worn out cells of the body.

It has the power of self-discipline through which it can form any desired habit and maintain it until it is taken over by the law of Cosmic Habitforce and is given automatic expression.

It is the common meeting ground wherein man may commune with Infinite Intelligence, through prayer (or any form of expressed desire or definiteness of purpose) by the simple process of opening the gateway of approach through the subconscious section of the mind, by Faith.

It is the sole producer of every idea, every tool, every machine and every mechanical invention created by man for his convenience in the business of living in a material world.

It is the sole source of all happiness and all misery, and of both poverty and riches of every nature whatsoever, and it devotes its energies to the expression of whichever of these that dominates the mind through the power of thought.

It is the source of all human relationships, and all forms of intercourse between men; the builder of friendships and the creator of enemies, according to the manner in which it is directed.

It has the power to resist and defend itself against all external circumstances and conditions, although it cannot always control them.

It has no limitations within reason (no limitations except those which conflict with the laws of nature) save only those which the individual accepts through the lack of Faith! Truly, "whatever the mind can conceive and believe the mind can achieve."

It has the power to change from one mood to another at will. Therefore it need never be damaged beyond repair by any kind of discouragement.

It can relax into temporary oblivion through sleep, and prepare itself for a fresh start within a few hours.

It grows stronger and more dependable the more it is controlled, directed to definite ends and used voluntarily.

It can convert sound into music that rests and soothes both the body and the soul.

It can send the sound of the human voice around the earth in a fraction of a minute.

It can make two blades of grass grow where but one grew before.

It can build a printing press that receives a roll of paper at one end and turns out a completely printed and bound book at the other end, in a few moments.

It can call back the sunlight at will, at any time of the day, by merely causing the pushing of a button.

It can convert water into steam power and steam into electric power.

The mind can control the temperature of heat at will, and it can create fire by rubbing two sticks together.

It can produce music by drawing a hair from the tail of a horse across strings made from the internals of a cat.

It can accurately locate any position on earth by observation of the position of the stars.

It can harness the law of gravitation and make it do the work of man and beast in ways too numerous for mention.

It can build an airplane that will safely transport human beings through the air.

It can build a machine that will penetrate the human body with light and photograph the bones and the soft tissues without injury.

It has the power of clairvoyance through which it can discern physical objects not present or visible to the naked eye.

It can clear the jungle and convert the desert into a garden spot of productivity.

It can harness the waves of the oceans and convert them into power for the operation of machinery.

It can produce glass that will not break and convert wood pulp into clothing.

It can transform the stumbling-blocks of failure into stepping-stones of achievement.

It can build a machine that can detect falsehoods.

It can accurately measure any circle by the smallest fragment of its arc.

It can produce rubber from chemicals.

It can reproduce a picture of any material object, by television, without the aid of the human eye.

It can determine the size, weight and material contents of the sun, over 93,000,000 miles away, by analysis of the sun's rays of light.

It can create a mechanical eye that can detect the presence of airplanes or submarines, or any other physical object, hundreds of miles distant.

It can seal hermetically any type of food and preserve it indefinitely.

It can record and reproduce any sound, including the human voice, with the aid of a machine and a piece of wax.

It can record and reproduce pictures of any kind of physical motion, with the aid of a piece of glass and a strip of celluloid.

It can build a machine that will travel in the air, on the ground or under the water.

It can build a machine that will plough its way through the thickest forest, smashing trees as if they were cornstalks.

It can build a shovel that will lift as many tons of dirt in a minute as ten men could move in a day.

It can harness the magnetic poles of the northern and southern portions of the earth, with the aid of a compass, and determine direction accurately.

Great and powerful is the mind of man, and it shall yet perform feats which will make all the foregoing seem as trifles by comparison.

Negative Thoughts Lead to Self-destruction

And yet, despite all this astounding power of the mind the great majority of the people make no attempt to take control of their minds and they suffer themselves to become cowed by fears or difficulties which do not exist save in their own imaginations.

The arch enemy of mankind is fear!

We fear poverty in the midst of an over-abundance of riches!

We fear ill health despite the ingenious system nature has provided with which the physical body is automatically maintained, repaired and kept in working order.

We fear criticism when there are no critics save only those which we set up in our own minds through the negative use of our imagination.

We fear the loss of love of friends and relatives although we know well enough that our own conduct may be sufficient to maintain love through all ordinary circumstances of human relationship.

We fear old age whereas we should accept it as a medium of greater wisdom and understanding.

We fear the loss of liberty although we know that liberty is a matter of harmonious relationships with others.

We fear death when we know it is inevitable; therefore beyond our control.

We fear failure, not recognizing that every failure carries with it the seed of an equivalent benefit.

And we feared the lightning until Franklin and Edison and a few other rare individuals, who dared to take possession of their own minds, proved that lightning is a form of physical energy which can be harnessed and used for the benefit of mankind.

Instead of opening our minds for the guidance of Infinite Intelligence, through Faith, we close our minds tightly with every conceivable shade and degree of self-imposed limitation based upon unnecessary fears.

We know that man is the master of every other living creature on this earth, yet we fail to look about us and learn from birds of the air and beasts of the jungle that even the dumb animals have been wisely provided with food and all the necessities of their existence through the universal plan which makes all fears groundless and foolish.

We complain of lack of opportunity and cry out against those who dare to take possession of their own minds, not recognizing that every man who has a sound mind has the right and the power to provide himself with every material thing he needs or can use.

We fear the discomfort of physical pain, not recognizing that pain is a universal language through which man is warned of evils and dangers that need correction.

Because of our fears we go to the Creator with prayers over petty details which we could and should settle for ourselves, then give up and lose Faith (if we had any Faith to begin with) when we do not get the results we ask for, not recognizing our duty to offer prayers of thanks for the bountiful blessings which we have been provided through the power of our minds.

We talk and preach sermons about sin, failing to recognize that the greatest of all sins is that of the loss of Faith in an all-wise Creator who has provided His children with more blessings than any earthly parent ever thinks of providing for his own children.

We convert the revelations of inventions into the tools of destruction through what we politely call "war," then cry out in protest when the law of compensation pays us off with famines and business depressions.

We abuse the power of the mind in ways too numerous

for mention, because we have not recognized that this power can be harnessed through self-discipline, and used to serve our needs.

Thus we go all the way through life, eating the husks and throwing away the kernels of plenty!

The Art of Accurate Thinking

Before leaving the analysis of self-discipline, which deals entirely with the "mechanism" of thought, let us briefly describe some of the known facts and habits of thought in order that we may acquire the art of accurate thinking.

1. *All thought* (whether it is positive or negative, good or bad, accurate or inaccurate) *tends to clothe itself in its physical equivalent,* and it does so by inspiring one with ideas, plans, and the means of attaining desired ends, through logical and natural means.

After thought on any given subject becomes a habit and has been taken over by the law of Cosmic Habitforce, the subconscious section of the mind proceeds to carry it out to its logical conclusion, through the aid of whatever natural media that may be available.

It may not be literally true that "thoughts are things" but it is true that thoughts create all things, and the things they create are striking duplicates of the thought-patterns from which they are fashioned.

It is believed by some that every thought one releases starts an unending series of vibrations with which the one who releases the thought will later be compelled to contend; that man himself is but a physical reflection of thought put into motion and crystallized into physical form by Infinite Intelligence.

It is also the belief of many that the energy with which man thinks is but a projected minute portion of Infinite Intelligence, appropriated from the universal supply through the equipment of the brain. No thought contrary to this belief has yet been proved sound.

2. *Through the application of self-discipline* thought can be influenced, controlled and directed through transmutation to a desired end, by the development of voluntary habits suitable for the attainment of any given end.

189

3. *The power of thought* (through the aid of the sub-conscious section of the mind) *has control over every cell of the body,* carries on all repairs and replacements of injured or dead cells, stimulates their growth, influences the action of all organs of the body and helps them to function by habit and orderliness, and assists in fighting disease through what is commonly called "body resistance." These functions are carried on automatically, but many of them may be stimulated by voluntary aid.

4. *All of man's achievements begin in the form of thought,* organized into plans, aims and purposes and expressed in terms of physical action. All action is inspired by one or more of the nine basic motives.

5. *The entire power of the mind* operates through two sections of the mind, the conscious and the sub-conscious.

The conscious section is under the control of the individual; the sub-conscious is controlled by Infinite Intelligence and serves as the medium of communication between Infinite Intelligence and the conscious mind.

The "sixth sense" is under the control of the sub-conscious section of the mind and it functions automatically in certain fixed fundamentals, but may be influenced to function in carrying out the instructions of the conscious mind.

6. *Both the conscious and the sub-conscious sections of the mind function in response to fixed habits,* adjusting themselves to whatever thought habits the individual may establish, whether the habits are voluntary or involuntary.

7. *The majority of all thoughts released by the individual are inaccurate* because they are inspired by personal opinions which are arrived at without the examination of facts, or because of bias, prejudice, fear, and the result of emotional excitement in which the faculty of the reason has been given little or no opportunity to modify them rationally.

8. *The first step in accurate thinking* (a step that is taken by none except those with adequate self-discipline) is that of separating facts from fiction and hearsay evidence. The second step is that of separating facts (after they have been identified as such) into two classes, viz.: important and the unimportant. An important fact is any fact which can be used to help one attain the object of his major purpose or any minor purpose leading to his major purpose.

All other facts are relatively unimportant. The average person spends his life in dealing with "inferences" based upon unreliable sources of information and unimportant facts. Therefore he seldom comes within sight of that form of self-discipline which demands facts and distinguishes the difference between important and unimportant facts.

9. *Desire, based on a definite motive, is the beginning of all voluntary thought action associated with individual achievement.*

The presence in the mind of any intense desire tends to stimulate the faculty of the imagination with the purpose of creating ways and means of attaining the object of the desire.

If the desire is continuously held in the mind (through the repetition of thought) it is picked up by the sub-conscious section of the mind and automatically carried out to its logical conclusion.

These are some of the more important of the known facts concerning the greatest of all mysteries, the mystery of human thought, and they indicate clearly that accurate thinking is attainable only by the strictest habits of self-discipline.

"Where," some may ask, "and how may one begin the development of self-discipline?"

It might well begin by *concentration* upon a Definite Major Purpose.

Nothing great has ever been achieved without the power of concentration.

How Self-Discipline May be Applied

The accompanying chart number one presents a complete description of the ten factors by which the power of thought is expressed. Six of these factors are subject to control through self-discipline, viz.:

1. The faculty of the will.
2. The faculty of the emotions.
3. The faculty of the reason.
4. The faculty of the imagination.
5. The faculty of the conscience.
6. The faculty of the memory.

The remaining four factors act independently, and they are not subject to voluntary control, except that the five physical senses may be influenced and directed by the formation of voluntary habits.

CHART No. 1

CHART OF THE 10 FACTORS WHICH CONSTITUTE THE "MECHANISM" OF THOUGHT.

OBSERVE THAT THE SUBCONSCIOUS SECTION OF THE MIND
HAS ACCESS TO ALL DEPARTMENTS OF THE MIND,
BUT IS NOT UNDER THE CONTROL OF ANY.

INFINITE INTELLIGENCE
• • •
The source of all power of thought, all facts, all knowledge, available through the subconscious section of the mind only.

SUBCONSCIOUS SECTION OF THE MIND
The connecting link between the mind of man and Infinite Intelligence.

Below is shown all departments of the mind, with the three sources of thought stimuli at bottom of the chart.

FACULTY OF WILL-POWER
"Boss of the mind"

FACULTY OF REASON
Master of all opinions and judgments

*FACULTY OF EMOTIONS
The Seat of most actions of the mind

FACULTY OF IMAGINATION
The builder of all plans

FACULTY OF CONSCIENCE
Moral guide of the mind

The three sources of thought which require the greatest amount of self-discipline are shown below

TELEPATHY	*THE FIVE SENSES	*MEMORY
The "sixth sense" or broadcasting station of the brain, connecting with other brains.	1—Sight These become 2—Sound reliable only 3—Taste through 4—Smell strict self- 5—Touch discipline.	Store house of all thought and sense impressions. Filing cabinet of the brain.

* Not always dependable. Must be under strict discipline at all times.

192

CHART No. 2

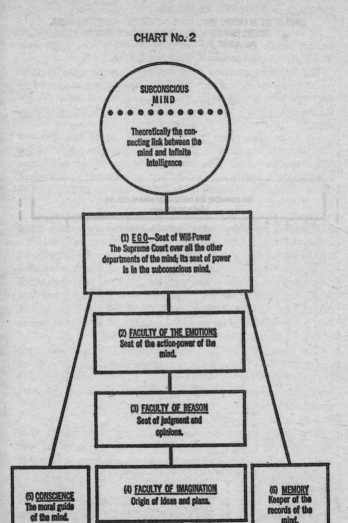

SUBCONSCIOUS
MIND
• • • • • • • • • • • • • • • • • •
Theoretically the con-
necting link between the
mind and Infinite
Intelligence

(1) E G O—Seat of Will-Power
The Supreme Court over all the other
departments of the mind; its seat of power
is in the subconscious mind.

(2) FACULTY OF THE EMOTIONS
Seat of the action-power of the
mind.

(3) FACULTY OF REASON
Seat of judgment and
opinions.

(5) CONSCIENCE
The moral guide
of the mind.

(4) FACULTY OF IMAGINATION
Origin of ideas and plans.

(6) MEMORY
Keeper of the
records of the
mind.

CHART of THE SIX DEPARTMENTS of THE MIND over which
Self-discipline can be maintained, numbered in the order of their relative importance.

In chart number two we have presented a perspective picture which reveals the six departments of the mind over which self-discipline may be easily maintained.

The departments have been numbered in the order of their relative importance, although it is impossible for anyone to say definitely which is the more important of these departments, for each is an essential factor in the expression of thought.

We have been given no choice but to place *ego*, the seat of will-power, in the first position, because the power of the will may control all the other departments of the mind, and it has been properly called the "Supreme Court" of the mind, whose decisions are final and not subject to appeal to any higher court.

The faculty of the emotions takes second position since it is well known that most people are ruled by their emotions; therefore, they rank next to the "Supreme Court."

The faculty of the reason takes third place in importance since it is the modifying influence through which emotional action may be prepared for safe usage. The "well balanced" mind is the mind which represents a compromise between the faculty of the emotions and the faculty of the reason. Such a compromise is usually brought about by the power of the "Supreme Court," the faculty of the will.

The faculty of the will sometimes decides with the emotions; at other times it throws its influence on the side of the faculty of reason, but it always has the last word, and whichever side it supports is the winning side of all controversies between the reason and the emotions.

And, what an ingenious system this is!

The faculty of the imagination has been given fourth place since it is the department which creates ideas, plans and ways and means of attaining desired objectives, all of which are inspired by the faculty of the emotions or the faculty of the will.

We might say that the faculty of the imagination serves the mind as a "ways and means committee," but it often acts on its own account and goes off on tours of fantastic exploration in places where it has no legitimate business in connection with the faculty of the will. On these self-inspired tours the imagination often has the full consent, cooperation and urge of the emotions, which is the main reason why all desires which originate in the faculty of the emotions must be closely scrutinized by the faculty of the reason; and countermanded, if need be, by the faculty of the will.

When the emotions and the imagination get out from under the supervision of the reason, and the control of the will, they resemble a couple of mischievous school boys who have decided to play hookey from school, and wind up at the old swimming hole, or in the neighbor's watermelon patch.

There is no form of mischief which these two may not get into! Therefore, they require more self-discipline than all the other faculties of the mind combined. Let us remember this!

The other two departments, the *conscience* and the *memory*, are necessary adjuncts of the mind, and while both are important they belong at the end of the list, where they have been assigned.

The subconscious section of the mind has been given the position above all of the other six departments of the mind because it is the connecting link between the conscious mind and Infinite Intelligence, and the medium through which all departments of the mind receive the power of thought.

The subconscious section of the mind is not subject to control, but it is subject to influence, by the means here described. It acts on its own accord, and voluntarily, although its action may be speeded up by intensifying the emotions, or applying the power of the will in a highly concentrated form.

A *burning desire* behind a Definite Major Purpose may stimulate the action of the subconscious section of the mind and speed up its operations.

The relationship between the subconscious section of the mind and the six other departments of the mind, indicated on chart number two, is similar in many respects to that of the farmer and the laws of nature through which his crops are grown.

The farmer has certain fixed duties to perform, such as preparing the soil, planting the seed at the right season, and keeping the weeds out, after which his work is finished. From there on out nature takes over, germinates the seed, develops it to maturity and yields a crop.

The conscious section of the mind may be compared with the farmer in that it prepares the way by the formulation of plans and purposes, under the direction of the faculty of the will. If this work is done properly, and a clear picture of that which is desired is created (the picture being the seed of the purpose desired) the subconscious takes over the picture, draws upon the power of Infinite Intelligence for the intelligence needed for the translation of the picture, gets the information necessary and presents it to the conscious section of the mind in the form of a practical plan of procedure.

Unlike the laws of nature which germinate seed and produce a crop for the farmer within a definite, predetermined length of time, the subconscious takes over the seed of ideas or purposes submitted to it and fixes its own time for the submission of a plan for their attainment.

Power of will, expressed in terms of a *burning desire*, is the one medium by which the action of the subconscious may be speeded up. Thus, by taking full possession of one's own mind, *by exercising the power of the will*, one comes into possession of power of stupendous proportions.

And the act of mastering the power of the will, so that it may be directed to the attainment of any desired end, is self-discipline of the highest order. Control of the will requires *persistence, faith and definiteness of purpose.*

In the field of salesmanship, for example, it is a fact well known to all master salesmen, that the persistent salesman heads the list in sales production. In some fields of selling, such as that of life insurance, persistence is the asset of major importance to the salesman.

And persistence, in selling or any other calling, is a matter of strict self-discipline!

In the field of advertising the same rule applies. The most successful advertisers carry on with unyielding persistence, repeating their efforts month after month, year after year, with unabating regularity; and professional advertising experts have convincing evidence that this is the only policy which will produce satisfactory results.

The pioneers who settled America when this country was only a vast wilderness of primitive men and wild animals, demonstrated what can be accomplished when will-power is applied with persistence.

At a later period in the history of our country, after the pioneers had established a semblance of civilized society,

George Washington and his little army of under-fed, half-clothed, under-equipped soldiers proved once more that will-power applied with persistence is unbeatable.

And the pioneers of American industry gave us another demonstration of the benefits of will-power backed by persistence. Men of their type who have made great contributions to the American way of life were men with self-discipline, and they attained it through the power of the will, backed with persistence.

Andrew Carnegie's entire career provides an excellent example of the benefits which are available through self-discipline. He came to America when he was a very young boy, and began work as a laborer. He had only a few friends; none of them wealthy or influential. But he did have an enormous capacity for the expression of his will-power.

By working at manual labor during the day and studying at night he learned telegraphy, and finally worked his way up to the position of private operator for the Division Superintendent of the Pennsylvania Railroad Company.

In this position he made such effective application of some of the principles of this philosophy, among them the principle of self-discipline, that he attracted the attention of men with money and influence who were in a position to aid him in carrying out the object of his Major Purpose in life.

At this point in his career he had precisely the same advantages that hundreds of other telegraph operators enjoyed, but no more. But he did have one asset which the other operators apparently did not possess: The will to win and a definite idea of what he wanted, together with the persistence to carry on until he got it.

This too was the outgrowth of self-discipline!

Mr. Carnegie's outstanding qualities were will-power and persistence, plus a strict self-discipline through which these traits were controlled and directed to the attainment of a definite purpose. Beyond these he had no outstanding qualities which are not possessed by the man of average intelligence.

Out of his will-power, properly self-disciplined and directed to the attainment of a definite purpose, came the great United States Steel Corporation which revolutionized the steel industry and provided employment for a huge army of skilled and unskilled workers.

Thus we see that *a successful man gets his start through*

the application of self-discipline, in pursuit of a definite purpose; and he carries on until he attains that purpose, with the aid of that same principle.

Self-discipline is a self-acquired trait of character. It is not one which can be appropriated from the lives of others, nor acquired from the pages of a book. It is an asset which must come from *within*, by exercise of one's power of will. These self-acquired qualities are just as effective in other forms of application as they are in the attainment of leadership in industry.

When Andrew Carnegie said that "the power of will is an irresistible force which recognizes no such reality as failure," he doubtlessly meant that it is irresistible when it is properly organized and directed to a definite end in a spirit of faith. Obviously he intended to emphasize three important principles of this philosophy as the basis of all self-acquired self-discipline, viz.:

    (a) Definiteness of Purpose.
    (b) Applied Faith.
    (c) Self-Discipline.

It should be remembered, however, that the state of mind which can be developed through these three principles can best be attained, and more quickly, by the application of other principles of this philosophy, among them:

    (a) The Master Mind.
    (b) A Pleasing Personality.
    (c) The Habit of Going The Extra Mile.
    (d) Personal Initiative.
    (e) Creative Vision.

Combine these five principles with Definiteness of Purpose, Applied Faith and Self-Discipline, and you will have an available source of personal power of stupendous proportions.

The beginner in the study of this philosophy may find it difficult to gain control over his power of will without approaching that control step by step, through the mastery and application of these eight principles.

Mastery can be attained in one way only, and that is by constant, persistent application of the principles. They must be woven into one's daily habits and applied in all human relationships, and in the solution of all personal problems.

The power of the will responds only to *motive* persistently pursued!

And it becomes strong in the same way that one's arm may become strong—by systematic use.

Men with will-power which has been self-acquired, through self-discipline, do not give up hope or quit when the going becomes hard. Men without will-power do.

A humble general stood in review before an army of tired, discouraged soldiers who had just been badly defeated during the War Between the States. He too had a reason to be discouraged, for the war was going against him.

When one of his officers suggested that the outlook seemed discouraging, General Grant lifted his weary head, closed his eyes, clenched his fists, and exclaimed: "We will fight it out along these lines if it takes all summer!" And he did fight it out along the lines he had chosen. Thus it may well be that on this firm decision of one man, backed by an indomitable will, came the final victory which preserved the union of the states.

One school of thought says that "right makes might!" Another school of thought says that "might makes right!" But men who think accurately know that the power of the will makes might, whether right or wrong, and the entire history of mankind backs up this belief.

Study men of great achievement, wherever you find them, and you will find evidence that the power of the will, organized and persistently applied, is the dominating factor in their success. Also, you will find that successful men commit themselves to a stricter system of self-discipline than any which is forced upon them by circumstances beyond their control.

They work when others sleep!

They Go The Extra Mile, and if need be another and still another mile, never stopping until they have contributed the utmost service of which they are capable.

Follow in their footsteps for a single day and you will be convinced that they need no taskmaster to drive them on. They move on their own personal initiative because they direct their efforts by the strictest sort of self-discipline.

They may appreciate commendation, but they do not require it to inspire them to action. They listen to condemnation, but they do not fear it, and they are not discouraged by it.

And they sometimes fail, or suffer temporary defeat, just

as others do, but failure only spurs them on to greater effort.

They encounter obstacles, as does everyone, but these they convert into benefits through which they carry on toward their chosen goal.

They experience discouragements, the same as others do, but they close the doors of their minds tightly behind unpleasant experiences and transmute their disappointments into renewed energy with which they struggle ahead to victory.

When death strikes in their families they bury their dead, but not their indomitable wills.

They seek the counsel of others, extract from it that which they can use and reject the remainder, although the whole world may criticize them on account of their judgment.

They know they cannot control all the circumstances which affect their lives, but they do control *their own state of mind and their mental reactions* to all circumstances, by keeping their minds positive at all times.

They are tested by their own negative emotions, as are all people, but they keep the upper hand over these emotions by making right royal servants of them.

Let us keep in mind the fact that through self-discipline one may do two important things, both of which are essential for outstanding achievement.

First, one may completely control the negative emotions by transmuting them into constructive effort, using them as an inspiration to greater endeavor.

Secondly, one may stimulate the positive emotions, and direct them to the attainment of any desired end.

Thus, by controlling both the positive and the negative emotions the faculty of reason is left free to function, as is also the faculty of the imagination.

Control over the emotions is attained gradually, by the development of habits of thought which are conducive of control. Such habits should be formed in connection with the small, unimportant circumstances of life, for it is true, as Supreme Court Justice Brandeis once said, that "the brain is like the hand. It grows with use."

One by one the six departments of the mind which are subject to self-discipline can be brought under complete control, but the start should be made by habits which give one control over the emotions first, since it is true that most people are the victims of their uncontrolled emotions throughout their lives. Most people are the servants, not the masters of their emotions, because they have never established definite, systematic habits of control over them.

Every person who has made up his mind to control the six departments of his mind, through a strict system of self-discipline, should adopt and follow a definite plan to keep this purpose before him.

One student of this philosophy wrote a creed for this purpose, which he followed so closely that it soon enabled him to become thoroughly self-discipline conscious. It worked so successfully that it is here presented for the benefit of other students of the philosophy.

The creed was signed, and repeated orally, twice daily; once upon arising in the morning and once upon retiring at night. This procedure gave the student the benefit of the principle of auto-suggestion, through which the purpose of the creed was conveyed clearly to the subconscious section of his mind, where it was picked up and acted upon automatically.

The creed follows:

A CREED FOR SELF-DISCIPLINE!

Will-power:

Recognizing that the Power of Will is the Supreme Court over all other departments of my mind, I will exercise it daily, when I need the urge to action for any purpose; and I will form habits designed to bring the power of my will into action at least once daily.

Emotions:

Realizing that my emotions are both positive and negative I will form daily habits which will encourage the development of the positive emotions, and aid me in converting the negative emotions into some form of useful action.

Reason:

Recognizing that both my positive emotions and my negative emotions may be dangerous if they are not controlled and guided to desirable ends, I will submit all my desires, aims and purposes to my faculty of reason, and I will be guided by it in giving expression to these.

Imagination:

Recognizing the need for sound plans and ideas for the

attainment of my desires, I will develop my imagination by calling upon it daily for help in the formation of my plans.

Conscience:

Recognizing that my emotions often err in their over-enthusiasm, and my faculty of reason often is without the warmth of feeling that is necessary to enable me to combine justice with mercy in my judgments, I will encourage my conscience to guide me as to what is right and what is wrong, *but I will never set aside the verdicts it renders,* no matter what may be the cost of carrying them out.

Memory:

Recognizing the value of an alert memory, I will encourage mine to become alert by taking care to impress it clearly with all thoughts I wish to recall, and by associating those thoughts with related subjects which I may call to mind frequently.

Subconscious Mind:

Recognizing the influence of my subconscious mind over my power of will, I shall take care to submit to it a clear and definite picture of my Major Purpose in life and all minor purposes leading to my major purpose, and I shall keep this picture constantly before my subconscious mind by repeating it daily.

Signed...

Discipline over the mind is gained, little by little, by the formation of habits which one may control. Habits begin in the mind; therefore, a daily repetition of this creed will make one habit-conscious in connection with the particular kind of habits which are needed to develop and control the six departments of the mind.

The mere act of repeating the names of these departments has an important effect. It makes one conscious that these departments exist; that they are important; that they can be controlled by the formation of thought-habits; that the nature of these habits determines one's success or failure in the matter of self-discipline.

It is a great day in any person's life when he recognizes the fact that his success or failure throughout life is largely a matter of control over his emotions!

Before one can recognize this truth he must recognize the existence and the nature of his emotions, and the power which is available to those who control them—a form of recognition which many people never indulge in during their entire lifetime.

There is an alliance of men known as Alcoholics Anonymous, with a membership that spreads throughout the nation. These men operate in local Master Mind groups in almost every city of the nation. And they are releasing one another from the evils of alcoholism on a scale which is nothing short of miraculous.

They operate entirely through self-discipline!

The medicine they use is the most powerful known to mankind. It consists of *the power of the human mind* directed to a definite end, that end being the end of alcoholism.

Here is an achievement which should inspire all men to become better acquainted with the power of their own minds. If the mind can cure alcoholism—and it is doing so—it can cure *poverty,* and *ill health,* and *fear,* and *self-imposed limitations!*

Alcoholics Anonymous is getting results because its members have been introduced to their "other selves"; those unseen entities which consist in the power of thought; the forces within the human mind which recognize no such reality as the "impossible."

This organization will live and it will grow, as all the forces of good must. The organization will eventually extend its service to include not only the elimination of the evils of alcoholism, but all other evils, such as the evils of fear, and poverty, and ill health, and hatred, and selfishness.

Eventually Alcoholics Anonymous will no doubt adopt the seventeen principles of this philosophy and provide its benefits for every member of that organization, as some of its members have already done with astounding effects.

It is a well known fact that *an enemy which has been recognized* is an enemy that is half defeated.

And this applies to enemies which operate within one's own mind as well as to those which operate outside of it; and especially does it apply to such enemies as negative emotions.

Once these enemies have been recognized one begins, almost unconsciously, to set up habits, through self-discipline, with which to counteract them.

This same reasoning applies also to the benefits of positive emotions, for it is true that a benefit recognized is a benefit easily utilized.

The positive emotions are beneficial, for they are a part of the driving force of the mind; but they are helpful only when they are organized and directed to the attainment of definite, constructive ends. If they are not so controlled they may be as dangerous as any of the negative emotions.

The medium of control is self-discipline, systematically and voluntarily applied through the habits of thought.

Take the emotion of Faith, for example:

This emotion, the most powerful of all the emotions, may be helpful only when it is expressed through constructive, organized action based upon Definiteness of Purpose.

Faith without action is useless, because it may resolve itself into mere day-dreaming, wishing and faint hopefulness.

Self-discipline is the medium through which one may stimulate the emotion of Faith, through definiteness of purpose persistently applied.

The discipline should begin by establishing habits which stimulate the use of the power of the will, for it is the ego—the seat of the power of the will—in which one's desires originate. Thus, the emotions of Desire and Faith are definitely related.

Wherever a burning desire exists, there exists also the capacity for Faith which corresponds precisely with the intensity of the desire. The two are associated always. Stimulate one and you stimulate the other. Control and direct one, through organized habits, and you control and direct the other.

This is self-discipline of the highest order.

Benjamin Disraeli, believed by some to have been the greatest Prime Minister England ever had, attained that high station through the sheer power of his will, directed by Definiteness of Purpose.

He began his career as an author, but he was not highly successful in that field.

He published a dozen or more books, but none of them made any great impression on the public. Failing in this field, he accepted his defeat as a challenge to greater effort in some other field—nothing more.

Then he entered politics, with his mind definitely set upon becoming the Prime Minister of the far-flung British Empire.

In 1837 he became a member of Parliament from Maidstone, but his first speech in Parliament was universally regarded as a flat failure.

Again he accepted his defeat as a challenge to try once more. Fighting on, with never a thought of quitting, he became the leader of the House of Commons by 1858, and later became the Chancellor of the Exchequer. In 1868 he realized his Definite Major Purpose by becoming the Prime Minister.

Here he met with terrific opposition (his "testing time" was at hand), which resulted in his resignation; but far from accepting his temporary defeat as failure, he staged a comeback and was elected Prime Minister a second time, after which he became a great builder of empires, and extended his influence in many different directions.

His greatest achievement perhaps was the acquisition of the Suez Canal—a feat which was destined to give the British Empire unprecedented economic advantages.

The keynote of his entire career was *self-discipline!*

In summarizing his achievements in one short sentence he said, "The secret of success is constancy of purpose!"

When the going was the hardest Disraeli turned on his will-power to its greatest capacity. It sustained him through the emergencies of temporary defeat, and brought him through to victory.

Here is the greatest of all the danger-points of the majority of men!

They give up and quit when the going becomes tough; and often they quit when *one more step* would have carried them triumphantly to victory.

Will-power is needed most when the oppositions of life are the greatest. And self-discipline will provide it for every such emergency, whether it be great or small.

The late Theodore Roosevelt was another example of what can happen when a man is motivated by the will to win despite great handicaps.

During his early youth he was seriously handicapped by chronic asthma and weak eyes. His friends despaired of his ever regaining his health, but he did not share their views, thanks to his recognition of the power of self-discipline.

He went West, joined a group of hard-hitting outdoor workers, and placed himself under a definite system of self-discipline, through which he built a strong body and a resolute mind. Some doctors said he could not do it—but he refused to accept their verdict.

In his battle to regain his health he acquired such perfect discipline over himself that he went back East, entered politics, and kept on driving until his will to win made him President of the United States.

Those who knew him best have said that his outstanding quality was a will which refused to accept defeat as anything more than an urge to greater effort. Beyond this his ability, his education, his experience were in no way superior to similar qualities possessed by men all around him of whom the public heard little or nothing.

While he was President some army officials complained of an order he gave them to keep physically fit. To show that he knew what he was talking about he rode horseback a hundred miles, over rough Virginia roads, with the army officials trailing after him, trying hard to keep pace.

Behind all this physical action was an active mind which was determined not to be handicapped by physical weakness, and that mental activity reflected itself throughout his administration in the White House.

A French Expedition had tried to build the Panama Canal, but failed.

Theodore Roosevelt said "the canal shall be built" and he went to work then and there to express his faith in terms of action. The canal was built!

Personal power is wrapped up in the will to win!

But it can be released for action only by self-discipline, and by no other means.

Robert Louis Stevenson was a delicate youth from the day of his birth. His health prevented him from doing any steady work at his studies until he was past seventeen. At twenty-three his health became so bad that his physicians sent him away from England.

Then he met the woman of his choice and fell in love.

His love for her was so great that it gave him a new lease on life, a new motive for action, and he began to write, although his physical body was scarcely strong enough to carry him around. He kept on writing until he had greatly enriched the world by his writings, now universally accepted as masterpieces.

The same motive, love, has given the wings of thought to many another who, like Robert Louis Stevenson, has made this a richer and a better world. Without the motive of love Stevenson doubtless would have died without having made his contributions to mankind. He transmuted his love for the woman of his choice into literary works, through habits of self-discipline which placed the six departments of his mind under his control.

In a similar manner Charles Dickens converted a love tragedy into literary works which have enriched the world. Instead of going down under the blow of his disappointment in his first love affair, he drowned his sorrow through the intensity of his action in writing. In that manner he closed the door behind an experience which many another might have used as a door of escape from his duty—an alibi for his failure.

Through self-discipline he converted his greatest sorrow into his greatest asset, for it revealed to him the presence of that "other self" wherein consisted the power of genius which he reflected in his literary works.

There is one unbeatable rule for the mastery of sorrows and disappointments, and that is transmutation of those emotional frustrations, through definitely planned work. It is a rule which has no equal.

And the secret of its power is self-discipline.

Freedom of body and mind, independence, and economic security are the results of personal initiative expressed through self-discipline. By no other means may these universal desires be assured.

You must travel the remainder of the distance alone. If you have followed the instructions I have given you, in the right kind of mental attitude, you are now in possession of the great Master-Key.

Now I shall reveal to you a great truth of the utmost importance: The Master-Key to Riches consists entirely in the greatest power known to man; the power of thought!

You may take full possession of the Master-Key by taking possession of your own mind, through the strictest of self-discipline.

Through self-discipline you may *think* yourself into or out of any circumstances of life!

Self-discipline will help you to control your mental attitude. Your mental attitude may help you to master every circumstance of your life, and to convert every adversity, every defeat, every failure into an asset of equivalent scope. That is why a Positive Mental Attitude heads the entire list of the Twelve Riches of Life.

Therefore, it should be obvious to you that the great Master-Key to Riches is nothing more nor less than the self-discipline necessary to help you take full and complete possession of your own mind!

Start right where you stand, and become the master of yourself. Start now! Be done forever with that old self which has kept you in misery and want. Recognize and embrace that "other self" which can give you everything your heart craves.

Remember it is profoundly significant that the only thing over which you have complete control is your own mental attitude!

For this is the Master-Key to Riches!

My Highland Rogue

The girl she'd been, so desperately in love, still lived deep inside her. That girl wanted to banish everyone, go to him, and kiss him in homecoming. He smiled and something bloomed in her chest. A memory, perhaps, or a wish. She wanted to re-create those nights at the loch when they'd been in each other's arms.

Jennifer wanted, desperately, to touch him, to assure herself that he was real. This wasn't a dream fervently to be wished for five years.

Gordon was standing only feet from her.

If they'd been alone, she would have gone to him, put her arms around his waist and her cheek against his chest. In that instant all the troubles in her world would have been lifted from her.

Yet would he have welcomed her? Even now he didn't look pleased to see her.

The smile she determinedly wore was getting more and more difficult to maintain. Tears were just below the surface.

By Karen Ranney

My Highland Rogue

A Highland Fling Novel

KAREN RANNEY

AVONBOOKS

An Imprint of HarperCollinsPublishers

MY HIGHLAND ROGUE. Copyright © 2020 by Karen Ranney, LLC. All rights reserved. Printed in the United States of America. No part of this book may be used or reproduced in any manner whatsoever without written permission except in the case of brief quotations embodied in critical articles and reviews. For information, address HarperCollins Publishers, 195 Broadway, New York, NY 10007.

First Avon Books mass market printing: August 2020

Print Edition ISBN: 978-0-06-301992-8
Digital Edition ISBN: 978-0-06-300356-9

Cover art © Alan Ayers
Author photo © Susan Riley Photography

Avon, Avon & logo, and Avon Books & logo are registered trademarks of HarperCollins Publishers in the United States of America and other countries.

HarperCollins is a registered trademark of HarperCollins Publishers in the United States of America and other countries.

FIRST EDITION

20 21 22 23 24   QGM   10 9 8 7 6 5 4 3 2 1

My
Highland
Rogue

Prologue

June, 1865
Adaire Hall, Scotland

I'll be damned if I know why she did it, but the Countess of Burfield left you a bequest."

Gordon McDonnell turned from the window and stared at the man who'd just spoken.

Richard McBain was the advocate for the Adaire family. For a number of years, he'd also served as the guardian for the underage Earl of Burfield, who'd ascended to his title at the age of five.

Gordon had had a few encounters with McBain in the past. Whenever they happened to meet—or he was called into the study—it was never to his advantage.

At first he thought that McBain had somehow discovered his relationship with Jennifer Adaire.

Jennifer was Lady Jennifer, the daughter of the Earl and Countess of Burfield. Gordon was only the gardener's boy, a title he'd been called ever since he was little. He'd grown to heartily despise it.

He had plans for his life, plans that didn't include becoming a gardener like his father. Gor-

don didn't care if anything bloomed or grew under his care. He preferred the wildness of the terrain surrounding Adaire Hall to the cultivated plants in the various gardens.

His mind registered what McBain said, but it still didn't make any sense. "What do you mean, the countess left me a bequest?"

"Evidently, the woman saw something in you I don't understand."

McBain had always talked to him in that same tone. He'd learned to ignore it.

"I didn't expect that," Gordon said.

Perhaps he should have. The countess had always been kind to him, and he'd always liked her. Their unusual relationship had begun when he was only seven.

One day, he'd seen her nurse wheel her out to the terrace so that she could enjoy the sunshine in the garden. He had dared his father's anger and had plucked some flowers for her, then walked up the three steps and thrust them at her.

"It's a bunch of posies, ma'am, to make you smile."

"You'll address her correctly, boy," the nurse had said. "It's Your Ladyship to you."

Gordon hadn't corrected himself, merely continued to stare at the countess.

The countess's vision had been badly damaged in a fire. She saw shapes and some colors, but little more. That day she'd reached out and felt his face, placing her palms against his cheeks.

"What is your name?"

"Gordon, ma'am. Gordon McDonnell. Your Ladyship."

"Sean McDonnell's lad."

"Aye, the same."

"And you picked your father's flowers to give to me."

"I think they're your flowers, ma'am. Your Ladyship. I merely borrowed them for a time."

The countess had taken the flowers and brought them to her face, telling him that they smelled of spring.

From that moment on, whenever the countess came to the garden Gordon went to see her. Their relationship was less that of the gardener's boy and countess than it was friendship, of a sort. He told her of his dreams. She shared some of her thoughts with him. In addition, she taught him a number of things that he'd never have learned otherwise, like how to handle his anger and how to speak properly.

He turned back to the window, unwilling to let McBain see his expression.

Her death hadn't been any easier than her life. After she'd died, he'd heard more than one person say that it was a blessing she'd finally been released. His first reaction to that comment had been anger. The world was less interesting because she was no longer in it. It was certainly less friendly.

"I tried to talk her out of it," the advocate said. "I don't know what you're going to do with the money, but I doubt you'll put it to good use."

Then McBain mentioned an amount that had Gordon turning and staring at him incredulously.

"How much?"

McBain repeated the amount.

"And it's all mine?"

"It's all yours."

He'd just been given a fortune.

"It's the perfect time, I think," McBain said, "to tell you that you're no longer welcome at Adaire Hall." The advocate smiled, an expression that reminded Gordon of a cat that had just devoured a plump mouse.

"It's been brought to my attention, McDonnell, that you have ideas above your station. I've been asked to explain to you that any further advances to Lady Jennifer are unwelcome. Therefore, the easiest thing for everyone would be for you to leave Adaire Hall immediately."

He stared at McBain.

"It's no secret that you've been causing Lady Jennifer trouble. You've been too persistent in your attentions."

"I don't understand." Jennifer wouldn't have made that comment.

"It's simple enough," the advocate said, standing. "That relationship is over."

"I don't believe you."

"Spare the young woman some embarrassment, McDonnell. Pretend, in this instance, that you have the manners of a gentleman. She's just left for Edinburgh and expressly asked me to convey to you that she would like you gone before she returns. She's not the only one who's anxious for your departure. The Earl of Burfield feels the same way."

The Earl of Burfield. That was a laugh. Jennifer's brother had always been an idiot. In the

past few years he'd coupled his idiocy with being an ass.

"I might add that your father agrees."

Was he supposed to be surprised at that news? He and Sean had clashed ever since he was a child.

"Maybe my father and Harrison want me gone," Gordon said, "but not Jennifer."

Just last night they'd met at the loch, spent hours talking, and ended the night by kissing. She couldn't have changed her mind in a matter of hours. Not Jennifer.

"She's not going to return from Edinburgh until you're gone. Your father has packed your belongings, McDonnell. The sooner you've left, the better for everyone. You've been a disruptive influence around here for too long. Unfortunately, the countess didn't agree with my assessment of you."

Evidently, he had one more reason to be grateful to the countess.

"Neither of your parents have expressed a wish to see you before you leave. Nor has the earl. There's a carriage at the front door. It will take you to Inverness."

"I'm not leaving until I talk to Jennifer."

McBain approached him slowly. "Understand this, McDonnell, Lady Jennifer doesn't want anything to do with you now or in the future."

Gordon faced the older man down. He was nearly a foot taller and bigger than the advocate. He wasn't intimidated.

When he didn't speak, McBain continued. "She

regrets meeting you at the loch, McDonnell, and allowing you to kiss her. Is that plain enough for you? Face it, man. You were an amusement and now you're not."

McBain's tone had softened, and there was something that sounded like pity in his voice.

Had he been wrong? Was it possible that Jennifer felt that way? No, McBain was an idiot to think he'd believe that of Jennifer.

The advocate returned to his desk, reached into the drawer, and pulled out a stack of notes. Gordon immediately knew what they were. He and Jennifer left notes for each other all over Adaire Hall. In the coop, in the forks of a tree they'd learned to climb just beyond the house, in a loose brick in the fireplace in a room adjacent to the schoolroom—anywhere they could find that would be private. If Gordon couldn't meet Jennifer after his work was done, or if she couldn't join him because of her obligations, they always communicated with each other.

Jennifer told him recently that she'd kept all of his notes to her, that she considered them precious.

No longer, evidently.

McBain amused himself by reading some of them aloud. The silly poetry Gordon had written for Jennifer seemed even more foolish now.

It was the ultimate act of betrayal.

McBain didn't say a word as Gordon left the study. Less than an hour later he was in the carriage on the way to Inverness, a letter to the bank in his pocket detailing his bequest. For the first

time in his life he had some wealth, but it was balanced by the empty feeling in his chest.

May, 1867
Adaire Hall, Scotland

IT HAD TAKEN nearly three months to get the information Jennifer needed, but now that she had it, she sat at her secretary staring down at the blank piece of stationery.

How could she possibly write this letter?

How could she not?

Ever since Gordon had disappeared, she'd been filled with anger, despair, and disillusionment. For two years there'd been no word. No inkling if Gordon was alive or dead. She didn't know whether to wish him to perdition or pray for his safety.

Some months ago her brother had let something slip, and she'd had the first hint that Gordon hadn't left the Hall of his own accord.

All he'd said was, "McBain got rid of the bastard."

When she'd questioned him further, all he'd said was, "McDonnell isn't coming back. Ever."

"What do you mean, he's never coming back?"

Harrison hadn't answered her. Nor had Sean been any more forthcoming. All he'd said was, "The boy wanted more from life than Adaire Hall. More fool he."

Consequently, she'd written Mr. McBain asking him how, exactly, Gordon had chosen to

leave Adaire Hall. Mr. McBain hadn't answered her questions, either, which was all she needed to know. Something had happened. Something had precipitated Gordon's departure.

What had they told him? What had they said?

She'd finally realized that Gordon's banishment had been an act of pure spite on Harrison's and McBain's part. Harrison had always resented Gordon, because he'd been sent to study with the two of them in the schoolroom on the second floor. Their tutor consistently ignored Gordon, but the truth was that he was better at math and science. Plus, people liked him. He had friends everywhere and was forever being greeted by someone, even when she wanted to be alone with him. Harrison wasn't thought of with such kindness. If anything, her brother was tolerated, but nothing more.

She picked up her pen. What should she write? *Dear Gordon. My dearest Gordon. My love.*

No, she couldn't do that, could she? She had to be more circumspect. After all, there was her pride to consider. He had simply left her without a word. One moment he was there, and the next he wasn't.

When she'd returned from Edinburgh, the first thing she'd wanted to do was to see Gordon and have him hold her. To feel solid and safe again in his arms. Only to be told that he was no longer at Adaire Hall. That he had simply left one night and no one knew where he was.

She picked up her pen again and wrote: *Dear Gordon.*

There, she'd actually written something. Her heart was fluttering, and there was a feeling in her stomach as if she'd eaten something slightly off. Now that she knew how to contact him, she couldn't delay. She had to write him and tell him the news. She had to let him know. It was the kindest thing she could do.

Her mother would have told her that it was a task that she should perform. But her mother would be so much better at this than she was.

She picked up the pen one more time, thought about the words she wanted to say, and wondered if there was a way to soften the news. This was Gordon. He had featured in her earliest memories. He'd been her friend, her companion, her playmate, and then so much more.

She bit her lip and prayed for guidance, before writing:

It is with great sadness that I am writing you. Your mother succumbed to a fever last week and died quickly.

The circumstances were not terribly different from her own mother's death, but Mary had lingered for nearly a month, the pneumonia finally claiming its victim.

I have received your address from the bank, which was kind enough to supply it to me.

I wish that I could offer you comfort at this time, Gordon, especially since you were such a solace to me when my mother died.

Again, I am sorry to have to convey such sor-
rowful news to you.

With my best regards,
Jennifer

London, England

GORDON STARED AT the letter in his hand. Jennifer. He would have recognized her distinctive script anywhere.

He read the letter again and then a third time. Finally, he folded it and placed it in his pocket, knowing that he would read it again.

He was sorry about Betty, but in actuality his mother had spared little attention or affection for him. It was as if one day she'd been presented with a baby and didn't quite know how to treat it. As a stranger? As an imposition?

She'd done both.

He would say a prayer for her, not because it was anything that Betty had taught him, but because it was something the countess had once said. *It serves us ill to be unkind to those who are not kind to us, Gordon. Instead, we should treat them with love, demonstrating what we've been taught in the Bible.*

He withdrew the letter from his pocket and stared at it again.

Two years. It had been two years since he'd seen Jennifer. Two years of wondering why she'd given McBain his notes to her. Why had she betrayed him like that?

Yet the woman who'd written him didn't sound like someone who'd believed him beneath her. Or someone who'd wanted him gone or considered him an intrusion in her life.

Perhaps she'd changed in the past two years.

As far as her news, he saw no reason to return to Scotland now.

Or ever.

Chapter One

Autumn, 1870
London, England

"You've gotten a letter," Maggie said, standing in the doorway of his office.

He glanced up at her.

"A letter?"

She entered the office and handed it to him.

"I opened it by mistake," she said. "I'm sorry, Gordon. It's bad news."

She came to stand by his chair, her hand on his shoulder as he read.

"Is there anything I can do?"

Her enunciation was perfect, but then she'd been practicing for the past five years. She'd wanted to eliminate all traces of the east end from her voice. She had already done miracles with her dress and personal hygiene.

Maggie had been his introduction to London. The minute he'd stepped off the train he'd been robbed.

No doubt he'd given off an aura of being naive and gullible. After all, London had been nearly

overpowering for someone who'd spent his life in the Highlands. However, he'd never been truly naive, thanks to Betty, and he was becoming less gullible with every moment.

He'd known who robbed him immediately, had caught up with her and grabbed her wrist, spinning her around and staring down into her face.

She wasn't young. If anything, she was the same age or thereabouts as his mother. He doubted, however, if she had washed in the past fortnight. Or even eaten, for that matter.

"I'll have my money back."

She'd attempted to pull away from him, but his grip was too tight.

"My money."

She answered him in a nearly indecipherable voice. It wasn't that he couldn't hear what she was saying. He couldn't understand her. It took several moments for him to figure out her accent and that she was denying the theft. He solved the problem by reaching into her cloak, finding the hidden pocket, and pulling out what she'd stolen from him.

When he let her go, he expected her to disappear into the crowd. Instead, she scowled at him.

"You're a fool if you keep it all in one pocket. Spread it out so that if you do lose something, it's not everything you have."

"Good advice," he said. "When was the last time you ate?"

She put her hands on her hips and said something he was certain was an insult.

"Come along, then, and I'll buy you a meal."

He didn't have any trouble deciphering what she said next. He'd used the same words when joking with the stable lads at Adaire Hall.

Gordon bit back a grin, turned, and headed for the exit out of the station. He glanced at her over his shoulder. "If you're coming, come, but no more insults, if you please. I've had enough of those to last a lifetime."

He thought it was curiosity more than anything else that had Maggie following him. From the way she'd eaten that day, he was right about thinking that she was nearly starving.

He'd suspected that Maggie had earned most of her money as a prostitute, but he'd never asked and she'd never confessed to it. From the beginning he'd wanted to help her. When he thought about it, he couldn't help but wonder if it was the countess's influence. There were times when he could almost hear her voice guiding him to do more and to be a better person.

To his surprise, Maggie had become a friend. It was Maggie who directed him to cheap lodgings, and Maggie who first took him to the Alhambra. He'd been fascinated by the acts as well as the fact that the establishment seemed to be a resounding success. Music halls were evidently the newest entertainment in London, and they were filled to capacity with people out for an evening of fun.

For six months he'd attended every music hall in the London area, studied the layouts, made a list of the acts, the fare charged to enter, and the

various drinks served at the small bars inside. By the time he'd rented a building himself, he was prepared and determined to duplicate—on a smaller scale—what he'd seen at the Alhambra.

The Midlothian had a small orchestra, a stage where scenes could be changed simply by a quick rotation, and a series of trapezes attached to the framing of the roof. Instead of simply hiring a male trapeze artist, he employed women who'd been trained in the skill. They also doubled as dancers in the last act, appearing on stage clad in numerous petticoats and performing a dance classified as French and therefore moderately scandalous.

He never hired prostitutes and he made that clear to everyone from the beginning. Whatever arrangement they made with the clientele was their business, but he didn't condone it. Nor would anything of that sort be done on the premises. In addition, he ensured that the women in his employ were always treated with dignity. They had a carriage to take them home, most of the time in the wee hours of the morning. Their safety was important to him, especially when tales came to him of horrendous deeds in other parts of London.

In the past year the Midlothian had been expanded to seat eighteen hundred people. Originally, the only patrons had been men, but over the past two years he'd opened it up to include women, providing entertainment for them as well as during what he called Ladies Fridays. It was a familiar sight to see a group of women

seated by themselves, eyes widening as they took in the trapeze artists, roaming singers, or the elaborate show on the stage.

The Dundee was his second music hall, but due to the success of the Midlothian, he'd had it built from the ground up. It had been designed by a Scottish architect with a taste for whimsy. The Dundee had soaring columns and a painted ceiling resembling a heather-strewn glen. A dozen private boxes jutted out from the walls around the stage. The building was filled with gilt and crimson, and attracted every kind of patron from artisans to working men and their wives to young toffs who declared themselves too filled with ennui to be charmed, but were, nonetheless.

The jewel of his empire, however, was the Mayfair Club, a private club catering to wealthy gentlemen. There were strict criteria for inclusion—each potential member had to be vetted by ten current members. Yet the stringent requirements had attracted exactly the sort of clientele he'd wanted. Now the Mayfair Club was the most prosperous of his ventures. A great many peers were members, including one royal personage.

The sixth Earl of Burfield was a member as well. Harrison wasn't aware that it was Gordon's club, however. Nor did Gordon have any intention of informing the man that every cent he lost at the Mayfair Club went into his pockets.

As he became successful, Gordon made sure Maggie wasn't left behind. He'd discovered that she had an affinity for numbers that rivaled his bookkeeper's. In addition, her knowledge of Lon-

don had proven to be invaluable. She'd been his first employee and was responsible for hiring the women who worked for him.

In that first year her appearance had changed drastically. She was no longer painfully thin. Her complexion had improved, as had her hair. One day, on walking into her office, he realized that Maggie was a beautiful woman. Her appearance had previously been dulled by her circumstances and something else: a lack of hope.

She wasn't starving now, but she had that same look in her eyes as when he'd first met her. As if she was trying to figure something out that was alien to her.

"Will you be going back to Scotland?" she asked now.

The letter was indeed bad news. His father was ill. Jennifer had written him again, the second time she'd done so.

Gordon pushed back his chair and stood before Maggie could hug him. She believed in effusive physical demonstrations of affection.

He glanced at her. "Yes, it's time I went home."

Adaire Hall, Scotland

"Are you very certain that this isn't a new cradle, Lady Jennifer?"

Jennifer directed the footman to place the cradle in the corner of the room, bit back a sigh, and turned to the midwife.

"Yes, Mrs. Farmer. It's the Adaire cradle. It was the one I was put into."

She hoped Mrs. Farmer didn't inquire further about the cradle. The midwife didn't need to know the tragic history of Adaire Hall.

When her brother was an infant, a fire destroyed the north wing where the nursery was located. A nursery maid had died in the fire and her mother had been severely injured and nearly blinded attempting to save her son. She bore the scars from that night for the rest of her life.

"It's just that it's bad luck for the child to be placed into a new cradle."

She knew that, but she'd been placed in a new cradle. It hadn't done her any harm.

The midwife had a range of strange beliefs, including her request that a live hen be placed in the empty cradle to ensure that the child was a boy. Jennifer absolutely refused to carry a chicken into Lauren's suite. The laundress had hand-washed the lace adorning the cradle and, per the Adaire custom, Jennifer had placed a silver coin under the pillow.

She had ordered a wheel of cheese, to be cut by Mrs. Farmer after the baby was born. In addition, she'd given orders to the cook and her staff to prepare a selection of currant loaves. One loaf, along with a bottle of Adaire whiskey, would be given to each visitor to the Hall for a month after the child's birth.

A great many other traditions—or superstitions, depending on your opinion—accompanied the birth of a baby.

Mrs. Farmer, being the renowned midwife that she was, should depend less on superstition and more on her medical expertise. That was

not, however, a comment Jennifer was going to say to the esteemed lady. Mrs. Farmer also had a temper.

The woman excused herself, no doubt to go and badger the cook or Mrs. Thompson, the housekeeper.

Lauren had dropped off to sleep again, being nearly to term. She slept a great deal, which was, according to Mrs. Farmer, a good sign for a propitious birth. Jennifer had every intention of leaving the room without disturbing her sister-in-law, but when she reached the doorway, Lauren spoke.

"Are you going to leave me to Mrs. Farmer?"

Jennifer glanced back at the bed, then at the doorway.

Mrs. Farmer had unexpectedly shown up on their doorstep two weeks ago and announced that Hamish Campbell, Lauren's father, had hired her to care for his daughter. Since Jennifer had been under the impression that Mr. Campbell was in America, she'd been surprised, at least until talking to Lauren.

"My father plans everything," she said. "He leaves absolutely nothing to chance." She'd smiled down at her burgeoning stomach. "Not even his grandchild."

That is how Mrs. Farmer had come to rule their days and nights. Both Jennifer and Lauren were somewhat in awe of the woman, who didn't seem to understand the word *no*. Nor did she accept excuses, regardless of the topic. Therefore, it was just easier—for Jennifer—to avoid the woman.

Poor Lauren had no such escape.

Jennifer walked toward the bed. Lauren scooted over so she could sit on the edge of the mattress.

Her sister-in-law was petite, nearly dwarfed in the massive four-poster. Her hair, black and normally lustrous, had dulled in the past few months. Her distinctive blue eyes were rarely filled with laughter now.

Jennifer put that down to Harrison's absence. It had been obvious from the beginning that Lauren adored her husband. Unfortunately, it had been as telling that Harrison barely tolerated his bride.

"How are you feeling?" she asked.

Lauren smiled. "Like I'm all baby and nothing else."

"Mrs. Farmer said that the baby should be born shortly."

Lauren sighed. "I do hope so, if for no other reason than not to disappoint her." She levered herself up, then swung her legs off the bed. "I feel that everything I do is somehow wrong."

"Nonsense, you're perfect. I'm the one who gets lectured every hour of the day. Adaire Hall is too large, too sprawling, too cold, too hot, too isolated, too filled with strange noises. We have creatures, in her words. Animals creeping past her window all hours of the night."

"She's in the room next to me," Lauren said, her brow furrowing.

"Exactly. How can anything creep past her window on the second floor?"

Lauren's smile was delightful to see. "Maybe it's a bat."

"Or a bird. Maybe some type of Highland monster ferret with wings."

"She truly doesn't seem to enjoy the Highlands very much," Lauren said.

"Or Adaire Hall."

"Silly woman. It's a beautiful place."

Jennifer smiled at the other woman, feeling in perfect accord. She loved her home, and it had been evident from the beginning that Lauren had taken to the Hall as well.

She'd been as surprised as anyone when her brother announced, two years ago, that he was about to be married. She'd learned later that Harrison had met Lauren because of an introduction from Jennifer's godmother. Normally, he went out of his way to be unpleasant to Ellen whenever she visited Adaire Hall. However, Ellen knew a great many people in Edinburgh, with the result that Harrison had married an heiress, the only child of a wealthy Scottish industrialist.

From the moment Jennifer was introduced to Lauren, the two had been friends. In all honesty, she thought Lauren was a better wife than Harrison deserved. The fact that he had ignored his bride for the past eight months was proof.

Jennifer helped Lauren on with her shoes. Although Mrs. Farmer would have been content for Lauren to remain in bed until her confinement, the younger woman refused. She very carefully navigated the grand staircase once a day and back up in the evening. Although the trips were becoming more difficult, Lauren had a streak of stubbornness that was nearly the match of Mrs. Farmer's.

"How long do you think she'll stay?"

"After the baby is born?" Jennifer asked. When Lauren nodded, she added, "Much longer than we want her to."

It was the perfect moment for Mrs. Farmer to enter the suite again.

"I've been told to tell you that a carriage is approaching, Lady Jennifer."

She glanced at Lauren. Her eyes were lighting up even as she reached for the brush on the table beside the bed.

With any luck it was Harrison, having remembered he was about to be a father at last.

Chapter Two

$\mathcal{G}$ordon had dreamed of returning to Adaire Hall in triumph like Caesar home from a successful battle. In his imagination he saw all of them standing at the front entrance: his father, his mother, McBain and Harrison, as well as all of the servants from the lowest to the highest. Most importantly, Jennifer would be there, smiling at him.

He would drive up in his new carriage, ebony with dark blue upholstery, four brass lanterns hanging on the outside. The horses would be two matched pairs with the driver resplendent in livery. He would be welcomed with awe and apologies.

The only plausible item in that daydream was his carriage.

Peter hesitated at the top of the hill as if Gordon had instructed him to stop there.

Five years ago, the carriage carrying him to Inverness had stopped in almost this exact spot. He'd looked back for long moments, the sense of loss nearly suffocating him. Not for the house or even most of its inhabitants. Only for Jennifer.

For him, the grand house in the glen had been the source of all the misery in the world.

He tapped on the grate and waited for Peter to open his side of the window.

"I'll get out for a few minutes," he said.

Peter, like all well-trained servants, didn't question him further. It wouldn't be the first time he'd requested something odd from his driver. Peter had been in his employ for the past three years, ever since he'd begun to make his mark on the world.

He'd never thought that his driver would take him this far from London, however. He couldn't help but wonder if Peter thought it odd as well. However, bringing his own carriage on a flat car from London was easier than having to rely on a hired vehicle.

After opening the door, he kicked the steps down and strode to the middle of the road.

The gardens his father had worked on all his life were dormant now in the autumn of the year. Yet the approach to the Hall was carefully manicured, laid out over plans executed in the last century. The oaks had been planted decades earlier and created a shadowed approach for the visitor.

Adaire Hall was known throughout this part of Scotland. First of all, it was the largest of the great houses. Secondly, it was the seat of the Earls of Burfield, men who'd been prominent in Scottish history for generations.

The house spread out below him like one of the queen's castles. The sprawling red brick Hall was the third structure to grace this particular spot, the first having been razed in battle in the eleventh century, and the second torn down to

make way for the new home in the fifteenth. This version of Adaire Hall was only three hundred years old, but looked to last a thousand years.

Over the years the red brick had deepened in color. The white of the window trim had dulled like an old lady's white lace collar fading to a pale yellow.

The oldest part of the house was the largest, with two wings built later, making the Hall look like three sides of a square. The north wing had been destroyed years earlier and never rebuilt. In the middle of the open space was yet another garden, one he knew well. To the rear of the Hall was the river and beyond that Loch Adaire, a spot that had been a haven during his childhood.

Two dozen chimneys spewed clouds of smoke into the pristine Highland air. Hundreds of windows watched him in the afternoon light, seeming to blink in the gold reflected glare.

He'd never had a future here, but when he said that to his father one day, Sean had turned on him angrily.

"What do you think you're going to do with your life, then, boy?"

"I'm going to be rich," he'd said.

The sound of Sean's derisive laughter echoed in his mind.

He was no longer Gordon McDonnell, gardener's boy. He was McDonnell, wealthy, successful, and, according to the gossips, ruthless. A Highland rogue, someone who was determined to succeed at whatever he chose.

He was back for more than one reason. He'd give his father whatever he needed before he

died, be it absolution or compassion. He understood Sean as he hadn't five years earlier. Some men did not possess the capacity to love another human being. Sean hadn't any interest in the gardeners under him, or even his wife or son. Any emotions he had were directed toward the flowers he grew and the vegetables that flourished in his care.

That didn't make Sean a bad person. Nor did it make him someone to pity. His father was perfectly happy being who he was, and if he had any regrets now, Gordon doubted they centered around people.

He didn't want to be like Sean, however. Nor had he been for the past five years. He had friends, both male and female. He had men working for him that he cared about. He knew their wives, their sweethearts, and their children. Sean might have chosen plants, but Gordon preferred people.

Turning, he walked back to the carriage, nodding at Peter before opening the door once again.

A few minutes later they descended the hill.

JENNIFER GLANCED AT Mrs. Farmer. "Will you be all right without me for a few minutes?"

"Of course we will, won't we, Your Ladyship?" The frostiness in the midwife's voice was unmistakable.

In other words, Jennifer shouldn't have asked. Of course Mrs. Farmer didn't need her. How dare she assume such a thing?

How was she supposed to endure the woman's company until the baby was born?

Jennifer made it down the sweeping staircase

in record time, remembering when she was a child and the three of them had made a game of trying to slide down the wooden banister. They'd been lucky they hadn't fallen and injured themselves. Gordon was the bravest one, Harrison next, while she, as the youngest, often won the race.

The years had brought about a great many changes. Gordon had left Adaire Hall. Harrison had discovered vice and occupied himself with all types of debauchery. She was the only one who hadn't changed, other than growing older.

She got to the front of the house just as Michaels was opening the door. The carriage at the bottom of the wide steps wasn't one of theirs. She'd expected Harrison, since she'd sent him a scolding letter reminding him of his responsibilities. Instead, the vehicle was a shiny black, obviously new and well equipped. At first she thought her godmother had come to visit, but Ellen hadn't written to expect her.

A man stepped out of the carriage and time telescoped in on itself. She wasn't five years older. Instead, she was a young woman flush with love.

She could barely breathe for the memory of it, of him. He was older. His shoulders looked broader, his chest wider. He looked as if he'd grown two inches. He'd always been so much taller than she, but now he dwarfed her.

Gordon.

She was certain that she said something to the majordomo. She must have made some comment, but she had no idea what it was.

He walked up the steps, hesitated only briefly

at the door, then entered, removing his hat. His hair was slightly mussed, reminding her of all those times when she'd run her fingers through it. His coat was a fine wool, equal to anything Harrison wore. His shoes were brightly shined, and his shirt was so blinding white that she almost asked who did his laundry.

How dreadfully inappropriate.

"Gordon."

He turned and looked at her and time seemed to stop.

Mrs. Thompson was suddenly in the foyer, along with two maids. No, three. Oh dear, it seemed as if the whole of the downstairs was suddenly there, greeting Gordon like the prodigal son. Why shouldn't they? He had always been kind to every member of the staff, never seeing the hierarchy that naturally developed in large houses where scores of servants were employed. He'd been a favorite five years ago and it seemed that nothing had changed.

She could see the housekeeper smiling out of the corner of her eye. Mrs. Thompson had always had a soft spot for Gordon.

He removed his gloves and the majordomo immediately took them, placing them beside his hat. The man wouldn't have shown the gardener's boy such respect five years ago.

Yet the young man was gone, and in his place someone who was almost intimidating. Suddenly Gordon was a stranger. Had he always had that direct look in his eyes? Or that air of self-possession?

He'd been handsome as a young man, but

there was something new about him. Some quality that made the maids simper and giggle. Even Mrs. Thompson, nearly fifty, had red cheeks as she greeted him.

Jennifer wanted to banish them all so that she could greet Gordon alone, but of course she didn't. Instead, she stood back, watching. The foyer was crowded with people now, all of them forgetting their places for the pleasure of welcoming home one of their own.

He glanced at her and then away, almost as if he didn't recognize her.

She hadn't changed that much in five years. Five very long years.

He might as well have been a stranger to her, not someone she once knew. Not the man she'd repeatedly kissed on the shore of the loch. She could still recall the press of his lips on hers, how his face felt beneath her fingertips. This man had featured in her dreams for years. As a girl, she'd wanted to love him, to give him her innocence. She'd planned to do exactly that, but he'd disappeared, leaving her alone, confused, and heartbroken.

Here he was, standing before her, looking prosperous and healthy. Had he married? She wished she could produce a husband. One who was gloriously in love with her, who thought she was the epitome of all things a man wanted in a wife.

This imaginary husband didn't exist. There was no one to praise her or smile at her with tenderness. All anyone could say was that she'd been a good chatelaine for Adaire Hall.

Hardly words to incite any man's jealousy.

For five years she'd missed him every day, while Gordon had probably forgotten about her the moment he'd left Adaire Hall.

Every birthday and Christmas for the past three years she'd written him, telling him of life at Adaire Hall, mentioning people he'd known. In that way she'd felt connected to him, even though he'd never written her back. She should never have written him again. Yet if she hadn't, he wouldn't be standing only feet away from her.

She was not going to remain here and act the part of lovesick idiot. She had her pride and she was going to wrap it around herself like a shawl before she said or did anything that made her look the fool.

Jennifer looked at Mrs. Thompson. "Is the Blue Suite ready?" she asked, an unnecessary question. All of the guest suites were kept ready in case Harrison arrived with a party of his friends.

During Lauren's pregnancy, when the poor woman had felt ill most of the time, Jennifer had assumed the role of mistress of the house. In actuality, she'd been the one to whom the servants had come ever since her mother became ill. Harrison, when he was in residence, was too volatile to be dependable. Nor did any of the staff want to be the subject of his rages.

The housekeeper nodded. "Yes, Miss Jennifer."

If Harrison was here, he would have chastised Mrs. Thompson and the rest of the servants for addressing her so informally. *She is Lady Jennifer,* he would have said, his booming voice capable of being heard many rooms away. Jennifer pre-

ferred the informality. It made her feel as if the staff was an extension of her own dwindling family.

With the birth of Lauren's child there would be one more Adaire, however. Even if the child's father wasn't here to see it.

No one said a word to her about putting Gordon McDonnell in one of their most impressive guest suites. He didn't look like the gardener's boy who'd left five years ago. Maybe it was his height or the fact that his shoulders were so broad. Or maybe it had nothing to do with his physical appearance, but simply how he stood there, commanding the foyer.

She hadn't said one word to him. Nor had he spoken to her.

The girl she'd been, so desperately in love, still lived deep inside her. That girl wanted to banish everyone, go to him, and kiss him in homecoming. He smiled and something bloomed in her chest. A memory, perhaps, or a wish. She wanted to re-create those nights at the loch when they'd been in each other's arms.

Jennifer wanted, desperately, to touch him, to assure herself that he was real. This wasn't a dream fervently to be wished for five years.

Gordon was standing only feet from her.

If they'd been alone, she would have gone to him, put her arms around his waist and her cheek against his chest. In that instant all the troubles in her world would have been lifted from her.

Yet would he have welcomed her? Even now he didn't look pleased to see her.

The smile she determinedly wore was getting

more and more difficult to maintain. Tears were just below the surface.

Had his eyes always been that blue? She could see the imprint of the boy's face in the man, but the man was so much more arresting.

She felt as if she were standing in the middle of a storm happening all around her. She was in an enchanted circle, and although she could see the darkness and the lightning racing from cloud to cloud, nothing touched her or could affect her in any way. Here, there was only stillness and a sense of eerie calm.

"Mrs. Thompson will show you to your room." There was something wrong with her voice. It sounded thin, as if she were suffering from some malady. A cold, perhaps. That's what she'd say if questioned.

The majordomo looked at her sharply, then turned his attention to directing the actions of the footmen.

"I know where it is, Jennifer," Gordon said. "Five years have not made me forget Adaire Hall."

They'd played in the house on inclement days. As children they'd chased each other—as quietly as possible so as not to disturb her mother. They'd giggled behind their hands and hid in closets. One eventful day Gordon had embraced her, pulled her close and kissed her cheek.

She'd thought about that kiss for days. The next time they were alone in a dark place, she'd stood on tiptoe, put her hands on Gordon's shoulders, and her mouth on his.

His indrawn breath had startled them both, enough that she'd jumped back.

He might not have forgotten the Hall, but it was obvious that he'd forgotten her.

"Yes, of course," she said now, hearing the words leave her mouth. She hadn't the slightest idea how she'd formed them or how the thought had made it from her mind to her lips.

She took a step back, away.

Gordon thanked the people in the foyer, including Mrs. Thompson, nodded to the major-domo, who assured him his valises would be moved to the Blue Suite, then turned and walked back out the front door.

Jennifer watched as he descended the steps, then turned to his left, heading for the head gardener's cottage.

Since Mrs. Thompson had disappeared, Jennifer guessed that the housekeeper was, even now, inspecting the rooms Gordon would occupy.

Jennifer turned on her heel and left the foyer.

Gordon hadn't written to tell her he was coming. She should have expected his arrival, of course, especially after her letter telling him about Sean. Perhaps it would be wise to remember that he'd never written her for five years. Five years of silence from him when a simple word would have eased her broken heart.

Now he was home again, but it didn't look as if anything had changed. He still wasn't speaking to her.

Chapter Three

*J*ennifer headed for her suite. Several years ago she'd moved out of the family wing and into one of the older parts of Adaire Hall. In addition to several modifications to her chamber, she had the estate's carpenters create a doorway to the room next door, expanding it into a sitting area.

Harrison hadn't seemed to mind. He was so rarely home that she wasn't even sure he knew what she'd done. He was never involved in the upkeep or the day-to-day maintenance of the house, the grounds, the lands, or even the management of the crofters.

All Adaire Hall was good for was a place to come when he needed to escape some drama in London. She suspected that he had borrowed money against the estate, but she'd never gotten him to admit it. Twice in the last five years they'd had visitors from both Edinburgh and London. The men had all been bankers and they'd inspected the property with the diligence one would expect from an owner. Whenever she'd questioned Harrison about the financial stability of Adaire Hall, he'd responded with anger.

No one raged quite as well as Harrison.

Her brother wore a great many facades, de-

pending on the person and the circumstances. Sometimes, she wondered who he was truly. Did he show his real face to anyone?

Harrison played at being earl, shunning any responsibility in favor of amusements in Edinburgh and London. He spent only a few days each quarter at home, and that only because of their mother. After she died, he hadn't even pretended to be responsible.

The fact that his wife was due to give birth shortly to his first child hadn't made Harrison return, but Gordon's sudden appearance might accomplish that miracle.

The two men didn't get along.

Even as a child Gordon had been filled with plans. He'd wanted to be more than the gardener's boy. He'd been tall for his age, with a yearning in his eyes, but he'd always had time for her. He'd been kind, too, always looking out for her when Harrison was cruel.

Ever since the nursery fire, her mother had been reluctant to see anyone other than her husband, children, and Ellen, her closest friend. After Jennifer's father's death, Gordon had been the only other person to penetrate Mary's isolation. Sean tried to stop Gordon from approaching her, but more often than not Mary Adaire was the one who sought out the gardener's boy.

When Gordon appeared in the schoolroom one day and told the tutor that he was to learn along with them, Jennifer knew it was her mother's idea. While Jennifer had been ecstatic, Harrison had had a tantrum and marched out of the room, only to be forcibly returned by his guardian.

The three of them had spent years in the schoolroom on the second floor of the east wing, a room not far away from where she lived now.

It had always been her and Gordon against Harrison in any match of wits. More than once Harrison had instigated a fight, but whenever Gordon fought back, Sean was there to yell at his son. The gardener never forgot that Harrison was the earl.

Gordon had been her constant companion, her friend, and her confidant until they'd begun to feel more for each other. Then, one day, he was gone. As if he'd never existed.

Now Gordon was back, but the young man she'd known didn't seem like the same one who'd entered Adaire Hall a few minutes ago. He didn't have a ready smile. Nor was there warmth in his beautiful blue eyes.

Had he changed? Had she been in love with someone who no longer existed?

ELLEN THORNTON SENT her maid a censorious look, which had no effect on Abigail's whining.

Abigail always whined in a genteel fashion. If she wasn't entirely certain Ellen had heard her, Abigail repeated her complaints.

She really should fire the woman, but Abigail had been with her for a great many years. In addition, she was certain that her maid had nowhere else to go. She was not about to send the woman out in the snow when her only sin was a dour personality. Ellen could be the same herself from time to time. At least Abigail never complained about her moods.

Today, however, Abigail was outdoing herself. So far, the day was excessively chilly, the meal had disagreed with her stomach, and she was certain that Fortune would not smile on this errand. Ellen thought that Fortune held more prominence in Abigail's life than God.

She didn't disagree with her maid about this errand. However, there were times in life when one must do what one must do. This was one of those occasions. She was about to trade on her reputation as the widow of a substantially wealthy man in order to bring Mary Adaire's son to heel.

Last week she'd received a letter from her goddaughter, and in it Jennifer had explained that Harrison's wife was due to give birth in a month or so. You would think that such an event would have interested the sixth Earl of Burfield. However, Jennifer was certain that Harrison was still in London, living a hedonistic life as he tried to empty the Adaire coffers with his gambling habit.

Harrison had never impressed her as having much sense, even as a boy.

She had a great deal of influence, and she intended to bring all of it to bear against the owners of Harrison's favorite gaming establishments. So far, she and Abigail had visited three, with the owner of the last one giving her the information that the Mayfair Club seemed to be Harrison's latest haunt. To that end, she had sent word of her intention of visiting that business. Now the carriage stopped in front of an exceedingly proper-looking building. In fact, if she hadn't known its

purpose, she would have thought that this entire row of buildings was given over to town houses, and quite lovely architecture it was, too.

Her home was in Edinburgh, but she also had a house in London. In fact, she had houses in seven large cities, thanks to Mr. Thornton, who had gone on to that great salmon fishing river in the sky.

Colin had been a great deal wealthier than she'd realized when she agreed to marry him. The fact that he was as rich as Croesus hadn't entered into their union at all. She had liked him, at first. He'd amused her, then charmed her, and once they'd become friends, she'd found herself anticipating his presence.

"You are insidious," she'd told him once. "You're very sneaky. I find myself depending on your counsel and craving time with you. I don't know how you do it."

"It's a secret," he responded. "I'm not about to tell you how. Then you might learn that I am but an ordinary man, worshipping at the feet of a goddess."

She'd laughed at the time, but that's exactly how he had treated her in the seven years of their marriage—like a goddess, or an angel. As if she could do no wrong and even when she did make a mistake, he forgave her so quickly and easily that she fell in love even more.

When he died, she hadn't thought she'd recover from the loss. It had been Mary who'd made her see the joy of life again, or at least the possibility of it.

If Mary could make her life have meaning, then surely she could.

It was for Mary that she was here now, preparing for an encounter with the owner of the Mayfair Club.

She turned to her maid. "I'd prefer that you remain in the carriage, Abigail. Especially given the delicate state of your digestion."

Just as Abigail was about to begin a new litany of complaints, no doubt accompanied by comments about how Fortune would not look kindly on her being left alone, Ellen hurried out of the carriage.

Her driver, who'd taken on the position of bodyguard—or duenna, as she secretly thought—since Colin died, preceded her up the stairs and insisted on announcing her arrival. Instead of using the brass knocker, he pounded on one of the black panels. Since Harry was a man of considerable girth, she was very much afraid the door was going to lose in this battle of brawn.

Fortunately, it was opened a moment later by the porter, a man looking every bit as proper as someone employed in a duke's household. The previous three establishments had not boasted of a man so tall, thin, and possessed of a shock of white hair like a barrister's wig.

"I am Mrs. Colin Thornton," she said, before Harry could say a word. "I believe I'm expected."

The porter bowed from the waist at the same time he sent a frown in Harry's direction. For the next two minutes the two men scowled at each other.

She shook her head at both of them. She understood Harry's possessiveness. He'd worked for Colin for years, and once he'd died, Harry had transferred his loyalty to her. It wasn't difficult to understand that the porter might have some pride in his own position as well.

The problem was, their mutual antipathy was preventing her from accomplishing her goal. Namely: finding Harrison Adaire and taking him home.

"Would you please announce me? I need to speak with your owner," she said before turning to Harry. "If you'd go and make sure Abigail is all right?"

There, she'd given each man a task, and after one last fulminating look, they went to do just that.

Chapter Four

$\mathcal{F}$ive years had passed since he'd seen Jennifer and, although Gordon had expected her to change, he hadn't anticipated that she would grow more beautiful. Even her voice was different, soft and musical. When she'd spoken his name, it had been a honed weapon, sliding into his heart.

She was . . . His thoughts ended in an odd blankness. He didn't know what the word was to adequately describe her now. It seemed to him that it was *lush*, although that didn't quite fit, either. Her lashes were thicker. Her lips were fuller. The color on her cheeks was not quite pink but closer to coral. Her figure was different, too. There the word *lush* fit perfectly. Her waist looked as small, but her breasts were larger.

The desire to take her into his arms and greet her properly had been so strong that he'd found it easier to avoid looking at her.

He'd wanted to touch her, to feel the shape of her back again as well as the slender beauty of her arms. Most of all he'd wanted to kiss her, even if everyone stared. Let them stare. After an hour or so he'd have enough of kissing Jennifer, but only for a while.

He'd thought she would greet him, but she hadn't. After saying his name, she'd not addressed him at all. He'd never thought Jennifer cold, but she hadn't said a word to him. Nothing to indicate that he was welcome.

Evidently, McBain had been right all this time.

He followed the path around the east wing, his gaze on the panorama of branches overhead. Autumn had already come to this part of the Highlands and stripped the trees of their leaves. It was a sign of Sean's illness that they hadn't been gathered up lest they mar the perfection of the grounds of Adaire Hall.

To his left was a large bed of Whin, or *Conasg*, in Gaelic. He'd learned all the Gaelic names of Sean's plants for the countess, a bit of bragging he was pleased to do for her sake. The Whin had been one of the flowers he'd given her that first day. It wasn't a particularly attractive plant, but when all its flowers bloomed, sometimes even in winter, they produced a golden-yellow, almond-scented array.

The land dropped down, undulating toward the river. Most of the outbuildings were located behind one of the rolling hills in a spot where they weren't easily seen from the Hall. The gardener's cottage, along with the ghillie's residence, was situated at the end of the path he took.

He was nearly at the home of his childhood, the place he despised above all others.

He'd learned a great deal at Adaire Hall, but even more once he was away from it.

He discovered that the wealthier a man was, the less he tipped. The best tippers were those

who'd escaped complete poverty and were on their way to some measure of success. Men who had the most to lose were often the least guarded about their actions. Having a title wasn't a predictor of a man's character. How a man treated a woman had nothing to do with his rank or status in life. Sometimes, the most vicious man was also the most exalted. Women could be as brave as any man, and just as resourceful.

In the past five years he'd also learned a great deal about himself. For long swaths of time he could forget about his past, but it still came back to haunt him at odd times. He was prosperous, whispered about, and the object of speculation. He enjoyed cultivating an aura of mystery. The more people wondered about him, the more apt they were to come to one of his music halls or club. Yet there was something lacking in his life, something that had to do with this place.

In the time it took to walk the graveled path, time reversed itself. He felt like he was eight years old again, forming his knowledge of the world and of himself one bit of truth at a time.

His relationship with his father had always been tenuous at best. He and Sean had always clashed. Nor had his father ever expressed anything other than disappointment in him. Never once had he said, "Good job, Gordon." Or, "I'm proud of you, boy." He'd never heard Sean say anything affectionate to Betty, either.

Sean was only happy when he was working in the earth, when he'd coaxed a bloom in the spring or a line of hedge he recently planted flourished. His happiness was measured by the order he cre-

ated in the Celtic Knot garden or any number of places at Adaire Hall. The great house was his life. The gardens were the source of all his love.

The moment he'd read Jennifer's letter, Gordon knew he'd have to return. His reluctance had been instant, borne of a memory of a scrawny child hoping for any crumbs of kindness from the two people in the world who should have cared for him but hadn't.

The cottage huddled like a mushroom on the landscape. The new thatching made it appear even more top-heavy. Two front windows let in the light on either side of the rounded wooden door and appeared like eyes gleaming in the fading sunlight.

Jennifer had told him once that she thought the cottage looked as if it were enchanted. Like special brownies lived inside. She was only nine at the time, and he ten, but even then he hadn't wanted to tell her the truth. The cottage had never been a happy place.

Sean hadn't approved of his friendship with Jennifer. His father always went on and on about how the guardian wouldn't like it, how the earl would disapprove, never mind that the earl was ten-year-old Harrison, already well on his way to being a prig.

However dislikable Harrison was, Gordon was told to treat him—and any of the members of the Adaire family—with the respect due their rank, understanding that he was the gardener's boy, nothing more.

He tried to obey, but he never could when it came to Jennifer. Whenever he could escape

Sean, he would steal away and Jennifer would meet him, either on the shores of Loch Adaire or one of the paths through the hills. She'd been his partner in adventure, his friend, and then so much more.

Now he knocked softly, but when he didn't hear anything, he grabbed the latch and pushed open the door.

The cottage was surprisingly spacious, having a main room, a small kitchen, and two rooms in the back. One of those had been his, and the larger one had belonged to his parents.

After closing the door behind him, he stood in the main room looking around. He had the curious sensation of having stepped back in time. Nothing had changed in five years.

No, there was one change. Betty was no longer here.

He walked to the fireplace and picked up a framed charcoal drawing on the mantel. Years ago, an itinerant Irish worker had come to Adaire Hall. He'd worked for Sean, who had labeled the man a drifter. He hadn't spent his time playing cards or drinking. Instead, the man was given to scribbling in a book of blank pages.

When he left the Hall, he'd given Gordon one of those scribbles, a portrait of Betty. He'd been eleven years old at the time and amazed at the man's talent. Now, looking at the lifelike portrait, he could almost hear his mother's voice.

Betty had never been maternal. Everything she'd done for him, from sewing a rip in his shirt to feeding him, had been accompanied by grumbling, condemning looks, and a switch more

than once. He'd wanted to ask why she disliked him so much, but the question would have been answered with another beating.

The portrait was uncannily accurate and not the least complimentary, a fact that Betty evidently hadn't seen. Her cheeks were full, her face round. Her mouth was small, pursed in this portrait just as it had often been in life. Her eyes were brown and narrowed, an expression that was commonplace. As if Betty didn't see anything pleasing about the world around her.

Her voice was raspy, the tone always this side of exasperated.

He remembered one incident when he was eight years old and had broken a bowl. He hadn't meant to do it; it had been an accident, but Betty didn't see it that way.

"You clumsy, worthless, disgusting piece of trash! See what you've done now?"

She reached for the strap by the door and proceeded to beat him until his legs bled. When she was done, or her arm tired, she'd thrown the shards of the bowl at him, one of them cutting his cheek. He still had the scar to remind him of his mother.

Yet she was as given to worshipping the Adaire family as Sean. No one was as handsome as Harrison or as talented. No one's future looked brighter than the boy made earl.

When Gordon had gone to study with Harrison and Jennifer, she hadn't been impressed at the countess's generosity.

"You'll get ideas above your station, boy. You just remember he's the earl."

Although he doubted that he'd ever need Latin or debate Pythagorean theory, he was determined to be educated, to learn as much as Harrison knew or even more.

Yet he'd never appreciated, until he'd been nearly grown, Betty's influence. She'd given him something he'd not expected: independence. He'd been forced to depend on himself, to grow a skin thick enough to endure his own mother's antipathy.

For that he would have thanked Betty, had she still been alive.

"If you're not a ghost, then you must be himself."

He turned to see his father leaning against the doorframe of his bedroom, one hand clutching it to hold himself up.

Sean was the one who looked like a ghost. Clad in his nightshirt, he was rail thin, his pallor so great that Gordon put the frame back on the mantel and walked quickly toward him.

"You shouldn't be out of bed, I'm thinking," he said, reaching his father.

He put his arm around Sean's waist and walked with him back to the bed.

"I'll not have you playing nursemaid."

"Someone obviously has to," Gordon said.

"I've got a nurse, thanks to Lady Jennifer. She insists on sending me a girl around the clock. I think she's afraid I might die without someone notifying her."

He should have known that Jennifer would ensure that his father was cared for.

"Where is this nursemaid of yours?"

Sean took a moment to answer, the effort evidently tiring him. "She went to fetch something from the Hall."

Gordon helped him into bed, covered him, then reached over to arrange his pillow.

"What does the physician say?" he asked, realizing he should have asked Jennifer that question.

"Damn fool. Same thing they always say. They don't know, but I should take this tonic or that medicine. Just in case, you understand."

Sean looked as if he'd lost nearly half his body weight. He was so frail a stiff wind might blow him away. His hair, once the color of straw, had thinned until there were only strands covering the bald patches.

"He had to have said something."

"My insides aren't working like they're supposed to," Sean said, scowling at him. "I'll not tell you more than that. I'll keep my own counsel, thanks."

Gordon pulled the chair close and sat.

Sean looked over at him. "So, you've been living in London all this time, boy? What makes you think you need to come home now?"

His father hadn't changed. Nor had Gordon expected that illness would soften Sean in any way.

"I take it Jennifer told you where I lived."

"It's Lady Jennifer to you."

Gordon didn't correct himself.

Sean turned his head away.

For a moment Gordon was tempted to recite a litany of his accomplishments to his father, but he realized it wouldn't make any difference.

Sean would never acknowledge that he'd done anything right or worthy of praise.

"So, you've come back to see me die, is that it?"

Gordon sat back in the chair, knowing that Sean would probably not be surprised by the truth. His father's illness had been just an excuse. In his heart he knew that he'd come back for one reason. To see if he'd been wrong all this time and McBain had been right.

Had Jennifer loved him as he'd loved her?

Chapter Five

The interior of the Mayfair Club was impressive with its soaring columns and three-story foyer. It reminded Ellen of a Roman bath she'd once seen. Although there wasn't a pool of water at the base of the columns, all the other details were intact.

She couldn't hear anything. No indication that this was a place for men to come to ogle women and lose a fortune at gambling. No doubt they were also fed well, and she'd come to understand that there were even living quarters on the upper floors for those who could afford them.

Thanks to Colin's indefatigable secretary, who had remained in her employ, she'd gotten some advance information about the Mayfair Club. Unfortunately, however, there was little she could discover about its owner. The man, who was rumored—according to her sources—to own various entertainment establishments throughout the city, was cloaked in secrecy.

She was therefore surprised when he agreed to meet with her so readily. Of course, she had mentioned Harrison's name, title, and the fact that she was a dear friend of the family. She didn't think it necessary to mention that she was Jenni-

fer's godmother. Nor that Mary had been her one close friend, someone she mourned every day.

Some things about her life were too important to be used, even as a negotiating point.

She had every intention, however, of putting pressure to bear against the ownership of the Mayfair Club if they refused to cooperate with her. She had no doubt that Harrison had proved to be an exemplary member. Not only had he taken up residence in one of the apartments on the upper floors, but she suspected that he'd lost a great deal of money gambling. Ascending to his father's title had not granted Harrison any sense.

Before her death, Mary was at her wit's end about her son. Ellen felt that this errand was more for both her friend and her goddaughter than it was for Harrison's benefit.

The porter escorted her to a parlor looking out over the street. The walls were thankfully not covered in that dreadful red flocking that was all the rage. Nor was there any indication that the owner of this establishment had an affection for gilt. Instead, this room was tastefully decorated in shades of beige and brown, giving her an indication that it was a masculine retreat.

A maid entered the room, bobbed a curtsy before stepping aside for another maid to enter, laden with a tea tray. Both girls were extraordinarily pretty and although they were dressed as modestly as they might have been in a London household, Ellen couldn't help but wonder if they had additional attire for the evening

hours. As the sun set was their modesty also put to rest?

She smiled her thanks and watched as they turned and left the room, still speechless. What a very strange encounter. Had they been taught that women were better seen than heard? If so, that was a mark against the owner of the Mayfair Club.

Rather than wait for her host, she served herself some tea as well as two biscuits. Age had something to recommend for it. She truly didn't care if her waistline expanded a bit. Not too much, of course, but she wasn't about to turn down a biscuit with currants along with her tea.

She was on her third biscuit when the door slid open again. She brushed off her fingers, blotted at her mouth with the embroidered napkin, and prepared to do battle.

The woman who entered the room was dressed as richly as anyone in the upper echelons of London society. In fact, Ellen was quite sure that she had seen a similar pattern from her own dressmaker. The woman's gown was perhaps a little much for afternoon wear, but since it was only an hour or two before dinner, she could be excused.

Her hair was blond, perfectly coiffed, in an ornate style that would have required a talented lady's maid to arrange.

Abigail was not quite as skilled, but Ellen made do with her inadequacies. After all, she herself wasn't perfect. Why should she require her staff to be without flaws?

Given that this woman's dress was immacu-

late and her hair was without criticism, it didn't seem quite fair that her figure was shapely, and her face . . . Well, the woman was of a certain age, that was without doubt. Yet she was still strikingly beautiful.

Ellen immediately fell victim to a surge of jealousy, supplanted by the wish that she had tried more with her own toilette before arriving here.

Who knew that she would be meeting Helen of Troy?

"I do apologize for keeping you waiting. We had a situation that required my presence, otherwise I would not have been so rude. Please, forgive me."

The woman floated across the room and sat at the end of the settee opposite Ellen. Each gesture was made with grace and delicacy. No doubt everything the woman did was performed in exactly the same way.

Ellen was without words. She wanted to tell the woman that she was expecting the owner of the Mayfair Club, someone hopefully ugly. She would very much like to see a normal human being in the next few minutes.

However, before she could form a word, the goddess spoke again.

"Oh, I'm so glad that you served yourself some tea. Should I call for some more hot water?"

Ellen shook her head dumbly, since the power of speech had not yet returned to her.

"The currant biscuits are my favorite, too."

"Who are you?" Ellen asked.

Speech had returned to her, yet it was shrouded

in rudeness. She wanted to call back the words the minute they were uttered, but the woman opposite her only smiled.

"We have started wrong, haven't we? I'm Maggie Boyland. I know you were expecting the owner, but unfortunately he's been called out of town. I manage the Mayfair Club, and I thought that I might be able to assist you in some way."

Ellen reached for another biscuit, not because she wanted one, but she needed to do something other than stare at the woman. She had never heard of such a thing. A woman, managing the Mayfair Club. She didn't quite know what to think. Of course, to manage such a successful establishment would require brains, charm, and a great many other attributes, some of which Ellen was certain she didn't know or understand.

Would you have to be good at gambling yourself? Certainly you would need to know something about cards and card players, for that matter.

Ellen was subjected to a sweeping inspection.

What did Miss Boyland see when she looked at her? A woman past her prime, no doubt. Fashionably dressed, with enough jewels on her rings to give the impression of wealth, certainly. Someone who did not get out often, because she had been tongue-tied ever since the woman entered the room.

Of the two of them, Maggie was the more polite, not to mention eloquent.

Ellen had never felt as out of her element as she did now.

She finished the biscuit, placed the plate back

on the tray, then used the napkin to blot her mouth once more.

"I have been exceedingly coarse," she said. "Please let me convey my apologies. Perhaps we can attribute my boorishness to the errand itself. I am at a loss and I need your help, Miss Boyland."

"How can I help you?"

"I'm a friend of the Adaire family. It's because of that fact that I'm here now."

Maggie reached for a currant biscuit and nibbled it delicately as she listened. The woman didn't have a crumb on her.

"I understand that Harrison Adaire is a member here."

Maggie did not confirm or deny that fact.

"He needs to come home," Ellen said, letting her utter disgust for Harrison show. "His wife is about to have their first child, and he hasn't come back to Scotland in months."

"What do you expect us to do about that, Mrs. Thornton?"

She waved her hand in the air. "Something. Can't you tell him that he's no longer wanted? Can't you refuse to allow him any more credit?"

Maggie looked momentarily startled before her face fell into perfect lines once again.

"Harrison has always been a lamentable card player," Ellen said in explanation. "And a gambler, for that matter. If there was one horse destined to come in last, that is the one that Harrison would pick. He cannot wager to save his life, and the only thing that has proven to be an asset for him is the Adaire fortune. You can't tell me that

his luck has changed. I don't believe it. Luck is the province of fools and beggars."

Maggie just stared at her.

Ellen continued. "I've been told that Harrison is doing everything in his power to diminish that fortune. I do not doubt that you consider him one of your best members, but I also suspect that he owes you quite a bit of money."

Maggie looked straight at her, blinked twice, then smiled. Such a blinding expression that Ellen almost wanted to close her eyes. Or beg the woman to direct her charm to something else, a far wall, perhaps.

"You're right. Harrison does owe us quite a bit of money. We have extended him credit, but there's no worry that we won't be paid."

They should worry. Harrison didn't have the sense God gave an ant.

"I am willing to pay his debts," Ellen said. "On the condition that you send him home."

Maggie looked momentarily surprised once more. "How do you suggest that we do that, Mrs. Thornton?"

"Refuse to let him gamble here for a month. If that doesn't work, rescind his membership."

"Why on earth would we do that? If we had twenty more Harrisons, we'd be the most successful club in all of England."

"For decency's sake?"

Maggie didn't say anything for a moment, making Ellen wonder if she had pushed too much.

Finally, the other woman nodded, just once.

"He'll still be responsible for paying his own markers, Mrs. Thornton. I wouldn't expect you

to do that. However, a certain situation did arise concerning one of our hostesses. It would be best, perhaps, if Harrison remained away from the club for a while. Just to let things settle."

Although she was curious, Ellen told herself not to ask. Harrison was already possessed of a lamentable character. She really didn't want to know that he'd done something untoward to a young woman. Or even engaged in an adulterous affair.

"So, you will send him home, then?"

"Yes, I will."

"Will he listen to you?" Unsaid were the words—because you're a woman.

Maggie smiled again, but this expression was not as amused.

"I speak for the owner. Every member here knows that. If Harrison disputes my words, I do have the ability to throw him out on his ear, earl or not."

The words were spoken in a delicate voice, but Ellen heard the steel in her tone.

She was beginning to like the woman more and more. Perhaps even enough to overlook the fact that, next to Maggie, she was rendered exceedingly plain.

"What a pity that we won't get to know each other better," she said. "I think I should like you very much."

"Never discount the future, Mrs. Thornton. Perhaps circumstances will arrange themselves."

She had been in the woman's company less than an hour, but she already suspected that whatever Maggie wanted, Maggie got.

That thought led to another: exactly who was the owner of the Mayfair Club? He must be an extraordinarily talented man and one imminently secure in himself. Otherwise, Maggie would've had him for breakfast.

Chapter Six

*G*ordon remained with his father, sitting on the ladder-back chair as Sean fell asleep.

"Begging your pardon, sir," a voice said.

He turned to see a girl standing in the doorway, a white apron over her dress. Her hair was caught up in a bun that had come loose, spilling bright red curls over one shoulder.

"Who would you be, sir?" she asked softly, after casting a glance in Sean's direction.

"Gordon McDonnell," he said, standing and moving to the door. "Sean's son."

She bobbed a curtsy, spreading out the apron like it was a ball gown.

"Pardon me for asking, sir. It's just that he's under my care."

They left the room, Gordon closing the door behind him.

"Can you tell me what's wrong with him?"

She seemed torn, looking at the closed door then back at him.

"It's a cancer, sir. The doctor says it's in the bowels."

Her face pinked up as she spoke, making Gordon wonder if she'd been a nurse for very long.

"What is your name?"

"Sally Farrell, sir." She smiled, the expression a pleasant one.

"Come and talk to me, Sally, and tell me what I need to know."

He led the way to the small kitchen table beneath the window. There had never been more than two chairs here. As a child he'd had his meals after his parents were finished. He'd grown accustomed to sitting here alone, staring out the window at the Hall in the distance. He'd always wondered at Harrison and Jennifer's life in that great house.

Now he pulled out the chair for Sally, and after she sat, he joined her.

"He's in a lot of pain, isn't he?"

"The herbs help, of course, and the laudanum."

Was there more that could be done? After speaking with Sally for a few minutes, he realized that it was probably stubbornness that had kept Sean alive. There was no hope for a cure, according to the Adaire family physician summoned to examine Sean. Something else Jennifer had done.

"We try to make him as comfortable as possible, sir. Plus, people come to visit. Ned comes to see him almost every day and finds a question to ask him. Something about the land or the gardens. Something to make Sean feel as though people care that he's still here. Everyone needs to feel important, sir, even in the midst of their pain."

He wondered if Sally was espousing beliefs that she held or if she was parroting what she'd heard. It sounded like something Jennifer would say.

He was rarely at a loss for words, even though there were times when he deliberately kept silent. It was better to let someone wonder at his thoughts than to let them fall on deaf ears. Now, however, he didn't know what to say to Sally.

Finally, the words seemed to birth themselves.

"Is there anything that I can do? Anything that I can bring him?"

Her brown eyes warmed. "Nothing, sir." She hesitated before speaking again, but finally did, the words coming slowly. "It's the knowing of it that's difficult. It won't be long now."

He'd already figured that out for himself. He reached over and patted her hand where it lay on the table.

Standing, he thanked her before making his way to the door.

"What would be a good time to visit him again?"

She turned in her chair and her young face looked suddenly older, more mature. He had a vision of what she might look like as an old, old woman. A lined face, a furrowed brow, but kind, gentle eyes.

"There is no good time, sir. Anytime would be best."

He nodded. "Then I'll come after dinner," he said.

"Moira will be here then. I'll tell her about you. She's the night nurse. Miss Jennifer didn't want Sean to be alone, so there's one of us here at all times."

One more reason to thank Jennifer.

JENNIFER HAD PLANNED to have a dinner tray brought to her in her sitting room. However, Lauren had sent word that she'd invited Gordon to dinner.

Perhaps it wasn't entirely proper for a woman in the last month of confinement to attend dinner with a stranger, but Lauren was determined. Jennifer thought it was a combination of being heartily tired of her room as well as Mrs. Farmer. Plus, she was probably sick of thinking about Harrison. Would he ever come home? Would he ever be a true husband? Questions like that must keep her miserable.

For the first time in her life, Jennifer was going to sit down to dinner at Adaire Hall with Gordon. When Mr. McBain had been in residence, that would've been impossible.

As the new Countess of Burfield, Lauren could command anything, and no one would think the less of her.

He was here. After all these years, Gordon was here. The thought echoed in Jennifer's mind and harnessed itself to her breath and her heartbeat. He was here. Even if he was different, he was Gordon. He'd finally come home. He was here.

Yet he hadn't returned for her, but for Sean. To do his duty by his father.

She sat at her vanity and stared at herself. She looked tired, but she'd wanted everything done for the celebration of the birth. They'd cleaned Adaire Hall from top to bottom, including all the windows. She was a little too pale, and there was an expression in her eyes that hinted at sadness.

Her life was enjoyable in a great many ways.

She had her books, her painting—or her dabbles as Harrison called them. She walked every day, not only around the Hall, but a path into the hills surrounding the house. Sometimes she sketched or painted or read. Occasionally, if her duties allowed it, she simply sat and watched as the sun traveled over a summer sky and the shadows grew deep, leading to the endless days of a Highland summer.

She'd always return home slowly and perhaps a little reluctantly. She loved her home, but she knew, only too well, that it didn't belong to her. She was here because she had nowhere else to live and no one wanted her. The estate belonged to Harrison, and if his child was a boy, he would inherit Adaire Hall, the title, and all that accompanied it.

That was the way of the world and she understood it. Even though she had always cared so much more about their home than Harrison, she knew she'd never be more than an afterthought in its history. Perhaps a footnote: *Jennifer Adaire, the sixth Earl's spinster sister, was instrumental in managing the estate for a number of years.*

Time had been kind to the house. There weren't many indications that five years had passed as far as the estate was concerned. Perhaps the trees had grown a little taller. There was dry rot in one of the drawing rooms. The roof had been replaced on one of the wings. Other than that, nothing had changed.

As for her, she was older than most of the women on the marriage mart. If she was firmly on the shelf, she had no one but herself to blame.

Gordon hadn't limited her life. He hadn't restricted her to Adaire Hall. She'd done that on her own.

We're better off without him. He was a disruptive influence.

Those were Harrison's words after Gordon left. Harrison had seemed fiercely glad that Gordon was no longer at the Hall. He'd told her, on more than one occasion, to stop staring out the window like a forlorn puppy.

Her godmother was the only one who seemed to understand.

"I miss him so much. Sometimes I don't think I can stand it. Why did he leave? Why?"

Ellen had patted her on the back, then kissed her on the forehead. "I didn't know your Gordon," she said, "but I imagine that the world was calling him. From what you've said about him, perhaps he would never be content to take an easy path in life."

Ellen had been right. He needed to find his own place, his own way in the world.

Had he done that?

He was a man you would notice when he walked into a room. He would stand in the doorway and every pair of eyes would gravitate to him. The men would feel immediately intimidated, and the women would want an introduction.

There was something in his gaze that hadn't been there before. A wariness coupled with something else. Knowledge, perhaps, of himself. This was a man who gave you the impression that he

knew exactly who and what he was, and was prepared to defend himself to anyone.

She had not expected that he would have that kind of impact on her. Or that she would feel suddenly inept and shy.

She stood in front of her wardrobe, selecting first one dress and then another. Nothing looked good enough. Everything she selected was too plain and serviceable. She had a few dresses that Ellen's seamstress had made for her, but if she wore one of those, she would look garishly over-dressed.

What a choice: to wear something utterly plain or much too formal.

The white lace blouse and blue skirt were going to have to suffice. She attached a ruby brooch to her blouse and surveyed herself in the pier glass.

She looked like a governess.

Perhaps she should put her hair up. If she took the time to do that, she'd probably be late for dinner. It was simply going to have to do. Besides, why was she being so foolish? Gordon had ignored her earlier.

He would probably not even notice she was at dinner.

Chapter Seven

Before she went downstairs, Jennifer stopped by Lauren's room to see if she needed some assistance. There was no one in her suite, which meant that Lauren and her maid had already descended the stairs.

She did the same, all the while counseling herself not to show any outward excitement. A placid demeanor, that's what was called for. If he could be distant, so could she. If he could ignore her, she'd do the same to him. She would not be the Jennifer of five years ago. Instead, she would be someone Gordon had never met, a mature Jennifer. Composed, calm, someone who wasn't overly emotional, but who let logic rule, instead.

He was here. A dozen feet to the dining room door and she would see him. How many times had she imagined him back at Adaire Hall? Too many to count.

She made it to the door of the winter dining room before her heart started to race. She was finding it difficult to breathe, and any thought of being unaffected by Gordon's presence flew out the window.

Lauren and Gordon were engaged in conversation. They seemed at ease with each other de-

spite the fact that their acquaintance was only minutes old.

A fire had been lit in the fireplace in the opposite wall. This room was used whenever the weather turned nippy because the other family dining room didn't have a fireplace. The formal dining room was almost never used unless Harrison brought guests down for hunting or a week's worth of drinking. It could accommodate two dozen guests with room to expand the table even further.

Her mother had loved this room because the windows looked out over the rolling hills leading down to the river. Jennifer had often sat here, staring through those same windows and wishing to be gone, either desperate to meet Gordon by the loch or to follow him up through the hills.

Now she stood in the doorway, uncertain. Gordon noticed her and stood.

"You look lovely," he said. He'd always been polite, even as a boy. He would have said the same thing to a stranger. Or a woman past the first blush of youth. Or someone unfortunately plain.

She forced a smile to her face.

"I see you've met Lauren," she said, glancing at her sister-in-law. She moved to the middle of the table next to Lauren and opposite Gordon.

"I have. We've discovered that we have quite a few friends in common in London."

"Oh?"

She wouldn't have known any of Lauren's friends in London. She'd only visited the city twice in her life, and she'd spent most of the time

awestruck by the monuments, the museums, and the sheer number of people.

Most of her time had been spent at Adaire Hall with visits to Edinburgh. She wasn't nearly as cosmopolitan as Lauren, or evidently, Gordon. Part of her wanted to flee the room. Instead, she sat, thanking the footman who'd pulled out the chair for her.

Lauren, who hadn't had an appetite for the past week, certainly made up for it tonight. Both she and Gordon masked the fact that Jennifer wasn't eating much. Nor did she have anything worthwhile to offer to their sparkling conversation.

Lauren had lived in Edinburgh most of her life, but her father also had a house in London, where she stayed during the season.

The only thing Jennifer knew well was life at Adaire Hall, and that was too boring a topic. She could quote how many sheep and cattle they owned, the various acreages being farmed, and whether the salmon were plentiful this year. She knew hundreds of separate details pertaining to the history of her home, none of which she mentioned. Lauren only saw Adaire Hall as Harrison's home, and there was never a doubt of Gordon's dislike for the estate.

He'd dressed for dinner. The black suit favored him, making his blue eyes even more vibrant. His was a strong face, with individual features that nevertheless seemed to fit perfectly. His nose reminded her of a Roman statue. His chin was squared. His brows were thick, but so were his eyelashes, keeping his face from being too rough.

At the same time, he looked like a Scottish warrior, someone transplanted into the present from the tenth century.

Over the years she'd often seen him wearing a kilt and he'd looked perfect in it. Once, he had hefted a broadsword in the clan hall. She'd never forgotten the sight of him lit by sunlight, the muscles in his arms pulled tight against his shirt. In that moment he'd been a member of her clan, proud, brave, and willing to fight.

He'd never known how often she had thought of him that way. Or how it had stirred her.

Lauren sat with her hand on the mound of her stomach. It was a protective gesture that she had started making about two months ago. From time to time she would pat her expanding girth as if to reassure the baby that she hadn't forgotten he was the most important person in her life. This dinner might well be the last time she was able to make it down the stairs until her child was born.

While she was probably a terrible person for resenting their easy camaraderie, Jennifer found it difficult to contribute to the conversation. She was being childish, as foolish as when she was five years old and refusing to eat her porridge to punish her mother. Lecturing herself didn't seem to make any difference. It was quite obvious that Gordon liked Lauren and that her sister-in-law felt the same way about him.

All she had to do was bring Harrison's name into the conversation and the tenor of it would immediately change. Lauren would look sad, and Gordon would no doubt scowl at her. For

that reason, she remained mute, wishing she were a better person. Or that she wasn't feeling miserable and overjoyed at the same time.

He'd always had that effect on her. A smile from Gordon was enough to make anything tolerable. It was the same with his anger. If he was mad at her, nothing would make the day brighter.

"Are you not feeling well?" Lauren asked. "You've hardly eaten anything and the salmon is especially good."

Her sister-in-law was one of the sweetest people she'd ever met. Plus, she noticed things. Even being heavily with child, she didn't withdraw into herself. Instead, she wanted to know about her maid's love affair with one of the footmen. Or how Mrs. Thompson's arthritic knee was doing. She might have been the daughter of a wealthy man, but she'd never put on airs.

Her question made Jennifer feel even smaller and more petty.

"I find that I'm not very hungry," she said, smiling at Lauren. She changed the subject immediately, looking at Gordon.

"How did you find your father?" she asked.

"Worse than I anticipated, frankly. Thank you for your care of him, Jennifer. No one could have done more."

"He's part of Adaire Hall," she said. "Besides, he's come to mean a great deal to me over the years."

That wasn't a lie. When she was a girl she was, if not afraid of Sean, then cautious around him. He had a tendency to say exactly what he thought to anyone who was nearby. The only people he

seemed to respect were her mother and Harrison. Yet as she grew, and especially after she had taken on the management of Adaire Hall, they had come to a meeting of the minds. He told her exactly what he thought, as usual. She did the same. They felt a grudging respect for each other, supplanted by a growing affection. She'd been as surprised by that as he.

"Sally said the physician has been to see him?"

She nodded. "Mr. McPherson. He treated my mother."

"Is there anything more that can be done?"

Although the topic was not one normally discussed at dinner, she wasn't going to dissuade Gordon from asking questions. At least he was talking to her.

"Not according to the doctor."

The prognosis for Sean was grim. In actuality, he had outlived the doctor's estimation. No doubt because proving him wrong would give Sean some satisfaction. The man might be ill, but his stubbornness was still firmly intact.

In that regard Gordon was just like his father.

JENNIFER WAS BARELY looking at him, and the only conversation they'd exchanged had been about Sean. Even Lauren glanced at her from time to time, as if Jennifer's behavior was unusual. Nor was she eating. She merely pushed the salmon around her plate a few times.

He'd always been able to read her, and if he wasn't wrong, she was angry.

"Do you think the cook has made any tarts for dessert?" Lauren asked.

"I'll go see, shall I?" Jennifer smiled, and before the footman could get to her chair, pushed it back and stood. In seconds she was gone from the room, leaving him alone with Lauren.

"I think she's upset," Lauren said, staring after her. "I don't know why."

"It's me." Gordon smiled at her, but the expression of worry remained on Lauren's face.

Her complexion was the color of cream, her soft brown eyes surrounded by long lashes. Her features were small, especially her rosebud mouth, but she was a pretty girl. No doubt she'd been raised to believe that being pretty was her most important attribute.

She did everything prettily, as if she'd rehearsed the most pleasing aspect of each task. She'd sat at the table, taken up her napkin, and eaten her dinner in the same fashion. Even the way she'd half walked, half swayed to the table had been done in a pretty way.

He'd thoroughly enjoyed Lauren's company. At the same time, he knew that she would drive him to distraction in a matter of weeks.

She was, regrettably, one of those women who didn't have a single original idea or thought. She parroted well, plus she'd hung on to his every word for the entire dinner. All in all, the characteristics of a perfect hostess.

If Jennifer had been herself, she would have argued with him by now. She would have challenged his assumptions or his observations. Except that Jennifer was barely talking to him.

She returned in minutes to announce that there was pudding for dessert, but no tarts. Lau-

ren looked disappointed, but her smile was back in minutes.

"I probably shouldn't have had a tart anyway," she said, glancing at Gordon then Jennifer.

He stood, excusing himself and explaining that he wanted to get back to the cottage to see Sean. Both women nodded at him.

Jennifer kept her gaze on the floor. Evidently, the patterned carpet held a great deal of interest for her.

He would have asked her what was wrong if she'd been the same person he'd known all his life. It was evident that she'd changed in the past five years. Gone was the girl he'd loved, and in her place was a woman he didn't recognize.

All these years he'd held out hope that McBain had lied. This homecoming was a great deal harder than he'd anticipated.

He left the room without another glance in Jennifer's direction.

Chapter Eight

*J*ennifer had never been a coward. Granted, she lived a safe existence at Adaire Hall. When she was a child, she'd had to be brave to be Gordon's companion. Grown, however, she faced few challenges.

At dinner tonight she'd been a shadow of herself, when all along what she wanted to do was to ask Gordon why he'd never answered one of her letters. Why hadn't he returned before now? And, the most important question, why had he simply left without a word to her?

Had her brother and Mr. McBain been right all along? Had he tired of her? Or, had he thought his future was more interesting than she was?

All of those questions needed to be answered, but all she'd done was simply sit there mute, listening to Gordon and Lauren's conversation.

When she had participated, her comments had been downright drivel.

Where was her courage?

Yes, this Gordon was different, but so was she. In the past five years she'd shouldered a tremendous responsibility. She'd made decisions that were important for the well-being of everyone who lived at Adaire Hall.

Why, then, had she acted the coward around Gordon?

The fact that she was pacing in front of the window was a symptom of her annoyance. So, too, the fact that she hadn't readied for bed. How could she possibly sleep, being as irritated as she was?

Without thinking, she grabbed her shawl and headed for the door.

GORDON WAS SURPRISED that nothing he'd seen so far had changed. It was as if time had simply stopped at Adaire Hall. No additional cottages had been built. No more of the land had been set aside for gardens or any other use.

He'd felt a yearning for Scotland over the years, wanting to feel the wind through the strath, see the lights in the sky in the winter, and experience the endless days during summer in the Highlands.

He'd always tamped down that longing, but now it was back in full force.

Outside of the area cleared for the Hall, the land was wilder. The woods took over just beyond the stable, stretching down to the river. On the other side the land rose to the hills.

Gordon preferred the blaeberry in the forest, or the thick growth of ling heather. Even a juniper thicket was preferable to those plants that were tortured into growing in one of the Adaire Hall gardens.

Sean never made time for anything other than his work, something that Gordon hadn't truly understood until he went to London. He'd been accused of the same thing and had tried to tell

people that he enjoyed what he did. His goal of amassing a fortune had entertained him. Maybe Sean's gardens were the same for him.

He ducked his head as he entered the cottage once more. The girl standing at the kitchen sink turned and looked at him.

"You'll be Gordon, I'm thinking," she said.

"And you're Moira."

"Aye, that I am."

She jerked her head in the direction of Sean's bedroom. "Himself has had his dinner. He's still awake, although it's time for his pain medicine."

"The laudanum?"

She nodded. "It's the only thing that gives him peace, but even so he rarely sleeps the night."

He'd been involved in his own life in London and hadn't given much thought to his father. He certainly hadn't considered that Sean's descent into death would be an agonizing one.

He nodded, excused himself, and went to Sean's door, knocking softly on it. He entered to find his father sitting on the edge of the bed, holding a cane in his right hand. He used it to laboriously stand and face Gordon.

"I'm tired of my bed. I'll be sleeping forever soon enough."

Gordon didn't even try to hide his smile at this proof of Sean's stubbornness. It was so much like the man he knew that he was thrust back into his childhood.

"Do you give your nurses this type of grief?"

"Nurses? Bah! Both those girls are younger than some of my shirts. Silly lasses they are, too. Always laughing and telling stories, leading the

footmen and the stable boys on as well. My lads are smarter than that."

That sounded like Sean, too.

"They seem to care for you, Da. Would it be so hard to be a little grateful?"

"Like you? Aye, I felt your gratitude all these years."

Now was not the time to fight with his father. Nor was he going to offer excuses for himself. He was no longer the gardener's boy, but Sean would never see him differently.

Going to his father's side, Gordon gave him his arm. Sean refused to take it. Instead, he made one shuffling step and then another toward the door. Before he got there, however, he started to sink toward the floor. Gordon picked him up, startled at how frail this strong and vibrant man had become. Gently, he helped him sit on the chair beside the bed.

"So, you've made something of yourself, then."

He glanced at Sean. "Yes, I have."

Sean didn't respond, merely looked toward the open door.

"You've given up any fool idea of her?"

They both knew who the *her* was in his question. The same woman who'd been in his thoughts and dreams for decades. The woman who'd barely spoken to him since he arrived.

Sean had said something similar many times, telling him that he was not of Lady Jennifer's station. He would be more sensible baying at the moon. In other words, he wasn't good enough. He'd never be good enough for Jennifer.

For the past five years he'd had one goal: to

prove Sean wrong. Perhaps to prove them all wrong. Yet, maybe it wasn't Sean's approval that mattered. The one person he wanted to impress was Jennifer.

He wanted to offer Jennifer the world and anything she wanted within it.

"I don't have any fool ideas anymore, Da. Just good ones."

"Then you've gotten some sense about you, finally."

Sean began to cough, then he grabbed his midsection. As he bent over, the cough turned into a moan. Gordon went to his side, picked him up, and placed his father in the middle of the bed. Once he was settled, Gordon went to the door and called for Moira.

"It's the excitement," she said, bustling into the room with a brown bottle in her left hand and a spoon in her right. "Whenever he gets excited the pain is worse."

She looked up at him. "If you'll help me sit him up, it will go a little easier."

He did as she asked, his arm supporting Sean's back. He could feel his father's spine through the thin nightshirt. He had the impression that the cancer was eating him from the inside out, feasting on his flesh the way a carnivore would.

After Sean took two spoonfuls of the laudanum, Gordon sat beside his bed and waited for it to take effect. From what he knew of the opium-based tincture, it eased chronic pain for a while, but also delivered hallucinogenic dreams to the patient. He hoped that Sean would be given a few hours of relief before the dreams began.

They managed to talk of innocuous subjects: the change of seasons, and the new servants at Adaire Hall.

His father unbent enough to compliment Jennifer on her running of the estate. "The girl has a good head on her shoulders." Gordon made a mental note to tell Jennifer that she'd earned one of Sean's rare bits of praise.

If she would talk to him.

Finally, Sean fell asleep. Gordon sat there for a little while, thinking about the years he'd spent in the cottage. When his father died, he'd be an orphan, but he'd felt like that the majority of his life.

He stood and left his sleeping father, closing the bedroom door softly behind him.

"Is there anything you need?" he asked of Moira. She was sitting on a chair in the living room, Betty's favorite place.

"I'm just fine. You go along now and come again in the morning. I know he'll want to see you."

He wasn't entirely certain that was true, but Gordon thanked her as he left the cottage.

JENNIFER APPROACHED THE gardener's cottage slowly, hearing the gravel crunch beneath her shoes. It was late. No doubt too late for this confrontation, but she didn't care. Not one more night would pass without answers.

She'd already waited too long.

The cottage was located some distance away from the main house, but she knew this way so well that she could navigate it even in the dark.

Tonight the full moon cast the area in blue-gray shadow. An owl called to her as if wanting to know why she was out and about. The cry of a fox reminded her of when she was a girl and used to leave food for them, at least until the ghillie found out and gave her a severe lecture. Even today she was tempted to leave some table scraps. Not because the foxes at Adaire Hall were starving. They weren't. However, she did admire them because they were beautiful and cunning creatures.

There were lights on in the cottage, and shadows visible in the windows. She hoped that Sean was having an easy night, although those had been few and far between lately.

At least Gordon had come back soon enough to say goodbye to his father.

The relationship between the men had always been difficult. As a girl she thought that Sean went out of his way to taunt his son, or to criticize him for things that were unfair and unwarranted. One day when a shovel was left outside to rust, it was Gordon who was punished. He hadn't been responsible. Instead, it had been one of Sean's apprentices. It hadn't mattered to Sean, however. Nor had he apologized for beating his own son.

"My father doesn't say he's sorry," Gordon said one day. "He thinks an apology is a sign of weakness."

She hadn't known what to say. That hadn't been the first sign of Sean's intolerance toward his son. Nor had it been the last.

Now she stood near the trunk of an oak, watch-

ing the cottage and wondering if Gordon was going to spend the night in his old room. Maybe he preferred it to the suite at the Hall.

She leaned against the trunk, folding her arms in front of her. She'd only worn her shawl and the night was proving to be chilly. Was she an idiot to be standing here like this? Probably. She'd never been that wise when it came to Gordon.

In the past five years she'd gone to Edinburgh often. Ellen had insisted on inviting some eligible men to dinner in a not at all subtle hint to Jennifer. Yet no one she met ever fascinated like Gordon had. She didn't want to know what those men thought or their opinions on various things. Not one of them ever made her dream about kissing them or losing herself in an embrace.

Perhaps she might have been considered almost a spinster, but she was an earl's daughter and an earl's sister, with a respectable income of her own, thanks to her father's planning. Plus, she was Ellen's goddaughter, and Ellen was not only exceedingly wealthy but quite popular in certain social circles.

She couldn't help but compare everyone she met, from a very nice industrialist to a cousin of a duke, against Gordon. They weren't tall enough or witty enough or kind enough. Their voice didn't have a velvet edge to it. They weren't nearly as handsome or strong. They didn't make her feel feminine simply by standing near her.

Nor did they make her heart race.

She loved him and she would probably always love him.

In the past five years the longing for him had

grown so fierce that she was certain her heart was being torn in two.

Gordon had always been there for her, and suddenly he wasn't. There was no one to turn to when Harrison was being incorrigible. No one to explain how much she missed her mother. No one to hold her or kiss her or tell her that their futures would be brighter than their pasts had been.

What if he didn't care? What if he'd fallen in love with someone else? She didn't think she could bear it. Or maybe she would learn to endure his betrayal until she grew to hate him. Hating Gordon might be easier than loving him for the rest of her life.

After a little while she realized that he might be remaining at the cottage tonight. She should go back to the Hall and see him first thing in the morning.

As she turned to leave, however, the door opened.

Jennifer could hear his voice but not the words. A moment later he ducked his head beneath the frame and closed the door behind him.

Chapter Nine

Jennifer waited until Gordon was nearly upon her before stepping out of the shadows. Without giving him a chance to speak, she stepped up to him and poked his chest with her finger.

"How dare you come back here and not explain yourself."

The moonlight revealed his frown. She didn't care. She'd gone too long without an explanation. The time had come for him to tell her why he'd left. She refused to go to bed confused, uncertain, and heartsick.

"At least you're speaking to me," he said.

She stepped back. "Why, Gordon? Why did you leave five years ago?"

"You know why I left, Jennifer."

"No, I don't. No one would tell me. Not Sean, not Harrison. Not even Mr. McBain. All I know is that you were there one moment and gone the next. Without a word."

"Why should I leave you a note, Jennifer, when you were just going to give it to McBain?"

"What do you mean?"

"You know all those notes I left for you, the ones you thought were so precious? McBain showed them to me, proof that you wanted me gone."

"I wanted you gone? How could you think such a thing?"

"What was I to think? You'd left for Edinburgh without a word to me."

"I gave Betty a letter for you."

They stared at each other.

Her world had been destroyed on that spring night when Gordon left. She could still remember what it had been like upon her return from Edinburgh to wait for him right here, only for him never to appear. She'd tapped on his window in the gardener's cottage, but he hadn't opened it and whispered, "Hush, Jen, my mother's in a mood."

Betty had always been in a mood. She was a disagreeable person, but she hadn't changed overmuch when Gordon disappeared. Jennifer had never seen her cry about her missing son.

"Your notes disappeared from my desk," she said. "Harrison said he destroyed them."

"Betty never gave me your letter."

It had been a concerted effort to separate them. McBain, Harrison, and Sean had all lied. They had simply rearranged her life and Gordon's without any thought to how they would feel.

"I didn't know," Jennifer said. "I didn't understand when I returned and you were gone. Mr. McBain said that you'd wanted to make your way in the world." She didn't tell him what else the advocate had said, that Gordon had probably become bored with his life here at Adaire Hall.

"Why didn't you answer any of my letters?" she asked.

"I only got two," he said. "Only that first one and the one about Sean."

"I wrote you every year on your birthday and Christmas." She'd probably been too open in those letters, pouring out her heart, hoping to remind Gordon of what they'd shared for years.

"You never once wrote back."

"I never got them, Jennifer. I'm sorry."

He offered her his hand. As if they'd been transported back in time, they began to follow the path to the loch, the same one they'd taken for years. They didn't speak as they topped the hill.

Moonlight made the surface of the loch appear like molten silver. Farther to the east was a dock and a rowboat they used from time to time. On this side of the loch, however, she'd had a bench built, placing it near a stand of pines overlooking the water.

She took the lead, guiding him to the bench. It was only about three years old, one of her favorite places to come, sit, and remember. Once there, she sat at one end, pulling her skirts to the side. He joined her and still they remained silent, both looking out at the water.

She clasped her hands tightly in front of her, the constriction in her throat nearly choking her. She felt on the verge of tears.

He finally began to speak. "I was only the gardener's boy, a young man who was occasionally punished for thoughts above his station. How many times did my parents say that to me? I lost count."

"So you left and stayed away five years. Five years we could have had together."

He glanced at her. "Where, Jennifer? Where could we have had those years? In London?" He shook his head. "You don't know what those early years were like. I wouldn't have subjected you to that."

"You don't understand, Gordon. I would have done anything, gone anywhere, just to be with you."

"And I wouldn't have asked that of you."

"So, your type of love has to be perfect? Everything pristine and without flaw? Nothing's that pretty, Gordon. I would have gone with you. Don't you understand?"

"How could I have taken you from here? You were an earl's daughter, an earl's sister."

"I was myself, first," she said, uncaring that the words were too loud, nearly echoing in the silence of the night.

"I was told that I wasn't good enough for you. Just the gardener's boy. Not suitable for Lady Jennifer of Adaire Hall."

She shook her head. "You were Gordon. My Gordon. You were eminently suitable for me."

"All three of them were at the door, Jennifer. All of them watching as I left. McBain, Harrison, and my own father."

She stood and moved away from the bench, the one place she'd come when she couldn't bear the loneliness anymore, when the hurt over his behavior made her cry.

"Jennifer." He stretched out his hand toward her.

"That didn't stop you from writing me. You could have written me. You could have said, 'Jennifer, I'm in London. I'm well. Don't worry about me.' Did you never think of me?"

"Every day."

"You couldn't have," she said, shaking her head. "You couldn't have and never let me know where you were or what you were doing. Five years, Gordon. Five very long years. I didn't even know if you'd found someone else. If you'd fallen in love or married."

"Of course I didn't. I was too busy."

She looked at him, wishing that the moon hadn't gone behind a cloud. His face was shrouded in darkness, and she couldn't read his expression.

"What about you, Jennifer? Why haven't you married? Do you have a sweetheart somewhere?"

No one but you.

"No, no sweetheart."

"In all this time you might have met someone. You might have married, Jennifer. Had your own home."

"I was given the chance. My godmother took me to see London and also insisted on my having a season in Edinburgh. I did everything any young woman would do."

"Except get married and have your own family."

"There was no one I liked well enough to marry," she said, giving him the truth. Besides, she'd held out hope that he would return. "Everyone was too interested in the fact that I was an earl's sister. Not to mention that more than one suitor seemed interested in the legacy from my

father. What would I be bringing to the marriage? Not simply myself, but how much of an income could they expect?"

She turned and faced the loch. "Besides, how could I be sure that I wouldn't be abandoned again?"

Perhaps that's why she felt so sorry for Lauren. She knew what it felt like to love someone who left you.

"Jennifer."

She moved back to stand in front of the bench.

"Forgive me. You're right. I should have written you and asked."

"You abandoned me, Gordon."

"Not because I wanted to."

He stood and walked toward her.

"Forgive me, Jennifer."

He opened his arms and she walked into them. They stood like that for a long time until she stepped back and looked up at him.

What could she say? What words would soften the cruelty of that moment five years ago? All she could do was put her hand on his arm, connecting with him. The man wasn't so far removed from the boy. Gordon's pride had always been fierce.

The answer to why he'd stayed away was in his voice. He'd been told that he wasn't good enough for her, and the shame of that had remained with him. Not only McBain had told him that, but his own father had evidently said something similar. The fact that Gordon had returned to Adaire Hall at all was an indication of the strength of his character.

She loved him. How could she not? Five years had not diminished those feelings. What did he feel for her? He hadn't said and she wouldn't ask.

The courage she felt earlier had dissipated, faded into nothing.

He could go back to London as easily as he came, without another word to her. He could leave and return to the life he'd created for himself and what would she do? Endure another abandonment?

She stepped back. She was determined not to let him see how emotional she felt. As a boy he'd always teased her when she cried.

"Jennifer."

She turned and left him, walking as fast as she could back to the Hall. She half expected him to follow her, but he didn't.

That made her cry even more.

SHAME WASHED OVER Gordon.

He'd allowed McBain to tell him a story, and he'd believed it. Even worse, he'd never written Jennifer to get her side. Why, because he didn't want to know? Anything was better than McBain's version of events.

He had a great many burned bridges to rebuild. The question was, could he?

As far as his grandiose plans about impressing her, she hadn't even asked about his empire.

What had he thought to do, coming back to Adaire Hall? He'd wanted to mend the rift with Sean. Perhaps he'd even wanted to impress him, too. Finally, he would prove that he was as good as one of the Adaires.

More than that, he'd wanted to find out, once and for all, if he'd been a fool to keep Jennifer in his mind and heart all these years. He certainly hadn't done anything to mend that rift tonight, had he?

He'd learned to change his destiny in London. He'd fought and scrapped for the future he'd wanted. The men he'd bested in London called him a rogue. As far as they were concerned, he was a Scottish ruffian who was determined to succeed, even if that meant he followed his own rules and not theirs.

He outbid, undercut, and paid higher wages, all of which made him an irritant to other businessmen. He also dared to employ women in high positions, something that wasn't normally done. According to one wag, he was undermining how business was done.

If he could do that, he could bridge the gulf that now existed between him and Jennifer.

He wasn't going to lose the woman he loved.

Chapter Ten

*J*ennifer spent a restless night, barely sleeping. She went over and over her conversation with Gordon, both understanding why he'd stayed away and annoyed and hurt that he had, and furious that he'd never written her.

She didn't have any words to ease what had happened to him. She felt anger on his behalf, but to whom did she express it now? Not Mr. McBain. He'd moved back to Edinburgh. Not Sean, because he was dying. Betty was beyond any human emotion.

Where did they go from here? After Sean died, was Gordon simply going to go back to London?

Did he feel anything for her?

She was up before dawn, dressed, and making her way to the loch. Here, on this bench where they'd sat last night, was the place she came when she wanted to think. No one from the house followed her here, as if they knew she needed to be alone.

She sat there for some time, watching as the rising sun bathed the horizon in light.

"You're right," Gordon said.

She turned her head to see Gordon standing there.

"You're right. I should have written you and asked how you felt."

"I can see how you'd believe McBain, especially if he had the notes I'd saved."

"You were the only good and decent thing about my life here all those years. I couldn't bear the idea of you verifying McBain's words and turning all of that into dust."

He came and sat beside her.

"I wouldn't have," she said. "You were the best part of my life, too." She smiled faintly. "When you left, it was like all the life went out of every day."

He placed his hand on hers.

"I couldn't stop what I felt for you," she said, "even when you didn't write me back. Perhaps I was foolish."

"If you were, then I'm grateful for it."

"Why stay away five years, Gordon McDonnell? Why make me long for you all these years? Unless it was to bedevil me. And confuse me. And make me cry entirely too much."

"I wanted to return a success. You're Lady Jennifer. I was the gardener's boy."

She looked up at him. "That sounds like Sean talking or McBain. Not you."

His quick smile surprised her. "You always did know how to insult me."

She reached over and slapped him on the cheek with one gentle palm.

"I worked hard to prove something to you. That you wouldn't have wasted your life with me."

She bent her head, wishing she didn't feel so close to tears.

"I never thought that," she said.

"I wasn't ready to give you the world, and now I am."

"I didn't want the world. I never wanted the world. I only wanted you. Didn't you know that?"

He looked at her. She'd never been studied in quite that way before. What did he see? Someone desperately in love and hurting with it? Until he'd left, she'd never realized that love could be a sword, or that it could wound so deeply.

"There's never been a time in my life that I didn't love you and want you," he said.

A spear of light traveled through her, illuminating all the dark and shadowed spots.

He reached out and wrapped his arms around her. She bent her head, resting her forehead against his chest as he tightened his arms around her. She sat with him in the dawn light, the seconds perfect in their simplicity. He was here, with her, and the world was suddenly friendly again.

The years slid away. The air was chilly just as it had been that last day she'd seen him, five years ago. It was like time had stopped.

Now he pulled back, just far enough to look into her face. She raised her head and returned his look. Let him see how much she loved him, how difficult these past five years had been. She didn't want to hide anything.

The truth—the inescapable truth—was that she loved him. There'd never been anyone else for her but Gordon McDonnell, and there would never be.

"What did you do in those five years, Gordon?"

She felt as though they were tiptoeing through the words, bridging the divide that five years had created. She wanted to know everything about those missing years, but didn't know if he would tell her.

"I built my empire," he said. "I have two music halls with another being planned, plus a gentlemen's club in Pall Mall."

She'd been to a music hall in Edinburgh and been startled at the size of it, not to mention all the entertainments offered there.

"Why music halls?"

He nodded. "I went to the Alhambra when I first went to London. I wanted to create the same experience, but with a Scottish theme. I've the Midlothian and the Dundee."

"And a gentlemen's club."

"The Mayfair Club."

"So the gardener's boy is now a successful businessman. I'm not surprised."

He turned and looked at her.

He'd made himself worthy, not understanding that she'd never felt that he was unworthy. He'd always been Gordon to her, her equal in all ways.

"Oh, Gordon, we've wasted so much time."

He bent his head and kissed her. Passion bloomed between them instantly, making her breathless, intensifying the need she'd always felt for him.

Kissing Gordon was like being given a treasure after years of searching for it.

GORDON PULLED BACK, finally, although he wanted to continue kissing Jennifer.

Her hand came up and pressed against his face, her fingers tracing the curve of his ear.

"I've missed you so much," she whispered. "I cried for weeks and months and years."

There'd been an emptiness inside him that had lingered for years. For the longest time he'd felt as if the world around him was gray, that he didn't belong to it or wasn't part of it. The revelation had come only months ago, when he'd questioned himself why he was so adamant about purchasing a certain house or why he wanted to acquire land in Scotland on which there was a romantic ruined castle.

Jennifer.

When he'd left the Hall, it had been with the taste of shame in his throat. His own father had repudiated him, as well as McBain and Harrison. He'd been called names that he didn't like to think about, even now. All because he'd loved Jennifer. All because he wasn't a peer or a relative of one.

He'd wanted to come back to the Hall triumphant and wealthy, landed and successful, showing that he'd multiplied the countess's bequest to him a hundred times over.

In the past five years he'd met a sizable number of women, from the landlady's daughter when he first arrived in London to the sister of one of the inveterate gamblers frequenting the Mayfair Club. Each one of them had, by their actions and words, indicated that they would not be insulted if he called upon them. He hadn't taken them up on their unspoken offer, holding out for a dream.

A vision, a wish, fervently felt all these years.

Jennifer.

She was beautiful, the promise of the girl maturing to fruition. Her eyes were a clear green with the capacity to see through to his soul. Her hair, thick and curly dark brown, had featured prominently in his daydreams. How many times had he imagined it on his pillow?

When she smiled, revealing white, even teeth, a dimple formed on the left side of her mouth. Her nose, chin, even the shape of her face was perfect.

He kissed her again, unable to stop himself. When she moaned, he pressed his palms against her face, tilted his head, and deepened the kiss. Kissing Jennifer was the only thing that mattered in the entire world at this moment.

"I love you," he softly said. "Never doubt that, Jennifer. I've always loved you."

"Oh, Gordon." That's all she had a chance to say before he kissed her again.

"We should go," he said reluctantly sometime later.

"Must we?"

He'd pulled her onto his lap and that's where she was now, her arms wrapped around his shoulders.

He didn't want her to move. Nor did he want to stand and walk back to the Hall. In fact, that was the last thing he wanted.

However, it was past dawn. The Hall was waking up. No doubt most of the servants were awake.

When he said as much, she answered with a sigh, "I have been exceedingly proper for five

years, Gordon. I now want to be exceedingly improper."

Gordon stood, bent, and kissed her, then held Jennifer in his arms. "I don't want to leave, either, but I have to go see Sean."

"And I have a list of tasks to be accomplished," she said, wrapping one arm around his waist.

He bent to kiss her again, then resolutely headed back. At the fork in the path they separated, him for the gardener's cottage, and Jennifer for the Hall, just like they'd done for years.

Chapter Eleven

Gordon would go and do his duty to his father, however much Sean wouldn't appreciate it. He might even take his carriage into the village and visit the church. He'd take some of the late blooming flowers and place them on Betty's grave. He could say a few words of regret. Not that he hadn't been the son she wanted, but that she hadn't seen anything good about her life.

The day was a cold one with a wind blowing through the strath and into his bones. When he was a child, autumn was his favorite season. Now it was spring. Autumn seemed to him to be a slow dying of the earth, the withering of leaves, the chill in the air until breathing was nearly unbearable, and the crunch of ice on the grass in the mornings. Spring was rebirth, the reemergence of life in the form of the foxes from the burrows and the plants from the soil. Spring was a promise that however much it seemed the earth had died in winter, it came back again and would continue to do so for eons.

A mist flirted with the ground, climbed to his knees, then subsided as he walked. In time the morning sun would burn off the mist, and

maybe they'd see a blue sky. Either that or the gloom of the dawn would continue.

On days like today he always occupied himself with as many tasks as he could. That was always the best way to prevent the weather from having an impact on his mood. Today, however, there were no tasks he could set himself, other than sitting vigil at Sean's bedside.

When he opened the door, Sally was already bustling around the cottage. A teapot was sitting in the middle of the square table beneath the window. She smiled brightly at him when she said good morning, then pointed to the teapot.

"Have yourself a cuppa," she said. "Sean's already had his first and is tucking into his breakfast."

"How is he feeling this morning?"

Her smile was brighter than the shy sun.

"I think your being here has made a world of difference, Gordon. He's better than I've seen him in weeks. In fact, he wants to get out of his bed again and come sit in the front room."

Instead of making himself a cup of tea, he entered Sean's room, standing at the doorway. Sean was propped up in bed with two pillows behind his back. In front of him was a tray of plates filled with food. Sally was right, Sean had a great deal of interest in his breakfast and it took a few moments for him to look up.

"I hear you're feeling better today. That's great news."

"Aye, that I am."

"And the pain?"

"Better, but not gone."

Gordon wasn't fool enough to think that the improvement would be permanent. Nor did he believe that it had much to do with his appearance. If anything, it was probably that Sean had been given a distraction to take his mind off his condition.

"We could play cards today, if you've a mind to."

Sean tilted his head a little and studied him. "It's cards that got you in trouble with McBain as I recall."

"I didn't take anyone's money, Da. They gambled and lost. I won."

"McBain always said you cheated. Is that true?"

"Never. Not once. I had no need to cheat. I was just better than they were."

He returned his father's look, then said, "Besides, that's not what got me into trouble with McBain. You and I both know it. It was Jennifer."

Sean nodded. "But you don't still have that foolishness in you."

He wasn't going to discuss Jennifer with his father.

"I'm going to return to the Hall and have my own breakfast. I'll come back afterward."

"Do as you wish."

He nodded, wondering what had soured Sean's disposition in a matter of moments. Or maybe it was his fault, seeing an earlier warmth that hadn't really been there.

ELLEN THANKED GOD all the way out of London that she was not Harrison Adaire's godmother. Thankfully, Mary had chosen another one of her

close friends for that dubious honor. Ellen spared a thought for the poor dear woman, now dead.

Mary had been an exemplary mother to both her children. Although the last part of her life had not been easy, Ellen couldn't be grateful for her friend's death. There were too many times that she'd said to herself, "*Oh, I must tell Mary this.*" Or: "*I must write Mary about this immediately.*" Only to be brought up short as she remembered that Mary was no longer alive.

They'd been sisters, of a sort. They'd embarked on their season together. Ellen's father had been wealthy enough to give his daughter a certain cachet. The same had been true for Mary's family. Neither one of them were at the height of the matrimonial market that year. They were neither heiresses nor raving beauties. Mary had gone on to fall in love with an earl and become a countess, while Ellen had a less positive outcome to her failed social season.

Her parents had become involved with the Church of Scotland to a fanatical degree in their later years. What had been normal they now considered sinful. Therefore, she was withdrawn from any further social events, her wardrobe changed for anything dark brown and dull looking, and her friends told her that she could no longer associate with them. Within a month or two she was a pariah to everyone. Of course, she'd rebelled, but only secretly.

Mary had stood firm against her parents. By that time, she was a countess with some influence. She'd possessed the type of loyalty that's spoken about in war dispatches. For that reason,

Ellen couldn't turn her back on Harrison now, no matter how irritating, annoying, and bothersome the man was being.

Ellen had sent Abigail directly home from London because her maid never enjoyed the visits to Adaire Hall. It was simply easier to send her back to Edinburgh by train to pout by herself.

As for Harrison, she recognized a fellow traveler on the road to self-destruction. She'd traveled that thoroughfare herself, resulting in disastrous consequences. Mary had saved her there, too.

For most of the journey Harrison had sat slumped in the corner of the carriage, his hat pulled low over his face. For all she knew he was leveling disgusted looks in her direction. He had already told her exactly what he felt.

"I don't know what you did, Ellen, but I would appreciate it if you would refrain from interfering in my life."

"I wouldn't have to, if you remembered certain salient facts about that life, Harrison. Namely, that you're a husband and soon to be a father. Your presence in that role is required."

"Why? I can't birth the babe."

She closed her eyes and prayed for patience, deciding then and there that there was no point trying to engage Harrison in any semblance of adult conversation. Nor in talking to him until he was sober. The man was disagreeable, surly, and was behaving like a twelve-year-old.

Ellen had stayed at the Hall for weeks in order to help Mary when Harrison was only two weeks old. In that terrible time, they hadn't even known if she would survive. Alex was distracted

by his wife's fight for life, leaving Harrison in the care of a wet nurse.

She hadn't known anything about infants at the time. All Ellen had done was cuddle the baby after he'd been fed and consulted the doctor who came nearly every day to care for Mary.

She vividly remembered the day that Mary was finally well enough to sit up in her bed. Ellen had taken her child to her, sitting on the edge of the bed and holding Harrison close so that Mary could touch him. The burns on her friend's face and arms had been terrible, stripping Ellen of her composure. She'd sat there with Harrison in her arms, tears flowing down her face, grateful that Mary couldn't see her. Alex had had to step out of the room. She'd watched him leave, thinking that women were stronger, sometimes, than men.

Mary had survived, although she never regained most of her sight. The burns had faded somewhat over the years, making her arms and face look almost like dough when it was being kneaded.

Ellen had never told Harrison that she'd cared for him when he was only a few weeks old. Nor had she ever confided in him that his mother was, to her, the bravest and most inspirational person she'd ever known.

Now she glanced at him and wondered why he'd become the antithesis of everything Mary had been. Was it his father's heritage? Alexander Adaire had always appeared to be a strong man. Perhaps too strong in many instances, but he was dependable, honorable, and decent, to both his family and those who relied on him. When

he died after being thrown from a horse, Harrison was only five. Hardly old enough to assume the mantle of responsibility becoming the Earl of Burfield had thrust on him.

He was not up to the task even now.

Harrison hadn't taken much from either of his parents. He was a dilettante, on his way to becoming a sot, a gambler, an adulterer, and a wastrel, for all that he was the sixth Earl of Burfield. She didn't respect him one jot. Nor did she like him, but he was still Mary's son, and for that reason she would ensure that he did his duty. At least she would get him home so that he would be there when his child was born.

Chapter Twelve

A little before noon, Jennifer headed for the cottage.

She wished the day didn't hint at sorrow. Or winter. Too many wintry days were like this one, gray and dull without a hint of the sun. She wanted the world to explode into color, the yellows, reds, and oranges of a typical Highland dawn. She wanted to see a blue sky, clear of clouds or hints of rain. Most of all she wanted to hear the birds, now strangely silent as if they waited for something precipitous to happen.

When she got to Sean's home, she could see Gordon through the window, talking to a smiling Sally. Her heart eased a little. Sally wouldn't be smiling if Sean was worse or had spent a bad night.

Her palms were damp even though the morning was cold. She tucked her hands underneath her arms for a moment, grateful that she'd worn her cloak.

When the cottage door opened, she stepped forward, chastising herself for her shyness. As a girl she'd been braver. She'd pushed her boundaries just as Gordon had shoved against his. They'd been rebels together, but never with each

other. They'd constructed a bubble around the two of them, a protective shield that no one could penetrate.

She'd missed him those five years, so desperately that the ache of it lingered even now.

He looked up, his attention no longer on the path.

"Jennifer?"

She smiled. "Gordon."

"Did you come in search of me?"

"I did."

He was wearing a white shirt and dark trousers beneath his coat. Plain clothing, but he'd never looked as handsome.

She didn't move as he came even closer. Instead, she reached out, her fingers brushing the sleeve of his shirt. She couldn't help smiling at him. The world was suddenly a beautiful place. Who cared about the weather?

She wanted to throw herself into his arms and hug him as she had so many times. Once he would have embraced her, then they would have kissed. After this morning, however, she knew that once she started kissing him, she wouldn't want to stop.

He didn't move. Nor did she. Finally, she stepped back, sending him a tremulous smile.

"Are you ready for lunch?"

"I am," he said. "Let me get my coat." A moment later he held out his arm for her and she took it. Together, they headed back to the Hall.

JENNIFER PULLED HIM into the kitchen to introduce him to the new cook. Then she gave her the

ingredients for a treat they'd devised as children, a cross between tablet and shortbread.

"Could you make that for us, Doris?"

"Aye, I could, Miss Jennifer. Is it something you'll be wanting for today?"

"Most definitely for today," Jennifer said. "Isn't it the most marvelous, glorious day, Doris?"

The cook smiled at them. It seemed to him that everyone was smiling in their direction. He took it as a sign that Fate itself recognized that a terrible wrong had been righted.

They ate their lunch together, the meal punctuated by laughter.

Jennifer sat next to him, her chin propped on her hand, her breakfast forgotten as he told her about his rise in London. She hadn't looked away since he began his story.

"I didn't want to waste your mother's bequest," he said. "It had to count for something, so I considered it my principal. I always repaid it so that it didn't get smaller."

She reached over and grabbed his hand as if she wanted to ease his circumstances all these years later.

He told her his plans for the future on land he'd already purchased. His newest music hall, currently being designed by an architect, would rival the Alhambra. He employed over three hundred people. The responsibility to ensure their salaries continued uninterrupted was a constant pressure, yet he seemed to thrive on it.

Jennifer stood and walked to the sideboard. She took a plate from the stack, then replaced it,

picked up a cup then put it back. He watched her, wondering if he'd said something to disturb her.

"Look what you've accomplished in only five years, Gordon. No one knowing you would be amazed. My mother certainly wouldn't be. She'd say something like, 'I always expected it of Gordon.'"

"Is that a bad thing?" he asked, genuinely confused.

"Of course not, but in comparison I've done absolutely nothing. You've built an empire while my life has remained the same. No, if anything it's gotten smaller. I think my life has been incredibly dull compared to yours."

"How can you say that?"

"Because I did nothing," she said. "Other than a few trips to Edinburgh I haven't ventured far from Adaire Hall. I've been its chatelaine when there was no one else, and since Lauren has been indisposed. I have no grand adventures to recall. Nothing about which I'm proud. At the very least I should have something to be ashamed about."

"How can you say that? You've kept the Hall running when Harrison was off playing in London for most of the year. I'd be willing to wager that you're the single most important person at Adaire Hall."

"How did you know about Harrison staying away so often?"

He wasn't about to start lying to her now. "Harrison frequents the Mayfair Club. Not to mention that he has rooms there. He's known to be voluble when he drinks."

"Does he talk about Adaire Hall with you?"

He shook his head. "I only visit the club on Monday mornings. To go over the accounts. But I hear about him from my staff."

There was another part of that he needed to tell her.

"I've been careful not to let Harrison know who owns the Mayfair, Jennifer. Nor has he figured it out."

"My brother is foolish, but he isn't stupid, Gordon."

Harrison cared more about himself than anyone else. The man's single-minded pursuit of pleasure blinded him to most truths.

"Let's just say that Harrison doesn't care who owns the Mayfair Club. All he cares about is whiskey, cards, and women, not necessarily in that order."

She returned to the table and sat.

They spent the rest of the day together. For the first time in years Gordon had no obligations, no duties, no responsibilities other than assisting Jennifer. Since Sean was feeling better, he didn't feel any guilt for leaving his father alone for a time. Besides, the longer they were together, the more they clashed. That hadn't changed in five years.

Jennifer was rarely left alone. Everyone came to her for answers, from Robbie Stewart in the stable inquiring about the winter feed to a milkmaid who reported a problem with one of the cows. There was the secondary storeroom to unlock for Mrs. Thompson and the instructions to be given to the upper maids about removing some excess furniture and storing it in the attic.

The main cistern had to be inspected because there was ceiling damage in one of the third-floor rooms and suspicion that the lead cistern had sprung a leak.

The only place she seemed to be without someone tugging on her had been at the loch. When he mentioned that to her, she got a curious look on her face.

"I think it's probably because whenever anyone found me there, I was crying. So, I think the word went out not to bother me if I'd gone there."

He didn't ask the reason for her tears, because he was all too afraid he was the cause. How could he ever make those years up to her? Perhaps simply by refusing to leave her again.

In the afternoon she had to inspect the linens.

"We have so many guest rooms. Granted, they aren't used much now, but they once were."

"And you have to do this why?"

"Because it's good stewardship. Just like moving the sheep from one glen to another. You don't use the same set of sheets all the time, for fear of wearing them out. Some of them were purchased from France and were very expensive."

"Do you have to do it? Why can't Mrs. Thompson? Isn't that her responsibility?"

"Yes," she said, smiling at him. "But Mrs. Thompson can't make decisions about what should be retired or what should be mended. In actuality, it isn't my task at all, but Lauren's. Nor is it something we do often, only once a year. But it's scheduled for today, and if I don't do it today, then that means I will have to wait until tomorrow, which means that I might not finish

the inspection of the larder. We could be low on foodstuffs of a certain type. That wouldn't please Doris."

He leaned up against the wall, folded his arms, and studied her. He'd never before considered that running a house, especially one the size of Adaire Hall, could be a full-time occupation.

"Do you have a chart?" he asked. "One that tells you what you need to do at a certain time?"

"I do," she said, nodding. "It's my annual journal."

He kept a calendar himself, one for each of his establishments. There were things that he needed to do regarding maintenance and upkeep of the properties. It was the only way he could oversee everything.

"Did you take on all this when Lauren couldn't?"

She shook her head. "No, earlier than that. After you left."

The words hung in the air.

"Both our lives changed, then," he said.

She nodded. "When I wasn't in Edinburgh, being paraded through the marriage mart. My godmother married late, but she was still determined to find me a husband."

"No likely candidates?" he asked, smiling.

She shook her head. "Besides, they weren't you."

"For which I'm eternally grateful."

She didn't say anything, merely tilted her head slightly.

"Did you expect me to be an idiot and say that I'm sorry you couldn't find a husband? I'm not that much of a hypocrite."

"Are you being a dog in the manger, Gordon

McDonnell? You didn't want me yourself, but you didn't want anyone else to have me—is that it?"

"Who said I didn't want you, Jennifer Adaire?"

He smiled at her and stood aside so that she could enter the linen room. She didn't get a chance to say anything further because Mrs. Thompson and one of the maids were standing there waiting for her.

IT WAS TRULY unfair. He couldn't say something to her like that when she couldn't respond. Jennifer frowned at him, but that didn't stop Gordon from smiling.

Who said I didn't want you?

"Miss Jennifer?"

She could feel her cheeks warming as she looked at the housekeeper.

"Yes, Mrs. Thompson," she said briskly. "Shall we get on?"

The annual inspection of the linens wasn't a complicated task, but it was time-consuming. They had to open each folded sheet and inspect its condition. If it needed mending, it would go in one pile to be given to the seamstress and her assistants. If a sheet was deemed too damaged it went into another stack. They were either sent to be used in the servants' quarters or torn into rags.

Gordon didn't stay with her, but left to write a letter to one of his managers and then to check on his driver. He'd always been solicitous of other people and evidently that hadn't changed over the years.

Mrs. Thompson asked her about two sets of French linens, one of which predated her grand-

mother. They had faded to an ecru color, were worn to the point that they were almost thread-bare in certain places, but they were festooned with a four-inch band of beautifully crafted lace at the top.

"Set those aside for my chamber, Mrs. Thompson. It's a shame to get rid of them just yet."

The rest of the inventory took nearly two hours. At the end of it she was heartily tired of unfolding and folding sheets, but they wouldn't need to do this task again until next year.

By that time Gordon had joined her again. He took her hand and walked with her to the main staircase. "What do you have to do now? Inspect the dairy? Oversee the delivery of a litter of piglets? Shoe a horse?"

She laughed. "Not quite all of that."

Gordon pulled her into the alcove beneath the bend of the stairs and kissed her.

She wrapped her arms around his neck, stood on tiptoe, and gave in to the feeling. Passion flowed through her, caressing her like velvet, dancing a pattern on her skin.

When he murmured her name against her lips, she gripped him even tighter.

Finally, he pulled back, leaving her standing there, her breath ragged, hands still clasped around his neck.

"I need to go see Sean," he said.

She nodded, grateful that she didn't need to talk right at the moment. She didn't think she could.

A moment later she dropped her arms. "I need to go see Lauren. I'll see you at dinner."

When she went to check on Lauren, she found her sister-in-law in some discomfort.

"I don't know why, Jennifer, but I'm not feeling well."

"That's nature's way of announcing that your baby will be born soon," Mrs. Farmer said.

"I'll send a tray up for you," Jennifer said.

Lauren shook her head. "I don't think I could eat. I haven't an appetite and I feel odd, Jennifer."

"Would you like me to stay with you?"

She wanted to be with Gordon, but Lauren needed her right now.

"Could you?" Lauren stretched out her hand. Jennifer covered it with her own.

"Of course I can."

She would send word to Gordon. That would mean that he would eat alone. Or perhaps he would prefer a tray in his room as well. Or, he might still be with Sean.

She left to manage dinner. She returned a few minutes later to find Mrs. Farmer sitting in the corner, occupied with a book. When Jennifer offered to sit with Lauren while she went to eat her own meal, the midwife considered the matter for a moment before nodding.

"I'll be gone only a short while, Lady Jennifer. I believe that the birth of the countess's child is imminent."

Poor Lauren looked terrified.

Jennifer stayed with her sister-in-law long enough for Mrs. Farmer to eat her dinner. Mrs. Thompson sent two trays up to the suite, one for Lauren and one for Jennifer. Unlike Lauren, she had an appetite.

She offered to read a book Lauren had begun, thinking that it might take her sister-in-law's mind from the impending birth. She kept reading for two hours until Lauren fell asleep.

Jennifer finally tiptoed out of the room, waving to Mrs. Farmer. The midwife barely returned a nod.

Chapter Thirteen

Jennifer entered her suite and lit one of the lamps in her sitting room. She walked to the windows and stood there a moment. Here, the view overlooked where the north wing had once been, the expanse of open area and the rolling hills. Tonight, she barely saw it as she stood there.

For several moments she thought about what she was considering. Her mother wouldn't approve. Neither would Ellen. The world would label her as some kind of fallen woman, but wasn't she considered a spinster now? Someone who was unloved and unwanted? What did it matter what other people thought?

She wanted and needed to be with Gordon more than decorum or morality or decency or any word that someone might use to condemn her.

She bathed, put on perfume, then donned her loveliest nightgown and peignoir, a gift from Ellen on her last birthday. The pale yellow silk floated like a cloud over her body, almost feeling like Gordon's fingers on her skin.

Her body hummed and her skin felt hot. Even the delicate silk felt like too much covering.

After donning a cotton wrapper and her slippers, she left her rooms. Adaire Hall seemed

even larger as she descended one staircase and ascended another to get to the main wing.

Jennifer was almost at Gordon's room when a footman stepped out of the shadows and bowed to her. She stifled a yelp and grabbed the neck of her wrapper with one hand.

"Good evening, Lady Jennifer."

After what had happened to the north wing, her father had put precautions into place. Consequently, a half dozen footmen were stationed throughout Adaire Hall, their primary duty to ensure that fire wasn't an ever-present danger.

Evidently, this footman had decided to lurk around the guest chambers.

"Is there anything I can do for you, Lady Jennifer?"

For a fleeting second she debated what she would say, then reasoned that she didn't need to offer him any excuses for being here past midnight. In the next moment she changed her mind, knowing that gossip flowed through Adaire Hall like whiskey at a clan gathering.

She was trying, desperately, to come up with some excuse when one of the double doors to the earl's suite opened to reveal Lauren.

"Jennifer? Is everything all right?"

"Everything is fine. Are you feeling better?" Jennifer asked, walking toward her sister-in-law.

"I am. Mrs. Farmer says that what I felt was false labor. It's very common, evidently."

For a moment she wondered if Lauren would question her presence in the corridor. Instead, Lauren looked beyond her to where the footman stood, then glanced at the end of the hall where

the Blue Suite was located. There was no doubt in her mind that her sister-in-law knew exactly where she'd been headed. The footman probably knew as well.

She was torn between disappointment, irritation, and acute embarrassment. It was one thing to decide to be a fallen woman without an audience. Quite another to have to come up with an explanation for her presence in the hallway wearing her bedclothes.

When Lauren turned and walked back through the open door, Jennifer followed her.

"Don't worry, Mrs. Farmer isn't here," Lauren said, passing through the sitting room and heading for her bed. "She's gone to bed." She climbed the three steps up to the mattress, then sat heavily on the edge, patting the spot next to her.

"It's not that I'm afraid of her exactly," she continued. "It's just that she's very domineering."

"I'm quite in awe of her myself," Jennifer said as she went to sit next to her sister-in-law. "She has a presence about her."

Lauren glanced at her, then away. "Nothing would dare go wrong with Mrs. Farmer around."

"Nothing's going to go wrong. You will have a healthy, happy baby. I can't wait to become an aunt."

"You should be a mother yourself, Jennifer. I don't know of anyone who would be a better mother."

She'd heard that comment before, but it had always been coupled with a recommendation for a husband. Lauren knew a great many people since her father was so wealthy. She was all for

marrying Jennifer off and wasn't the least bit shy about her intentions.

"Tell me about Gordon."

"Gordon?"

"Yes, Gordon. The exceedingly handsome man whose room you were going to. The same man who's made you starry-eyed."

Jennifer didn't know whether to faint, claim a sudden unbearable sickness, or pretend a blinding headache. None of those maladies, however, would be sufficient to keep Lauren from satisfying her curiosity.

"There isn't much to tell," Jennifer said. "He used to live here. We knew each other as children."

"No, Jennifer. You forget. We're friends. I've lived at Adaire Hall for a year now. During that time I've gotten to know you. I've always wondered why a woman as lovely and personable as you was unmarried. Is Gordon the answer?"

Jennifer slid off the bed and walked to one of the bedroom windows, parting the heavy velvet curtains. This room was almost oppressive in the richness of its furnishings. Everything was crimson. The curtains were crimson. The bedspread, even the skirt on the vanity was the same bloodred color.

Any other shade would have made the large room with its inlaid panels and ornate ceiling seem more welcoming.

To her surprise, however, Lauren loved the color, claiming that it was her favorite. She'd also been under the impression that Harrison liked it. To the best of Jennifer's knowledge Harrison

didn't care what color Lauren had redecorated their suite, as long as he didn't have to spend much time in it.

"Yes. Gordon's the reason."

"You love him."

She glanced at Lauren. Her sister-in-law wasn't smiling any longer. Instead, there was an expression on her face that was oddly poignant, as if she understood in that moment. Maybe she did. Maybe Lauren realized that Harrison didn't feel the same about her, that she was simply a wife, a life change that needed to happen.

Every young man married, especially a titled one. He had an obligation to bring an heir into the world and his wife was with child. After that requirement was satisfied, there would be no place for Lauren in his life.

For the first time she suspected that her sister-in-law recognized the truth only too well.

Lauren looked down at her feet, now bare of slippers. "Does he love you? I mean, really love you, not simply tell you that he does? If he has, how do you know? How does anyone know?"

"Yes." Jennifer walked back to the bed, stepped up, and sat on the edge of the mattress again. "I think you have to believe, don't you? I don't know what it's like *not* to love Gordon. I've loved him ever since I was a child."

For a moment Lauren didn't say anything. Jennifer didn't know if she should interject a comment or say something calming about Harrison. What could she say about her brother that would explain his behavior? He'd treated Lauren abominably.

"Sometimes, you can fool yourself," Lauren finally said. "It doesn't matter what your mind says. Your heart will do as it wishes."

They had never discussed Harrison before, even in such opaque terms.

"Sometimes," Lauren continued. "Most of the time, in fact. My heart refuses to listen to anything else other than how it feels."

Implicit in that comment was a request, one that Jennifer heard and understood. *Please don't tell me the truth.* Don't tell her that Harrison was probably not capable of caring for anyone other than himself.

The truth would not be Lauren's friend in this instance.

"Gordon is a very personable man. I found him exceedingly charming."

Jennifer smiled. "That is not a word I have ever heard anyone use about Gordon. Except for my mother. She found him charming, too."

"But he wasn't the same toward you?"

Jennifer stared at the opposite wall. "He was just himself. He was angry sometimes. And funny. He could do the best impressions of people, including our tutor. He had a wonderful sense of humor. He was also passionate about a great many things. I don't find it odd that he's made a success of himself. I always knew he would."

"Tutor?"

"My mother insisted that he be educated along with Harrison and me. Harrison was sent away to school, but he didn't do well there. His guardian decided that a tutor would be good enough

for him. My mother was the one who insisted on me being educated as well."

"My father would have approved, but then he's an egalitarian. How did you feel about it?"

Jennifer smiled again. "I was thrilled, but then I had been Gordon's friend for a long time by that point. We studied together often. He was always determined to do better on a test than I did. Or Harrison."

Harrison fussed. He complained. He insulted Gordon at every opportunity. He made jokes about his education being wasted on a gardener's boy. She doubted that Mr. McBain was in favor of the arrangement, either, but he deferred to Jennifer's mother. After all, she was still the Countess of Burfield, a woman beloved and considered a heroine by most people.

"Both Gordon and Harrison were determined to show the other one up. At least until Harrison went away to school again. This time he stayed."

"What happened then?"

"Plans were made for me to have a season, even though I didn't want one."

She'd known exactly what she wanted in life, to be Gordon's wife. To live with him where they'd have the freedom to love each other.

One day she'd said as much to her mother. She couldn't remember the reason for the comment, only that Mary Adaire hadn't said anything for some time.

When she'd finally spoken, Jennifer wasn't surprised by what she said.

"My dear, darling girl, you might change your mind. You're young and that happens."

"Did you? Did you change your mind about Father?"

Her mother's lips had turned up on one corner, the only kind of smile Mary could express with the terrible burns on her face.

"No, I didn't change my mind."

That had been that. They'd never spoken of Gordon after that day. The strangest thing was that her mother had never told her that he wasn't good enough for her, or that she was foolish for loving the gardener's boy. Instead, when she spoke of Gordon it was with admiration for his achievements in the schoolroom.

She had a feeling that her mother would have been proud of Gordon's other accomplishments as well.

"But he left you," Lauren said.

"Yes, he left me, but he returned."

Nor was she going to let him leave her again.

"It's time for bed," she said. "Sweet dreams, Lauren."

Lauren reached out and placed her hand against Jennifer's cheek. "Don't be foolish, Jennifer."

Jennifer only nodded. There wasn't much she could say. If she went to Gordon's room now, everyone would know about it in the morning.

Reluctantly, she left the earl's suite, nodded to the footman, then headed back to her rooms.

Chapter Fourteen

*J*ennifer had taken care with her appearance, wearing a dark red dress the same color as a thread in the Adaire tartan. She hadn't put up her hair, but instead kept it down like she'd worn it all those years ago.

Before she left to find Gordon, Jennifer knocked on Lauren's door.

Lauren was in bed, and the minute Jennifer entered the room, her sister-in-law held out her hand.

"It's time, Jennifer. This time it really is."

Mrs. Farmer was bustling about, telling the maid where to put the stack of linens and preparing to help Lauren out of bed.

When Jennifer questioned the midwife, Mrs. Farmer turned an irritated look on her.

"This is the ancestral bed, Lady Jennifer. Would you have us ruin the mattress with blood?"

Jennifer looked at Lauren, who returned her glance with wide eyes.

"It's important that the countess be moved to a chair until we can ready her bed."

She nodded and helped Lauren to a chair not far away.

"The woman terrifies me, Jennifer," she whispered. "She always has. I do wish my father hadn't hired her."

It was a bit late to be concerned with Mr. Campbell's arrangements.

"What if she's sent word to him?"

"I thought he was still in America," Jennifer said.

Lauren shook her head. "He told me that he'd be here, and whenever my father says he'll be somewhere, he's there. He never breaks his word. Never."

The two women looked at each other.

It wouldn't look good if Lauren's father arrived at Adaire Hall before her husband. Jennifer could just imagine his reaction if Harrison wasn't here.

However, the man had been more than willing to marry his daughter to an earl. Or perhaps she'd misjudged Mr. Campbell's desire for a title. Or, since Lauren hadn't made any secret of the fact that she adored Harrison, maybe her father had consented to the match simply to make his daughter happy.

Mrs. Farmer and the maid were stripping the bed down to the mattress. Once that was done, several sheets were folded in half lengthwise and stretched across the width of the mattress before being tucked in on the sides. The middle part of the bed was covered in lengths of toweling before an older set of sheets was placed over everything.

Another troubling detail was that Mrs. Farmer had a length of sheet tied to each of the two upper bedposts. She didn't say what they were for,

but Jennifer had an idea that Lauren would be using them before her labor was over.

"We need a comfortable nightgown for the countess. Do you have something older yet still serviceable?"

Jennifer doubted it, since her sister-in-law had arrived last year with seven trunks of new clothes, most of them made for her in Paris.

"I do," she said, leaving the room to retrieve the garments.

Once in her own suite, she went to the bottom drawer of her dresser and took out two cotton nightgowns, both of them worn and nearly threadbare. Before returning to Lauren's room, she took a moment to compose herself.

Women died in childbirth. One of their closest neighbors had died two years ago giving birth to a little boy. He, too, had perished. A friend she'd made in Edinburgh had also died of childbirth fever a few months ago.

Yet more women survived. She had to remember that. Lauren was young, healthy, and Mrs. Farmer was reputed to be an excellent midwife.

She said a quick prayer for Lauren as she rushed back to the earl's suite.

Once Lauren was changed Mrs. Farmer escorted her back to the bed, making sure she was tucked up and comfortable with two pillows behind her.

Where was Harrison? He'd evidently ignored her letter just as he'd ignored his wife. Was he going to ignore his child as well?

Perhaps that would be for the best. When he

was at Adaire Hall, Harrison was difficult, critical, complaining, and generally a misery to be around. Yet Lauren loved him and missed him.

Even as isolated as they were in the Highlands, gossip still filtered to the Hall in the form of London newspapers. Harrison, as the Earl of Burfield, was occasionally mentioned, and not in a way that would please a wife.

"He seems to like London a great deal better than Scotland," Lauren had said, just in the past week.

"He does at that," Jennifer said.

"It's because there aren't as many entertainments here as there are in London. Harrison's often bored. His mind is such that it craves stimulation."

No, it was because there weren't any gambling establishments locally like there were in London. Harrison was a gambler. He'd always been one for wagering on anything. The worst of it, however, had started after he'd been sent away to school. Ever since, he'd done everything in his power to empty the Adaire coffers and, to her dismay, might be succeeding.

She didn't say that to Lauren, however. What good would it do to point out some difficult facts to the woman? There was nothing Lauren could do about the situation that she hadn't already tried. Charm hadn't worked. Understanding certainly hadn't.

Not for the first time, she wished her brother was a different kind of man, someone who wasn't as involved with his own pursuits. Someone who

cared about those around him. Yet wishing for
him to be different was silly. He wasn't going to
change.

"Now, Lady Jennifer, while I appreciate your assistance, this is not the place for a single woman."

"I beg your pardon?"

"It's time for you to leave."

Jennifer didn't understand why Mrs. Farmer
was being so restrictive. She'd assisted in the
birth of the scullery maid's child, a secret hidden
until the moment the girl went into labor. There
hadn't been time to summon anyone else, and
Jennifer had been the only one available to help.

Everyone had been ridiculous about that event.
They didn't seem to care that the poor girl had
been so terrified that she would be struck off for
being pregnant that she'd hidden her condition.
No, what everyone paid attention to was the fact
that Jennifer was unmarried and therefore too
virginal to have witnessed the event.

What nonsense.

How could she possibly leave now with Lauren looking at her with such pleading eyes?

"Mrs. Farmer, I will concede that you have a
great deal more experience than I, but Lauren is
not just my sister-in-law. She's my friend. Surely
it isn't necessary for me to leave right this moment?"

Just when she was certain that Mrs. Farmer
was going to have her bodily removed, Lauren
looked up at the midwife. "Please, Mrs. Farmer.
May I stay just for little while."

"Very well, Your Ladyship." She didn't look
happy about the concession, however.

Right at the moment, Jennifer didn't care about the midwife's feelings.

"Now I'm hungry. Isn't that awful?" Lauren whispered. "Who's hungry when they're having a child?"

When Jennifer asked Mrs. Farmer if Lauren could have something to eat, the midwife just frowned at her.

Jennifer would have left to fetch Lauren some mints she'd purchased in Edinburgh, except for one thing. She wasn't sure Mrs. Farmer would let her back into the room.

"Could you read some of the book you were reading before?"

Jennifer nodded and picked up the book. She noticed, as she read, that Mrs. Farmer seemed to listen along as well. Anything to keep her from mentioning how long the labor was going to be.

For most of the morning, nothing further happened. Then Lauren's face suddenly contorted. She gripped the sheets with both hands, her eyes wild.

Jennifer turned to find the midwife. "Mrs. Farmer!"

The woman looked over at the bed. "It's only the birthing process, Lady Jennifer. She'll have plenty of those pains before the bairn is born."

Yet the contraction seemed to last forever. When it was over, Lauren sagged against the pillows, her face damp with perspiration.

More women lived than died during childbirth. She had to keep that thought in her mind. It became even more difficult during the next hour as Lauren experienced three more labor

pains. During the last one she cried out, and all Mrs. Farmer did was bathe her forehead with a damp cloth.

"Isn't there something you can do?" Jennifer asked.

"This is why I don't like to have young misses in my birthing rooms," the midwife replied. "You don't understand the pain that a woman has to go through in order to bear children. It's something that God decreed. Would you have the countess be spared?"

"Yes," Jennifer said. "Queen Victoria had the use of chloroform. Why shouldn't Lauren?"

The midwife looked decidedly disapproving now.

"I think it's time you left."

"On the contrary, I'd like to stay."

"As I told you earlier, Lady Jennifer, Her Ladyship will probably be in labor for quite some time."

"Is there anything she needs, Mrs. Farmer? Or anything I can get you?"

"Rest and patience. The good Lord will bring this child into the world on His timetable, Lady Jennifer. Not ours. In the meantime, your presence here is scandalous. You're a single woman."

"It's all right, Jennifer. Truly," Lauren said. She looked exhausted and it had only been an hour. Her hairline was damp. Her face was pale except for spots of color on the top of her cheeks. Even her lips looked a little bluish.

She made a gesture with her finger and Jennifer bent close.

"Don't make the dragon mad," Lauren whispered. "She'll be even more unbearable."

"Are you very sure?" Jennifer asked, holding her sister-in-law's hand.

"I am. You can go and welcome my father, who I'm sure is going to be here any minute."

"And Harrison."

They smiled at each other, and Jennifer hoped she wasn't lying.

Where was her brother?

Chapter Fifteen

Since she didn't want to disturb Gordon when he was with Sean and it was too early for lunch, Jennifer left the Hall, her destination the bench beside the loch.

Nothing here ever changed. The years passed in tranquility; the beauty of the Scottish scenery remained as awe-inspiring as it had for centuries. The loch didn't dry up. The hills didn't crumble. Nothing ever changed.

She'd come to this spot when it was evident her mother wasn't going to recover from the pneumonia that was sapping her strength. She'd come here after she'd made all the funeral arrangements, since Harrison didn't seem to want to accept any of his responsibilities. It was here she'd come when he brought his carousing friends home, some of whom had wandering hands. She'd had to slap a young man because he'd made an advance toward her. Her brother hadn't said a word to him.

They were only a year apart, and when they were small, they'd played together and been friends. As they grew, however, they'd grown apart as well. Harrison was only too cognizant that he was the sixth Earl of Burfield. All other

lesser mortals, even a sister, were beneath his notice.

She didn't know if Mr. McBain had anything to do with Harrison's arrogance or if he'd gained an inflated opinion of himself away at university. She suspected it was a combination of the two.

Once his education was finished, Harrison spent more time in Edinburgh and London. Nor did that change after their mother's death. He'd attained his majority, so there was no further need for a guardian. All restrictions on the Adaire fortune were released as well. Harrison seemed to think that his only task was to live a life of hedonism.

She understood, in a sense. Adaire Hall was isolated, one of the jewels of the Highlands, but not a place that a young man might wish to spend all his time. Yet even after Harrison returned with news that he was to be married his behavior hadn't changed. After the wedding he'd simply deposited Lauren here and gone off to live the life he'd established in London.

Now his wife needed him and he was nowhere to be found.

"Are you angry about something?"

She turned to see Gordon standing there, one hand on the back of the bench.

"Do I look angry?"

He came around the bench and sat. "As a matter of fact, you do. You're glaring at the loch."

"I am angry," she confessed. "About Harrison."

He didn't say anything, which she appreciated. He never tried to talk her out of feeling what she was feeling or offering her a rational explanation

when she was feeling emotional. She'd always been able to be herself with him.

"Lauren needs him and he isn't here."

He still didn't say anything.

She glanced at him with a smile. "You've learned tact in the past five years, Gordon. The young man I knew would have launched into a speech about how selfish Harrison had always been."

He shrugged. "Why say something twice when it's already been said?"

She shook her head, her smile disappearing. "At least my mother isn't here to see his behavior. It would have disappointed her greatly."

He squeezed her hand. "Perhaps he's been delayed for some reason. His carriage could've lost a wheel. He could have missed the train."

"He could have been set upon by pirates. Or robbers. Perhaps his trunks were set afire and he had no clothes."

They smiled at each other.

"Perhaps he'll shock us both," he said, taking her hand and turning it over to inspect the palm.

What did he see? It was the hand of a woman who often forgot to use the lemon-scented cream on her vanity.

"The last time I heard from him he was annoyed, but then he often is with me. I did something to anger him."

"What did you do?"

"I told him to be a better husband. Evidently, I'm not to ever criticize Harrison."

"Or spend too much time with me. That always set him off."

He curled her fingers toward the palm and then covered them with his hand.

"You were my best friend, Gordon. I was just thinking how many times I came here in the past five years and wished I had you to talk to." She stole a glance at him. "I have so much to learn about those missing five years."

"And I have so much to tell you. Is it just Harrison that has you upset?"

She shook her head. "I've been banished from the birthing room because I'm single. Unmarried. Therefore, I am too innocent to view my niece's or nephew's birth. Mrs. Farmer evidently believes that I would run screaming from the room."

"Who's Mrs. Farmer?"

"A very interfering midwife Lauren's father hired from Edinburgh. The woman does not tolerate any disobedience, from Lauren or me, for that matter. Lauren should have one member of the family with her. If Harrison could not be bothered, there is always me. However, Mrs. Farmer refuses to allow me admittance. God forbid I should discover how babies are born." She looked up at the sky. "Does the woman not realize that Adaire Hall has a great many horses, cows, pigs, and sheep?"

"But Harrison wouldn't be in the birthing room, either."

She nodded. "You have a point. But the woman doesn't have to be so annoying."

His laughter surprised her and made her grateful that he could turn aside her anger and worry.

Mrs. Farmer was right in one respect. There

was nothing she could do to speed up Lauren's labor. The baby would come when the baby would come.

She glanced at him and then back at the water. "I missed your laugh the most, I think."

"While I missed laughing with you."

"Do you think we've changed, the two of us?"

"Life changes us," he said.

"Absence changed us," Jennifer added.

"Longing does as well."

She dared herself to look at him again. "What have you longed for, Gordon?"

"Do you really need to ask me that question?"

She looked away again, this time at the ground between the bench and the shoreline. It was littered with various sizes of brown and black stones. When they were younger, they'd challenged each other. Who would be better at skipping stones across the water? He almost always won, but she'd had years of practice.

"I missed you so much. When you left, it was like you took my heart with you."

He startled her by reaching over and grabbing her around the waist and hauling her onto his lap.

"What are you doing?"

"Being rash and reckless. It's been years since I allowed myself to be either."

"And you expect me to be rash and reckless as well?" She couldn't help but smile at him.

"Last night you wanted to be."

"Ah, but you counseled restraint," she said.

"More fool me. Do you want to move?"

She shook her head. "Do I look foolish?"

Should she tell him that she'd gone to him last night? For a moment she considered remaining silent. Then that same daring spirit that had been awakened around him pressed her to speak.

"I came to you last night," she said, feeling her face flame. "I dressed in my prettiest nightgown and was intent on seducing you."

He didn't say anything, but his smile faded as they looked at each other.

"I was awake most of the night. I would have remembered if you'd come visiting."

She shouldn't have said anything because now she had to tell him the rest of the story.

"The footman saw me. He and I spoke and then Lauren opened her door."

"So you were well and truly found out."

Now she knew her face was bright red. "I was. I retreated to my room after that."

"You shouldn't have come."

"I know, but I'm not sorry. I only wish the footman hadn't been there."

"Me, too. But perhaps I'm foolish to wish that."

"I should dismiss all the footmen."

"What will you do about Lauren?" he asked with a smile.

"She'll be having her baby soon. Surely he will keep her busy. I don't need a chaperone."

"After last night I'm more than sure you do," he said with a smile.

GORDON WASN'T DEMONSTRATIVE by nature, having been trained that it was best not to show emotion. Betty had been his teacher, followed by

Sean. Yet around Jennifer he'd always been different, freer to be himself, perhaps. Or it could be that she brought out the best in him.

Mary was always touching her children, smoothing her hand across Harrison's sleeve, reaching up and placing her palm against Jennifer's cheek. He'd been envious of that easy familiarity, that sign of caring. More than once she stopped Harrison, called him back, and made him bend down so that she could smooth his hair away from his forehead or kiss his cheek. When that happened and he saw it, Gordon couldn't help but feel a twinge of jealousy. The only time Betty touched him was to give him the back of her hand.

Jennifer was like her mother. She'd always touched him, her fingers brushing his wrist. Sometimes she'd placed her hand on his shoulder in a wordless gesture of comfort.

Now she placed her palms against his face, encouraging him to lose his mind like he had last night. Yet it was daylight and there were people milling about. Reason enough to keep his head. Yet a part of him, atavistic and wild like Highlanders of old, wanted to pull her behind the nearest bush and make her his.

He'd always given the illusion of being somewhat civilized with an undercurrent of strength. The kind of man who didn't accept orders from anyone, but gave them. The kind of person who didn't tolerate cheaters or liars.

For years McBain's scalding words had been buried deep inside him. All this time he'd been determined to prove him and Sean wrong. For all

of that effort, for all of those years, he'd been rewarded. Not simply with Jennifer's understanding and love, but the knowledge that nothing or no one would ever be able to separate them again.

"I love you," he said softly. Words he'd once found difficult, but were easy to say to her.

She looked at him solemnly, her smile fading.

He wanted to be her hero, but he didn't want to pretend that he was more than he was.

"I've done things in the heat of anger, Jennifer, but I've learned from my mistakes. I've never deliberately harmed another human being, but I've been called ruthless. Maybe I am. I need you to know that. I know that I'm no angel."

Her knuckles brushed his cheek. He placed his hand on the back of hers, pressing it against his skin.

"I never wanted you to be a paragon of virtue, Gordon. Only to be yourself."

He smiled, the expression coming up from the inside of him. He couldn't remember the last time he felt this happy or carefree. "I've never been anyone but myself."

"I'm so glad for that."

He kissed her softly. "While you've always been an angel."

She pulled back. "I'm not a paragon, either, Gordon. You mustn't make me out to be that way. I have a temper."

"I remember," he said with a smile.

"I get annoyed from time to time."

"Again, I can attest to that."

"I get impatient."

He remained silent.

Even as they sat there still embracing, the day was brightening and warming. As if nature had taken a hint from their joy and was now replicating it.

He lowered his head and softly kissed her. Five years ago they had been more circumspect. Now he didn't care. Let the world watch them; it didn't matter.

How had he lived for five years without kissing Jennifer?

His arms tightened around her.

Yes, he'd laughed. He'd greeted each day with enthusiasm, eager for that day to be a success. Something had always been missing, however. Maybe the essence of hope. Or Jennifer, being close to him.

Now he almost felt drunk, as if he'd imbibed an entire bottle of wine. Bubbles of excitement raced through his veins.

This was the woman he loved, had always loved, would always love. No one would ever know her as well as he did. No one would ever understand him like Jennifer. They had the rest of their lives to love each other, and that thought was both heady and exciting.

"I'll come to you tonight," she whispered.

"No."

"No? Don't you want me?"

"Don't want you? I've wanted you every day since I first knew what it was to want a woman. How can you ask me that? But one of us has to be sensible."

"Why?" She wrapped her arms around his waist, placing her cheek against his chest.

"Jennifer."

She stood and stepped back. "Then go. I wouldn't want you to appear dishonorable to anyone."

"You've done that ever since you were a girl," he said.

"Done what?"

"Started a fight when you were in the wrong."

She frowned at him. "I'm not wrong now. I'm annoyed at you. I'm irritated. And I am, if I must admit, more than a little hurt. I offer myself to you, and all you can say is I'm picking a fight."

"I love you."

That stopped her in midtirade.

He stood and joined her. "I love you and I don't want to do anything to dishonor you."

"And you think loving me would dishonor me?" She shook her head. "Never, Gordon."

He dropped his head, his cheek against hers. "Here I am, struggling to maintain my honor, and you're doing your damnedest to be a temptation."

"Very well," she said. "Will you, at least, join me for dinner?"

"All alone, just the two of us?" he asked. "Whatever will the servants say?"

"Do you care?"

"Not one jot," he said, smiling.

She had a glint in her eye. He knew that look. Jennifer would be up to mischief. Or perhaps seduction.

Chapter Sixteen

*J*ennifer took her time dressing for dinner. She wore one of her newer garments, something Ellen had insisted she include in her wardrobe.

"Who am I going to wear new dresses for?" she'd said at the time.

"You never know what's going to happen," Ellen had responded. "You need to ensure that you have a wardrobe commensurate with any activity."

"My activities consist of taking care of Adaire Hall. Occasionally, I'll ride out to visit a neighbor. Or I'll take a carriage to Edinburgh to see you. Beyond that . . ." Her words had trailed off to meet Ellen's frown.

"You're not on the shelf, you know," her godmother said. "It's still possible for you to find someone to fall madly, deeply, passionately in love with."

Jennifer hadn't responded. She was already madly, deeply, and passionately in love with Gordon. Just because she hadn't confessed that fact to Ellen didn't change the reality of it.

However, arguing with Ellen was a losing proposition.

The only time she'd wanted to get a new ward-

robe was after her mother had died, but Ellen had been adamant about honoring Mary's wishes.

"Wearing one color or another will not make you mourn your mother more or less. Besides, she was insistent that you not wear mourning for more than a month. You know that well enough."

"It doesn't seem right," Jennifer said at the time.

"It was right for Mary. It was her only wish. She didn't want to see you buried beneath yards of crepe. How does that show respect?"

She had looked at her godmother. "Then why did you wear black for Colin for so many months?"

"That was entirely different."

Even though she thought she'd been rational, she'd lost that war with Ellen.

This dress was emerald, a shade of green she especially liked. The collar was lace, as were the cuffs. Although it was three years old, it was still flattering, accentuating her waist and both the curve of her hips and her bosom.

She did her hair herself, pulling it up and pinning it so that it fell in a cascade. If she was more talented with curling tongs, she would've used those, but every time she tried, she burned herself. She didn't want to mar this evening by being in pain.

A touch of rouge to her lips and a final inspection and she was done.

How had she lived without seeing Gordon every day? How had she been able to sleep, rise, do all those tasks that needed doing without the promise of being able to talk to him, embrace him, and kiss him?

The Hall was too large, too filled with people, too oppressive and demanding. It required sacrifice and she'd done exactly that for years. Now she was tired of it, and pushing back for the first time.

She didn't want the responsibility any longer. She wanted Lauren to have her baby and take over her rightful duties as the Countess of Burfield. Jennifer didn't want the staff to come to her with problems or issues.

All she wanted was to be with Gordon.

He had already told her so much about those missing years, but she wanted to know everything. Whom he met, the people he employed, what he did every day—she wanted to share every aspect of his life.

Everything in her life had changed in the past two days. It was like living in a world filled with clouds, and all of a sudden, the sun shone through. Or having no hope, and suddenly being suffused with it.

She smiled at herself in the mirror and left the room, anxious to see Gordon again.

INSTEAD OF GOING into the drawing room to wait for Jennifer, Gordon remained at the base of the stairs. He felt strangely out of place in this Adaire Hall. Five years ago he'd known every inch of the place. He and Jennifer had haunted the upper floors, explored the attic, and as children, had taken over an unused room as their own private domain.

The countess had never fussed at him for being here. Or at the both of them for being hooli-

gans in the house during rainy or snowy days. Instead, she would ask what they were playing at, and he would stop to explain.

He was only five when the earl died suddenly. All he knew about that time was that the countess took to her rooms and didn't leave them for two years. It was Harrison who'd coaxed her out of her hermitage, but not out of kindness or concern. He'd been expelled from his father's alma mater and sent home in disgrace.

Gordon had often wondered if the countess had put all three of them together in the schoolroom to force Harrison to behave. Jennifer loved reading and had a natural ability for recall, often putting the two boys to shame. He was better with numbers and mathematics. Harrison's talent was in feeling slighted. As the new Earl of Burfield he made sure that everyone knew of his elevation in rank. Even as a child he'd been insufferable.

The countess had once been a beautiful woman. One side of her face was unmarred by the fire that had nearly taken her life. The other resembled a melted candle. He'd been fascinated by her scars as a boy, had wanted to reach up and touch her face, but had never done so. He had asked her, once, if it hurt.

She'd tilted her head and regarded him through her one good eye. He knew that she couldn't see well enough to read, although she could discern shapes and colors.

"Not now," she said. "It did in the beginning."

She'd been his tutor in many things, giving him an education he hadn't received from either

of his parents. She taught him how to speak to people properly, to treat a woman with respect, and even corrected his table manners.

Evidently, he'd reminded her of her younger brother.

"He was as stubborn as you," she often said. "Impatient, too. As if he couldn't wait for life to start for him."

"Does he live in Edinburgh?" he'd asked.

"No," she said, sounding sad. "He's gone to live in New South Wales."

He'd patted her hand that day, feeling a compassion for her that had startled him.

Adaire Hall wasn't the same without the countess. It was like the house's heart had been extinguished.

He wished there was a way to tell her how much he appreciated everything she'd done for him, especially in educating him. He'd often wondered if she'd had to go against McBain's wishes to do so. Had the man acceded to her request out of respect for her? Or simply because the issue hadn't been important to him? For whatever reason, Gordon had received an education in excess of his position in life, and for that he would always be grateful.

He had reason to be thankful for her lessons in other subjects, especially in the past five years.

One day, the countess had been doing an inventory of the silver in the butler's pantry and had called him over to the table.

"Do you know what this is, Gordon?" she'd asked, holding up a curious looking piece of silverware.

"It's a knife."

"It's not just a knife. It's a butter knife."

She taught him how to identify various spoons and forks as well. He learned when one was used and how he was to use it. Because of her, he learned not to stuff his napkin in his collar or slurp his soup.

She'd never been unkind to him. Never once had she mentioned his station in life, or uttered a harsh word. Whenever she corrected him, it was done with grace and sometimes humor.

He'd grown to feel more for the countess than any other adult at Adaire Hall.

Going from the Hall to the gardener's cottage had always been a jarring journey. He was learning how to have manners at the Hall only to return to the cottage to see that neither of his parents cared overmuch about polite behavior.

What would the countess say to see him now? He'd thought of her from time to time in London, as he had risen in reputation. She'd given him something that had taken him years to identify: confidence. He knew how to handle himself in a great many situations, all because of the Countess of Burfield.

Because of her, he wasn't intimidated by a title or a man's birthright. Instead, he was impressed by a man who was determined in the face of obstacles.

A sound caused him to look up. Jennifer was descending the stairs, her eyes not veering from his face. She was even more beautiful than she'd been in his dreams. Her green eyes were sparkling at him and a small smile curved her pink

lips. The dress, an emerald green, revealed her curves and matched the color of her eyes perfectly.

He moved to the bottom of the stairs, holding out his hand.

She placed hers in it and smiled up at him.

"You dressed for dinner," she said.

He had changed into a black suit and white shirt.

"As did you. I like your dress."

He brought her hand to his mouth and gently kissed her fingers.

"What a shame no one else can see you as I do. You should live in Edinburgh, and reign over a literary salon. People from all over Scotland and England would come to see just you."

"You've learned flattery, Gordon."

"No, only to speak the truth."

He walked beside her to the small dining room only a short distance from the kitchen. Until that first dinner with Lauren, he'd never taken a meal with Jennifer there. They'd eaten together at the loch, mostly sandwiches she'd made for him, or whatever treats Cook had given them. Never here at the Hall.

One of the footmen helped her with her chair, a task he wanted to do. If his hand slipped and grazed her upper arm, he would be able to measure if his touch gave her goose bumps. Perhaps he might even bend and brush away the hair at the nape of her neck and kiss her exposed skin.

It seemed to Gordon that there were entirely too many people in this small dining room, all of them pleasant, smiling, and essentially intrusive.

Finally, after the first course, Jennifer dismissed them with a smile and they were alone.

"How is Lauren?" he asked.

She blew out a breath and shook her head. "I haven't the slightest idea. The midwife says that everything is proceeding as it should be, but I can't see how that's right. It seems to be taking entirely too long."

"I have to confess my ignorance about labor and birth. However, didn't you tell me that Lauren's father hired Mrs. Farmer?"

She nodded.

"Surely he would have selected the best person available?"

She frowned at him. "You're being entirely too logical." Her frown melted into a smile. "The woman is annoying and I want to be annoyed at her."

"You can still think she's a gorgon. Just a skilled gorgon."

They smiled at each other.

"Any moment now you'll get to meet Mr. Campbell. I'm certain that the gorgon sent word to him that his grandchild was about to be born. I only hope that he arrives after Harrison does. Otherwise, there's bound to be trouble."

Perhaps it was time someone held Harrison to account. He'd always been treated as if he was better than anyone else. More privileged, more talented, more adept at everything, even though he wasn't. It had begun back in the schoolroom they'd shared. Their tutor had a tendency to forgive Harrison's behavior as high spirits. When the man started scoring Harrison's tests with the

same willful disregard for the truth, Gordon realized that the tutor was afraid. Not of Harrison, but of the guardian. Bringing the young heir's inadequacies to McBain's attention might cause the tutor to be dismissed. Therefore, Harrison was allowed to get away with a great deal more than Gordon or Jennifer.

The safest way to handle any discussion of Harrison was simply not to say what he thought. His opinion hadn't changed in the past five years. In fact, he'd grown even more disgusted with Harrison's behavior, because he had it on good authority that the man wasn't faithful. The vows he'd taken in a church were simply suggestions for other men. They didn't apply to him.

Wait until Harrison learned that Gordon wasn't so lax. He had every intention of demanding payment for the debt Harrison owed him.

Chapter Seventeen

During the second course Gordon told her about some of the people he employed in London. More than a few of them were fascinating individuals. Men who had come up in life through sheer grit and determination. Women who'd turned their backs on their individual pasts in order to believe in a better future.

His life wasn't here, but by marrying him Jennifer would have to leave Adaire Hall. Was she prepared to do that? Would she trade the life she knew for one with him?

Now was not the time to ask her to be his wife. That was for later, perhaps. Or even tomorrow beside the loch. He had planned what he would say. The words wouldn't be difficult. In fact, they'd be the easiest ones he'd ever speak.

"What the hell is this, Jennifer?"

They both looked toward the doorway. Harrison stood there.

The current Earl of Burfield was a big man, tall with broad shoulders, but he'd recently started going to fat because of his indolent life in London. He slept most of the day, spending his nights at either the gaming tables or in a private card game. When he wasn't gambling, he was

drinking or eating or involved with one of the women he brought to the Mayfair Club.

Harrison had tried to entice every one of Gordon's female employees to his bed. They'd all refused him. Gordon had a rule that fraternizing with customers was grounds for being fired. That hadn't delayed Harrison all that much. He'd simply gone outside the club to find his female companions.

His eyes were bloodshot, his face puffy. He looked twenty years older than his age. Even his blond strands were thinning and hinting at baldness in the not-too-distant future.

He was a perfect picture of a man who lived a dissolute lifestyle.

Gordon stood as Harrison entered the room followed by a woman he vaguely recognized. It took him a moment before he placed her. Mrs. Thornton, Jennifer's godmother. They'd never been introduced, but he'd seen her before. He'd always disliked watching her arrive because it meant that she was going to take Jennifer away for weeks at a time.

"McDonnell. The gardener's boy," Harrison said.

"The same," Gordon said, nodding to Mrs. Thornton.

Jennifer stood. "Where have you been?" She glanced at her godmother. "Are you responsible for bringing him home?" Before Mrs. Thornton could answer, Jennifer turned to her brother again. "Is that the only reason you're here? I think you should care less about who my guest is and more about how your wife is faring."

"She's having the baby. That's how she's faring."

"Go and see her. Now. We'll talk later, but for now you need to see your wife."

Harrison sent a fulminating glance toward him, then turned and left the room without another word.

The kitten had tamed the bear.

"I'm not entirely certain Mrs. Farmer will let him in, earl or no earl," Jennifer said. She turned back to her godmother. "Ellen, I'd like you to meet Gordon McDonnell. Gordon, my godmother, Mrs. Thornton."

Mrs. Thornton looked somewhat bemused. "Pleasure," she murmured.

"Mrs. Thornton," he said, inclining his head slightly.

"Would you like to join us?" Jennifer asked.

Gordon pulled out a chair between them. Ellen smiled as she took it, removing her gloves and hat.

"Indeed I should. I'm famished. I wanted to get here as quickly as possible, so we rarely stopped. Has Lauren had her baby?"

Jennifer rang the bell on the sideboard. Before the servants arrived, they spent the next few minutes in a conversation that Gordon would have avoided if he could. It consisted of talk about labor pains, the travails of women, and the mechanics of birth, none of which he wanted to know.

A few moments later Jennifer glanced at him.

"I think we're scaring Gordon," she said with a smile.

He wasn't frightened, but he didn't want to be privy to this particular conversation. Thankfully,

Jennifer took pity on him and changed the subject.

They talked of London, the journey to Scotland accomplished by train as well as carriage, anything but childbirth.

It turned out that Ellen owned a home in London not far from his own town house. He wouldn't be surprised if they had acquaintances in common as well.

"Are you related to the Adaire family?" he asked Ellen.

She thanked the maid for delivering her soup, then glanced at him.

"You and Jennifer have the same green eyes."

"How odd. I was just thinking that you reminded me of Alex, but perhaps it's just coloring."

"How were you able to convince Harrison to come home?" Jennifer asked.

"It wasn't me at all, I'm afraid," Ellen responded. "But the woman who manages Harrison's favorite club. She was instrumental in convincing him it was time to return home. I think she might've threatened him, actually. I'm not exactly sure how she accomplished it, but I'm grateful, nonetheless."

He shared a glance with Jennifer before asking Ellen, "Are you talking about the Mayfair Club, Mrs. Thornton?"

"That's it, exactly. How did you know?"

Jennifer looked at him again. "Gordon owns the Mayfair Club."

Ellen looked startled. "Does he? How very strange. Talk about coincidence."

Maggie had evidently cut Harrison off, which

meant that he had no ready money with which to gamble. Gordon didn't blame her for the decision. He would have done the same if Ellen had come to him.

"However it was accomplished," Jennifer said, "I'm grateful, too. He should have been back a week ago."

"London is a lure for men like Harrison," Ellen said. "They're young, titled, and wealthy."

"He's also married and has responsibilities. Do those simply vanish because he wants to spend his time gambling and even worse?"

Thank God for men who liked to gamble. Without them he wouldn't be as wealthy as he was. However, there were actually few men as irresponsible as Harrison in his coterie of customers. Most men recalled their duties and performed them without being reminded.

The rest of the dinner conversation centered on people that Ellen and Jennifer knew in Edinburgh. When dinner was over, he excused himself, leaving the two women alone to discuss birth and Harrison's peccadilloes.

Since it was late, Gordon decided not to go back to the cottage for fear of waking Sean. Instead, he stopped in front of the library, recalling the countess the moment he opened the door.

The myth of Adaire Hall was that it was a place of enchanted happiness. He'd known that was false when he was ten years old and realized how desperately unhappy the Countess of Burfield was. No one else seemed to realize how much she still missed her husband. Either that or she cloaked it well in front of everyone else.

She'd always been honest with him, and he'd reciprocated with telling her how he'd learned the basics of mathematics by playing cards with the footmen. He'd attended the village school, but only until he was nine. The education he'd received there had been considered adequate for his station in life. It was the countess who'd expanded his boundaries.

One day he'd confessed to her that he'd stolen into this library once, just to see all the books. He'd taken one, bound in burgundy leather, and sat with it between his hands, opening it to random pages and wondering at all the words. He hadn't known many of them. To his surprise she asked him to fetch that same book one day. From then on, she spent at least an hour each day teaching him some of those words. He would say the letters aloud for her, and she would say the word, then they would practice sounding it out and spelling it.

"You need to know about men who've dreamed great things," she told him once. "Philosophers and mathematicians, among others."

Because of her, he'd started reading the books in the library. She'd given him one a week and expected him to finish it in that time. When Sean said something about the time he spent reading, Gordon had responded that the countess wanted him to do it. Neither Sean nor Betty commented after that.

Now all of those memories coalesced. He could almost see Mary Adaire sitting there in her chair, holding a book with her fingers trailing over the spine, her palm flat against a page, almost

as if she were willing herself to read the words through her fingers.

She'd never complained to him, but he felt that losing the ability to read was something she regretted the most.

He and Jennifer had taken turns reading to her. He'd always felt embarrassed when it came to poetry, but he had kept on, for fear that one of them would consider him a coward for not continuing.

He headed for that section now, daring himself. One book especially seemed to have been her favorite. He pulled it from the shelf, smiling as he opened it.

"What the hell are you doing back here?"

He carefully placed the volume back on the shelf before turning to face Harrison.

"Wasn't the money my mother left you enough? Are you thinking you'll get some more from my sister? She may be a fool, McDonnell, but she's not your fool."

As a boy he'd handled the problem of Harrison by pushing his face into the dirt. He was sorely tempted to do the same right now.

There were several places in the Mayfair Club where he could see the members without them being aware that they were being watched. He'd observed Harrison often. The man was a bully. One who'd supposedly been taught manners, but who remembered them only when it was personally convenient.

"Does it make you feel better to insult your sister?"

"What the hell are you doing back?"

Gordon folded his arms and wondered how far this conversation would go. He didn't resort to violence unless it was absolutely necessary. Neither was he physically afraid of Harrison. He was his match in height, plus he'd taken boxing lessons in the past year. In a fair match he'd beat Harrison, he was sure. However, Harrison wasn't above bending the rules.

"My father is dying," he said.

That silenced Harrison, but only for a moment.

"You aren't wanted here, McDonnell."

"That hasn't changed."

The current situation could be altered with only a few words. All he had to do was tell Harrison that he owned the Mayfair Club, that the markers that may well bankrupt Adaire Hall were in his possession. It wouldn't alter Harrison's contempt for him, but it might well shut him up.

He knew when to use an advantage, and tonight was not the time.

"Get out," Harrison said.

"Your sister has invited me to stay. I believe your wife seconded that invitation."

"I don't care. Get out."

He could argue with the man, or he could simply get his belongings and take them to the gardener's cottage.

Gordon strode toward the door, anticipating that Harrison would do something. He wasn't disappointed when the other man's arm reached out. Before Harrison could strike a blow, Gordon struck first, hitting Harrison in the chin with his left. He stumbled, which was enough for Gordon.

"Anytime you want a fair fight," Gordon said, "let me know."

Harrison rubbed his chin and glared at him. "The sooner you leave Adaire Hall, the better, and don't return."

"I doubt I'll have any reason to do so, Harrison."

Unless he owned Adaire Hall, which he could do with a flick of a wrist.

He'd wanted to return triumphant and in a way he had. He had a noose around Harrison's neck, and the idiot didn't even recognize his hangman.

Chapter Eighteen

Gordon knocked softly on the door to the cottage.

Moira opened it. "Here you are with the manners of a duke, I'm thinking. Knocking on the door of your own home."

The cottage had never felt like home to him. However, since he was carrying his valises and needed a place to stay, it seemed a foolish thing to say.

"Your father's having a bad night," she said, her eyes filled with concern. "I've had to give him a second dose of laudanum, but it doesn't seem to help."

"I thought he was doing better."

"He was, but that's how it sometimes goes. The better they do one day is how much worse they are later."

"Is there anything I can do?"

"Hot pads," she said. "They're the only thing that seems to help even a little."

He put his valises in the empty second bedroom. The only furniture there was the cot he had used as a boy. He returned to the kitchen area, where Moira showed him how to dunk rags

in boiling water and then wring them out using two sticks.

"Take care that you don't burn yourself," she said. "I'm not wanting another patient tonight."

He promised with a smile, then realized that he shouldn't have been so quick to reassure her. Getting the rags wet wasn't a problem. Retrieving them from the boiling water and then manipulating the two sticks proved to be a challenging task. By the time he finished with one, Moira was returning to his side with rags that had already cooled.

Sean's moans kept him working. Finally, several hours later, Sean fell into a drug-induced sleep. Moira sat at the table and placed her head on her arms. Gordon let her rest while he removed the pot of boiling water from the stove and dumped it out. Once that was done, he wrung out the rags and hung them on the line beside the window.

From what he'd witnessed during the past few hours, he suspected that the end was probably near. Perhaps it might even be a blessing.

He stood in the doorway of Sean's room for a few minutes, looking at the drawn and pale face of his sleeping father. The soft knock on the door made him turn his head. Jennifer entered and talked with Moira for a moment before approaching him. Her hand reached out and grabbed his arm in wordless comfort.

"I didn't know what Harrison had done, Gordon. I'm so sorry."

"Don't worry. It was best that I was here anyway."

Together they entered Sean's room. Jennifer sat

as Gordon picked up the second chair beneath the window and moved it to the other side of the bed. He covered Sean's work-worn, gnarled hand with his own, grateful that the Adaire family had cared for his father when he hadn't.

A moment later he looked over at Jennifer. "Tonight has taught me something. How fleeting life can be. Marry me. Marry me, Jennifer. Be my wife. Be my partner. Be my sounding board and my most trusted ally. Be my friend and my lover."

She stared at him wide-eyed.

"We would have to live in London, but hopefully that isn't a problem. If it is, I can make other arrangements. I have a few managers I trust implicitly."

"London?"

He nodded. "I'll give you the world. Whatever you want, Jennifer. You won't suffer for anything. I promise."

He was babbling. If it had been anyone but Jennifer, he would've stopped himself before now. It sounded as if he was begging, and he probably was. Yet he didn't have any pride when it came to her, not when she looked at him with such radiance in her eyes.

She had to say yes.

"Marry me," he said again. "I promise you we'll be happy. As happy as we were all those years ago. Happier, perhaps."

"Oh, Gordon, don't you know how much I love you? You don't even need to ask. You could simply take my hand and lead me to a carriage, and

I'd go anywhere with you. These last five years without you have been miserable."

"You'll marry me?" He wanted the exact words. He wanted her to say it in such a way that there was no question.

She squeezed his hand. "Yes. A thousand times yes. A thousand times a thousand times. Yes, I'll marry you. Do you know how many times I've dreamed of being your wife?"

Sean blinked open his eyes. He looked up at the ceiling, then seemed to realize where he was.

"I've something to say," he said, his voice raspy.

"Don't tire yourself," Jennifer said, smoothing the sheets over Sean's chest.

He turned his head at her voice, then closed his eyes, sighed, and remained silent.

"What is it, Da?"

"Naught," Sean said. "Naught at all."

They remained there long enough to be assured that Sean had no intention of speaking. He fell into an uneasy sleep, his hands occasionally twitching on the sheet.

Finally, they stood and left the room, leaving Sean to rest.

"You look as tired as I feel," she said, smiling up at him.

"It's been a long night."

"Will you meet me later?" she asked. "At the loch? I'll bring a lunch for us."

He nodded.

She turned to leave him, her hand brushing his. He wanted to reach out and grab it, pull her to him, and hold her. Just that, to hold her for a

few minutes, to allow himself the luxury of being with the one person in the world he loved unconditionally.

When the door closed behind her, he turned to Moira. "I'm going to sleep for a bit. If I'm needed, please come and get me."

"Aye, that I will, but for now you go and get some rest. There's time enough for worry later."

When he woke, he would see if Sean felt like talking and find out what he wanted to say but couldn't in front of Jennifer.

LAUREN'S DAUGHTER WAS born in the wee hours of the morning which, according to Mrs. Farmer, was not unusual. The baby was healthy, already expressing her displeasure about having to wait a moment to be fed, and was instantly adored by her mother and her aunt.

Jennifer said a fervent prayer of thanks. She'd known that first births were long, but she'd never thought that it would take this many hours. The baby was perfect, however, even if she was loud. The two of them, Lauren and her daughter, were a picture she would not shortly forget.

She was careful not to compliment her niece. Doing so would summon all sorts of bad luck including being *forespoken*. To prevent such a thing from happening, the infant was passed through the nightgown that Lauren had been wearing at the time of her birth three times. Then Mrs. Farmer washed the baby in ice-cold water. Great care was taken so that the water didn't touch the baby's palms. Otherwise, any luck the child might have in acquiring worldly goods as an

adult would be washed away. Finally, the infant was wrapped in her father's shirt before being turned over to the nurse Jennifer had hired a week ago. Alice was barely older than a child herself, but she was bright, eager to please, and was well thought of in the village.

Harrison would be invited to visit his wife and their daughter as soon as Lauren was dressed in a clean gown and the linens changed once more.

Jennifer went in search of her brother now, knowing that despite the early hour Harrison was probably awake.

He was in the library, the first place she looked, his feet propped up on the desk that had been commissioned by their great-grandfather, a snifter of brandy in one hand and a cigar in the other.

She stood in front of the desk until he looked up, saw her, and nodded. Evidently, that was the only recognition she was going to get.

"You have a beautiful baby girl, Harrison."

He took a sip of his brandy, then waved his cigar in her direction.

"Not an heir, then. Pity."

She understood his need for an heir, but at the same time she couldn't help but feel a surge of irritation. Lauren had been in labor a day and a half and he could at least come and visit her.

Nor had he inquired as to his wife's health in the past eight months. If Ellen hadn't gone to London to get him, would Harrison have even come home? She had the sinking feeling that he wouldn't have bothered. Perhaps he would have sent some type of gift to Lauren, a string of pearls to mark the occasion, but little else.

Gordon had once said that Harrison was the epitome of a perfectly selfish person. She'd always tried to find something about her brother to admire, but he'd been making it more and more difficult in the past few years.

"You need to come and see the baby."

"Why? She won't know I'm there. Babies aren't real people until they're six or seven or so."

How had he made that judgment?

"Lauren will know. You need to see her, too. Pretend you're married, Harrison, just for a few minutes. Surely you can do that."

His eyes narrowed. "Has being a spinster turned you into a harpy, Jennifer?"

"Is it being a harpy to remind you of your duty?"

"Who the hell are you to tell me what to do?"

Jennifer didn't bother answering him. He'd evidently been drinking steadily ever since he'd arrived. Harrison, inebriated, was even more irksome than Harrison, sober.

She was turning to leave when he spoke again. "I got rid of him. The gardener's boy. I told him to get out."

"Yes, I know. Or did you think someone wouldn't tell me? I know most of what happens at Adaire Hall. Unlike you. You had no right to ask Gordon to leave. He was a guest."

"You've always been a fool about him, Jennifer. He knows that. He takes advantage of it."

"How exactly has he taken advantage of it, Harrison? I invited him to stay at the Hall. He didn't ask. Nor did he expect it."

Harrison only waved his hand in the air. "This is my home and I won't have him here."

"It's only your home when you remember. It's my home, too, Harrison. Who do you think manages Adaire Hall while you're off in London?"

She left before he could respond. The less she saw of her brother, the better.

Chapter Nineteen

It was nearly dawn by the time Jennifer got to sleep. She woke only four hours later, her thoughts on Gordon. She realized she was smiling, the sensation so unusual that she pressed her fingers against her lips. How long had it been since she was this happy? Five years. Five long years.

She sat up, then swung her legs over the side of the mattress. The hours just after dawn were the most productive for her. She liked to get a start before most of the inhabitants of the Hall were up and about. She had time to plan her day before any of the normal complications arose.

Now, however, all she could think about was Gordon. They were going to be married.

She dressed while still smiling. She even laughed at herself in the mirror. Happiness made her pretty. Her cheeks were pink. Her eyes sparkled.

She knew exactly what she had to do today, all of it written out on a list she had made the month before. Her habit of making lists, keeping a calendar, and scheduling every task was how she managed everything to be done at Adaire Hall.

Today, however, it didn't matter how much she had to do. She didn't care. She would do every single item on her list with a smile on her face and with a warm swelling joy in her heart. She hadn't felt like this in years—as if happiness was making her buoyant.

The only drawback to her happiness was Sean's health. She wished she could somehow pray enough that he'd be magically healed, but God made those decisions, not her.

She couldn't wait to marry Gordon. She didn't want a large wedding. Nor did she want a ceremony that would take ages to plan. All she wanted was to be Gordon's wife, to start their lives together.

Instead of eating breakfast, she grabbed some oatcakes and wrapped them in a napkin. At the cottage she tapped lightly on the door.

Gordon opened the door. Although it was obvious that neither of them had gotten much sleep the night before, the sight of him made her heart expand.

She offered him the oatcakes. "You haven't had time to come to the house for breakfast."

"I doubt if I would have been welcomed," he said, taking the napkin from her.

"If Harrison behaves as he always has, he won't wake until noon."

"Thank you. I think Sally will have her hands full caring for Sean today."

"I'm so sorry." Sean's illness took a little luster from her happiness.

Gordon reached out and enfolded her in a one-

armed hug. "I know you are. No one could have done more to help him. I thank you for that, Jennifer."

She hugged him back and walked inside the cottage, sitting at the table with him. When he offered her one of the oatcakes, she shook her head. Happiness had taken away her appetite. It was enough for her to be here with him, close enough to reach out and touch his arm, to see him smile and make quick work of his small breakfast.

The oatcakes gone, Gordon folded the napkin and handed it back to her.

"Do we have to wait?" she asked. "I know the circumstances, but couldn't we have a small wedding? Here, in the cottage, so that Sean could see?"

"I don't want a hole-and-corner affair, Jennifer. When I marry you, I want it with all the villagers and every person who works at Adaire Hall to witness it."

Warmth swept through her.

He leaned over and kissed her gently. She placed her hand on his cheek, feeling his early-morning whiskers. Just think, she would be able to see him whenever she woke. He would be part of each day. She would be able to tell him what had transpired, people she'd met, things she thought. He would be part of her life and she had missed that for five years.

Sean's door opened and Sally came out, carrying a basin. Gordon stood and helped her with it, placing it on the counter.

"How is he?" Jennifer asked.

Sally shook her head. "Last night was bad. I hope he can get some sleep today."

Was she selfish by wanting to wed now?

Gordon walked her to the door.

"I'll stay with Sean for a little while."

She understood. "I'll send a note to our minister," she said. "If you're sure you haven't changed your mind?"

He hugged her again. She really didn't want to leave him, but she had other duties to attend to today, and he needed to be with Sean.

When she returned to the Hall, Ellen was eating her breakfast in the dining room.

Jennifer joined her, and for a while Ellen wanted to discuss the latest fashions she'd seen in London. Although Jennifer didn't have any interest in fashion, her godmother had an amusing opinion on everything. In addition, she was a font of knowledge on almost any subject.

"You're like a walking library," Jennifer had told her once.

Ellen had laughed. "What a compliment, my dear Jennifer, and very prettily said. Thank you."

Today was no different as Ellen recounted tales of her adventures in selecting a new wardrobe. After the maid took away Ellen's dishes, her godmother sat back in the chair and smiled at her.

"Tell me all about Gordon," Ellen said. "Does he really own the Mayfair Club?"

Jennifer nodded. "As well as two music halls."

"How interesting. And he used to live here?"

"I've mentioned him before."

"Yes, you have," Ellen said, "but you left out a

great many details. For example, how handsome he was or that he was quite an overpowering personage."

"Overpowering?"

"There are people you meet who give off a certain quality," Ellen said. "I'm not entirely sure I can explain what it is. They are either more ambitious or talented, but whatever it is, it's not that they're better than the rest of us. It's simply that they're different." She looked at Jennifer sharply. "I've never met anyone who's less a gardener's boy than Gordon McDonnell."

"He's always been his own person," Jennifer said.

"Now that doesn't surprise me," Ellen said. "It's quite daunting how he looks at you. I don't believe I've ever had a man look at me that way. Not even my darling Colin."

Jennifer didn't know what to say.

"Oh, it's not a bad thing," Ellen continued. "But I do believe that anyone who tried to come between you and him would suffer a terrible fate."

Jennifer couldn't help but smile. "I've always adored him. After mother died, Mr. McBain sent him away."

"That man was a prude in many ways. I never liked him. I don't think your mother did, either. However, your father's will assigned him as guardian, so we were stuck with him."

That was a surprise. No one had ever offered up any criticism of Mr. McBain. To most people he was a paragon of virtue.

"What about now? Your Gordon has returned."

"His father is ill."

"Is that the only reason he's here? Do you still adore him?"

Jennifer smiled.

"Never mind, I have my answer from your face. I know he feels the same just from the way he looks at you."

"Yes, he does," Jennifer said, feeling her face warm. "He's asked me to marry him."

"Like hell you'll marry the bastard."

They looked up to see Harrison leaning against the doorjamb. Her brother was wearing the same clothes he'd worn the day before, now badly wrinkled. His white shirt was stained in two spots, and his hair disheveled as if he'd threaded his fingers through it many times. Lines of dissipation were already beginning to show on his reddened face. The wrinkles around his bloodshot eyes belonged to a man several decades older.

The odor of alcohol wafted off Harrison so strongly that it was nauseating.

"I'll be damned if you marry McDonnell," he said. "You're not going to shame the family like that."

"You've done your share of shaming the Adaire name, Harrison. Besides, you have no say in who I marry."

"I'm the head of the family, Jennifer."

There was more than one way to marry in Scotland. If necessary, she and Gordon could simply stand before witnesses and declare their wish to be man and wife. Harrison could do nothing to stop it.

Jennifer stood and looked at Ellen.

"Forgive me, Ellen," she said. "I've just remembered some urgent tasks that need to be done."

When she got to the door, Harrison didn't budge.

"I mean it, Jennifer. I won't have you marry that bastard."

"You don't have anything to say about it."

When he still didn't move, she shoved him out of the way.

Behind her, she heard Ellen address her brother.

"Must you always be so boorish, Harrison?"

She didn't stay to hear Harrison's response.

Chapter Twenty

"Would you like me to fetch you some tea?" Sally asked.

"I'll make it," Gordon said. "You don't need another duty."

She smiled at him, gratitude in her expression. He joined her in the kitchen, watching as she made Sean a cup of tea, putting some whiskey in it.

"Have you been caring for him long, Sally?"

"Two months now." She looked toward Sean's door and then leaned closer to Gordon. "Poor man, he's been so ill. I don't think it will be long now."

"No," he softly said. "I think you're right." He took the cup from her. "Why don't you go and get some air. I'll take this to him."

"Are you sure? He's been in and out for a while now. Sometimes, he doesn't know who people are."

"I'm sure. I'll go and sit with him."

"Well . . ." She looked toward the window and the encroaching sunlight like freedom beckoned.

"Go," he said.

She left the cottage with an eagerness he completely understood. If he could be quit of this

place, he would, but responsibility held him here. Or perhaps it was honor. Or maybe the love a young boy had once felt for his father.

Sean was lying straight in his bed, the covers folded and tucked neatly beneath his arms. His pose and pallor were reminiscent of a man being laid out for his funeral.

Since he'd returned, he and Sean hadn't talked about Betty. Sean hadn't said anything about him missing her funeral. It was as if Betty had simply vanished from not only their daily lives, but their history together.

Sean looked to have fallen into an uneasy doze. Gordon was content to sit there for as long as necessary. If Sean was asleep, then at least he'd been given a respite from pain.

He and Jennifer were going to be married. He was filled with plans. He wanted to show her everything he'd built and introduce her to everyone who'd helped make his music halls a success—Maggie, the other people who filled his daily life. He hoped she liked his house, but if she didn't, he'd buy another. Jennifer would never lack for anything. Nor would she ever regret marrying him.

He couldn't give her a title, but he could give her a home the equal of Adaire Hall. He'd build a house for her on the land he'd purchased in Scotland. She could tell the architect to design it however she wished. Whatever Jennifer wanted, he was going to ensure she received.

His life would finally be exactly how he wanted it, shared with the woman of his dreams. He and Jennifer would never be apart. He couldn't wait

to spend his life with her, to ask her advice, or to listen to what she thought of people they met.

Sean moaned, the sound bringing him back to the present. Gordon reached over and covered his father's hand. Sean's eyes fluttered open, blinked up at the ceiling, then slowly he turned his head. His eyes were dull and there was no recognition there.

"It's Gordon, Da."

Sean's eyes closed again.

"I have a cuppa here, with some whiskey. If you like, I can help you sit up so that you can drink it."

Sean didn't acknowledge his words. Nor did he speak.

Gordon continued to sit there, watching his father.

He'd never sat a deathbed vigil, but he knew that this was what it was. Now was not the time for recriminations or even questions. Instead, silence was the best recourse.

He wished that it was easier for Sean, that the end could have been swift and merciful. Instead, it was evident that Sean was in agony.

Even though he wished it, he couldn't magically erase Sean's pain. All he could do was be the best son he could be. Perhaps Sean didn't deserve it, but that wasn't a judgment he needed to make. All he had to do was to be here, at this moment, and ensure that Sean had everything he needed.

A few minutes later his father opened his eyes again. He blinked up at the ceiling before looking around the room. Finally, his gaze settled on Gordon.

"Boy."

Gordon could ruin a man by calling in his debts. A number of the peerage owed their current prosperous trappings to loans he'd given them. He employed over three hundred people in various positions. Yet Sean still called him *boy*.

Somehow, he managed to smile back at his father.

"How are you feeling?"

Instead of answering him, Sean made a sound in the back of his throat before saying, "You should have stayed gone."

Once Sean's words would have affected him. Yet he'd had years to acquire a thick skin as well as an understanding of human nature. Sean knew he was dying. His anger would have been directed to anyone in this situation. Gordon was only a convenient whipping boy.

"If you hadn't come back, everything would've been fine. There would be no need for it all to come out."

He didn't understand what his father was saying, but credited it to the laudanum.

"Why don't you drink your tea? Sally put some whiskey in it."

"If you'd only stayed away, everything would have been fine. Why did you even come back?"

"Because Jennifer wrote that you were ill. I thought it would be the right thing to do."

"You didn't come back because of me. I was just an excuse."

That comment had enough truth in it that Gordon remained silent.

"It's because of her that it has to come out, all of it. All of the secrets."

"Leave Jennifer out of this, Da. She doesn't have anything to do with us."

"Go away. Just go away. If you go away now, it might be all right. Promise me you'll leave now."

Nothing had changed since that night five years ago when Sean was eager to banish him from Adaire Hall because McBain and Harrison wanted it.

Not once had his father put up an objection.

McBain, Harrison, and Sean had stood on the steps of Adaire Hall as the carriage rolled beneath the oaks, cleared the gates, then made it up the hill. At the top he looked back to find them still watching, like he was a rabid dog they were afraid might return.

The anger rolled in from the past, anchoring itself beneath Gordon's breastbone.

"I'm not going anywhere. Maybe once you could throw me out of the Hall, but not now."

Sean didn't answer.

"I could buy and sell this place a hundred times over, but I still wouldn't be good enough for you, would I?"

Sean closed his eyes. "It's the girl. You still want her, don't you?"

"Hell, yes. When I leave here, Jennifer is coming with me. She and I are going to be married."

"You can't have her."

"Why, because I'm not good enough for an Adaire?"

"No, because she's your sister."

Chapter Twenty-One

"Did you hear me?"

Yes, he'd heard. The words didn't make any sense, however, unless Sean was hallucinating. Laudanum had that effect on some people.

He understood that. He was willing to accept any kind of behavior in this situation. However, telling him that he and Jennifer were related? That seemed more bizarre than a simple hallucination.

Did Death have a face? It was there in that room. He could almost see it superimposed over Sean's features. Pain lingered in his eyes, the set of his mouth, and the tense muscles of his neck.

The tea was cooling in the cup on the bedside table. Perhaps he should drink it. The whiskey might shock him out of this feeling of being disembodied.

"I did wrong by you," Sean said.

How very odd to hear those words from his father. He'd never expected to hear them. Evidently, Death was a hard taskmaster, requiring absolution.

"I didn't know until Betty was dying. She wanted to clear her conscience. Once I knew, I should have said something. I should have told

you, but what good would it have done by then?
You'd already gone. I didn't know you'd come
back for her."

"I don't understand," Gordon said, hearing
himself speak. His lips moved. Words flowed out
of his mouth, but he was curiously still calm and
detached. "Tell me what you meant. About Jennifer being my sister." The words were wooden
and without inflection.

All he had to do was concentrate on one word
at a time, one sentence. That and keep breathing,
even though he felt more and more like a statue
sitting there. He was growing colder, more immo-
bile, frozen into this position of leaning forward,
his hands clasped between his knees. It was easier
to focus on the sheet than his father's face.

"It was because of the fire," Sean said.

Sean didn't speak for several moments. Gordon didn't prod, simply sat there waiting, his
gaze on the bed.

"Betty became Harrison's wet nurse, since she
was also nursing our son as well. He'd been born
only days earlier."

Gordon still didn't speak.

"Not many people had seen the earl's son. The
only person who could have told Harrison from
our son was the countess and she was near death
herself. It was put out that she would probably be
blind if she did survive. Betty had an idea."

Sean moaned and clutched his stomach. Gordon stared at him, knowing he should summon
compassion from somewhere.

"The tea is cold," he finally said, "but the whiskey might help."

Sean shook his head. "No, I'll get through this."

He knew what Sean was going to say. Ridiculous as it was, he could almost say the words themselves. It matched perfectly with what he knew of Betty's character and her antipathy to him.

"Betty had an idea to switch the babies. She saw it as a chance for our son to prosper. She wanted more for him and she got her wish. He became Earl of Burfield."

Gordon's fingers were cold, but so were his feet. His heart was beating, but slowly. Perhaps he would die first and leave Sean staring at him in wonder.

"So what you're saying is that you're not my father."

"No."

"And Betty wasn't my mother."

How very placid he sounded, like the words he was speaking didn't mean anything. Perhaps he didn't have any emotions. No, that wasn't right. He could feel the rage building up beneath his skin. It would break free soon enough.

"And I'm the Earl of Burfield."

"Yes."

"Not Harrison."

"You are Harrison Adaire," Sean said.

"And he's your son."

Instead of answering, Sean grabbed at his midsection again. Gordon helped him sit up, then held the cup of whiskey-laced tea to his mouth. After Sean had taken several sips, Gordon lowered the older man back onto his pillows.

It was some time before Sean could talk again. Gordon sat there, his thoughts congealed, fo-

cused on imagining the night when flames had engulfed the north wing. He'd been inches from death, saved because of the actions of his mother. His mother. Because of a tragedy, everything had changed. Someone steeped in venality, hardened by circumstance, had altered the course of his history.

Sean's words were halting. "I didn't know what Betty had done until just before she died."

"You knew," Gordon said, his tone still calm. "Don't try to tell me you didn't. You've always known somehow. Maybe it was intuition or maybe it was something Betty said, but you knew."

"She wanted more for our boy."

He didn't have any kind words to say about Betty, even before learning what she did. Nor could he summon up any thoughts of a generous nature now.

"Betty died three years ago," Gordon said. "You've known ever since then."

Sean nodded. "I would have told you if I'd been able to find the words, boy."

"I'm not a boy," Gordon said, standing and walking to the window. "I haven't been a boy for a very long time."

His life could have been different with the countess and the earl as parents. With all the advantages they would have given him he could have had the world at his feet instead of clawing his way to the top.

And Jennifer . . .

His thoughts ground to a halt, held in abeyance by a sense of horror so acute that he felt his heart slow.

Jennifer was his sister.

Jennifer was his sister.

The woman he loved was his sister.

It didn't matter how many times he repeated the words, they didn't register. They couldn't penetrate the fog cushioning every emotion.

Gordon had only gotten a few hours of sleep, and no doubt that accounted for this strange sensation he was experiencing, as if he was here but not here. Yet he'd gone without sleep in London often enough without feeling like he was trapped in a soundless bubble. No, this was something different. A feeling of being separate from reality. Perhaps he'd accidentally ingested some laudanum himself.

Time slowed, then stopped. His face was oddly cold. Gordon couldn't hear his breathing. Nor could he feel it through the numbness that was spreading over his chest. His headache, strangely enough, had vanished. His eyes, however, felt as if each one held a spoonful of sand.

He wanted to find a comfortable place, perhaps beneath one of the pines at the edge of the loch. He would stretch out beneath it and take a nap, at least until the chilled air woke him. He'd dream for a bit. A dream that held more substance than this moment sitting at his dying father's bed. Not father. Sean wasn't his father.

Where was Sally? Was she going to stay away for hours, leaving him here? He needed to quit this room. He needed to be away from Sean, most of all.

He could hear noises, but they sounded as if they came from far away. He could feel the

shirt on his body, the cuffs at his wrist, even the shoes on his feet, but they were sensations that were oddly distant. As if they were happening to someone else. Or he was inhabiting a strange body that wasn't his own.

He looked down at Sean, a frail man, who looked even more fragile this morning.

"You stole my future. You stole my life. You lied." He turned back to the window and tried to compose himself. "I've seen a great deal in the past five years. I've seen how people could lie and cheat and walk over a friend or loved one to accomplish what they wanted. I've seen humanity at its worst, but this? This is so much more grasping and greedy than anything I've ever seen or imagined. Congratulations, Sean. You managed to shock me, and I didn't think that was possible anymore."

Sean didn't answer him. His eyes were closed and his breathing seemed more labored than before.

At least the man hadn't sent him a letter posted after his death. He'd had the courage to look Gordon in the face and tell him the truth.

Or maybe it wasn't courage after all. This confession was his attempt to get right with his Maker before his death, much as Betty had done to Sean. Is that all that was required? A confession at the threshold of death and all was forgiven?

Maybe he didn't need to pass judgment on Sean. A higher power would do that. For a moment he wanted to, however. He wanted to condemn him to living, but in continued agony.

He heard the door open and close. Sally was back. He walked to the doorway. Before he left, he turned to look at Sean.

Sean opened his eyes. "You did all right for yourself, even so."

Yes, he'd done all right for himself, without a father or a mother and now without the woman he loved.

He couldn't think of a single remark. Not one decent thing to say to a dying man. He couldn't lie and tell Sean that he forgave either him or Betty. He couldn't absolve Sean of his sins.

Instead, he turned and left the room.

Chapter Twenty-Two

*J*ennifer was hurrying through her tasks so that she could spare time to be with Gordon.

Today she needed to supervise the brushing of the ornate rugs in the formal dining room. Both carpets were woven for Adaire Hall in Belgium fifty years ago. They were still vivid, with borders of roses and thistles.

The skirling of the pipes sent Jennifer to the window. She opened it and sat on the window seat, pleased that James had dressed in the Adaire kilt and presented himself on a nearby hill without being reminded. It was an Adaire custom to welcome any child of the earl into the world with their march.

They would play when Sean died as well, only then it would be a dirge.

As they always did, the sound of the pipes made her heart swell. Something opened up in the cavern of her chest, a spot large enough to encompass the whole of Scotland. How could anyone hear the sound and not be thankful that they were Scottish, that a heritage so proud and fierce was theirs?

When her mother was alive, the two of them would sit together and watch the piper. Some-

times, they'd have a wee dram of whiskey to mark the occasion. She'd always felt such pride in being an Adaire and in living at Adaire Hall.

"I cannot imagine a more fitting send-off, my dear girl. Did you arrange for the piper just for me?"

She turned to see Ellen, dressed for travel, standing at the entrance to the dining room. She smiled at her godmother's quip. Ellen knew the traditions of Adaire Hall as well as Jennifer.

"Are you leaving so soon?"

"I must, my dear. I have things that require my attention in Edinburgh. Now that Lauren has had her baby, can I not convince you to come and stay with me for a while? We could plan your wedding together. Or do scandalous things."

She didn't want a large wedding. In fact, she'd like to be married in the next day or so, but didn't say that to Ellen. Her godmother would insist on an affair that took months of planning.

As for scandalous things, she doubted if Ellen had ever been scandalous a day in her life. Instead, she'd been rigorously proper, the only child of a very religious couple who followed the teachings of the Church of Scotland. The only truly shocking thing she'd ever done was to marry Colin Thornton long past the time that most women married.

"I may come for a visit," Jennifer said. "But not right now."

Ellen kissed her on the cheek and embraced her once again. "Well, if that's the best I can expect, then I shall expect it. No writing me and telling me that plans have changed."

"Thank you for bringing Harrison home. I'm not sure how you did it, but I am grateful all the same."

"I told you, it was your Gordon's Maggie."

Jennifer shook her head. "No, I think it was all you."

They hugged again before Jennifer walked Ellen downstairs and to the front door, where her carriage had already been brought around.

"Before you say a thing," Ellen said, "your housekeeper has already provided me with a basket of food for the journey. Plus, I was promised a delightful bottle of wine."

She wasn't the least bit surprised at her housekeeper's actions. Mrs. Thompson had always admired Ellen, saying on more than one occasion that the world would be a better place with more women like her.

Jennifer watched as Ellen's carriage pulled away from the main entrance and down the oak-shaded drive. The last of the leaves fell on the carriage roof, almost like a benediction of farewell.

She wished she'd been able to convince Ellen to remain for a few days. They didn't see each other often enough. When she was little, she always spent a few weeks at Ellen's home every few months. Now it seemed as if she went for half the year without seeing her godmother.

Ellen had been such a comfort when her mother had died. She had been there toward the last of her mother's illness, spending time with Mary, the two women talking in low tones. More than once she'd interrupted them and seen the signs that each had been weeping.

Every day brought a memory to mind. Her mother might have been restricted to her chair on wheels, and nearly blind, but she had an impact on everyone around her. Mary had made it a point to know as much as she could about every member of the staff. She had Cook make special treats for those having a birthday or some other special day of note. She inquired about their families, their health, or things they liked. She had a phenomenal memory and made it a point to ask something important when talking to each person.

To Mary, someone wasn't just a scullery maid, or a stable boy, or one of the footmen in training. Each was a person, separate and apart from his role in life.

Harrison wasn't as egalitarian as their mother. There were numerous occasions when her mother would stop and single out a member of staff either because his wife had given birth or they'd done something worthy enough to note or their smile was especially attractive. There would be a look in Harrison's eyes that made her think he wished to be anywhere but there. Yet he always forced a smile to his face for their mother's sake and added his words to hers.

Their mother's death had freed Harrison.

Yet Harrison never seemed truly happy, as if something important was missing in his life. She didn't know what it would be, since he seemed to have everything a man could possibly want. He'd been born into a title, a fortune, a magnificent home with a history that mirrored Scotland's. He

had a beautiful wife and now a daughter. What more could he possibly want?

What more could anyone want?

If someone looked at her life, what would they say? Before Gordon returned, they would have seen a woman content with her daily occupations, perhaps, but not entirely happy with her life. She had purpose, but no partner. No one to love, to care for. No one with whom to share her life, her hidden thoughts, or her observations of what went on around her. Not one person ever stopped her during the day, put his hand on her arm, and said, "Tell me what you're thinking, Jennifer."

No one seemed especially curious to know her thoughts. No one but Gordon. Dear, wonderful Gordon.

Everything had changed since he'd come home.

Now she was no longer going to be a spinster aunt, forever puttering around Adaire Hall. She'd be a wife, and perhaps a mother in time. Her life would be shared with the one man she'd always loved.

They'd live in London, unless Gordon wanted to open some entertainments in Scotland. Perhaps they'd become a well-traveled couple, with homes in both countries.

The world was suddenly open to her. They could do anything they wanted.

He loved her. She loved him. She was going to marry Gordon, and they'd never be apart again.

That thought warmed her as she went about her duties. There weren't any disagreements be-

tween the maids or problems with the footmen or stable boys. Harrison hadn't issued any impossible demands. Lauren didn't need her. The baby seemed well and, other than acting like a baby, was thriving.

When Lauren announced that they'd decided to name the baby Mary, Jennifer didn't hide her tears.

One day, she too would be a mother. She could almost see her little boy, nestled in the crook of her arm. Perhaps she and Gordon would have a large family. A boisterous group of children who filled their home with noise and love.

More than once she caught herself humming as she went about her duties. She greeted and smiled at everyone she saw. If Harrison had appeared, she would have even been cordial to him—that's how happy she was.

The world was a wonderful place and she was the happiest person in it.

Chapter Twenty-Three

The Elizabeth Chapel wasn't named for the period of time when it had been built or for any type of architecture. Instead, it had been named after a previous Countess of Burfield, Elizabeth, who was known to be devout almost to a fault.

Adaire Hall was laid out like a square, although after the north wing had burned down, it consisted of only two wings and the original part of the Hall. Behind the ruins of the north wing were a half dozen fair-sized outbuildings, plus the stable, dairy, and barns.

The chapel was located to the east of the Hall, at the end of a serpentine path winding through the statuary gardens.

Gordon opened one of the chapel's double doors. The squeaking hinges made him wonder how long it had been since anyone had entered the building. Perhaps the last time had been the countess's funeral.

His mother's funeral.

He could still remember the procession, pallbearers carrying the coffin through the chapel to the crypt. He'd stood in the back, wishing he could be with Jennifer to comfort her, to hold

her as she wept. She'd struck him as particularly alone, seated next to Harrison and McBain.

The rage that suddenly swept over him was boundless yet impotent. Who did he punish? Sean, a man dying in agony? Betty? She was already beyond any earthly penalties. The inescapable fact was there was no one to bear the brunt of his anger.

Since it was a bright day, the chapel was lit by yellow and red hues from the stained glass windows on three sides. The founding members of the family had been devout, but he didn't think that Harrison had ever invited a visiting minister here.

Gordon made his way down the central aisle, passing all the pews that had been filled on his mother's funeral. Like a larger cathedral, the chapel had an upper recess for the choir, its own impressive sounding organ, and an arched roof with crossed timbers. Above the altar was a stained glass window, one of three. Two doors sat side by side just beyond the altar. The one on the left led to the sacristy, the one on the right to the crypt.

He and Jennifer had explored the crypt once as children. They'd dared each other, and crept down the stairs. He remembered the musty odor that had seemed to cling to him for hours afterward. At the time, with a child's logic, he had thought it was because of all the long-dead Adaire bodies.

Now he knew that it was simply because the crypt was below the earth, and what he smelled was dampness. There were no windows to allow

sunshine to filter in. For that reason, there were candles in various spots, along with matches. At the base of the steps he found the nearest one and lit it, carrying it with him.

He went to stand before the wall facing east. One brass plaque was lighter than the others. He reached out with his right hand and placed his fingers over the incised letters. Mary Alice Adaire, Countess of Burfield. His mother. He wished he'd known. He wished he could have had the freedom of being her son, to embrace her, to kiss her scarred cheek. To tell her thank you for saving him. Thank you for caring more about him than her own safety or health.

Thank you for his life.

Yet, even not knowing who he was, she'd treated him with kindness and love. She'd been as maternal to him as she might have been knowing the truth. She had taught him well, preparing him for the day when he would have no one to watch over him or to care.

His heart ached in a way he could never remember feeling. After a moment he identified the emotion: regret. Perhaps he'd experienced it before, but never this way, never this deeply.

His earliest memories featured Jennifer. They were laughing, holding each other's hands as they were running up one of the hills behind Adaire Hall. Jennifer loved the woods, but she was forbidden to explore them. Even at five, he was more adventurous and probably manipulative. He always urged her to come with him, but she, a year younger, always pulled back, saying in that sweet, lilting voice of hers, "Mama said not."

More than once in his childhood he wished he had a mother like the countess.

He always seemed to interrupt his parents when they didn't wish to be bothered. Or ask questions for which there were no answers. Or tempt Betty to take out the switch she kept hanging by the front door for times when her patience was thin and his daring was great.

All his life he'd had a feeling that he didn't fit in, and now he knew why.

He was having a difficult time reordering his history. The process would probably take years instead of minutes. He wanted to howl, to scream, to claw at life itself, demand that those days, weeks, months, and years be returned to him.

Jennifer had always been an integral part of who he was. She'd been important to him, vital to who he knew himself to be. The day wasn't complete until he'd talked to Jennifer. No problem was that difficult once they'd talked it over. No anger so insurmountable once they'd spoken. She was so vital to his life that he couldn't remember any significant event without her presence in it. When she went off to Edinburgh to be with her godmother for weeks every few months, he'd suffered for her absence.

Betty had known. All those years when she'd seen the relationship developing between him and Jennifer, she'd known the truth. All those years when she'd criticized him for drawing breath, she'd known who he really was. Her selfishness had been stronger than her decency, so she kept silent.

He hated her, more than he ever hated anyone or anything.

What did he do with his rage?

Nothing. Betty was beyond him. He couldn't do anything to her. She'd never get justice.

He turned his attention to the brass plaque belonging to the fifth Earl of Burfield. His father had only lived a few years after the night of the nursery fire, succumbing to an accident while riding his favorite stallion.

Gordon had been five at the time and could barely remember what the man looked like. He tried to make sense of the fact that the earl had been his father, but he discovered that it didn't matter much. Alexander Adaire was only a shadowy figure to him. He couldn't remember much about the man, other than the fact that the countess had grieved for years after his death. No one had ever said anything bad about the earl. He'd been a good employer, a fair man, someone obviously beloved at Adaire Hall.

Two things had happened immediately following his death. Harrison had become the sixth Earl of Burfield, and Richard McBain had arrived at Adaire Hall to become his guardian.

An iron bench had been placed in the middle of the crypt. No doubt it was designed for people to spend some time in contemplation, to weep, or pray. He placed the candle beside the bench and sat. He wasn't weeping, but perhaps his thoughts were in the way of a prayer. He had to be able to handle this, but he was very much afraid it was the one task he'd been given that was greater than his strength.

How did he endure this?

For five years he'd done everything in his power

to remake himself, to become a success. He wanted to be worthy of Jennifer Adaire.

He stood, picked up the iron bench, and hurled it at the wall. When it crashed against the brick, he hauled up one end and threw it again. He wanted to destroy something, lay waste to it, create rubble. He overturned both iron candleholders, hearing them fall to the concrete floor with satisfaction, the candles rolling to rest against the crypt.

The candle sputtered out, leaving him in the darkness.

A moment later he grabbed the decorative trellis of the iron wall, his head falling between his outstretched arms.

"Why?"

God didn't answer.

"Why did this happen? Why did You let it happen?"

God was silent.

Gordon had taken everything he'd been given in his life and managed to overcome it. The only kindness he'd ever been shown had come from the countess and Jennifer. The countess died, and Jennifer had been taken from him, but he'd come back to her.

Now God had taken her away forever.

Sean's deathbed confession had altered the whole of his life.

He'd survived being the gardener's son. He didn't know if he would survive learning that Jennifer was his sister.

Chapter Twenty-Four

Jennifer knocked on the door of the gardener's cottage, but there was no answer. She waited a moment, then knocked again. When she still didn't get a response, she looked into the open window.

She couldn't see anyone in the main room. Sean's door was closed, as was Gordon's. Where was Sally? Sean was too ill to have gone anywhere. Nor did she believe that either Gordon or Sally would have left him alone.

She debated with herself for at least five minutes before putting her hand on the latch and pushing the door in slowly.

"Gordon?"

No answer.

"Sally?"

The window in the front room was wide-open, letting in the cold air.

She heard something, a noise from behind Sean's door. She was violating his privacy as well as Gordon's. With any luck they'd understand that it was worry that had prompted her to trespass.

She walked to Sean's door and stood there listening.

The door wasn't latched completely, and she heard Sally's voice. Not in conversation, but in prayer.

"Sally?"

The door suddenly opened and she was greeted by the sight of Sally standing there, her eyes red and tears on her cheeks.

Behind her the bedroom window was wide-open.

"Oh, Miss Jennifer, I knew it would happen, but it takes you by surprise anyway, doesn't it?"

"Sean? He's passed?"

Sally nodded, brushing at her wet cheeks. "Aye, and Gordon not here."

"Where is he?"

"I don't know," Sally said. "He left about two hours ago and I haven't seen him since."

He hadn't come to the Hall. Where had he gone?

She moved into Sean's room and sat on the chair beside the bed.

The traditions of death were more complicated than those for birth, but both would be observed at Adaire Hall this week. The piper would play the Adaire Lament to let everyone know that someone at the Hall had died.

Sally had already washed Sean's face, his thinning blond hair neatly combed. His ruddy complexion spoke of a life outdoors. The lines that had etched themselves into his face in the past two years were due to pain more than age.

He looked at peace now, his lips almost in a half smile. His hands had been folded, one on top of the other on the sheet. She reached over

and patted Sean's hand, surprised at how cold he felt.

She knew why the windows were open now. It was customary to open the windows at death to allow the soul to fly free.

Blinking back tears, she stood and leaned over the bed to kiss Sean's forehead.

Birth and death had come to Adaire Hall.

"Thank you for everything, Sally. I'll send Moira to help you with the rest of the preparations."

"It was a pleasure, Miss Jennifer. He was a gruff man from time to time, but that was the pain talking. He had a heart in him as well."

Several people, Gordon included, would dispute her analysis of Sean. One thing he had been, however, was unfailingly loyal to her mother and to Harrison.

Sally followed her into the front room. Soon the chairs would all be sprinkled with water. If there was any milk in the cottage it would be poured onto the ground, and a piece of iron would be thrust through any foodstuffs to prevent death from entering them. The mantel clock would be stopped and any pictures covered with a blanket or sheet.

Jennifer would send word to the minister and also inform her neighbors of Sean's death. He'd been an important man at Adaire Hall and they would attend the funeral.

First, however, she had to find Gordon.

GORDON CLIMBED UP the crypt steps slowly. When he emerged into the sunlight of the chapel he blinked at the brightness. Did anyone ever use

the chapel for a place of solace anymore? Did they look up at the altar and wonder if God lingered there?

He wished there was somewhere he could go, like a fox to his den, someplace safe where he could recover from the news he'd been given. Some haven where he could fit armor around his emotions and steady himself.

He had never felt this weak.

The cottage wasn't an option right now. Nor did he want to go to the Hall. He didn't think he could bear seeing Jennifer with his emotions as shredded as they were.

There were a dozen places he could go around Adaire Hall. He could take the path up into the hills like he and Jennifer had often done in order to escape Harrison's bullying and the watchful eyes of the adults. Or he could go past the stables, into the strath, and sit beside the river, watching the waterfall. Instead, he went to the one place that had always meant the most to him, the one spot he'd always gone when he was troubled.

The dock was new, the wood boards replacing those that had been rotting when he was a boy. He'd learned which ones to avoid, to step over, to get to the end, where the rowboat was moored.

He could always take the boat out to the center of the lake and sit there watching as the sun took its path across the sky. He'd be alone at least. No one could bother him. Or he could simply sit at the end of the dock soaking up the sun and feeling the heat on his back, a welcome change from being in the crypt.

This was a favorite place for some of the staff

to fish on their half days off or when their duties were done. No one was here today. Perhaps it would've been better if he'd had company. Anything but concentrate on the thoughts spinning in his mind.

His life was never going to be as filled with promise as he'd thought on rising this morning. He wouldn't have Jennifer with him. She would never be his partner, the mother of his children, the one person he trusted among others.

Loving her was wrong. His brain told his heart that, but his emotions hadn't yet caught up.

How could his life have changed in an instant? Yet it had happened that way five years ago. One moment he was at Adaire Hall, filled with amorphous plans to make something of his life. The next he was shown the door, a carriage bearing him away. Unwelcome, unwanted, and homeless.

Yet it had been the best thing that could have happened to him. He'd been forced to put his effort into all those plans he'd made. He'd remade himself. He could do it again. Except that this time it would be more of a challenge. Instead of a hill, Fate had given him a mountain the size of Ben Nevis to climb.

The sun warmed his back, but he still felt the chill of the day. He should go back to the cottage, gather up his belongings, and leave for London. No one at Adaire Hall would understand his abrupt departure, but he didn't think he could sit with Sean one more minute.

He'd never understood why Sean was so impatient, why he didn't seem to have any fatherly feelings. Everything was beginning to make sense,

like a pattern that had been blurry and was just now coming into focus.

Although Sean had sworn that he hadn't known about the switch until Betty's death, Gordon wasn't sure he believed him. Something must have made Sean suspicious.

Betty's interest and constant praise of Harrison was now understandable. Every time Harrison did something wrong, she was predisposed to instantly forgive him. For years Gordon had resented that preferential treatment, thinking that it was because Harrison was the earl. No, it was because Harrison was Betty's child.

She'd been lucky; everything had conspired to aid Betty in her ruse. There weren't any portraits remaining of the Adaire family since the portrait gallery had been housed in the north wing and had also been destroyed in the fire.

The wet nurse had perished that night. What about the other girl, the nursery maid? Where was she?

He hadn't asked Sean if there was anyone else who knew that the babies had been switched, anyone who could provide testimony as to what Betty had done. For that matter, he would need to record Sean's confession, at least have it witnessed by someone in addition to himself.

Without proof, he had nothing. Without proof, he had to believe Sean.

First of all, he would go back to the cottage, ask Sally to sit with him, and have Sean repeat what he'd learned from Betty. Then he would see if he could find the nursery maid. She'd still been

employed at the Hall when he lived there, but he wasn't certain where she was now.

After that he'd seek out the oldest members of the staff to see if any of them recalled that night so many years ago. There, something he could accomplish. A few tasks to do rather than sit and mull over Sean's confession. Anything but think about the future he wouldn't have.

GORDON WAS SITTING on the end of the dock, just as he had so many times in the past when she'd met him here. Once in a while she'd threatened to push him off the end of the dock. Once he'd done the exact same thing to her. Then he'd been so apologetic at her tears that he'd never done it again.

She'd gotten into trouble that day. It wasn't her mother who'd chastised her for acting like a hoyden. It had been Ellen, who had been visiting.

"Whatever have you done, Jennifer?"

"We were playing," she'd said.

That had not been enough of an explanation for her godmother.

"I don't know what game you are playing, Jennifer Adaire, but you'll soon be a young lady. You must remember your manners at all times. After all, you're Lady Jennifer."

That day had marked a change, not in Gordon's treatment of her, but in her realization that they were growing up. There wouldn't be too many more days like these in which they could play or meet each other to plot some way to avenge themselves on Harrison.

As she walked slowly to the dock, she wished that someone else could do this terrible duty. Yet there was no one close enough to Gordon. No one but her. She didn't want to cause him pain, but she must, simply with the news she brought him.

At least she was here, to offer whatever comfort she could.

GORDON HEARD THE tap of shoes on the dock and knew immediately who it was. He closed his eyes, wishing he had more time to prepare himself.

"Gordon."

Had her voice always been that low and sensual?

"I'd like to be alone, Jennifer."

"Then you know," she said softly. "I'm so sorry, Gordon."

He turned slightly, looking at her over his shoulder. "Know what?"

Know the secret that would forever separate them? Know the truth of his birth? Know that nothing would ever be the same again?

She startled him by kneeling on the dock, her arms reaching out to hug him. He stood, moving away from her before she could touch him.

"Gordon?" She remained on her knees looking up at him. "What's wrong?"

He shook his head, but took several steps away from her.

She stood. "I'm so sorry, but at least you were able to see him before he died."

"Sean's dead?"

She nodded. He stared at the water, the surface of it brightly lit by the sun. A dozen thoughts cas-

caded into his mind, chief of which was the realization that he wouldn't be able to get a witness to Sean's revelations. No one but him would hear the story of Betty's perfidy.

"Gordon?"

She was too damn close. He couldn't bear to smell her perfume, see the tears welling in her eyes, or her face melting into a look of compassion. He could only tolerate so much, and he'd reached his limit.

WHEN SHE WOULD have reached out for him again, Gordon took another step back, almost as if he didn't want her to touch him.

No doubt it was a reaction to the news she'd brought.

"I'll come with you to see him."

"No."

That was a surprise.

"It's all right. He looks like himself, only more peaceful and at rest."

"Death does not imbue anyone with virtue, Jennifer. Sean is Sean whether alive or dead."

He turned and started to walk away from her. He didn't stop to apologize for his behavior. Nor did he offer any explanation for it. She could only assume that grief was causing him to act as if they were strangers to each other, that they hadn't declared their love for one another just yesterday.

Later, after he'd had time to adjust to the news of Sean's death, she knew he would come to her. Until then, she'd wait.

Chapter Twenty-Five

*I*n the next two days, every maid, footman, and stable boy came to Sean's cottage to extend their condolences, and to stand in mute testimony of the fragility of life beside his coffin.

The cottage hadn't been empty since Sean's death. Because Gordon was his only close relative, the staff at Adaire Hall had taken up the duties of family. Sean's body was never left alone but was watched over by two women taking turns. In the morning Sally and Moira surprised him as the next to be Sean's guardians.

Gordon heard countless tales of Sean, vignettes of memory that painted the man as kinder than the person Gordon had known. Someone with a sense of humor that he'd rarely seen. He couldn't help but wonder if the stories had any basis in truth, or if people conjured up something nice to say about Sean McDonnell for his sake.

He thanked each one of them, never saying what was in his mind: that whatever he learned about Sean couldn't offset his greater sin. He didn't care about the man's sense of humor, or his fairness to underlings, or how he'd always personally selected the flowers for the countess's morning table. For three years—or longer—he'd

kept a terrible secret safe, and for that Gordon would never forgive him.

Most people who entered the cottage asked him if he'd heard the dead jack. Evidently, the sound, similar to the ticking of a watch, was an omen known to be present prior at most deaths. He hadn't.

Sean's body had been washed and wrapped in a winding sheet and laid on the *strykin* board provided by Adaire Hall's carpenter. The long flat board was wider and longer than any table in the cottage and would hold the body until the coffin was ready. The front room furniture had been rearranged, the *strykin* board supported on two chairs, and this was where Sean lay, candles kept burning beside him. When it was time, the *kistan*—the laying of the body in the coffin—was held, and close friends were invited to attend. A penny was placed on each of Sean's eyes and a plate of salt on his chest.

Jennifer had been one of the first to pay her respects. Gordon had forced himself to remain standing in the front room, but other than thanking her for coming, he didn't speak.

When he did address her, he found it easier to stare at the far wall above her head, someplace where he didn't have to look at her face, or see the expression in her eyes.

She'd been part of his life, even those five years when he hadn't been physically near her. He'd wondered about her endlessly, allowing his daydreams to carry him into her life at Adaire Hall. Somehow, he was going to have to exorcize her, see her not as someone with whom he could

share a future, but only someone he'd known in his past.

Harrison also showed up on the first day. No doubt because it was expected of him, or because Jennifer had lectured him on the duties of an earl. After sending a cursory glance in Sean's direction, he announced his real reason for coming to the cottage.

"The new head gardener will be moving in soon. You'll have to be quit of this place by the day after the funeral. You're not going to give me any trouble about this, are you?"

Gordon had been able to rein in his emotions for most of the day, but it had been difficult, especially with Jennifer. The last thing he wanted was to be pushed to the edge of his restraint by Harrison's words.

"Do you expect me to give you trouble? Why, do you think I want to fight for the right to live in the gardener's cottage? Don't be an ass. Or is that an impossible task, Harrison?"

Several people filed into the cottage and looked at the two of them curiously. Gordon didn't care. Let the world hear what he thought.

"You're an ass. You've been an ass as long as I've known you. When you were younger, you were a younger ass. Time has done nothing for your character, your demeanor, or your inability to get along with anyone. You look at the world as if it's filled with people who are supposed to identify your every whim, then serve it. You don't see people as they are. Half the time I don't think you even know someone else is around. I'm genuinely surprised that you ever married.

Perhaps your mother had something to say about that, wanting to see you settled before she died."

"Don't talk about my mother, you bastard."

He was so tempted to tell Harrison the truth in that moment. However, he wasn't about to give the other man either the upper hand or a warning. Instead, let him be blindsided by the court case.

"I've never been bothered by names, by the way. You can call me anything you want. I only give credence to those insults from people I respect. Believe me, you're not among that exalted group. You won't have any difficulty getting me to leave this accursed place."

He turned on his heel and left the cottage. Anywhere was preferable to being around Harrison.

SOMETHING WAS WRONG, and Jennifer didn't know what it was.

She hadn't seen Gordon for more than a few minutes since his father died. Some of that was understandable, because there were preparations that had to be made and Gordon needed to be part of those as Sean's son.

Twice she'd tried to see him, but had been told that he couldn't come to the cottage door. She saw him walking toward the loch one afternoon and almost caught up with him. She didn't, because she knew he'd seen her, yet he made no effort to flag her down or try to capture her attention.

He was avoiding her, but she didn't know why.

She had meals taken to the cottage. When Moira or Sally returned the trays, they made certain to

thank Cook, but didn't say if Gordon had eaten. She assumed he had, just one of many assumptions she had to make in the past few days.

Although she hadn't been able to talk with him, she made the funeral arrangements, just as she would have if he'd given her permission. She'd had the chapel opened and aired out, feeling a little shame that there hadn't been many services there in years. Her mother had been the one to invite the village minister to come and officiate. Harrison hadn't done it. Nor had she, an oversight that bothered her now.

She had fresh candles put on the altar and in the two chandeliers. An army of maids dusted and swept, polished the windows and ensured everything was spotless for Sean's funeral.

One of the maids told her that there had been vandalism in the crypt. Together they inspected it and found that things had been tossed around. It only took a few minutes to put everything back in order.

The day of the ceremony Gordon still hadn't said more than a few words to her. Even when she went to see Sean laid out, Gordon remained silent.

What had she done? Had she said something wrong? Even worse, did he regret asking her to marry him? Had he changed his mind?

There was every possibility that he found her boring. Her life hadn't been as cosmopolitan as his in the past five years. All she knew was Adaire Hall.

The fact that he hadn't come to her was more than troubling. They'd always reached out to

each other in times of difficulty. She'd always felt a sense of reassurance to know that Gordon was there for her, yet this behavior was more like those five silent years.

She knew that his relationship with Sean hadn't been an easy one. However, people handled grief in different ways. Perhaps he was mourning the fact that he and Sean hadn't been closer. Or it could be that he was realizing his own mortality. Becoming an orphan had that effect on you. At least it had on her.

By midmorning the minister arrived and pronounced all the preparations to his liking. Villagers and staff filed into the chapel until it was near overflowing. Jennifer stood at the door, waiting.

When Gordon entered the chapel, he was accompanied by Moira and Sally. The two nurses had evidently taken to him, enough to behave like his family.

She told him of the arrangements for the funeral and what would follow. Women did not accompany men to the churchyard. She would not be there for Sean's interment, but had provided refreshments for the men once they returned to Adaire Hall. She expected a sizable number of villagers to also be in attendance.

He only nodded when she finished speaking. She thought he murmured something that sounded like *thank you*, but couldn't be certain. Within moments, the three of them had found a seat in the front pew on the other side of the aisle from the one the family used.

He didn't say another word to her. Nor did he even look in her direction. He acted just like the

man who'd first arrived at Adaire Hall—like a stranger who was not predisposed to like anything he saw.

Blessedly, the service was brief. Sean wouldn't have expected any less. He wasn't overly devout. Nor had Betty been. There would be another service at the graveside, officiated by the same minister.

She and the rest of the women stood aside as the men gathered in a procession, led by Gordon. As the only male member of Sean's family, he would lead all of them in the walk to the village church.

She wanted to say something to him, especially standing there as isolated as he appeared. She wanted to go to him and shock the staff by hugging him in full view of everyone. Yet his behavior had been so strange that perhaps she should talk to him in private first. She needed to find out what was wrong between them.

Gordon was unapproachable and intimidating. She found it hard to believe that she had sat on his lap, kissed him, and told him how much she loved him. Or that she had ever once thought of seducing him.

AN OLD GAELIC proverb stated that *amaisidh an dall air an reilig.* A blind man will find his way to the burial ground. All during the walk to the churchyard Gordon thought of those words.

At the front of the procession was the beadle ringing the passing bell. Behind him came the coffin, hoisted on the shoulders of eight young men who'd worked for Sean, and then came Gordon.

From time to time—due to the distance to the churchyard, he'd been told—the pallbearers would stop, place the coffin on a spot above the ground, such as an overturned stone—and partake of a dram of whiskey.

He sincerely hoped that the two stops they'd already made would be sufficient to get them to the churchyard. Otherwise, he couldn't guarantee anyone's sobriety.

At least tradition had kept Jennifer from accompanying him. For a few hours he wouldn't have to see her. For some time, he could be spared the sight of her walking among the mourners, greeting each of them with the same grace the countess had possessed. He needn't hear her voice, gracious and kind.

Lady Jennifer. She'd never seemed to bear the title better than she had today. When she told him of the arrangements she'd made on Sean's behalf, her voice had been soft and caring. If he'd looked at her, he might've seen tears in her eyes. He knew that, if he'd given her the slightest indication, she would have patted his arm or squeezed his hand.

Or even hugged him.

That would have been unbearable.

He'd never truly lost anyone he loved deeply. Sean's death affected him because he was human. What was it the poet John Donne had said? "Any man's death diminishes me." Beyond that, he felt little.

But Jennifer . . . That was different. For the past week he'd endured. He'd walked and talked, yet felt as if he'd done so as a ghost of himself. He

imagined that what he was feeling was similar to deep grief. Not for Sean, but for Jennifer. He suspected that he would never get over this, but that he would learn to accommodate the enormous hole in his chest. He would never be the same person he had been before Sean's announcement.

How strange that he felt as dead as Sean.

Somehow, he would have to begin to plan his life, unlike Sean who had no such concerns. Unless there truly was an afterlife, and Sean was being called to explain himself even now.

As soon as he took care of his business here, he'd return to London. Jennifer wouldn't understand his departure. She'd thought he'd abandoned her five years ago; what would she think now?

He'd leave her a note. A letter, perhaps. A short written message of his intention to depart Adaire Hall and never see it—God willing—again.

In London he'd be safe from hearing Jennifer's voice, or catching sight of her. He'd never have to smell her perfume again or listen to her laughter. He'd be free of any reminders of her.

All he had to do was get through this interminable day.

Chapter Twenty-Six

$\mathcal{S}$ean McDonnell was put to rest beside his wife. Although the day was chilly, the sun was shining. Birdsong punctuated the ceremony, attended by most of the male inhabitants of Adaire Hall and a good portion of the village. Harrison hadn't bothered to attend.

Thankfully, the ceremony was nearly over, and Gordon would soon be gone from here. Until then, he was determined to stand here, respectfully silent and outwardly stoic.

He glanced at the tombstones around him. The church was one of the oldest in this part of Scotland. The inhabitants of this plot of ground had been here for centuries. Some of the stones were dark and weathered. Others looked to have been newly chiseled.

Who would make arrangements for Sean's stone? No doubt it was his responsibility. One of many that he didn't want to have.

The minister finished and nodded toward Gordon. He felt like an imposter, but he nevertheless scooped a bit of earth from the pile with the implement offered to him and dropped it over Sean's coffin before leaving the graveside.

He needed to be away. Away from the church.

Away from the solemn dirge of bagpipes. Just away.

Unfortunately, he needed to continue this charade for a little while longer. He joined with some of the men he knew from Adaire Hall on the way back. The return walk was not as somber, since they weren't accompanying Sean's coffin. After a few glances in his direction he even heard laughter.

At the Hall, the mourners were greeted with a lavish spread of food, whiskey, wine, and ale. Pipes and tobacco were offered as well. Sean had been an important person at Adaire Hall, and his passing was being treated as such.

"Gordon."

He reluctantly turned to face Jennifer.

"Are you all right? You've barely spoken to anyone."

"Yes, I'm fine."

"How was the churchyard?"

"Tolerable," he said. "Thank you for everything you've done, Jennifer. You've been exceedingly kind."

There, he'd managed to thank her in words that sounded polite. Now all he had to do was walk away, before he was tempted to look at her, to touch her, to pretend that Sean hadn't said what he had.

He'd recently learned that the nursery maid, the one who'd survived the north wing fire, still lived at Adaire Hall. His plan was to visit her tomorrow and receive some corroboration for Sean's story. After that, he'd leave this cursed place.

Jennifer did the one thing he hoped she

wouldn't. She touched his arm, her hand warm through his jacket. He gently pulled away.

"Is it because Sean died?" she asked. "Is that why you're acting so odd?"

It was torture being around her. He glanced down at her. Today she was wearing black in honor of Sean, and the color emphasized her creamy complexion and the brilliant green of her eyes.

"Have I done something wrong?"

He focused on the people around them. There was the stable master, dressed in his best suit, standing next to two of the boys who worked in the stables. Beyond him was Ned, the new head gardener who would soon occupy Sean's cottage. He even saw Harrison, who was holding court in the corner. Perhaps he should congratulate the man for deigning to make an appearance.

"What is it, Gordon? You're worrying me."

He finally directed his gaze back to Jennifer. She hadn't changed. She was still as beautiful as ever.

"Nothing's wrong. I simply have other things on my mind," he said, keeping his voice carefully neutral.

"I haven't seen very much of you recently," she said.

"We went five years without seeing each other. I'm sure you got into the habit. I know I did."

One hand went to her throat as she stepped back. Her eyes were wide and, if he was right, she was on the verge of tears.

He'd accused Harrison of being an ass, yet he'd behaved worse. He'd hurt Jennifer.

He turned and left her, striding away from the Clan Hall.

Jennifer watched as Gordon walked away from her. The change in him since Sean died was like sunshine and rain. One day he was passionate and romantic. The next day he was remote, inaccessible, and rude, someone she hardly recognized.

Something was terribly wrong and she didn't think it had anything to do with Sean's death. Had he received a letter from London containing bad news? Had Harrison said something to him?

Someone had to act as host for this gathering. Gordon had walked off, and she didn't think he was returning. Lauren still hadn't left her bed following Mary's birth. She wouldn't bother asking Harrison; he wouldn't do anything to help Gordon. Therefore, the duty fell to her. She went from person to person, thanking them for their attendance and their kind words about Sean. She gave orders for more whiskey to be brought up due to the volume of toasts given in Sean's honor.

If anyone thought it odd Gordon wasn't there, no one said as much to her. Perhaps his actions would be seen as normal, given that he hadn't returned home in five years to visit his father.

The man she'd known would've come to her and explained what was wrong. He would have told her how he felt, regardless of what it was. They'd always been open to each other, always forgiving. He could tell her anything, and if she didn't understand she would ask for more infor-

mation. Yet he knew—or at least he should've known—that he could say anything to her.

She loved him.

The man who'd faced her only minutes earlier hadn't wanted comfort or understanding. He hadn't even looked at her. Gordon had gone out of his way to be hurtful, and she'd never known him to behave like that.

Still, love wasn't convenient. It didn't vanish when things got difficult. Her love for Gordon hadn't dissipated after five years of separation. It wasn't going to disappear now. Besides, love was even more important during turbulent times.

The girl she'd been, sweet and perhaps naive, would have retreated to her room with hurt feelings. However, she'd had five years of experience to fall back on. Gordon had come back into her life. She wasn't going to let him walk out of it again. If he had any issues with her, if he was angry or annoyed, he was simply going to have to tell her what was wrong. She was not going to accept either silence or his absence again. He was too important to her happiness.

For the next hour she saw to her hostess duties, all the while hoping that Gordon would reappear. She didn't get her wish, but at least the guests at this gathering were replete with food, stories, and enough whiskey to make them wish that they hadn't raised their glass for another toast.

She escaped for a few moments to check on Lauren. Mrs. Farmer had told her—at excruciating length—that a gentlewoman, especially a

countess, did not leave her bedroom after giving birth for at least two weeks.

She didn't tell the midwife that her mother hadn't followed such an arbitrary rule. She'd heard stories of how Mary had arrived back at Adaire Hall carrying her. A combination of bad weather, a ruined road, and a broken wheel had kept her parents stranded at a friend's house. Instead of being born at the Hall, Jennifer had been born near London. However, her mother had always told her that it didn't make her any less of a Scot.

Mrs. Farmer was, unfortunately, still as jealous a guardian as she had been before Mary's birth. Jennifer had been given strict instructions that she wasn't to disturb the countess with any distressing news. Nor was she to ask any intrusive questions. She was to treat Lauren as if she were a delicate flower, easily bruised.

From what she'd seen, Jennifer didn't think that a delicate flower could survive childbirth, but she was careful not to say that to Mrs. Farmer.

She made her way to Lauren's bed, and despite the midwife's frown, sat on the edge of the mattress. Lauren had insisted that Mary's cradle be beside her, and Mrs. Farmer had grudgingly allowed such an arrangement. Lauren had also insisted on nursing her own child. Jennifer couldn't quite tell if Mrs. Farmer agreed or disagreed with such a decision. The woman's face underwent a series of expressions each time she lifted Mary out of her cradle and delivered her to Lauren.

"You've come at the perfect time," Lauren said

with a smile. "Mary's just gone down for a nap. Her tummy is full and her nappy isn't."

Lauren had always been a pretty girl, but giving birth had bestowed on her something, a quality Jennifer found difficult to describe. Perhaps it was radiance.

"I think she must've gained a great deal of weight already."

Tradition dictated that a baby was never weighed before her first birthday, so it would be a mystery until then. The baby did look extraordinarily healthy with a boisterous set of lungs.

"Are you hungry?"

Lauren smiled. "I'm always hungry lately," she said.

Jennifer went to the door, opened it, and waved two maids inside. She had prepared a tray for not only Lauren, but Mrs. Farmer. She'd also provided a selection of beverages. She wasn't the least bit surprised when Mrs. Farmer chose whiskey and Lauren opted for ale.

"Thank you for thinking of us," Lauren said.

The midwife unbent enough to add her thanks to Lauren's.

"Have you seen Harrison today?"

Lauren's face changed, ever so slightly, but it was enough to tell Jennifer what she needed to know. The baby hadn't changed Harrison's character. It was one thing to ignore an infant. Mary wouldn't know of her father's desertion—but Lauren?

"He's in the Clan Hall," Jennifer said, exchanging a glance with Mrs. Farmer.

Regardless of how Harrison behaved, Lauren would be a good mother, and Jennifer would be a good aunt. The newest Adaire wouldn't notice for a while that her father didn't seem to care for her.

Who did Harrison care about, besides himself?

Jennifer spent a while in conversation with Lauren and Mrs. Farmer before returning to the celebration in the Clan Hall.

Her brother was still in the corner, playing laird to a nonexistent clan. It suited him, just as it did to dress up in the Adaire tartan from time to time, as if to remind everyone exactly who he was.

"Where's the bereaved son?" he asked her, surveying the crowd.

She estimated that there were still at least a hundred people in the Clan Hall, even though it had been hours since the men had returned from the churchyard.

"He isn't here. Why, do you want to cause a scene with him?"

"I want him gone, Jennifer."

She deserved some say in what happened at the Hall. She'd served as its factor, steward, and chatelaine for the past five years without recognition or thanks. When she said as much to her brother, he sent her a quick look.

"Bored, Jennifer? Prefer to have your lover in residence? Don't worry. We have some new stable boys who might interest you."

She took a deep breath and told herself not to respond. Harrison's coarseness had always been

a goad. Conversation with him was often a blood sport.

"What? No rejoinder? Have you already sampled them?"

"Must you be so horrible, Harrison? On this occasion?"

"I don't know if you've noticed, Jennifer, but this is my home. Not yours. You live here on sufferance."

She always had, a comment she didn't bother to make.

Did he never give any thought to who would do the quarterly allowances if she didn't? Who would do the accounts? Who would ensure that the repairs to the Hall were made so that the bricks didn't fall down around their heads? Who would perform the inventory, instruct the housekeeper, meet with the majordomo and the stable master?

Harrison had no concept of how things ran. He probably thought that elves came out of the woodwork or brownies worked after midnight to polish the silver and clean the floors.

"Have you seen your wife today? Or your daughter?"

"Calling me to account, are you? A clever way to deflect from the point of this conversation, sister. However, I won't be questioned by you. See that he's gone. I would hate to have to escalate the issue."

Harrison was capable of doing anything. He believed himself to be a prince and Adaire Hall his kingdom.

"You really don't have any humanity, do you?"

"For McDonnell? Why should I? He's been spoiled, Jennifer. Someone should have pointed out to him exactly who he was. The gardener's boy. That's it. Nothing more."

"I would worry about your own behavior, brother. You haven't seen Lauren today, have you? Have you even seen your daughter? Or do you intend to ignore them completely?"

"I should like to know the answer to that question myself."

They both turned to see Hamish Campbell standing behind them, flanked by his two bespectacled secretaries, young men who rarely smiled but were assiduous in their note-taking.

Jennifer had only seen the man a few times, the first at Harrison's wedding. She didn't doubt that he would have been here more often if he hadn't been in America. The minute he'd heard that his daughter was about to become a mother, however, he'd changed his plans and booked passage home.

If nothing else, Hamish should be an example to her brother.

Mr. Campbell was short, stocky, and possessed a face that regrettably reminded Jennifer of an English bulldog. Yet what he lacked in physical charisma, he made up in genuine charm. She, herself, had been the object of his interest at the wedding dinner. She had the feeling that he'd wanted to assure himself that she was sufficiently proper company for his daughter.

"How is Lauren?" he asked, turning from Harrison to Jennifer. "She wrote me, Lady Jennifer,

and said that you were instrumental in her happiness. I thank you for that."

Jennifer felt a little odd. "Lauren is a friend of mine. We do what we can to help our friends."

He nodded. "That we do, Lady Jennifer. That we do."

He'd insisted on calling her Lady Jennifer despite the fact that she had urged him to dispense with the honorific.

"If you will tell me where my daughter is, I will leave you to your celebrations," he said.

Jennifer stepped forward and placed her hand on Mr. Campbell's arm. "I'm afraid it's not a celebration, sir, but a funeral supper."

"My apologies, then."

Jennifer told him about Sean as they walked up the stairs to the earl's suite. She glanced behind her to find that Harrison hadn't followed them. What was her brother thinking? Didn't he realize that Mr. Campbell was teetering on the edge of full-blooded anger?

She almost wanted to warn him, but then thought about what he had said. Perhaps it was time for people to stop protecting Harrison from himself. It was time he reaped what he sowed, and if that was Mr. Campbell's anger, then so be it.

Mr. Campbell, as a successful industrialist, was no doubt a financial genius. However, he didn't have as tight a rein on his temper as he did his empire, especially where Lauren was concerned. Over the past several months, Jennifer had exchanged several letters with Mr. Camp-

bell, all of them centered on his daughter's welfare. She'd hurried to assure him that Lauren was healthy and that Mrs. Farmer had made several visits to Adaire Hall to assure herself of that fact as well.

After entering the earl's suite, Jennifer witnessed a reunion that brought tears to her eyes. It was evident that Hamish Campbell was overwhelmed with love, not just for his daughter, but his new grandchild.

That little girl was not going to lack for anything, at least if her grandfather could provide it. Hopefully, that would make up for her father's indifference.

Chapter Twenty-Seven

"What's the bastard doing here?"

Jennifer looked up at Harrison, shocked. He rarely showed up for breakfast, but he'd evidently made an effort because of Mr. Campbell. Not much of an effort at that, because he looked as if he'd slept in his clothes and hadn't yet shaved. He employed a valet, but he'd probably left the man in London. Or else Ellen had refused to bring him in her carriage. She wouldn't put that past her godmother. Ellen was exceedingly determined when she wished to be.

Jennifer nodded to one of the maids and the girl rushed to put another place setting on the table. Thankfully, Mr. Campbell had already eaten and she'd had a tray taken to Lauren.

"Are you referring to your father-in-law?"

"Unless there's some other bastard who's arrived unannounced. Adaire Hall is getting as crowded as King's Cross station."

"He's Lauren's father. I should think that it would be perfectly understandable for him to be here, Harrison. Lauren is his daughter and Mary is his granddaughter."

"That's not why he's here," Harrison said, kicking out a chair. He sat heavily, propping his

elbows on the table. He looked as if he had continued drinking after the funeral supper for Sean had ended. "He's here to check on me. To ensure than I'm being a dutiful husband. The bastard thinks he has the right to dictate my life."

"Does he know how much time you spend in London? If that's the case, perhaps he does."

"You always were a disloyal bitch, Jennifer."

She bit back her irritation. "I'm only stating the truth, Harrison. You can't ignore your wife for eight months and have anyone think that's acceptable behavior."

"What do you know about it?"

"Why do you always have to be nasty when someone calls you out on your behavior, Harrison?"

"Because I'm tired of people telling me what I should do and what I shouldn't do. Especially you, Jennifer. You've turned into a scold."

She sat back against the chair, took another sip of her tea, and tried to compose herself. Every conversation with Harrison devolved into an argument.

"Spend a little more time home and less in London. Or gambling. Then Mr. Campbell won't have any grounds for criticism."

Yes, perhaps she was a scold, but she knew what her brother was doing to Adaire Hall. The Adaire fortune he'd inherited wasn't going to last forever, especially at the rate Harrison was going through it.

"Why do I need Campbell criticizing me when I have you, Jennifer? You don't know anything about my life in London."

She put down her cup, clasped her hands in front of her, and prayed for patience. "I know what I read, Harrison. You're in the papers more than you should be. If Lauren and I can read about your exploits, so can Mr. Campbell."

She stood and put her napkin beside her plate. She hadn't finished with her breakfast, but she wasn't going to sit there and argue with Harrison.

"Who do you want me to act like, Jennifer? Your precious Gordon?"

He got up from the table and advanced on her. She wisely took a few steps toward the door. She'd seen Harrison's temper up close, and she had no intention of being a victim of it again.

She'd always considered her brother a handsome man, but not this version of him. It was as if all of his insecurities, all of the hatred and envy and rage he'd ever felt was compressed into the look on his face now.

"First Gordon and now Mr. Campbell. You don't like anyone showing up at Adaire Hall, do you?"

"Not if they think they can dictate my movements."

"God forbid someone tells you what to do. You're so much better than the rest of us, aren't you?"

Harrison had struck her before, when he was inebriated. At least that's the excuse he'd given her the next day when he apologized. He'd claimed that she'd been in the wrong by goading him. The only thing she said was that he needed to watch his expenditures in London.

Now she stood where she was and folded her arms, looking up at him and praying for courage.

"What are you going to do, Harrison? Hit me for daring to question you? Would that make you feel better? It seems to me that it would be a hollow victory to hurt someone weaker than you."

He raised his fist and for a moment she thought he was going to carry through with the threat. A second later he turned on his heel and walked out of the dining room.

Only then did she take a deep breath.

For the first time she was grateful her mother was dead. At least she didn't have to witness what a bully her son had turned out to be.

BECAUSE OF HER actions the night of the fire in helping to save the countess, Margaret McBride had been treated as a heroine. For thirty years she'd worked directly for the countess until such time as age crept up on her and made accomplishing her duties more difficult. Since she'd been promised a place to live until the day she died, she essentially retired at Adaire Hall.

He remembered her as a tall, thin woman with graying hair, a sharp nose, and suspicious eyes.

He made his way to the third floor and, thanks to a friendly maid, found Margaret's room.

The woman sitting by the window in an overstuffed chair had aged a great deal in the past five years. Her hair, now almost entirely white, was worn in a tight bun. Her face had folded in on itself, a network of lines on top of lines. Her eyes, brown and still suspicious, focused on him.

"Miss McBride?"

She nodded, still studying him.

For a moment he wondered if she could see, then if she could see well enough to recognize him. It seemed as if she could, because she glanced away from him, then back again, and then finally fixed her gaze on the view outside her third-floor window.

"May I speak with you?"

"You're speaking, aren't you?"

Her voice was thin, as if the effort to talk took too much of her breath.

"I'm Gordon McDonnell," he said. "I don't know if you remember me, but I used to live here a number of years ago."

She buried her trembling hands beneath the yarn in her lap.

"Do you remember me?"

"If I do or if I don't, what does it matter?"

She didn't look at him. Instead, her attention was on a tree not far from the window. A squirrel ran up the branch closest to the sill, almost as if he wanted to come and visit before thinking better of the idea.

Gordon came and sat on the edge of her neatly made bed.

"I heard a story, Miss McBride, about something that happened after the fire. I understand that you helped save the countess and her son."

She didn't respond to his comment. Nor did it look like she was paying any attention to what he was saying. Had age addled her wits?

"Do you remember the fire?"

She finally turned to look at him. "Of course I remember the fire. How could I forget it, Gordon

McDonnell? A body doesn't forget something like that."

"I imagine it was a terrible time, but you were very brave."

Her eyes narrowed.

He could be charming when he wished, but he doubted if Miss McBride would succumb to blandishments. Perhaps the best approach was to be direct and honest with her.

"There were two babies at Adaire Hall back then, weren't there? The countess's child and one born to Betty McDonnell, the wife of the head gardener."

"What if there were? Are you thinking that it's unusual for babies to be born?"

"Sean died a few days ago, Miss McBride."

She simply stared at him. She didn't offer any condolences. Was the woman as cold and withdrawn as she appeared?

Or had he frightened her?

"He told me a story before he died. I'm trying to discover if it was the truth or not. Can you help me with that?"

She leaned back and closed her eyes. "I'm tired. Go away, Gordon McDonnell."

He wasn't going to leave until he got the answers he needed.

"You cared for the countess's son, did you not? You were one of the few people who knew what the baby looked like, Miss McBride."

"I'm an old woman and all I want now is a little peace. If you were a decent man, you'd leave now."

"Betty confessed something on her deathbed. Would you like to know what she said?"

"I'm too old and too tired for stories. Leave me be."

"Sean told me that Betty switched the babies after the fire. You were one of the few people who would know if that's true."

She opened her eyes, turned her head, and stared at him.

"What is it you want from me?"

"The truth. Did Betty switch the babies, Miss McBride?"

"She was a hard woman. I imagine you know that, Gordon McDonnell. She could put fear into anyone just with a glance. We weren't friends, in case you think that."

"Did Betty switch the babies, Miss McBride?" he asked again.

She looked away, staring out the window once more.

"We lost one of our own that night. A lass by the name of Maisie. She was a good girl, a strong girl. She'd had her own child just three months earlier. Her husband was as proud as could be that she got a place at Adaire Hall. I didn't even get to go to her funeral."

She looked up at him, and he was startled by the sheen of tears in her eyes.

"It took the countess months after the fire to leave her sickbed. It took me weeks."

She shocked him by pulling up her skirt to reveal her right leg. It was a web of scars, just like the countess's face. She wasn't done, however. She unbuttoned her cuff and rolled up her right sleeve. It, too, showed signs of being badly burned.

"I'm sorry. I didn't know."

"There was no reason for you to. I don't go around showing myself to other people."

She buttoned her cuff again, taking so much time with the task that he almost bent forward to do it for her. She wouldn't have welcomed that.

"To answer your question, Gordon McDonnell, I don't know. By the time I was well enough to take up my duties again, two months had passed. Whatever I suspected, I kept to myself."

He didn't believe her. There was something in the way she refused to meet his eyes that told him she was lying.

She closed her eyes again, effectively shutting him out. He couldn't pull words from her mouth or a confession from her soul.

"Would Betty have told anyone else?"

"Leave me, please. I am tired."

He stood and looked down at her. "Betty might have given her son the life he would otherwise never have known. To do that, she stole mine."

She finally met his look. "You've prospered all the same."

"I have."

"So who gets the credit for that, Gordon McDonnell? Betty, I'm thinking."

"Does she get the blame, too, Miss McBride?"

"If she does, it's too late to make amends."

There was his answer, shining clear in her rheumy eyes.

He wasn't Gordon McDonnell. He was the rightful heir to an earldom and to Adaire Hall.

And Jennifer was his sister.

Chapter Twenty-Eight

$\mathcal{T}$he time had come to leave Adaire Hall. Gordon would never return, even if Harrison bankrupted the estate. Other people would wander through the buildings and appraise the furniture and belongings. He wouldn't see it again.

He found himself walking toward what was left of the north wing. The countess—his mother—had told him that in addition to the nursery, there had been a gun room here, the portrait gallery, a spare larder, and a number of other rooms.

He remembered, when he was a boy, that a team of workers imported for the task had come to Adaire Hall. For weeks they'd pulled down the remaining bricks stained black by the fire. Sean had complained about them and Betty had told him that they were Irish workers.

"Starving, most like," she said. "Be glad you've got a meal in your belly, boy."

Even though they'd razed the black bricks, the foundation was still there, incised into the earth, a reminder of the tragedy that had happened all those years ago. When he'd been reborn as the gardener's son.

Sean had planted hedges and flower beds over the stones, and Gordon walked the outline of the

north wing now, imagining the chaos of that night. All of the servants had been able to escape the blaze, but none of them had thought to alert the nursery staff.

The countess had seen the fire as the alarm had gone out. Instead of staying safe, she'd climbed the steps, intent on reaching her infant son, only days old. She'd gotten to the nursery just as the fire had expanded, taking out half of the third floor. Three of them had tried to escape, but only the countess with her child—him—and Margaret had made it to the second floor. From there, he'd been told, they'd had to jump to safety. The countess had taken the time to rip her skirt into lengths. She'd tied them together before wrapping him securely in a bundle. Once she was certain he'd be safe she'd dropped him slowly to the rescuers below. Flames had surrounded her and only Margaret's quick wit in pushing her to safety and jumping afterward had saved their lives.

He glanced back toward the main building and the terraced gardens leading up to the older part of the house. He could remember the day he'd felt drawn to the countess, had walked up to her wheeled chair and presented her with a bouquet of flowers he'd hastily plucked from Sean's beds. He knew, at the time, that he'd probably be punished for doing so, but it was worth it. His gesture had drawn a smile from the countess, and he'd smiled back at her.

Had he instinctively recognized the woman who'd given him birth? Or was it simply that she was the antithesis of Betty?

Not only had she saved his life, but she'd changed it with her kindness. She'd given him an education that he wouldn't have gotten without her. She'd given him part of herself, not knowing that he was her son.

He was leaving today. He'd already sent word to Peter to prepare the carriage. He'd go back to London and begin his legal fight to reclaim his name and birthright. He would never use Harrison's name, but the title was his.

"Gordon?"

He heard her voice, but couldn't bring himself to turn and face Jennifer. He'd never considered himself cowardly, but seeing her at the funeral yesterday had been almost more than he could bear.

"We need to talk, you and I."

No, they didn't. The fewer encounters with Jennifer, the better. He hadn't even been able to write a note to her. The words wouldn't come. If he didn't see her, he could pretend that he was handling this situation with equanimity, that he was equipped to understand and even accept it.

"I really must insist."

Didn't she realize that you rarely got what you wanted in life? Life was a series of compromises. He'd learned that, even before leaving Adaire Hall.

He finally turned, wishing that he had been able to leave without seeing her.

They stood on opposite sides of the foundation. A curious place to have this confrontation, but perhaps the best spot of all.

"Gordon, what is it?"

Was there something on his face, some expression he couldn't control? Something in his eyes, perhaps, that indicated what he was feeling?

"I've been told you're leaving. Weren't you going to say anything to me? What's wrong? Will you at least tell me that?"

There, something he could respond to without feeling like his guts had been ripped from him.

"I have to return to London."

"Were you going to go without telling me?"

Yes, if he could have. It would be easier. It would have been better.

The morning sun danced on her hair, bringing out auburn highlights. Her cheeks were slightly pink, indicating her emotions. Her green eyes were too imploring, too filled with emotion for his comfort. She was wearing a burgundy dress beneath her black cloak and looked every inch like Lady Jennifer, perfect, beautiful, and once his.

"I have to go," he said. He sounded dispassionate enough. There was hardly any inflection in his tone.

She took another step toward him, and he almost turned and walked in the other direction. He couldn't be near her. He couldn't be close. Even now, knowing what he knew, he wanted to enfold her in his arms and comfort her.

A habit of a lifetime was difficult to break.

He should cling to those five years when he hadn't seen her. Five years when he'd had practice in missing Jennifer.

"Would you tell me what I did?" she said. "Are you angry with me? What is it, Gordon?"

He only shook his head, wishing she would return to the Hall.

"Thank you for everything," he said, his manners finally coming to the fore. "You've been very generous."

"Why are you treating me like we're strangers? You told me you loved me. You asked me to marry you."

He looked up at the clear blue, unforgiving Scottish sky. He would forever remember that color. This day, this morning with its winter chill would always strike him as the end. Not of life, but of innocence, perhaps. Or a certain era where he believed that it was possible to achieve his goals. To be happy as he'd always imagined. Those hopes were forever dashed.

"I can't marry you, Jennifer."

"Why?"

She was not going to let it go, was she? She was not going to accept that everything had changed until he said the words.

"I'm going back to London, Jennifer. It's best if we forgot this interlude. That's all it was. It didn't mean anything. It wasn't real."

She grabbed her skirt and stepped over the edge of the foundation, marching through the flower bed toward him.

Her cheeks weren't simply pink now. They were red, and there was fury in her eyes. She'd always had a temper, and it was out in full force.

"What do you mean an interlude?" Her voice was this side of a shout. "What, you came back to Adaire Hall to amuse yourself? Oh, my father is

dying, but in the meantime I can fool this poor bumpkin of a lass? Who in the blazes do you think you are, Gordon McDonnell?"

"That's the problem, Jennifer," he said, the words slipping out of him. "I'm not Gordon McDonnell." His voice was nearly as loud as hers.

"I don't understand."

"Neither did I. Until Sean spelled it out for me. I'm not who you think I am. I'm not even who I thought I was." He told her about what Betty had done. "Harrison is Sean's son. I'm the rightful Earl of Burfield."

He knew the second it occurred to her.

Her face turned ashen as her eyes widened. "Then . . ."

"Yes," he said. "I'm your brother."

SHE STARED AT him, unable to get beyond that one thought. It echoed in her brain the same way sound reverberated in the Clan Hall when it was empty.

"You're my brother." Even the words sounded wrong. "You can't be."

He didn't say anything, and it was his silence that overwhelmed the echo.

"You have to be wrong," she finally said.

He still didn't speak, only looked at her with his beautiful blue eyes.

"You have to be wrong," she repeated.

"Not according to Sean. He wanted to purge his conscience, tell me what Betty had done. I don't think he would have said anything if I hadn't told him we were going to marry."

She stared up at him.

"Betty wanted a better life for her child and stole mine. I could almost understand the impulse, but she played God. The worst thing was that she knew how I felt about you. She knew, and she never said a word."

"This can't be real."

His smile was soft and incredibly sad.

"We don't look alike," she said.

"You and Harrison don't look alike, either."

What if it was the truth? The horrible truth?

Her mind was beginning to wrap around the idea, even as she tried to repudiate it. This was why Gordon had been so different, why he'd avoided her. He, too, was coming to grips with Sean's confession.

Something died inside her, and she felt it as it writhed and curled and twisted in its death throes.

This was the man she loved. This was the man against whom all other men had been compared. This was the man she'd kissed and with whom she'd planned a future. She'd thought about the children they would have, the life they'd create.

She was suddenly so cold that the trembling was almost anticlimactic. She wished she'd worn her gloves, but the day had seemed too temperate earlier. She wrapped her arms around her midriff and fought back the nausea.

He took one step toward her, then seemed to think better of it, stopping where he was.

"You might as well know something else. I hold Harrison's markers. He's a gambler, but not a good one. Adaire Hall is essentially mine now."

A moment later he turned and walked away, leaving her standing there.

Life will give you lessons that seem too hard to bear, my darling girl. You must accept them anyway and become the stronger for it.

Her mother's words. Mary Adaire had lived a shadowy existence ever since the night of the fire. Yet she'd never complained, either about her deep, life-altering scars and infirmities or the fact that she could barely see.

Her mother was wiser than she. Stronger, too. Yet the loss of her husband had changed her. Grief had worn her down just as it was eroding Jennifer.

The cold wrapped around her like a blanket made of ice. She thought that Sean might be warmer in his grave than she felt at this moment.

Somehow, she had to take a step and then another. She was standing in a mulched flower bed. If Sean were alive, he would fuss at her now. She had to get to the Hall and then upstairs to her rooms without speaking to anyone. Without anyone coming up to her with an endless request for information or permission. She would shatter if anyone talked to her. She would disintegrate if she was forced to answer any kind of question.

The Hall loomed before her. All those steps seemed impossible to navigate. She couldn't do it. She fell to her knees in the flower bed. Better here than someplace private. There she might scream at God, demand to know what sick and horrid jest He had perpetrated on them.

She sat back on her heels, clutching her hands together. She was getting her cloak dirty and her best dress soiled as well. How very strange that it didn't seem to matter.

In that moment she wasn't Lady Jennifer Adaire of Adaire Hall. She was simply Jennifer, of the wild curls and abandoned laughter, who ran through the strath following Gordon, who found limitless things about which to be fascinated, who hoped and dreamed and wept when her love left her, only for him to return and destroy her.

She didn't know how long she knelt there, but she heard the sound of a carriage pulling away from the Hall. She wasn't able to see it until it had climbed to the top of the hill. Then it seemed to hesitate.

Did Gordon wave goodbye? Did he tip his hat to her in a final, horrible gesture of farewell?

She had to get up before someone saw her. She had to stand and make it to the Hall. A low, keening sound emerged from deep inside her chest. She wanted to silence herself but couldn't. The grief was too great, the sorrow too overwhelming. She finally grabbed the edge of her cloak and stuffed it into her mouth, unsurprised when her hands came away wet with tears.

"Lady Jennifer?"

Oh no. Oh no. He was the very last person she wanted to see. Yet even Mr. Campbell's presence wasn't enough to control her weeping. He bent and put his hands under her arms, helping her stand.

"Lady Jennifer, what's wrong? What can I do?"

His unexpected kindness was enough to summon another wave of tears. He pulled her into his arms, and she fell against him, both horrified and grateful for his presence. He didn't say anything else, simply let her cry there in a flower

bed. Occasionally, he would pat her back, but not a word passed between them.

Somehow, she returned to her suite of rooms. She wasn't entirely certain how it had happened, but it had involved, strangely enough, Mrs. Farmer who, along with Mr. Campbell, provided a wall of security around her.

She heard a few people questioning her appearance, but Mr. Campbell simply brushed them off. Then, she was in her bedroom, and Mrs. Farmer was helping her off with her cloak and then her dress before wrapping her in her dressing gown and sitting her in her favorite chair beside the window. Then that remarkable woman was rubbing her feet. Her bare feet that were as cold as a block of ice.

In the next few minutes a maid arrived with a tray of tea and biscuits. After that, she was wrapped in a blanket and tucked back into the wing chair. Once she'd curled her hands around the hot cup of tea, Mr. Campbell entered her room.

He came and sat on the footstool in front of her, Mrs. Farmer standing near.

"What can I do for you, Lady Jennifer? What service can I perform for you?"

She hadn't meant to, but she started to cry again. Mrs. Farmer clucked at her and said something to Mr. Campbell that made him get up and leave the room. When they were alone, Mrs. Farmer took his place on the footstool, holding her hands and looking earnestly up into Jennifer's face.

"You must tell me if you were importuned, my

dear. There are things that I can give you that would prevent any scandal."

It took a minute or two for Jennifer to understand what the midwife was saying.

"Thank you, Mrs. Farmer. Truly, but it's not necessary. No one did anything to me."

The midwife didn't say anything, merely kept holding Jennifer's hands as if she expected another tearful confession in a moment. There was nothing to confess. She'd done nothing. Neither had Gordon. They'd been innocent in this horror.

She gently pulled her hands free.

"Thank you, Mrs. Farmer, for your care of me. Please thank Mr. Campbell, too. And now I think I'd rather be alone for a while, if you don't mind."

She had every intention of crying some more and didn't want a witness.

The older woman stood, nodding down at her. She had the feeling that Mrs. Farmer understood exactly why she wanted to be alone.

"Thank you, again."

"You'll let me know if there's anything I can do to help you?"

If there was anything anyone could do, she'd be grateful for their assistance. She would beg them for it. Nothing, however, could make the situation better.

Nothing at all.

Chapter Twenty-Nine

Jennifer gave orders for tea to be delivered to the Mackenzie Parlor, named after a friend of the family several generations ago. All she truly wanted to do was remain in her rooms, but Mr. Campbell had asked her to meet with him. Why, she didn't know, she only hoped that their meeting would quickly be over.

She hoped Mr. Campbell didn't want to talk about Harrison. She had no influence over . . . Her thoughts stumbled to a halt. He wasn't her brother, was he? Even so, she didn't have any influence over Harrison. No one did.

She'd chosen this room because the Mackenzie Parlor was distant enough from the rest of the public rooms that they wouldn't be disturbed.

"Lady Jennifer?"

She looked up to find Mr. Campbell standing in the doorway. She smiled her welcome as he entered the room. Surprisingly, Lauren followed him and behind her was the nursemaid with little Mary.

Lauren sat on the end of the sofa, opposite the chair where Jennifer was seated.

"This is your first outing," Jennifer said. "How was it?"

Lauren smiled. "Other than the staircase, it was fine. I shall have to take my time with the stairs, however."

She hadn't been as good a hostess as she should have been in the past two days, preferring to stay in her room rather than see anyone. However, good manners dictated that she push her own grief to the side for a little while. She had the rest of her life to think about Gordon's words.

When she asked Mr. Campbell about his recent trip to the United States, he surprised her by being an excellent storyteller. He told of visiting Niagara Falls, and how he wanted to expand his travels to see the Grand Canyon.

Harrison entered the room and Mr. Campbell's story stopped, long enough for the older man to send him a look of barely veiled contempt. Lauren wouldn't glance in her husband's direction at all.

What had happened in the past two days?

Mr. Campbell concluded with a comment about how young the United States felt. "Everything is new. I find that I miss the history there."

History was one thing Adaire Hall had in abundance.

"If you have any time today and would like to see more of the Hall, I'd be happy to show it to you."

"Thank you, Lady Jennifer, but I'm afraid our plans will prevent that."

He and Lauren shared a look, one that excluded Harrison.

Something had most definitely happened, but since she'd retreated to her rooms, she didn't know what.

Mr. Campbell had a great deal of tact, and for that she was thankful. He hadn't asked her how she was feeling in front of Lauren. She'd realized she was grieving, but that grief was never quickly eased. She'd gotten a taste of that with her mother's death.

The rest of the staff thought that she had been suffering from a bad cold, one that sent her to bed. The tale of her illness hadn't been enough, however, to stop the parade of people from coming to her door. Mrs. Farmer, bless her, had proven to be a godsend in sending people packing.

What a pity that she'd left Adaire Hall to care for another patient this morning.

Harrison hadn't spoken a word since he'd entered the room. He'd studied them all in turn as if they were strangers. Jennifer had seen that look before, and it meant that Harrison was spoiling for a fight.

She wasn't up to a skirmish with him.

"You've lost your bridegroom, Jennifer. McDonnell left, if I'm not mistaken."

She didn't answer.

"I'm glad you came to your senses and obeyed me."

She'd never been a violent person, but if she'd had anything at hand, she would have chucked it at him. Thankfully, he didn't continue talking about Gordon.

"I'm returning to London," he said flatly.

His announcement had an effect on all of them. Lauren simply stared at her husband. Mary began to cry. Mr. Campbell's face took on the appearance of a thundercloud. No one looking at him

could have any doubt as to his feelings on the matter. He was incensed.

As for her, Harrison's words made her plans impossible.

Adaire Hall only had two carriages, one for the family to use and the other that Harrison took to London with him. Since Ellen had brought him home, there was only one remaining carriage.

If Harrison was intent on going back to London, that would trap her here.

"I've already made arrangements," Jennifer said, aggravated that Harrison had forced her to make the announcement like this. "I've sent word to Ellen that I'm coming for a visit. As soon as I arrive in Edinburgh, I'll send the carriage back. Surely you could wait a few days."

"No," Harrison said. "I can't. I choose not to be inconvenienced, Jennifer."

A different person might have asked why she was traveling to Edinburgh so precipitously, but Harrison never cared about anyone else's plans, especially if they interfered with his.

"It will only be a matter of days, Harrison. That will give you time with Lauren and Mary."

"I've already told you, Jennifer. I have no intention of being dictated to by you."

"I would think that someone would want to dictate to you, Burfield. Your manners are deplorable." Hamish turned to his daughter. "I bought you a pig in a poke, my darling girl. Forgive me, and I hope you'll note that I blame myself for this disaster of a marriage."

He stared at Harrison. "I'm taking my daughter back to Edinburgh, Burfield."

He turned to Jennifer. "Begging your pardon, Lady Jennifer. You have a lovely home here, and I'm sure its history is impressive. It's Lauren's husband—or whatever label he chooses to call himself—that I find objectionable. When Lauren's mother was alive, I didn't go out of my way to absent myself from my wife. I didn't live in another city in another country in order to avoid her or my responsibilities. I cannot countenance my daughter being treated with such contempt."

Mr. Campbell came and stood beside the sofa, extending an arm to his daughter to help her rise.

"You are welcome to travel back to Edinburgh with us, Lady Jennifer. In view of the recent developments we'll be leaving in the morning. Is that acceptable to you?"

She nodded, shocked by the turn of events.

Lauren didn't say a word. Nor did the young nursemaid whose eyes had gotten as wide as dinner plates. Even baby Mary had decided to stop crying. Jennifer watched as they walked out of the room in a slow procession before turning to Harrison.

"Are you truly that much of an idiot, Harrison? Are you willing to let your wife leave and take your child with her?"

He only shrugged.

"It's not a good idea to make an enemy of Mr. Campbell. He's a powerful man."

"There's nothing he can do to me."

"Do you really believe that he couldn't hurt you if he wished? You aren't the most important person in the world. Although you might be the most arrogant."

"I think this is your doing, bitch. You've soured Lauren against me."

"I haven't done anything, Harrison. This is all your doing. Or did you think that no one would ever ·call you to account for your actions? Believe it or not, you're not better than the rest of us. You're a deluded, demented human being. One day soon everything you have will be taken away from you."

"What are you talking about?

She only shook her head. She had no intention of telling him Gordon's story. Let him hear it in a courtroom. Or however something like that would be resolved. Would the Queen need to be involved? Gordon would discover that.

As she stood there, staring at Harrison, she realized that only one good thing had come from Betty's actions. Harrison was not her brother. She needn't claim him as a relative.

Nor would she, after today.

Chapter Thirty

$\mathcal{F}$or Gordon, life in London was not appreciably better than anywhere else.

He'd been back in the city for a number of days, but he might as well have been at Adaire Hall. He couldn't escape his thoughts. Nor was it possible for him to banish the memories that followed him wherever he went.

How did you kill love?

He didn't have it in him to think of Jennifer as a sister. Not when he'd held her and kissed her and had thoughts that were a sight more carnal. He'd wanted her to be his wife, to share the rest of his future.

With his words, Sean had taken from him the only woman he'd ever loved.

How did he overcome that kind of loss?

The only way he knew how to handle the tumult of his thoughts was by keeping busy. He immersed himself in his businesses, purchased another building on the outskirts of London, and finalized the purchase of land over which he'd haggled for a few months. He met with a potential manager, solved countless complaints, and resolved two important employee issues all while

managing to hold off Maggie and her insatiable curiosity.

They'd already argued a few times about what she considered his stubborn refusal to tell her everything that had transpired in Scotland.

"I knew it was a mistake to let you go to Scotland alone."

He stared at her. "What do you mean, let me go? Since when do I report to you, Maggie?"

"You evidently don't have any sense when it comes to that woman, Gordon."

His words were very calm and measured. "And what woman would that be?"

"You know who I'm talking about."

"My correspondence is none of your concern, Maggie. I pay you to manage the Mayfair Club, which you do quite well. I don't pay you to manage me."

She wasn't the least bit perturbed by his irritation.

"Something happened in Scotland. You're not the same person. You've been short with everyone, Gordon."

"I will attempt to have a more pleasant demeanor, for your sake, Maggie."

She only narrowed her eyes at him.

He'd told her about Sean's death when he returned. Consequently, she smothered him with compassion, making him feel a little guilty. She'd brought him a plate of scones, fetched him tea, and proceeded to cluck over him like a mother hen. He allowed that for a few days before deciding that it would just be easier to avoid her.

Unfortunately, that was proving more difficult every day.

One of the reasons he'd always valued Maggie was her unflagging loyalty. However, she also possessed a frankness that could occasionally be brutal. He wouldn't list that among her assets.

On the morning of the fourth day after he had returned to London, she entered his office at the Mayfair Club, planted her fists on her hips, and glared at him.

"It's time we talked."

"What about?"

"About what's wrong with you."

Standing, he walked around his desk and stood at the window, looking down at the London street.

This Pall Mall location was a prime one and had cost him in rent. Yet the Mayfair Club had turned a profit from the very beginning. Nor did it look like it was going to stop being a money-maker anytime soon. The young peers to whom he catered found it amusing to belong to a club that wouldn't automatically welcome their fathers. Here there was no heritage membership, no legacy extended simply because your father, uncle, or grandfather had joined. He'd deliberately crafted the rules of the club that way.

Being around Harrison had taught him about autocracy and the arrogance of a young man with a title and enough money to do damage.

He glanced at Maggie. "Has Burfield returned?"

They'd already spoken about her refusing Harrison additional credit. He'd commended her for her decision and given her a bonus for her actions. If the wife or a mother of a member ever

came to them in distress, he wanted it known that he would do what he could to help them.

She nodded. "Yes, two days ago."

"Cut him off. Rescind his membership. Send word that he isn't to be granted admittance. If it's a public ban, all the better."

"Is that wise, rescinding his membership?" Her look of surprise wasn't unexpected.

"I'd like it done as soon as possible."

"He spends a great deal of money here, Gordon."

"He loses a great deal of money here, Maggie. I've decided to call a halt to it."

"Then what about Peterson? And the Duke of Luton? They're both as profligate as Burfield."

"I don't care about them right now."

He didn't look at her again, but she was probably frowning at him. Maggie was a money person. She understood, as well as he, what it took to run the Mayfair Club.

If one of the young peers was insulted, he could do a lot of damage to their hopes of increasing membership. However, he knew that Harrison was as obnoxious to his acquaintances and friends—if he had any—as he was to his family. He doubted that banning him would have a detrimental effect to the club.

"Is this a result of going to Scotland, too?"

He returned to his desk. He'd made this office his base of operations because he knew that Maggie would leave him alone to work. However, that hadn't proven to be the case since he'd returned from Scotland.

Gordon really wanted to concentrate on the

report in front of him, but she came and stood in front of his desk. Maggie could be as stubborn as a stone.

He leaned back in his chair and regarded her. "If you have something to say, Maggie, say it."

"I don't know what happened to you in Scotland, Gordon, but I suspect it was more than losing your father. You hadn't spoken to him in five years. Yet suddenly you're a different man."

She was right. He was different. He would never be the same person he had been. What did he tell her?

He doubted he would ever be able to talk about it.

"I shall endeavor to return to my normal self," he said, sitting up and pulling a sheaf of papers in front of him.

"I don't know what's wrong, but if you don't tell me soon, I'm tempted to beat it out of you."

He looked up from his desk. Maggie was still standing there, her hands on her hips, glaring at him.

"Since when are you given to violent threats?"

"I've been out of practice lately," she said, her chin jutting up in the air. "However, there were many times when I had to cosh some idiot over the head."

Maggie had lived hand to mouth for years. She'd made herself over so well that he sometimes forgot about her past.

"What happened to you, Maggie? Why did you rob me five years ago?"

She stared at him for a long time. Finally, she crossed her arms in front of her. He'd seen that

pose before, too. It always preluded changing the subject.

This time, however, she surprised him. "I'd been kicked out of my lodgings for not paying the rent. The man I was with took all my money and left me to starve. See? It's not so hard to tell the truth."

From that he could deduce more than he was comfortable knowing.

"So you fell in love and it turned out poorly."

"Is that what you call it? I think I was a fool and an idiot."

"Sometimes that's one and the same, Maggie."

"So she hurt you?"

"No," he said, smiling slightly. "She didn't hurt me." He'd hurt her. He'd never be able to forget that look on Jennifer's face. Disbelief, shock, horror—the dawning of grief—he'd probably looked exactly the same way on learning the news he'd delivered.

"Even if you don't admit it, I know it's about her."

He sat back in his chair and looked at her. "How do you know that?"

"Because you've never been involved with a woman seriously here in London, and you've had a fair bit of women interested in you."

"Have I?"

"I've mentioned them before. You never seemed to notice them. I thought, at first, that it was because you were working too much. You were determined to get ahead to the detriment of everything else."

"If I admitted it was about a woman, would you leave me alone?"

"No. I'd just want to know more. Why isn't she here with you in London?"

"Maybe she will be in the future."

"No, she won't," Maggie said, shaking her head.

"Why do you say that?"

"Because you wouldn't have that look on your face if she was. Like a dog that's been kicked."

"I've not been kicked. I don't need advice, and I'm fine, Maggie."

She didn't move, only frowned at him.

"If she broke your heart, she's not worth the effort to be pining about her. There are plenty of English girls who are interested in you, Gordon McDonnell. Don't you forget that."

"I'm fine, Maggie. All I want to do right now is work."

There must've been something in his tone, because she didn't badger him further. Maggie only sent him another frown, turned on her heel, and left the room.

He wasn't fooled. She'd be back. She'd ask questions until he left and found another place to work.

Chapter Thirty-One

The journey to Edinburgh was accomplished with a minimum of fuss and a maximum degree of comfort. Jennifer had never ridden in as luxurious a vehicle as Mr. Campbell's carriage. In addition to being well sprung, the seats and back were thickly upholstered. Two clever little compartments along the side held flasks of brandy and wine, a mirror, writing materials, and a folding pair of binoculars in case one wanted to see the scenery with more magnification.

Every possible effort had been made to ensure her comfort—from the neck pillow she'd been given to the rounded brazier on the floor.

She truly couldn't have been more cosseted.

Even little Mary was adding to the pleasant nature of the journey. The baby hadn't fussed once, but that was probably because Lauren was holding her daughter. Jennifer hadn't had many occasions to be around new mothers, but she couldn't imagine a more perfect person for the role than Lauren.

What a pity that Harrison hadn't fitted into his role of father.

For over a year, Jennifer had thought that Lauren was a sweet, biddable young thing, so in love

with Harrison that she would forgive any of his sins. She'd also anticipated that the journey to Edinburgh would be spent with Lauren in tears, inconsolable at her father's actions.

Instead, the woman in the carriage was steely eyed and seemingly unperturbed about the fact that her husband had already returned to London.

Mr. Campbell, however, was doing his utmost to comfort his daughter. More than once Jennifer saw him patting Lauren's arm or hand. He'd only spoken about Harrison in passing, and that comment elicited a surprising response from Lauren.

"I'm so sorry, my dear," Mr. Campbell said.

"You didn't do anything wrong, Papa. It isn't your fault that my husband is devoid of character."

Jennifer hadn't said a word. In all honesty, there was nothing she could say to counter Lauren's assessment of her husband. If he'd showed any interest whatsoever in his daughter or demonstrated a little kindness toward Lauren, it might be a different situation.

She was simply grateful that she had somewhere to go and someone to be with. Everything about her life had been turned on its head. Perhaps that's why she needed Ellen. She wanted to be around someone familiar, someone who had known her since she was a child. Someone to whom she could say, "Do you remember . . ." and have that person match her memories. She had no doubt of Ellen's affection for her, and maybe she needed that right now as well.

The journey to Edinburgh was interminable, giving her too much time to think. Her mind

danced through the years. She was a child, racing through Adaire Hall, chasing Gordon in a forbidden game of tag. Or hiding from him, only to dart out and startle him, then burst into laughter at his expression.

Her childhood had been, for the most part, punctuated by laughter. There were times when she was sad, of course, when thinking of her father or even her mother's injuries. Yet children never stayed somber for long. There was always too much to see, do, and learn.

She and Gordon explored the hills beyond Adaire Hall. They'd made their own path through the woods. They fished in the loch and chased the sheep in the glen, earning a lecture from both the shepherd and her mother.

They'd had a bond, a closeness ever since she was a child. She had known that she could always go to Gordon if Harrison was being cruel. If she'd seen something funny or read something she wanted to share, Gordon was the first person she thought of.

She would need to alter her thoughts, expunge her memories, learn to think of him as someone else. Not the man she loved. Nor even her brother. It would be easier to not think of him at all.

How did she do that?

For the first time in her life she'd walked away from all her responsibilities. Let the housekeeper and the majordomo write Harrison and ask about the numerous and never-ending daily issues. What kind of punishment would be apt for the third-floor maid who had absconded with another maid's brooch? What were they to do

with a fourteen-year-old horse that had gone lame? The roof in one area desperately needed repair. Should they send to Inverness for the materials to do the work?

Let Harrison answer those questions. Let him—for once—assume some responsibility. Until such time, of course, as Gordon proved himself to be the true Earl of Burfield.

Thankfully, the other occupants of the coach did not seem inclined to talk. Mr. Campbell was making notations in a small notebook. His two secretaries had been sent back to Edinburgh the day after their arrival, but he seemed to have taken up the slack in note-taking. For a number of hours, Lauren had her eyes closed and either feigned sleep or dozed. Whenever baby Mary fussed, however, she took the infant from the nursemaid and calmed her with just a touch.

Seeing them made her heart ache. Unless Harrison drastically altered his character, Lauren was destined to be without a husband and Mary without a father.

Her eyes met Mr. Campbell's once, and she knew that he had the same thought. She wanted to apologize for Harrison, but there was nothing she could say to make the situation better than it was. If she could have changed Harrison's behavior, she would have done so years ago, before he began to waste so much money on his London pursuits.

Finally, she began to recognize landmarks that indicated they were nearing Edinburgh. Ellen's home, which had been owned by Colin's family since the seventeenth century, was located about

two miles from the center of the city. The lands on which it stood had been granted to the monks of Holyrood Abbey in the fifteenth century. The first time she'd visited Ellen and her new husband, Colin had given her a tour of the expansive property.

The original house, an L-shaped structure, dated from the late seventeenth century. However, because of extensive renovations and additions, none of the earlier house was visible on the exterior.

One of Colin's ancestors had surrounded the house with an expansive brick wall complete with towers. To enter, visitors had to come in through an impressive iron gate that was kept closed most of the time and opened by a man whose only duty was to maintain security for the family.

Colin had added his own touches to the property, which included a conservatory in the rear of the house and modernizing the interior with bathrooms and a cistern on the roof. In addition, Colin had added a series of ponds throughout the grounds.

"I've never seen a man so entranced with fish," Ellen told her on one visit. "We have a different variety of fish in each pond, and the silly man goes to check on each one of them every morning. He's even named some of them."

Although there had been exasperation in Ellen's tone, her eyes told a different story. It was easy to see that she adored her husband and that Colin felt the same about her.

Evidently, Mr. Campbell was well-known to

the man at the gate, because they were waved through to the courtyard without any delay. As soon as they approached the wide steps, the double doors at the top opened, and Ellen emerged.

As they pulled up and stopped, Mr. Campbell looked at Jennifer.

"I understand why you would wish to stay with your godmother, Lady Jennifer. However, I hope that you will find time to call on us before returning to Adaire Hall."

She forced a smile to her face. All she truly wanted to do was enter Ellen's house, close the door behind her, and forget about the rest of the world.

Yet because of his kindness, she only said, "That would be nice."

She glanced at Lauren. Even though Mary had an idiot for a father, she was blessed by having a devoted mother.

Although Ellen invited the occupants of the carriage to come inside, rest, and have some refreshments, they declined.

"Thank you for your kind invitation," Mr. Campbell said. "However, I think that my daughter would benefit by shortly being in her bed."

He was probably right. Lauren did look a little pale. It was unusual for a new mother to embark on a long carriage ride only weeks following a birth. Evidently, Lauren had been so desperate to leave Adaire Hall that she was willing to put up with a little misery.

Jennifer kissed Lauren on the cheek, promised to call on her shortly, and thanked Mr. Campbell for his kindness before exiting the carriage. It

was only due to him that she was here at all. Mr. Campbell's driver surrendered her valises to Ellen's footman.

She and Ellen waved goodbye until the carriage made it through the gates.

"I'm thinking that Lauren isn't the only young woman who needs to seek her bed," Ellen said, turning to her. "You, my dear, are looking exceedingly pale. Are you feeling all right?"

She was enfolded in a perfumed hug and suddenly wanted to cry. Ellen had always been a source of comfort to her, especially after her mother died.

Ellen pulled back and looked at Jennifer. "Are you certain you're feeling well?"

Jennifer nodded, forcing a smile to her face. She could feel her defenses falling too quickly to prepare herself. If Ellen said anything else, she might burst into tears.

In moments she was whisked inside the house, her cloak removed, and she was led into one of the oddest rooms in Ellen's home. Ellen called it Colin's Aerie. In addition to being fascinated with fish, Colin had also been interested in birds. There were a great many stuffed specimens in the sitting room, and they never failed to disconcert Jennifer. Each one of the birds had been encased in a glass dome, but that didn't lessen the effect of a dozen pairs of beady eyes staring at her as she sat on one of the sofas.

"If you are ill, my dear girl, I shall summon my physician immediately."

"I'm not ill, Ellen, truthfully. I'm just tired."

She didn't think Ellen believed her, but her

godmother didn't question her further. Ellen did, however, insist that Jennifer have a restorative cup of tea. The maid also brought in a tray filled with delicacies. Ellen's cook made exquisite pastries, and it was a miracle she didn't gain several pounds whenever she came to stay with her godmother.

Although she wasn't hungry, she made a point of taking a small cake. Either that or have Ellen watch her with eyes just as sharp as one of the specimens on the shelves around them.

"Will you tell me what's bothering you?"

She wasn't the least surprised that Ellen knew something was wrong. The older woman had a sixth sense where she was concerned.

"There won't be a wedding, Ellen. That's all I'll say."

"Not a wedding? Why?"

She simply looked at Ellen. She had no intention of discussing the matter any further.

"Not right now," she said. "Please."

Thankfully, Ellen only nodded, but there was a look in her eyes that said Jennifer had only been given a reprieve. Ellen would have the full story.

Jennifer couldn't give it to her. She didn't think she'd ever be able to speak the words.

Chapter Thirty-Two

$\mathcal{G}$ ordon waited a week before visiting his solicitor. He knew why he delayed: the moment he went to see Blackthorne, he'd make it real. Sean's words would no longer simply be a deathbed confession, they would become a legal matter.

He expected his solicitor to listen patiently, but tell him that, since he had no documented proof or witnesses, the tale of switching infants would be just a story.

Thomas Blackthorne, a man with whom he'd done business for four years, surprised him by nodding sagely when Gordon was finished.

"It's not the first time a title has been in dispute," Blackthorne said. "You'd be surprised how many there are about. Yours is simply one of many."

"So, you think I have a claim?"

"Most assuredly you have a claim. However, that's not the issue. It's a Scottish title and therefore would be adjudicated in Scotland."

"Which means?" Gordon asked.

"You need to go to Edinburgh to do it. I know a number of advocates in Scotland and would be pleased to provide you with some recommendations if you wish."

Armed with a list of three Scottish solicitors,

he left Blackthorne's office and headed back to the Mayfair Club.

He didn't look forward to telling Maggie that he was leaving for Scotland again, especially since he wasn't going to divulge the reason why. She didn't need to know everything about his life, although she'd dispute that.

There was every possibility that he wouldn't succeed. He wasn't foolish enough to think that justice prevailed in every situation. He didn't have any corroborating proof. Margaret McBride was not going to say anything. There weren't any other people at Adaire Hall who'd been there at the time of the fire. Or, if they had, no one had seen both infants.

All he had were the words of a man who wanted to clear his conscience.

He was going to leave in a few days. Time enough to take care of any lingering business matters and attempt to calm Maggie's ruffled feathers.

DAYS PASSED. DAYS during which Jennifer tried not to think or feel. She woke in the morning and got through the day, then finally retired to her suite to sleep.

Ellen spoke to her, tried to engage her in conversation, but she had nothing to say. Nor did she care anything about fashion, flowers, politics, the weather, or Adaire Hall. She couldn't even feign an interest in discussing Harrison, Lauren, or baby Mary.

What she truly wanted was to be left alone and allowed to sit in the grayness of the world

around her. She didn't want to hear laughter or conversation or even the wind. Everything felt like an intrusion.

She was inside somewhere, down deep, buried where no one else could find her. She knew, in an odd way, that she was protecting herself. That if she didn't feel or didn't think or didn't remember anything that she might survive this.

Or she might not.

Even if she could turn back time and change Betty's actions, it wouldn't give Gordon back to her. She would be raised with him as his sister. She wouldn't have fallen in love with him. He was forever gone. He was no longer hers. Whatever they felt for each other would be labeled wrong and a sin against God.

The most terrible part was that she knew that, but how did she convince her heart?

She couldn't forget the look on Gordon's face when he'd told her what Sean had said. He'd had a few days to absorb the words. Yet the stunned expression in his eyes revealed that he felt the same about the news as she did.

They'd been sweethearts. She loved him like a woman loves a man, not a brother. Would she have to do penance for that love or did ignorance mitigate her actions? She would not confess her sin to a minister for fear that he would pronounce some horrible verdict on her immortal soul.

How did she do this? The endless stream of days stretched out before her, none of them holding any significance or joy. Somehow, she was going to have to find meaning in something. How, though? How was she supposed to forget

Gordon? Was there a tonic she could take to induce a loss of memory?

It was easier to sleep than to endure each day.

ELLEN DIDN'T KNOW what was wrong with Jennifer, but something obviously was. First of all, she'd never left Adaire Hall for an extended visit without some coaxing on Ellen's part. Secondly, Jennifer was not the kind of woman who sat in a window seat and stared out at the world. No, she was the type of person other people watched.

Something had happened. Something drastic enough to have canceled the wedding and altered Jennifer's demeanor. She accompanied Ellen shopping, but she wasn't interested in purchasing anything. She didn't seem involved in their conversations. She rarely smiled. She was sleeping late and retiring early.

The past week had been a guessing game, and so far, Ellen hadn't come up with any answers. Harrison had returned to London, which wasn't a surprise. However, his young wife had come back to Edinburgh, which was. Since she'd introduced Harrison to Lauren, she felt a sense of guilt that was difficult to banish.

Jennifer wasn't ill, at least according to the answers she'd given Ellen. There was something weighing her down. That wasn't difficult to figure out. However, her goddaughter wasn't confiding in her.

The sad fact was that Ellen didn't know how to handle this situation. She didn't have anyone to go to for advice. This was Jennifer, after all, and she didn't discuss Jennifer with anyone.

Something had to be done. Colin had often said that in the case of difficult situations, assume the mantle of confidence and barge on through.

The only problem was that she didn't know what to say or do.

Although the wedding was off, Jennifer hadn't said why. Nor had she spoken Gordon's name once.

She had to admit that Gordon was a fascinating man. He reminded her of Colin, and it wasn't difficult to see why. Colin, too, had come from humble beginnings, but he'd prospered in his life, accomplishing more than most men she knew. Gordon struck her as having the same kind of determination and drive.

Mary had often spoken of the gardener's son in admiring tones. As far as Ellen was concerned, Gordon had impressed her because of his care and concern for Jennifer. She was more than willing to overlook his antecedents because Jennifer loved him.

However, something drastic had happened and Jennifer hadn't explained. Why was the wedding canceled?

Hamish Campbell had invited them to a luncheon. She would like to see Hamish again, renew their acquaintance, and see the baby as well. Mary would be so pleased to know that she had a granddaughter.

When Harrison had been smart enough to offer for Lauren, Ellen had been overjoyed. She'd given up thinking that he was going to do something right. However, he'd managed to be married only a year and the young couple was already having

problems. She didn't doubt that Harrison's living in London was the reason.

The distraction of a visit to the Campbells would do Jennifer good. If nothing else, perhaps she would confide in Lauren. When she informed Jennifer of the invitation and the fact that she was going to accept it, her goddaughter didn't say a word to her. She didn't even nod. All she did was smile wanly in her direction.

Ellen hated feeling inept. Nor was she happy about being unable to help Jennifer. She loved that girl more than anyone else on earth. Sometimes, she thought that Colin had been jealous of her affection for Jennifer. More than once he'd made the comment that she should've had her own children. She wished she could have had his child, but regrets were foolish, a lesson she'd learned long ago.

Chapter Thirty-Three

Gordon had always been proud to be a Scot. In fact, he even accentuated his brogue in conversations with obstreperous Englishmen. Yet he felt a curious reluctance to cross the border into Scotland.

He was too close to Jennifer.

He still hadn't called in Harrison's markers, but the moment he did, he would essentially destroy Adaire Hall. The estate might be entailed, but if there wasn't any money to operate and maintain it, it would only be a matter of time until the servants were disbanded, the house emptied of its treasures, and it became a home for ghosts.

He didn't care. He'd never live there. The memories would be too disturbing. Not of Sean or Betty, but of Jennifer.

Jennifer, laughing. Jennifer, her face earnest as she confided a secret to him. Jennifer, weeping on those rare occasions when sadness overwhelmed her. Jennifer, angry at Harrison. They were almost always angry at Harrison together.

No, he couldn't think of her. It was a habit he was going to have to learn somehow.

The minute he crossed into Scotland, he felt

himself tensing. Perhaps it was a godsend that the journey was so difficult, requiring changing trains, being concerned about his baggage and carriage, and the sheer noise and belching soot he was subjected to, even in a first-class compartment.

Adaire Hall was far enough away that he didn't have to worry about encountering anyone, yet he still found himself looking north.

He'd never been to Edinburgh. Five years ago when he'd left Adaire Hall, he'd headed south immediately, wanting away from everything that had reminded him of his upbringing.

Now he looked around him, feeling a sense of pride at what he saw. The city was crowded, but not as difficult to navigate as London. No doubt there were parts of Edinburgh that were less acceptable, but what he saw, from the castle on the hill to the prosperous homes and offices, was the equal of London architecture.

He should have come to the city before now. After all, he was a Scot and Edinburgh held the history of Scotland in her palm. He wondered if he should expand in Edinburgh. If he won his case, he'd be a Scottish peer. It made sense to come and live here.

He'd be too close to Adaire Hall, however.

The advocate's office was in a redbrick building aged by soot. It possessed a minimum of windows and a maximum of pomp and ceremony. A doorman attired in scarlet livery greeted him at the door and bade him remain on the steps until his appointment had been verified.

A few minutes later, the door opened again,

wider than before. Another man, dressed in a severe black suit, bowed slightly to him and invited him inside.

Gordon was immediately submersed in gloom.

He followed the man down a long corridor, then to the left. At the end of the hall was a window that barely lit the space.

The man hesitated midway down the hall and bowed again to Gordon before opening a door. He stepped to the center of the doorway, placed his gloved right hand on his chest, and intoned, "Mr. McDonnell to see you, sir."

A moment later, he stepped to the side, motioning Gordon to enter.

He found himself in a dimly lit office. There was a row of windows behind the massive desk, but they were heavily curtained, and no one had thought to open them and allow a little brightness into the room. The only illumination was two gas sconces on either side of the room that gave off a weak yellow glow.

The man seated at the desk was probably thirty years older than Gordon. His hairline had receded, and the wispy strands across the top of his head were only a few months away from departing. His severely arched nose stood in relief, almost like a handle for the rest of his long face.

He stood, stared at Gordon, then abruptly sat once more. As a greeting it was unusual. Gordon didn't know whether to announce himself again, stand there until the man regained his composure, or return the stare of the advocate, who was sitting there with his hands flat on his desk, wide eyes staring in Gordon's direction.

Evidently, the man didn't have new clients very often.

He strode forward, extending his hand. "My solicitor gave me your name and said that you might be able to help me, Mr. McNair."

The man shook his head a few times, almost as if he were dislodging cobwebs.

"Of course, of course," he said, standing again. The two of them shook hands before he gestured to a chair in front of his desk.

Gordon sat.

"I know Blackthorne well. A good man. I shall send him a letter thanking him for the referral."

Was this Scottish advocate partial to drink? Had he imbibed his breakfast?

The outcome of this case wouldn't rest on anything he did. Instead, it would be solely on his solicitor's expertise as well as the letter of the law. Betty had taken his name and his parents. He was damned if Harrison was going to go the rest of his life wearing Gordon's title. However, he wasn't entirely certain that he entrusted his future to this man.

McNair was still staring at him.

"You say your name is McDonnell?"

"That's part of my problem," he said.

He had told the tale twice. Once to Jennifer and once to his English solicitor. Circumstances dictated that he tell it again, but it didn't become easier with repetition.

"Until a few weeks ago, I thought my name was Gordon McDonnell. I believed that I had been born to the head gardener at the estate owned by the Earl and Countess of Burfield."

McNair tilted his head slightly, his pen hovering over the page. "Are you referring to Adaire Hall?"

Gordon nodded. "I was raised at Adaire Hall. Because of the generosity of the Countess of Burfield, I was educated with her children." He was not going to go into his relationship with Jennifer. It didn't have any bearing on his claim. Nor was it anyone's business.

"I left the estate five years ago and returned only recently when my father was dying."

McNair still hadn't written anything.

Gordon stared at the edge of McNair's desk. It was as old-fashioned as the building and the office in which he found himself. He wondered if it was something deliberate, an aura achieved to give the client the impression that they were reserved, traditional, and dedicated not so much to change as to maintaining the status quo. No doubt that reassured a great many people.

That same attitude might prove to be deleterious to his claim. Or it might even prejudice McNair against taking his case.

"The night before he died, Sean confessed." He corrected himself. "No, it wasn't so much a confession as it was a revelation. Betty, his wife, was the one who confessed to him on her deathbed. However, I have my suspicions that Sean knew what she'd done all along."

"And what was that, Mr. McDonnell?"

"There were two babies born that year, both within days of each other. One was the heir to the earldom. The other was born to the gardener and his wife."

"That would be you."

"So I thought," Gordon said.

He told the solicitor about the fire, the countess's heroic actions to save her child, and what it had cost her.

"The wet nurse died in the fire. Betty was asked to care for the countess's child while she was so ill. The infants were both only days old. Betty decided to switch the babies. Her son's future would probably be limited to following in his father's footsteps, but she wanted more for her child."

McNair put the pen down on his desk.

"No one was the wiser. No one would've known what she'd done had her conscience not bothered her shortly before she died."

McNair sat back in his chair, his note-taking evidently forgotten.

"You're telling me that you believe yourself to be the rightful heir to the earldom? That you're the son of the Earl of Burfield?"

Gordon nodded again. "I am. I find it a fantastical story myself, Mr. McNair. I wouldn't blame you if you doubted every word of it."

"Do you have any proof?"

"No. There's a woman who was there that night. She was a nursery maid, but she won't talk."

McNair adjusted his suit jacket, then his cuffs, before straightening his pen and the stack of papers in front of him. He reached for a blank sheet of paper, put it on his blotter, then folded his hands before looking at Gordon.

"I believe you, Mr. McDonnell."

Gordon looked at him, surprised. "Why?"

"Because when you walked into my office it was like seeing a ghost. Alexander Adaire was one of my closest friends. At school he and I were inseparable. I've been to Adaire Hall many times. When he died, he was still a young man, and there are many people who mourn him to this day. I'm one of them. You're the image of your father, McDonnell."

He hadn't expected that. He didn't remember the earl since he'd only been five when the man died. Nor were there any portraits of him anywhere.

"I am very sorry, however, but I can't take your case."

Gordon wasn't unduly surprised. However, he had two more names on his list.

"Thank you for your time," he said, standing.

"Please sit down," McNair said. "Aren't you curious as to why I'm not going to take your case?"

"It's not hard to understand. All I have is a story. I can't prove any of it."

"That's not why, Mr. McDonnell. I cannot represent you if I'm also going to appear as a witness."

Gordon sat, looking at the advocate. "A witness?"

"You're the mirror image of your father. I have a number of friends, men who knew Alex who would say the same. I don't doubt that they'll stand as witnesses as well."

He pulled a sheet of paper to him and began to write.

"In the meantime, I'm recommending another

advocate. Let me write a quick note to him, and you can take it now. He's just across the street. Tell him what I said. I don't think he'll have any reluctance to take your case."

McNair folded the note and gave it to him. True to his word, the advocate he recommended was anxious to represent him.

"If you have Robert McNair as a witness in your defense, your claim is as good as granted."

Gordon began walking back to the Waverly Hotel, feeling better about one part of his life. He'd never considered that he might resemble his father. If it was true that he was so like the fifth earl, enough that McNair was willing to be his witness, then perhaps it would make it easier to prove that the earldom had been stolen from him.

He'd never actively hated anyone. It seemed to him that hatred was a wasted emotion, requiring too much energy and reaping few rewards. In this instance, however, he allowed himself the luxury of hating Betty McDonnell and wishing her to eternal perdition.

Chapter Thirty-Four

"The Campbells' retiring room is always cold," Abigail said. "And their tea is never hot. No one who works there ever has any time for me, so I'm put in a corner to wait."

Abigail's complaints had begun the minute they entered the carriage. Ellen didn't respond, but then she normally remained silent. If you got into a discussion about anything Abigail said, the maid grew even more voluble.

"It's a dreich day, which means it'll be even colder. I don't think their housekeeper likes me, which is why I'm not given acceptable refreshments."

Jennifer looked up to find that Ellen was studying her.

"I think it would be best if you saw my physician, Jennifer. I've sent word to him and he can come tomorrow. I absolutely insist."

She knew why her godmother thought she was ill. She would admit that she was acting oddly, but how else was she supposed to behave? She couldn't cry. The pain was too deep for tears. It was easier to sleep or simply stare at the wall. She didn't want to feel anything, because it was easier that way.

"Very well."

She didn't care. Let a physician examine her. Let him ask her all sorts of intrusive questions. He would never ask the right one. He would never say to her, "Lady Jennifer, have you lost your will to live? Has everything in your life suddenly lost meaning?" No, he wouldn't ask those questions, would he?

Ellen didn't look away. "Do you know how worried I am about you?"

"You shouldn't worry," Jennifer said. The effort to speak was almost beyond her. "There's nothing you can do. There's nothing anyone can do."

Even Abigail turned to look at her. Jennifer closed her eyes, unwilling to see Ellen's expression or Abigail's curiosity. They felt as far away from her as the stars. How could she possibly explain the situation to them?

Although she didn't feel like going anywhere or seeing anyone, she also knew her godmother. When Ellen was determined on a point, nothing and no one could stop her. It was simply easier to give in immediately, which was why she was in a carriage going to Hamish Campbell's house. It was either this visit or spend the rest of the day arguing. She had neither the inclination nor the energy for that. Therefore, she'd go and see Lauren and Mr. Campbell and be as polite as possible. She would smile when she was supposed to and contribute to the conversation if she absolutely must, and when it was over, she would go back to her room and sleep.

Traffic in Edinburgh was not as bad as that in London, but it wasn't easily navigated, either. To-

day it was taking longer than it should have, according to Ellen, to reach Mr. Campbell's home.

She'd only been there once, for a dinner prior to Harrison's wedding. It was a lovely and impressive home, whose history paralleled that of Edinburgh itself. At another time, she and Ellen would have discussed the house or Mr. Campbell's penchant for displaying all sorts of weapons used in clan wars on every available wall.

Now she wasn't interested.

She stared out at the streets of Edinburgh. It truly was a lovely city. In the past, she'd always found something new to interest her. Now she simply didn't care about the scenery.

Their driver was evidently becoming impatient with the traffic because he asked permission from Ellen to take another route. She concurred, and they turned left at the next corner.

She wished Ellen hadn't insisted on going to the Campbells'. She didn't feel strong enough to feign politeness. All she really wanted to do was go to sleep.

A man on the sidewalk looked like Gordon, but it wasn't the first time she'd been reminded of him. Would she always think she saw him, as if her mind wanted to ease her heart with the pretense? This man had the same purpose in his stride. She sat up and looked harder. She only caught a glimpse of his face before the carriage turned, but he even looked like Gordon. She sat back. It couldn't have been him. Gordon was in London. The momentary glimpse of someone who resembled him made her feel even worse than before.

ELLEN THANKED THE maid for bringing her cloak and then smiled at Hamish, who helped her don it. He'd invited her to see the addition to his garden, and she would do almost anything to escape the atmosphere in the drawing room.

To her great surprise, Lauren was barely talking to Jennifer. Nor did Jennifer do anything to fill the silence. You would think that the two women had never met, hadn't been friends for the past year or, even worse, were archenemies.

"That was exceedingly uncomfortable," Ellen said as she took Hamish's arm.

She would never have made that remark to anyone other than Hamish, but he had been a friend for years. He'd known Colin well, and after her husband's death, he'd been exceedingly kind in helping her navigate financial waters. Plus, he had been kind in other ways, demonstrating that he, too, knew the power of grief.

"Indeed, it was," he said. "I think perhaps my daughter is more disturbed than she has let on about her marriage. I, myself, am bothered by the attitude Harrison has taken."

Ellen sighed. "I wish I could give you some advice in that quarter, Hamish, but I'm afraid I can't. He has proven to be a thorn in a great many people's sides. Yet he was raised by a wonderful woman."

"You can't always blame the parents, Ellen. Sometimes, a child will go astray for no reason."

"Jennifer has done her part to make the visit uncomfortable," she said, determined to be fair. Lauren shouldn't be blamed for the entirety of the strain in the drawing room. Jennifer sat on

the end of the sofa and stared at the carpet, rarely speaking. When she did, it was like someone had just awakened her. "She's been different ever since she came to visit. I haven't the slightest idea why, and I'm at my wit's end about it."

Hamish didn't say anything. His attention was suddenly on his footing, as if he was afraid he would trip in his own garden. His arm beneath her hand tensed.

"Do you know something?" She stopped and faced him. "Hamish?"

"Nothing that makes any sense, Ellen."

"Nothing has made sense since Jennifer arrived in Edinburgh. If you could tell me anything, I would appreciate it."

"I found her one day on the lawn. She'd evidently just been given some terrible news." Hamish didn't look at her but continued to stare at his shoes. "I've never seen anyone cry like that, Ellen. It was like her soul was wounded." He finally glanced at her. "She wouldn't tell me what was wrong, but I knew that something had happened. I never did learn what it was, but I'm not surprised that she hasn't acted herself."

"Are you certain you don't know what happened?" Ellen asked, more confused than before. "What about Mr. McDonnell?"

"Who?"

"Gordon McDonnell."

"I don't know who that is. I was never introduced to anyone by that name."

That was very strange, but everything about this visit was odd.

When Hamish showed her the new greenhouse,

she made admiring noises, all the while wondering exactly how to broach the subject of Gordon with her goddaughter. She was determined not to endure this state of affairs for much longer. Jennifer was simply going to have to tell her what was wrong.

MR. CAMPBELL CERTAINLY appreciated Scottish history, to the point that there were various framed documents scattered through the hallway and the parlor attesting to his family's participation in several battles. The Campbells also seemed to have been active in political movements through the years.

The Campbell tartan was everywhere in this parlor, from the sofa and chairs to the ottomans. Even the curtains were tartan. When Jennifer first walked into the room, it was like visiting a Scottish nightmare.

Lunch had consisted of a choice of clear or cream soup, salmon with dill sauce, venison with roasted vegetables, and a pudding topped with curls of chocolate.

Jennifer tried to eat so as not to be insulting to Mr. Campbell or his cook. She managed to eat a little of everything even though she didn't have an appetite.

After lunch they spent some time oohing and aahing over Mary, who'd grown in only one week. It was evident to anyone that Mr. Campbell was a proud grandfather. He was the one who carried Mary into the room, then returned her to the nursery.

Ellen and Hamish carried the conversation,

their interests surprisingly parallel in several areas. Ellen had a decided political bent that dictated Scotland should consider its interests first. Mr. Campbell concurred.

Neither she nor Lauren added to their discussion. When Ellen and Mr. Campbell left to tour the garden, she and Lauren simply looked at each other.

Something had happened in those two days she'd retreated to her rooms. Ever since then, Lauren had been withdrawn and distant. Their friendship had suffered as a result.

"I'm not returning to Adaire Hall," Lauren abruptly said.

Jennifer glanced at her. For several moments neither spoke.

"You're never returning?"

Lauren shook her head.

"Harrison feels only contempt for me, Jennifer. He told me so himself. How am I supposed to live with a man who says something like that?"

So that's what had happened in those two days.

"I'm his wife, and I'll remain his wife until one of us dies, but I'll not live with him."

Now was the time for her to launch into a speech about how people can change, except that she was certain that change was beyond Harrison. Even as a boy he'd been inflexible in his thoughts. Once he'd decided on something, it didn't matter how much evidence to the contrary you showed him, his mind was made up.

"Harrison doesn't want to be a proper husband and father. Mary and I will make our lives here in Edinburgh. If Harrison wants us, he

knows where we'll be." She took a deep breath and continued. "However, I have no hope of that ever happening."

Jennifer couldn't think of anything to say in response. Of course, she couldn't excuse Harrison's behavior. Nor would she. He'd treated Lauren abominably and would probably continue to do so.

No one had ever called him out on his actions. Her mother had tried, but it had been a futile effort, especially when Mr. McBain had backed Harrison in so many instances.

"I'm sorry, Lauren."

She stretched out her hand to Lauren. The other woman took it and for a moment they sat in silence.

"I want my husband to love me," Lauren said finally. "I thought Harrison was capable of that, but not now."

She glanced at Jennifer as she pulled her hand free.

"I don't want your life, Jennifer. I'm not that good of a person. You're the epitome of dedication and selflessness, but I don't want to have to take care of Adaire Hall without any promise of some type of reward. Like a husband who loves me and a sense of family."

She wasn't as virtuous as Lauren made her sound. Her mother's illness had dictated that Jennifer take on her duties. After her mother's death, she'd stepped up when Harrison had abdicated his responsibilities and had continued to do so for five years. When Lauren had arrived at Adaire Hall and had been almost immediately

pregnant—and debilitated—Jennifer had carried on, waiting for the moment when Lauren would take on the role of countess.

Now it looked like that day would never come.

She didn't blame Lauren for refusing to follow in her footsteps. Adaire Hall could not hug you in the evening or give you comfort at night. It couldn't greet you in the morning with a kiss or share a laugh. Yet someone had to care, to be the one everyone relied on.

Lauren was choosing her own life, one that would prove shocking to many people. Yet Jennifer couldn't help but wonder when she got to choose hers.

Chapter Thirty-Five

Ellen's patience ran out at dawn a week later.

Nothing had changed since the visit to the Campbells a week ago. If anything, Jennifer had become more withdrawn. She barely spoke and found excuses not to join Ellen for dinner. She'd refused, for two days now, to accompany Ellen on shopping trips.

Her physician had called on Jennifer and examined her goddaughter with Ellen in attendance. Dr. Ferguson pronounced Jennifer the picture of health.

While she was relieved that there wasn't anything physically wrong, she was still certain that something wasn't right. She was determined to get to the bottom of it.

Jennifer always had her morning tea in her bedroom. She had her own suite, something that Ellen had decorated herself in anticipation of the many visits Jennifer would make to her home.

Over the years, she'd changed the decor to suit her goddaughter. If Jennifer espoused a liking for flowers, the next time she visited, the coverlet of her bed, the curtains, and even the skirting around her vanity had been changed to a flowery pattern. The same was the case if she evinced

a preference for a certain color. One year it was yellow. The next year it was blue.

She hadn't changed the decor since Jennifer had expressed a preference for green. The skirting around the vanity was a green-and-white stripe that was mirrored in the drapery. The two chairs in front of the fireplace, both comfortably overstuffed, were upholstered in a very small pattern of green leaves on a background of white. The coverlet was the same.

Overall, it was a bright and cheerful room, the antithesis of its current occupant.

Ellen was determined to discover what was wrong and solve it.

After all, there was no problem that couldn't be rectified by a little calm thinking. Another of Colin's aphorisms, and one she sincerely hoped was true in this case.

ANOTHER WEEK HAD passed, another week in which the world was a gray formless void. Jennifer didn't think of the future, and other than memories of her mother, she didn't think of the past. As long as she didn't think of anything, she was fine.

She couldn't seem to surface from the black mood enveloping her. Or maybe it was simply the realization that God had played a magnificent jest on her. He'd said to her: *Here is Gordon, your friend and your companion. As you grow to know him, you will fall in love. You'll want to be close to him, to live the rest of your life with him, but wait. I'm going to take him away from you for five years, during which time you'll question and worry. You'll*

miss him desperately, but don't despair. I'll give him back to you for a few days of magic and wonder. I'll show you what life with him would be like. Just when you're certain that I'm smiling on you, I'll take it all away.

Did God know when people were furious with him? Did He somehow sense it in the lack of prayers sent in His direction? She didn't know. All she did know was that the world wasn't a kind or just place. Instead, it was vicious and cruel.

She couldn't help but ache for her mother. Mary had been disappointed in her son. Harrison had never returned voluntarily to Adaire Hall. Even when she'd been so sick toward the end, he'd only made a grudging appearance.

"Your brother has suffered for the lack of a father," she told Jennifer once. "I think he would have been a different kind of man had Alex lived."

Mary would've been proud to have Gordon as her son. She didn't doubt that he would've brought a lot of comfort to her mother in her last days.

Betty's actions had done more than destroy her life. She'd altered Mary's as well. Hadn't the poor woman suffered enough? First the fire, then the death of her husband, and the pain that she'd to endure for the rest of her days.

Perhaps it would've been charitable for her to forgive Betty, but Jennifer couldn't bring herself to do so. If God was displeased, she didn't care. What more could God do to her?

The maid brought her morning tray as usual.

Until Ellen appeared, she hadn't realized that there were two cups there.

"I've decided to take tea with you this morning, my dear girl. We're going to have a talk, you and I."

She'd heard that tone from Ellen before, but had rarely been the recipient of it. Ellen insisted on excellence from her staff and, for the most part, received it. When someone did a slipshod job or didn't follow instructions, they were lectured by Ellen in just that tone. She'd also heard her godmother face down a shopkeeper and had been grateful not to be the object of Ellen's irritation.

Her initial thought was to ask what she had done; then she decided not to say anything at all. Silence was always safer.

"I've been patient long enough, my dear. When you wouldn't tell me what was amiss, I told myself that it was a private matter. However, my patience is at an end. I've come to the conclusion that something is dreadfully wrong. Harrison has probably been an ass, but Harrison has always been an ass. Besides, you wouldn't have that look in your eyes about him. No doubt you're still missing your mother, but that is a pain that will last for the rest of your life. Yet I've seen you smile since Mary died. I haven't seen you smile recently."

"Do you miss Colin?" Jennifer interjected. "You don't speak of him very often."

Ellen looked taken aback. She poured them each a cup of tea, added sugar to hers, and sat back, concentrating on her cup for a moment.

"I miss him every day. It's like a hole in my chest, one that I can never hope to fill." She smiled. "My grief always surprises me, however. I wake up and my first gesture is to roll over to his side of the bed, but he isn't there. Does that answer your question?"

Jennifer nodded.

"I don't know what I thought marriage was," Ellen continued. "I saw your mother's marriage to your father, but I believed they were so compatible because it was Mary, and Mary was a generous and loving soul. I had my own parents' marriage as a lesson, you see." She shook her head. "I think that's why I rejected marriage myself, at least until I met Colin."

She took another sip of her tea, her gaze far away.

"I was expected to be a dutiful spinster daughter. My parents only unbent and allowed me some freedom because of my friendship with Mary. By that time, she had become a countess." She smiled in memory. "It was your mother who introduced me to Colin. Did you know that?"

Jennifer shook her head.

"My marriage was unlike anything I'd expected. It was like being with your best friend, the most favorite person in your entire life every day. We laughed a great deal. We kissed a great deal. I knew him better than I knew anyone, and I know that he felt the same about me."

Jennifer didn't know what to say. That was the exact relationship she had envisioned having with Gordon.

"It was a complete surprise when he wore me

down, but I think your mother knew, from the beginning, that he was the one man for me. I never asked her, but I should have." Her smile faded. "When Colin died unexpectedly, it was a shock. I think I believed that I would always be as happy."

Jennifer reached over the tray and grabbed her godmother's hand. "I'm so sorry, Ellen. I shouldn't have asked."

"I'm glad you did. I don't speak of Colin very often, but I should. He was a fascinating, loving, generous, kind man, and by not speaking of him, I've helped to erase him from the world. I shall not do that in the future, because people deserve to remember him. Or if they didn't know him, to learn of him anyway."

"I liked him very much," Jennifer said. "We had the most wonderful conversations."

Ellen smiled. "He liked you, too. In fact, he said he thought you were the second most intelligent woman he had ever met. Me being the first, of course."

Neither said anything for a moment, each adrift in their memories.

"Why did you ask about Colin?" Ellen asked, looking straight at her.

There was always something perceptive about Ellen's glance, as if she could see beyond the layer of lies or wish to obfuscate or pretend. Even if she'd tried, Jennifer doubted she would have ever gotten away with anything as a child. Ellen took her role as godmother seriously. When Mary wasn't feeling well, Ellen took it on herself to ensure that Jennifer knew her manners, was

being educated well, and that her character was being formed correctly.

"Is it because of Gordon?"

Jennifer forgot to breathe for a moment. "Do you know?"

"All I know, my dear girl, is that you aren't yourself. Something's happened and you have studiously not mentioned Gordon's name ever since arriving in Edinburgh."

Jennifer stared down at her hands, clasped them together, then released them.

"You haven't been very communicative, Jennifer. When pressed, you've told me about Harrison and Lauren and baby Mary. You've been very descriptive about Sean's funeral, Mrs. Thompson and her expertise, and even your cook. Gordon is the one person you haven't spoken of. Has he gone back to London as well?"

Jennifer didn't think she could say the words. If she said them, it would magically change everything about her past. Make all those interludes with Gordon something terrible, something about which to be ashamed, instead of memories she'd always treasured.

How could she possibly tell Ellen when she could barely face the truth herself?

"Did he hurt you in some way?"

"No, Gordon would never hurt me." Not deliberately.

"Then will you tell me what it is? Misery shared is misery eased, sometimes."

Jennifer only shook her head.

"Are you certain you don't want to tell me?"

Jennifer stood and without another word

headed for the bedroom. She closed the door firmly behind her, hoping that Ellen hadn't seen her tears.

ELLEN STARED AT the closed bedroom door, wishing that she hadn't pushed the issue. She'd upset Jennifer, and it was the very last thing she wanted to do.

She placed her cup on the tray, then went to the bellpull, and signaled for the maid to come. She would have to apologize later this morning and then work on her patience for a little while longer.

Jennifer hadn't said anything about wanting to go back to Adaire Hall, another change. In the past, Jennifer had always put a limit to her visit almost immediately on arriving in Edinburgh. Plus, she always went on about enhancements that she wanted to make to the Hall or to the gardens or to some aspect of the estate.

Jennifer had always taken such pride in her home, more than Harrison ever had. All he cared about was gambling, which was a fool's exercise.

She would have to be very judicious about her questions of Jennifer in the future, but she wasn't going to curb her curiosity.

Chapter Thirty-Six

$\mathcal{G}$ordon had never been feted at a dinner like the one he attended tonight. Four friends who'd known Alex Adaire insisted on buying him an extravagant meal, then finishing it up with a round of drinks.

Gordon learned that his father had an ear for voices, and that he kept his classmates amused and entertained by mimicking their professors.

"It's only because he was brilliant that he got away with it, of course," Michael McTavish said. "He was smarter than all of us."

"I used to ask him if he ever studied," McNair said. "He answered that he did, sometimes. Hardly ever, though."

Over the next several hours, Gordon was regaled with stories of Alex's generosity, too. How he'd spent many sleepless nights quizzing friends for exams. Or how often he'd loaned money to a classmate and never asked for it back.

All four of them had gone to Adaire Hall for his funeral and even now missed him.

It was odd to be examined so closely, especially when they pretended not to be looking at him. Evidently, even some of his gestures were similar to his father's.

Each man had an abundance of Alex stories and insisted on telling them. By the end of the evening, he was filled with regret that he hadn't known the man they knew and never would.

Gordon had, however, acquired four new friends, men who promised to help him find property for sale if he wanted to expand in Scotland. From what he'd been told, Edinburgh would be the perfect venue for a new music hall.

He managed to say enough to indicate his interest, but not why he would probably never come back to Scotland to live. That confession was too raw; that loss too much to bear.

He finished his whiskey and nodded when asked if he wanted another. One thing alcohol could do: erase your memories, at least temporarily.

"I LOVE HIM," Jennifer said.

Ellen turned to see her goddaughter standing in the doorway, dressed for bed.

"I've always loved him. I dreamed of being his wife. I wanted to share the rest of my life with him. I wanted to bear his children. I was used to sharing my thoughts with him, and hearing his. A day wasn't right without him being there."

"Gordon?"

Jennifer nodded. "When we were children, we never tried to keep our friendship a secret. There was no need. My mother liked Gordon very much. She spent a lot of time with him. I think she saw him as a good influence for me. Or hopefully for Harrison, although he and Gordon never got along."

Ellen went to Jennifer's side and gently pulled her into the sitting room. She'd been ready to retire for the night, but not now, especially in view of Jennifer's distress. She could feel Jennifer trembling and wanted to hug her, but instead led her to the sofa.

"When we got older, Mr. McBain began to object to my seeing so much of Gordon, so it was just easier to slip away to meet him. Harrison always tried to remind me that he was the gardener's boy, never realizing that Gordon would always be more than that for me."

Jennifer had left her rooms barefoot. Now Ellen draped a throw over her goddaughter's feet.

"I knew he would eventually leave Adaire Hall, but not the way he did."

Ellen wanted to hurry her goddaughter along, to ask her what had gone so bad between them, but she had the feeling that the story had to be told in Jennifer's way, not hers.

She grabbed one of Jennifer's hands, disturbed at how cold it felt.

"And then he went away. For two years, I didn't know anything. Harrison kept telling me that Gordon had left because he was tired of me, that he was bored. That I had misinterpreted everything, that I'd been played for a fool. I never believed Harrison, but I still wondered, simply because there was no word from Gordon. Then, when his mother died, I got his address from the bank and wrote him."

Two tears fell down her face. Ellen wondered at the power of those tears. They had the ability to etch a path through her heart.

"I wrote him every Christmas and on his birthday, but he never wrote me back." Jennifer looked over at her. "He said he didn't get those letters."

Ellen kept silent.

"I wanted him to come back. I was desperate for him to come back, but he didn't."

"Is that why you never wanted to meet any young men when you came to visit?"

Jennifer nodded. "I was waiting for Gordon."

"But he never returned to the Hall."

She shook her head. "Not until recently. I wrote him again and told him about Sean, who was dying." She glanced at Ellen again. "He wanted to be a success when he returned to Adaire Hall. He wanted to prove that he could make something of himself to Sean and maybe Harrison."

"But never to you?"

She shook her head again. "He never had to prove anything to me. He never had to be anyone other than who he was, Ellen. He was Gordon. That was enough."

Ellen's attention was on their joined hands. "That's a very romantic notion, but it isn't real, Jennifer. Gordon knew that. In order to offer you something, he had to have something to offer. I admire him for knowing that and putting actions to ideas."

"I know that," Jennifer said. "I knew that Gordon always had plans for his life—for our life—but I never thought that he would stay away so long. Or that it would be so painful."

"But he came back. He returned to you. So what is wrong?"

Jennifer squeezed her hand, released it, then stood and walked to the other side of the room. The drapes had already been closed, but she pushed one side open and stood there, looking out at the night.

"I love him." A few minutes later she spoke again. "But I can't love him. It's wrong. It's a sin."

Ellen kept silent only because she had a feeling that if she spoke, Jennifer would burst into tears.

"I don't think I can tell you," Jennifer said, her voice faint. "The words won't come."

That didn't sound like her goddaughter at all. She'd always faced every situation directly and with determination, from Mary's illness and subsequent death to managing Adaire Hall and handling Harrison.

"You can always tell me anything, Jennifer."

Slowly, Jennifer closed the drapes again and turned, facing Ellen.

"I love him. I love him with all my heart, but it's wrong to feel that way."

"When is love ever wrong?" Ellen asked. "Because he doesn't have a title? That seems unlike you."

"No, because he's my brother."

Ellen blinked a few times, but the words were still there, almost floating in the air between them.

"Your brother?"

Jennifer nodded.

"Gordon is your brother?"

"Yes."

For the next several minutes, Ellen heard the

most outrageous story about a woman named Betty McDonnell, who'd done something hideous. Perhaps she'd even label it evil. She'd taken Mary's child and replaced him with her own.

When Jennifer was done speaking, Ellen stared at her wordlessly. Not one comment came to mind. In a world of words, she had nothing reassuring or comforting to say. Now, at this one particular point in time, she should have been able to murmur something, but nothing penetrated the maelstrom of her thoughts.

"If Betty hadn't done what she did," Jennifer added, "then Gordon and I would've been raised as brother and sister. I wouldn't have come to feel for him what I do. Somehow, I'm supposed to only feel a certain way for him now and no more. How am I to do that, Ellen? How do you kill love?"

This young woman she loved so dearly was suffering.

"I don't know," Ellen said helplessly.

No wonder she was predisposed to like Gordon. He was Mary's child. She'd known Mary's husband well, but she'd only been in Gordon's company once, for a short time. He'd startled her at the time by remarking on how her eyes were like Jennifer's.

Poor Mary, to have never known who Gordon was. Harrison had proved to be a poor replacement.

"There, I've told you the truth, but it doesn't make the situation easier to bear. Misery shared isn't necessarily misery eased, Ellen."

"Certainly not in this situation," Ellen said.

"There's something else you need to know. I've made a decision. I'm not going back to Adaire Hall. I can't go back there. I can't see the places where Gordon and I spent so much time. I can't pretend that my life is the same. It isn't."

She didn't have anything to say to that, either.

Jennifer bent and kissed her on the cheek. "I'll see you in the morning."

Before she straightened, Ellen pressed her hand against Jennifer's cheek, smoothing away the tears. "Oh, my dear girl, I'm so sorry."

"I know you are, Ellen. I wish it made a difference."

Jennifer closed the sitting room door behind her, leaving Ellen alone.

She turned her head and stared into the bedroom, at the large bed that she and Colin had shared. An enormous creation, it sat on the dais, dominating the room. Colin had been a big man and had wanted his comfort. The bed had been specially made for him, to his specifications. Each time she climbed the steps, she thought of him.

She missed him desperately right now. He possessed a core of common sense. In some ways he was like a child, feeling excitement and enthusiasm for travel, new discoveries, and inventions. In others, he was an old soul, wise beyond his years.

What would he say to her dilemma?

He'd always wanted to know her thoughts and had valued her opinion. They had laughed together, and at night they had loved each other. She respected him more than anyone she had ever known, but she'd never told him the truth.

Only four people knew the entirety of it, and two of them had died. She didn't know what had ever happened to the midwife. She wasn't even sure she could remember the woman's name.

She'd promised Mary that she would never tell the story. It had been a vow that she had been willing to give at the time. How was she to know that a woman named Betty would cause that vow to be upended?

Oh dear God, what did she do?

Jennifer was in pain, and it was a pain that only she could ease. The question was, did she have the courage to do so.

How could she not?

Chapter Thirty-Seven

*E*llen managed to get through the night with the help of some brandy from the cut glass decanter on the sideboard in her sitting room. Colin occasionally liked to have a drink after they'd retired, and she'd kept up with the practice.

No doubt the brandy would shock Jennifer. The truth was that she had a great many bad habits. After all, she was a mature woman who'd had an eventful life. What was she supposed to be, pure, virginal, and perfect? No, she was definitely not an angel. Even though her parents had sincerely wanted a saint for a daughter, they hadn't gotten one.

She even had some regrets, but not many since learning that regrets were a waste of time. Every single person who'd made it to her age had moments in which they were blithering idiots. She was not exempt.

Life had visited sorrow on her, too, just like it did everyone. It had occurred to her, more than once, that sorrow was perhaps a payment for the joy you experienced in life. If that was the case, then she would reluctantly accept the sorrow, because she'd also experienced great joy.

This time it wasn't Jennifer who retreated to

her rooms. She stayed in her suite, even banishing Abigail. Ellen wasn't in the mood for complaints or general grousing.

It wasn't that she had a decision to make. She'd already made it. That was the easy part. Yet speaking the words would change everything, and that's why she needed to muster her courage. She understood Jennifer's silence now more than ever, yet at the same time she thanked God that Jennifer had found the strength to tell Gordon's story.

Finally, she was ready. She'd sent the dinner tray back uneaten and poured herself a brandy in preparation for this meeting.

When Jennifer entered the room, Ellen smiled, then indicated the end of the sofa.

"You wanted to talk to me, Ellen? If it's about not returning to Adaire Hall, I can't be talked out of my decision."

"Nor would I try to do so, my dear girl. We need to discuss something much more serious."

Jennifer looked at her inquisitively, but didn't speak as she sat.

Ellen raised the brandy snifter. "Can I interest you in one of these?"

Jennifer shook her head. Ellen wondered if she would change her mind after a while. A little brandy did wonders in difficult situations.

Once Jennifer was settled, Ellen sat back and said another prayer. She'd been praying most of the day.

"Mary Adaire was one of the most wonderful people I've ever known," she began.

Jennifer nodded.

"She was kind. She was understanding. Even if she didn't condone a certain behavior, she tried to see beyond it to the human being who'd performed it. She was gracious. She was the perfect countess. When she married Alex, I thought it was a wonderful union. It was evident, to everyone, how much they loved each other. I never knew anyone like her. She even charmed my parents, who'd become very strict Church of Scotland. They liked her. Even better, they respected her. I think they secretly admired her as well. You didn't know her the way I did, Jennifer, but she was a beautiful woman. She had this glorious auburn hair and these beautiful blue eyes."

Ellen stared down at the brandy, remembering how jealous she'd been when first meeting Mary and how quickly that feeling had dissipated in view of the woman's charm and grace.

"My parents allowed me a season. They hadn't found religion yet, you see. I was an only child, expected to be the apple of my parents' eye. I was to be perfect, but I fell far short of that."

She was going too far afield. Jennifer was too polite to ask why she was suddenly talking about people she had never met.

"You know about the fire, of course."

Jennifer nodded again. She leaned forward, clasping her hands, intent on Ellen's words. Did she have some kind of precognitive ability? Did she realize that what Ellen was going to say next would change her entire life?

"What you don't know is that the fire altered their marriage. Not the fire, exactly, but what happened when Mary fell from the second floor.

They couldn't be together any longer. It was too painful for her."

She knew how much that had mattered to both of them. Yet she doubted if Alex would have ever been unfaithful to his wife. He loved her too much. In addition, the man was a paragon of virtue himself. He was a good man, and it was evident that Gordon took after him.

"As I said, Mary was very understanding. Perhaps the word isn't *understanding*. Perhaps it's *compassionate. Generous. Kind.*"

She took another sip of the brandy and realized that it wasn't going to help. She was simply going to have to tell this story, as difficult as it was.

"All around me, my friends were getting married, but I did not have any affection whatsoever for any of the young men who seemed interested in me. It was all too evident that I was going to remain a spinster, caring for my parents until their elderly days. Maybe that's why I did what I did." She shook her head, determined to be honest. "No, that's not why. I was entranced and flattered and pleased. A handsome young man began to pay me attention, and it went to my head, I think. That was before I learned my own value. I didn't respect myself enough. So I fell for his blandishments, ardent as they were, and found myself in a precarious position. Especially since he decided to marry an heiress and leave me without a backward glance."

She could still remember the humiliation of learning of Ronald McCormick's betrothal. First had come the hurt, then the panic.

"I confided in Mary. I was, in fact, about to

shame my parents by causing a massive scandal. I was about to have a child out of wedlock. Perhaps such things would be acceptable in some families, but not Church of Scotland members." She smiled without any trace of humor. "My parents would have thrown me out on the streets."

She'd been worried about her child. Even then, her baby had acquired a supreme importance. She would have done anything to protect him.

She could remember every moment of that visit to Adaire Hall. Mary had just acquired her wheeled chair and she was no longer imprisoned in her room. They had been sitting on the terrace, and Ellen had tearfully confessed her sin to her friend.

"Mary had an idea. She could no longer have children, and here I was, about to have a baby."

She forced herself to look at Jennifer. There was a dawning awareness in the younger woman's eyes. Her cheeks were becoming pink, and Jennifer's hands were clasped together in what looked like a death grip.

"Mary asked my parents if I could accompany her to England. That's the story we gave out. Because of her fragile condition, I was going to be a nurse/companion. Alex accompanied us, of course."

Even if she stopped right now, Jennifer would know the truth, but that would be sheer cowardice on her part. Instead, she continued.

"We stayed at a small house that belonged to a friend of Alex's. Only one other person called on us—the midwife. When my child was born,

Mary and Alex claimed her as their own. We named her Jennifer."

Where had the tears come from? She hadn't thought to weep, but suddenly she was.

Jennifer didn't say anything for a long moment. Neither did she look away. The color rose on her cheeks, but when she still didn't speak a moment later, Ellen almost begged her to say something, anything. She had tried to anticipate Jennifer's reaction to the news, but she hadn't thought that the younger woman would break the silence with a question.

"Did everyone accept that I was their child?"

Ellen nodded. "We were gone long enough. I had been able to hide my condition. No one knew us in the English town where we stayed. Alex even sent word back to the Hall that the reason they were staying away so long was Mary's pregnancy and how difficult the journey home might prove to be."

"Did he go along with the story?"

Ellen smiled. "You have to understand how much Alex loved Mary. Whatever she wanted, he was willing to do. Plus, I think he wanted another child as well. He never saw you as different. He always loved you as the child of his heart."

She had to make Jennifer understand. "Mary did this for me, not for herself. She knew what would happen if anyone found out. It would be a scandal that I wouldn't be able to live down." She cleared her throat. "Everyone loved Mary. Even before the fire she was beloved by not only the staff of the Hall, but by Alex's friends and their

acquaintances in Edinburgh. I've never heard a bad word spoken of her. So, if there were any suspicions, no one voiced them."

She blinked back her tears and cleared her throat again.

"The three of us vowed that it would remain a secret, that no one would ever know that you weren't Mary's child. She wanted me to have a place in your life, so I became your godmother. In a sense, we shared you. You spent time with me and lived at Adaire Hall."

Jennifer nodded. "I never knew. I never suspected."

"Oh, my darling girl, you were never to suspect. Mary was a wonderful mother. I couldn't have found anyone better. If I couldn't be with you, then she was the perfect substitute."

She watched as the full ramifications of her confession occurred to Jennifer.

A moment later, Jennifer came and knelt at Ellen's feet. She grabbed Ellen's hands and said, "Are you saying that Gordon isn't my brother? He's not my brother? We're not related?"

Ellen nodded. "I couldn't have you suffer for my sin, Jennifer."

"Oh, Ellen, Ellen."

Whatever else she might've said was buried in the hug Jennifer gave her. A few minutes later, Jennifer pulled back and looked at Ellen, her face awash with tears of joy. Her next words didn't surprise Ellen in the least. In fact, she'd already given orders for the carriage to be brought around early the next morning.

"I have to go to him, Ellen."

"And we shall, my darling girl. As fast as the train can carry us."

"Who is my father?" Jennifer asked as she stood.

"His name is Ronald McCormick. I lost track of him years ago. I don't even know if he's still in Scotland. Does it matter to you?"

"No," Jennifer said. "Did he ever know about me?"

Ellen shook her head. "Only the three of us did. It was the only way our plan would work."

"You must've been terrified. Unmarried, uncertain of the future."

"Petrified and overjoyed," Ellen said with a rueful smile. "My parents were very strict, so I had no doubt about their reaction. At the same time, I felt that I'd been blessed with you."

"I know that your parents died a few years ago, but do I have any other relatives?"

"Cousins."

"I don't suppose I could go to them and introduce myself, could I?"

"Honestly, I thought your Gordon guessed my secret. He kept looking at us the night Harrison and I arrived at Adaire Hall, almost as if he saw a resemblance."

Jennifer startled her by kneeling again. She took Ellen's hands in hers. "Thank you. Thank you for telling me. It can't have been easy."

"It was infinitely easier than seeing you in pain, my darling girl."

The night seemed to call for tears. When she embraced her daughter again, Ellen didn't hold back this time.

Chapter Thirty-Eight

Jennifer's whole life had been a lie. She suddenly knew, exactly, how Gordon had felt. When the foundation of your life turned out to be built on shifting sands, you questioned everything.

Taking the train to London was not an easy journey, but they would get there a day earlier than by carriage. Every day mattered.

She kept glancing at Ellen, but she hadn't changed in appearance. Nor was she a different person now than she'd been yesterday. Yet the way Jennifer saw her had changed.

Their noses were the same. Their eye color was surprisingly similar. Why hadn't she seen that before now?

All these years and she'd never guessed. She'd thought that Ellen was simply conscientious about being her godmother. She'd never realized that all the advice, all the concern, all the love was for another reason. She was Ellen's daughter. Yet she was Mary's, too. She was Lady Jennifer only because of the kindness of the Countess of Burfield and her husband.

Yet she'd loved them with all her heart. Just as she loved Ellen.

It didn't seem fair that she'd been given so much love, and yet it had been stripped from Gordon. She would simply have to make up for the lack.

She thought back to all of those occasions when she'd been sent to Edinburgh to be with Ellen. Mary had been emphatic on the point, her rationale being that Jennifer needed to have a bit of experience with the world, and seeing Edinburgh and being with her godmother would provide that. When, in actuality, Mary had been insistent that Ellen get some time with her daughter.

Would she have been brave enough to give away her child? For that matter, would she be generous enough to take the child of a friend and raise it as her own? The two important women in her life had been true examples of courage and kindness.

She looked up to find Ellen studying her.

"Do you hate me?" Ellen asked. "Now that you know the truth?"

"How could I ever hate you?" Jennifer asked. "You gave me life. You've loved me. So did Mary. I've been twice blessed. I had not just one mother, but two."

Ellen began blinking, and Jennifer realized she was trying to hold back tears. She moved to sit next to Ellen, grabbed her hands, and held them tightly.

"I was a fool," Ellen said. "I was young and naive, but I thought myself in love."

"I think love must make you foolish," Jennifer

said. "But it also makes you brave and kind and generous."

The two of them smiled at each other.

Jennifer looked down at her gloved hands. Outwardly, she probably appeared calm. Inwardly, however, her stomach was jumping and her breath felt tight. She couldn't wait to reach Gordon, to tell him the truth.

The journey to London seemed interminable. One good thing was that Abigail had been left behind. Jennifer could just imagine the trip with the maid's constant complaints.

Would Gordon want to live in London? She didn't particularly like the city, but if sacrifice was necessary to be with Gordon, then she was willing and eager to accept whatever price she had to pay. Perhaps it wouldn't be easy, but a great many things that mattered weren't particularly easy. And Gordon mattered, more than anything else in her life.

GORDON THANKED HIS new advocate, stood, and made his way out of the office with the sheaf of papers he'd been given. He had suspected that claiming an earldom would not be an easy process, but he hadn't realized how much paperwork would be involved. He had signed a half dozen documents attesting to what Sean had told him. His advocate had also suggested that Margaret McBride could be encouraged to testify and was sending an associate to Adaire Hall for that purpose.

Had the countess sensed a resemblance? He couldn't help but wonder if things would have

been different if her vision hadn't been so badly damaged.

Circumstances had been perfect for Betty's deception. His father had died when he was five. His mother had been badly injured. There were no close relatives to see a resemblance and because of the countess's injuries, visitors had not flocked to Adaire Hall as they had in earlier days.

But for Sean's honesty, he would never have known his true identity. For that, he should probably be grateful to the man, but that emotion was currently beyond him.

Two weeks had passed, and he was intent on getting back to work. His claim would snake its way through the courts. No doubt at some point it would reach the newspapers. Before that happened, however, he was going to call in Harrison's markers.

He would have to let Jennifer know. He didn't want her blindsided by his actions. He wouldn't be able to sell Adaire Hall, but he could empty it to pay Harrison's debts.

He'd write her. Somehow, he'd manage not to feel anything, and if he did, he'd simply quash that emotion before it had a chance to break free.

The rain echoed his mood, made Edinburgh dark and gloomy.

According to his advocate, he had a good chance of pleading his case to the court and even winning. It wasn't enough to offset the greater loss of the woman he loved. Somehow, he would have to overcome that, but he suspected it would be years in the making.

WHEN THEY FINALLY reached London, their first destination was Ellen's home.

Jennifer wanted to change her dress, fix her hair, and ensure that she looked her best. She raced through all those preparations and was slowed only by Ellen's refusal to leave the house without a decent meal.

"I do not consider having an apple in the train station to be sufficient nourishment. If you don't want to faint at Gordon's feet, you will at least take some soup."

She sat reluctantly and agreed to eat a hearty vegetable soup with an accompaniment of bread and butter. Ellen was probably right, because she did feel better immediately. She wasn't nearly as shaky, and her stomach had stopped doing that curious trembling.

Gordon was only minutes away. She was finally going to see him. All she had to do was wait a few minutes, that's all. An hour at the most.

Finally, they were on their way.

Jennifer had given the driver Gordon's address. When they pulled up in front of the town house, she was surprised for two reasons. First of all, Gordon's residence was only a block or two from Ellen's house. Secondly, it was the equal in size, if not slightly larger.

"I would say that your Gordon has done quite well for himself," Ellen said.

"I like it when you call him my Gordon. He is my Gordon. He always has been."

Ellen smiled at her. She had been doing that a lot for the past two days. Could it be that she had

wanted to reveal her identity for years, but been constrained by her promise to Mary?

Gordon's home was designed like so many town houses, in that it was predominantly brick with a black door and white framed windows, sparkling in the afternoon sun. The approach was formal, however, the path lined by an ornate wrought iron border.

All this time she'd been thinking of Gordon living in London in a small house or flat. She'd never considered that he would own such a spacious dwelling. It was a sign of his character, perhaps, that he hadn't bragged about his acquisition.

Ellen's driver opened the carriage door and unfurled the steps, helping them out to the street. Together, they walked up the broad steps to the front door.

"I shall not be intrusive," Ellen said. "I'll leave and give the two of you time to talk."

Jennifer sent Ellen a look of gratitude.

The door was opened by a very short man, who was very broad as well. He looked almost as wide around as he was tall. However, he was blessed with a bright smile that he flashed at them.

"Good afternoon, ladies. And how could I be helping you?"

Jennifer certainly hadn't expected someone quite so Irish.

She pulled out one of her cards and handed it to him. "I should like to see Mr. McDonnell, if it is possible."

"And sure, it would be possible if he was here."

"He isn't here?"

Of course, he wouldn't be. He'd be working. Except that she didn't know where, exactly, he would be working. When she said as much to the strange majordomo, he grinned at her again.

"Well, now, that could be anywhere, couldn't it? He's got two music halls with one being built, plus a hoity-toity club with another on the way. Although I think the hoity-toity club is the best place to be looking for him. If he's back from Scotland, that is."

He immediately launched into a long discussion of solicitors and travel and the appointments Gordon had evidently missed in the past two weeks, not to mention the volume of callers he'd had.

"Do you know when he'll be back?" Ellen asked, cutting through the voluminous explanation.

"Well, now, he's gone back to Scotland and him just returning from there. You could ask Maggie. She'd probably know."

"Maggie?" Jennifer said. "Where could we find Maggie?"

"Where she is most of the time. At the hoity-toity place."

"The Mayfair Club," Ellen said. "It's where I found Harrison."

They thanked the majordomo, descended the stairs, and entered the carriage again.

"Why has Gordon gone back to Scotland?" she asked, biting back her impatience.

"Perhaps Maggie will tell us," Ellen said. "The

Mayfair Club is where Harrison likes to gamble. He even has lodgings there."

"No," Jennifer said. "It's where he likes to lose money, according to Gordon."

Thankfully, Harrison's actions no longer needed to concern her.

Chapter Thirty-Nine

The Mayfair Club didn't look anything like Jennifer had expected. It wasn't appreciably different from the street on which Gordon lived. All of the carriages either parked there or letting out their passengers were fancier than most. She even saw a ducal crest on one.

The porter at the door wasn't Irish this time, but quintessentially English with a very proper way of speaking. There was a glint in his eye, however, as he greeted Ellen. Evidently, she'd made an impression on her first visit.

"We should like to meet with Miss Boyland," Ellen said.

The porter motioned them to an upholstered bench.

"I will see if she is available."

Jennifer looked around her, impressed at the entranceway and wishing she could see the rest of the club. However, from both Harrison's and Ellen's conversations, such establishments were not open to women, unless they were employed on the premises.

They couldn't hear anything. No raucous laughter or shouting. No clinking of glasses. No indication of the activities that were going on behind

closed doors. The only thing that hinted that the club might be a masculine province was the faint smell of tobacco.

A few minutes later, they could hear the click of the porter's shoes on the marble floor. When he appeared before them, his cheeks were slightly reddened. Either the exertion up the stairs had caused him to become flushed or announcing their presence to Maggie had resulted in some difficulty.

"If you will come with me, please," the porter said, bowing once more.

They followed him up a staircase that rivaled the one at Adaire Hall. This one might even be fancier, with its carved wood balusters and brass handrail. Even the risers were decorated with thin strips of embossed brass.

The runner on the second floor was crimson, woven with blowsy roses on either side. There were four doors in the corridor, all of them closed but one. Jennifer couldn't help but wonder what activities went on in those rooms.

The porter led them to the open door, then stood aside, bowing once more. "Miss Boyland," he said as a way of introduction.

"Thank you, Ellison," Maggie said, standing and coming out from behind the desk. "What a pleasure to see you again, Mrs. Thornton. Have you come about Harrison? If you have, I'm afraid I have bad news for you. He's no longer a member of the Mayfair Club. Nor does he have lodgings here."

Jennifer and Ellen looked at each other. Evidently, Gordon had kicked him out. Jennifer

wondered if he'd been able to find other lodgings. If not, would he return to Adaire Hall?

At the moment, that was not her problem.

Maggie Boyland was not a young woman. Although she was wearing powder, rouge, and something to make her lashes appear darker, she applied the products with an expert hand. Yet there were still lines at the corners of her eyes betraying her age, as well as a softening of the skin beneath her chin.

For some reason Jennifer had thought Maggie was Gordon's age. Not someone old enough to be his mother.

"And you are?" Maggie asked, her thin lips formed into a smile that didn't reach her eyes.

"Jennifer Adaire."

A name not unknown to Maggie, from the flash of recognition in her glance. "Oh yes, Gordon's little friend."

Gordon's little friend?

Ellen stepped between them. "We're here for information, and I hope you can provide it. Do you know when Gordon is returning to London? The majordomo at his house said that he had returned to Scotland. Is that true?"

"It is. That's as much as I can tell you. Anything more than that would be considered confidential. I couldn't betray a trust."

That last was said with a quick look in Jennifer's direction.

She'd never had such a reaction to anyone so instantly, but Jennifer did not like Maggie Boyland. It was an instinctual feeling, and one that she would have to investigate later, but for now

she forced a smile to her lips. The woman was not going to have the ability to rile her. Or goad her to say something Jennifer would regret later.

"Are you certain you can't tell us where he's gone?" Ellen's voice was positively dripping with sweetness.

Jennifer almost rolled her eyes but kept her gaze on the floor.

"It is quite important that we reach him."

"I believe he's gone to Edinburgh," Maggie said, unbending enough to give them that information. "Beyond that I can't say."

"Have you no idea when he'll return?" Ellen asked.

"I didn't say that. I said that I wasn't going to divulge anything further."

"Why not?" Jennifer asked, unable to keep silent. "We mean no harm to Gordon. Surely you know that. If you know my name, then you realize that Gordon and I have had a relationship of long standing."

"I know that you have had a difficult relationship," Maggie said. Her smile altered character, becoming almost a sneer.

Once again, Ellen tried to calm troubled waters. "We truly do need to reach Gordon. It's on a matter of some importance."

"I really can't say," Maggie said.

"You really *won't* say," Jennifer said, stepping to the side so that Ellen was no longer between them.

Maggie was slightly taller, which was annoying. Jennifer would have liked to tower over the woman.

"Why should I tell you anything, Lady Jennifer? Yes, I know exactly who you are."

Ellen stepped between them again. "I commend your loyalty, Maggie, but believe me when I tell you that it's misplaced in this instance. Gordon will not be pleased to learn that you've turned us away without information."

Instead of looking chastened, Maggie smiled again, a smug, self-satisfied smile.

"My loyalty has never been misplaced, Mrs. Thornton, and it isn't in this case. Now, if you don't mind leaving, I have work to do."

"Thank you for giving us your time," Ellen said, her voice decidedly frosty.

Neither woman spoke as they left the office. As they entered the carriage, Ellen said, "What a disagreeable woman. She didn't appear that way when I first met her, I can assure you."

"She didn't like me, but that's all right," Jennifer said. "I didn't like her."

Ellen gave instructions to her driver to take them home.

"What are we going to do now?" Jennifer asked.

"There is nothing to do but reconnoiter. Is there anyone else in London who might know where Gordon is and when he will be returning?"

Jennifer shook her head. "I don't know."

"We'll find him. It may not be the reunion you wanted. You might have to wait a few days or even longer, but he'll return to London shortly, I'm sure."

She glanced at Ellen. "If I had been more pleasant, do you think she would've told us? Is it my fault that she didn't?"

"I truly don't think it would've made a difference. She's extremely protective of Gordon."

Jennifer stared out the window at the passing scenery.

"I shall send a note around to the majordomo at Gordon's home and ask him to inform Gordon that we are in London. I'll also give him my address so that when he returns, he'll come to see you."

"If he will," Jennifer said. "There's every possibility he'll avoid me. He doesn't know the truth, you see."

Ellen frowned. "There's that." After a moment she said, "Never mind. I shall think of something."

Jennifer sat back against the seat. *Disappointment* was not a word that adequately described her feelings at the moment. It was deeper than that. She had been so excited about coming to London, overjoyed to be able to tell Gordon that nothing stood between them anymore. Now his absence felt like another barrier that needed to be torn down. She was growing excessively tired of people and situations preventing her from being with the man she loved.

Chapter Forty

The change in Jennifer was remarkable. It was as if someone had turned on a switch and made life appear in her eyes. She smiled. She'd even laughed in the past day. She'd stood up to Maggie in a way that had completely surprised Ellen.

Why, though, should she be startled at Jennifer's behavior? Her daughter was a strong woman. She'd cared for Mary without complaint, even as Harrison had ignored them all. For nearly a year before Mary's death, Jennifer had taken on the duty of Adaire Hall, continuing when Harrison had abdicated all responsibility.

Ellen couldn't help but recall the night she and Harrison had arrived at Adaire Hall, interrupting Jennifer and Gordon at dinner. In that moment, seeing them together, she'd known that Jennifer was in love. Gordon's five-year absence was the reason why Jennifer sometimes looked inconsolable. His presence brought out the sparkle in her eyes and a rose to her cheeks. Nor had she stopped smiling during the entire dinner. Not only that, but she'd glanced at Gordon often and stretched out her hand toward his, as if she couldn't bear not touching him.

Love was not in such abundance in the world

that it could afford to be quashed. Nor was she going to allow her daughter to be hurt. She was going to obtain Gordon's location, and if they had to return to Scotland immediately, that was fine, too. She had unlimited funds at her disposal and time to act as Cupid.

Therefore, Ellen found herself in front of the Mayfair Club once again. She'd waited until after dinner, when Jennifer had retired to her suite. Then she'd called for her carriage, and she was more than prepared to go to war with Maggie Boyland.

A few minutes later, she was knocking on the door of the Mayfair Club once again.

"Good evening, Ellison," she said, evidently surprising the man who probably hadn't expected her to learn his name.

"Ma'am," Ellison said, bowing slightly.

"I should like to see Miss Boyland again. Would that be possible?"

Demands rarely accomplished anything. Sweetness, on the other hand, often accomplished more.

"I shall not take very much of her time," she added.

Ellison opened the door wider, stepped back, and bowed slightly again.

"If you will remain here, ma'am, I shall inquire."

"Thank you," she said, smiling brightly at the man as she sat at the end of the bench.

In a flash he was up the stairs.

She was quite proud of herself. No one looking at her would guess at the level of rage she was hiding at the moment.

First of all, she was tired. The journey from Edinburgh had been long, difficult, and taxing. Although her dinner had been excellent, she was still hungry. She craved a tray in bed and perhaps a snifter of brandy. After that she fully intended to sleep for a day or two.

She had reached her quota of emotion. She wanted no more histrionics of any sort, which made her thankful Abigail had stayed in Edinburgh. She wanted things done the way they should be. She was heartily tired of the world running counter to what she thought was right, proper, and just.

No one should stand between Gordon and Jennifer any longer. They'd both been through too much in the past few years. She certainly wasn't going to allow Maggie Boyland to be a harpy, when kindness would be just as easy. She didn't care what kind of resentment Maggie felt for Jennifer; withholding information about Gordon at this point was simply cruel.

Ellison suddenly appeared in front of her.

"Miss Boyland only has a few moments, but she's willing to spare them for you."

No doubt Maggie had said those exact words to him. Ellen stood, smiling again.

"How very kind of her." Hopefully, Ellison did not hear the sarcasm in her voice.

He escorted her up the stairs again and down the corridor. This time the door was closed and he knocked three times before they heard Maggie's voice.

Ellison opened the door, stepped back, and bowed once more.

She thanked him again with a smile. With a placid expression firmly in place, she sailed into the office. The minute Ellen closed the door behind her, her smile disappeared. When Maggie stood, Ellen shook her head and waved her back into her chair.

"Let's not mince words, shall we? I don't want any of your hail-fellow-well-met false cheer. Nor will I pretend to be polite and diplomatic."

"That would be a welcome change," Maggie said. "I despise being a hypocrite."

"As do I. You know where Gordon is, just as you know when he's due to return. I want that information. In fact, I insist upon it."

Maggie smiled. "Or what? You'll shout the house down? You'll get down on the floor and kick your heels?"

"Yes. Ellison is an excellent porter. He looks large and strong enough to remove any miscreant from the club. No doubt that's part of his duties. How, though, will he handle the situation with a woman?"

She smiled brightly. "I know, quite well, how to defend myself. Plus, I have a very wicked-looking hat pin in my reticule. I would hate to have to use it on the poor man, but I shall. I shall also scream. That should summon an audience as well. I will simply refuse to leave. Poor Ellison will have to transport me bodily from here, and that surely won't do the reputation of the Mayfair Club any good. I'm well-known in London. Or at least in financial circles. You see, my husband was a very wealthy man. His word carried a great deal of weight. As his widow, I have some

cachet. Whatever would happen if word got out that I was treated badly by you?"

She advanced on the desk. "If you care as much about Gordon as I think you do, you wouldn't allow his reputation to suffer such a fate."

Maggie's lips thinned, a sure sign that her temper was rising. Ellen didn't care. Besides, it was only fair that Maggie was an enraged as she was.

"Tell me where Gordon is and when he's returning."

She sat in one of the chairs before the desk and waved Maggie back into her chair.

"I absolutely refuse to leave until you do. Where is Gordon?"

"I told you. He's in Edinburgh."

"When is he returning?"

"Why should I tell you?"

"Because it's the decent thing to do?"

Maggie only smiled at her.

She had an idea, something that had occurred to her after a conversation with Jennifer.

"Jennifer used to write to Gordon. Every Christmas and every year on his birthday. He never received those letters. Are you aware of that?"

Maggie looked at her, no expression on her face.

"I can't help but wonder if you took those letters, Maggie. Were you so overprotective of Gordon that you intercepted his correspondence?"

For a moment, Maggie didn't speak. Finally, she said, "She was intent on ruining his life."

"So you did take them."

"Someone had to protect him from her."

"That wasn't your decision to make. Now you're

determined not to tell us where Gordon is. Why? For the same reason?"

"There's an old adage I learned as a child that eavesdroppers never hear any good about themselves."

They both turned toward the door. Ellen hadn't heard it open, and evidently neither had Maggie.

Gordon stood there. "To answer your question, Mrs. Thornton, I've just returned. What can I do for you?"

Ellen was not going to divulge her history in front of Maggie. She had the impression that the woman used any scraps of information as a weapon.

"If I may speak to you in private, I have some information that I think would be of interest to you. No, let me rephrase that, Gordon. I think it would change your life."

"I've had one too many conversations like that recently. I'd prefer not to have another."

She stood, walked toward Gordon, grabbed his arm, and pulled him out of the room. With her other hand, she slammed the door shut.

"You're not her brother."

Gordon blinked at her several times, but didn't speak.

"You're not Jennifer's brother. Would you care to hear why?"

He nodded, but surprised her by turning and walking down the corridor, opening a door and stepping aside so that she could enter. There was enough light from the sconces in the hallway that she could see him go to the sideboard and light

a gas lamp. This room, too, was an office but a more expansive one than Maggie's.

A wall of windows overlooked the street. The curtains hadn't been closed, and the streetlamps were like golden glowing stars forming intricate patterns.

The desk itself was massive, heavily carved, and a beautiful piece of furniture. Strangely enough, it reminded her of Colin's desk. She had never been able to get rid of it, or even change his study in any way. This room reminded her of her husband with its shelves filled with well-read books, the brass inkwell, and the leather blotter. There were four stacks of papers across the front of the desk, each topped with a brass paperweight. The carpet beneath her feet was something that reminded her of the Orient, another similarity with Colin's study.

Gordon pulled out one of the chairs in front of the desk and she sat, watching as he took the chair opposite. He met her gaze straight on, as if he had nothing to hide. A good sign as far as she was concerned.

"Do you love Jennifer?" she asked.

"How I feel about anyone is not your province, Mrs. Thornton. I would prefer to keep my emotions to myself."

"While it is very important that I get an answer to that question, Gordon. Do you love Jennifer?"

"Why do you want to know?"

"Because she's my daughter."

She had to hand it to him. Gordon had evidently learned to school his features. There was

nothing in his face or demeanor that indicated that she'd surprised him. Nothing but a quick blink of his eyes. She might've missed it if she hadn't been looking so closely.

She told him the story of when she'd been a fool for love. He listened intently, not looking away once. He leaned forward, his elbows on his thighs, his hands clasped between his open knees. Yet he never allowed his gaze to move from her face.

"So, you see," Ellen concluded, "you are not related. Even remotely."

He didn't say anything for a moment, just sat back, his gaze finally moving from her to the windows. He took a deep breath and exhaled it.

"Where is Jennifer now?"

"At my house. I have a home here in London." She withdrew one of her calling cards and, taking the pen from the desk, wrote her address on the back of it.

"As you can imagine, she was quite disappointed not to find you here. She couldn't wait to come to you to tell you the news."

She handed the card to him, and Gordon only stared at it for a minute.

"Are you certain, Mrs. Thornton?"

For the first time in an hour, she smiled with genuine amusement.

"That I gave birth? Most definitely. That the Earl and Countess of Burfield took Jennifer as their own? Again, most definitely. I could never forget those details, Gordon. Nor would I lie to you. I do have a question for you, however."

"Yes, I love her. I've always loved her."

She smiled as she shook her head. "I'm glad to hear it, but that wasn't the question. What are you still doing here?"

He stood, looking down at her. He was a handsome man, but the smile he gave her lit up his eyes. Suddenly, it was like he was radiating light from within.

"Then, if you'll pardon me . . ."

She waved him away. "Go. Go," she said, watching him leave with a smile.

JENNIFER ENTERED HER sitting room, thanking the maid for lighting the lamp here and in her bedroom and for laying the fire. It was going to be a chilly night, the beginning of winter. Still, if she were at Adaire Hall, she wouldn't have lit the fires quite yet. Nor would she have ever left a gas lamp burning without being attended.

The fire in the nursery wing had caused a great many changes at Adaire Hall, all of them geared to making the countess feel safer.

This sitting room, like her chambers in Ellen's Edinburgh home, had recently been decorated. It seemed to have a theme, if the mural on the far wall was any indication. It depicted the ruins of Rome with a few columns standing, but most broken on the ground. The predominant color reminded her of sand with perhaps a little pink mixed in. The sofa, the two chairs, the curtains in both rooms, and the bedcover were all in that shade with varying patterns.

Ellen certainly did her part to keep the seamstresses in London busy.

Jennifer began to pace, creating a path around the sofa, in front of the windows, back to the door, and to the sofa again.

She should have been more polite to Maggie. She should've groveled, if nothing else. Had the man she'd seen in Edinburgh been Gordon? When was he returning? Would Maggie tell her where he was staying? She didn't mind retracing their steps and leaving for Edinburgh tomorrow if she needed to.

How was she to bear this? Until two days ago, she'd been miserable, unable to think about anything other than how terrible she felt and how horrible a future without Gordon would be. Then Ellen had told her the truth of her birth and she was overjoyed. The journey from Edinburgh had been endless, but she'd endured it, only to be told that he was no longer in London.

She wanted to scream.

She couldn't even begin to think of readying herself for bed. Sleep was the furthest thing from her mind. All she wanted was to find Gordon. She opened the sitting room door and left the room.

Chapter Forty-One

$\mathcal{M}$iracles did happen. The refrain stayed with Gordon during the short carriage ride to Ellen's house. Miracles did happen. For the past weeks he'd been simply existing, doing his best to perform those duties that needed to be done to seem functional and rational to other people. For weeks he'd been living a lie, unable to tolerate the life he'd been given.

Miracles did happen. His mind replayed Ellen's words. He could easily see the countess agreeing to take on another woman's child as her own. Mary Adaire was one of the kindest and most generous women he'd ever known, and she was his mother.

At Ellen's door he was greeted by an officious majordomo who insisted on announcing him to Jennifer. He kept his patience with difficulty. At first he thought the man was escorting him outside again before he realized that Jennifer was standing on a terrace at the rear of the house.

"Lady Jennifer," the majordomo announced, "Mr. Gordon McDonnell."

Jennifer turned, so slowly that it felt like a dream. She was wearing her cloak, probably the

same garment she'd worn the last time they met. For a second it was like time was replaying itself.

He took a few steps toward her.

In the weeks since he'd seen her, she'd become even more beautiful.

The faint light from the house illuminated her face, hinted at the color of her eyes, and darkened her hair.

She didn't rush to greet him. Nor did she smile. Instead, she stared at him as if she hadn't seen him for years. Too many years.

Why the hell hadn't he rushed back to Scotland for her? Why had he allowed five years to pass before they were together? Pride, that's why. His foolish, idiotic pride.

He didn't have any pride right at the moment.

"I saw Ellen," he said.

"Did you?"

He nodded.

She smiled. "I'm a bastard. Isn't that the most glorious news?"

A surge of love for her nearly felled him.

In the next instant, she was in his arms and he was kissing her.

She was his friend, his companion, the playmate of his childhood, the woman to whom he had confided all his fears and hopes and dreams.

Ever since Sean's revelation, he'd thought that he would have to go the rest of his life without her. Now he didn't. Now it was as if the rain had stopped, and a rainbow stretched across the sky, so accessible that he could reach out and grab the pot of gold at the end.

His love for her was colored blue, red, and green with sparkling silver and gold threads. It encompassed him, shivered through his body, and touched the hooks in his soul. He held her close, feeling her breathe against him in wonder. She'd been everything for him, and everyone, and for too long a time she'd been forbidden him.

His life suddenly made sense. All of the worry, the deprivation, the sacrifices he'd made, the sleepless nights, and hours of planning. All of it made sense as his future slipped into place.

Jennifer made it worthwhile and gave meaning to everything.

She pulled back and looked up at him.

"You belong to me, Gordon. I belong to you. I'm not going to let anything else separate us. We've gone through so much already. Five long years apart and then this latest horror, believing that we were brother and sister. No more."

With that, she wrapped her arms around his neck, pulled his head down, and kissed him.

As a child, she'd been fearless in following him. She was always there, right behind him, when he climbed a tree or explored a cave. More than once, he thought he'd led her into danger, but Jennifer refused to be left behind. As she grew, she became more circumspect, the lectures from Mary taking root, but she'd never lost her courage.

Now she demonstrated it again by grabbing his hand and pulling him with her.

Although he'd never been to Ellen's home

before, the layout was not substantially different from his own. Jennifer led the way up the back stairs. He stopped before they reached the second-floor landing.

"Jennifer, what are you doing?"

"I'm refusing to wait one more moment, Gordon."

She was one step above him, and now bent down to kiss him again.

Heat shot between them, intoxicating and luring. He wanted her as he always had, but where he'd been controlled in the past, he wasn't sure he could be now.

It would be simpler, better, and wiser if he left for the night and returned in the morning, when they could discuss their future.

He got a few words of that explanation out before Jennifer kissed him again.

"No," she murmured against his lips. "No."

"Jennifer." Her name was a caution, a restraint.

"Gordon," she said, turning the tables on him and enticing him. Her tongue danced against his mouth.

He'd taught her how to kiss, but now it felt like she was teaching him.

She broke off the kiss and smiled down at him. "My love. My darling Gordon. Please don't say no. I won't live one more day without you. I'm ready for happiness. We had two short days of joy, Gordon. Only two days in the past five years. I want more than that. I want happiness from now until the end of my life."

His hands framed her face.

"Jennifer."

"No, I don't want to be wise, Gordon." She put her hands on his wrists, but didn't pull his hands free. "Let me be brazen and shocking. Come to my bed, and let me show you how much I love you."

"Jennifer, you're making it very difficult for me to be honorable."

"I don't want you to be honorable, Gordon. Tonight, of all nights. Or, if you insist on being honorable, then I'll be shocking. Just lie there, and let me do as I will."

She pulled back and looked down at him. "Don't you want me, Gordon?"

"Don't be daft. I've wanted you since I first knew what it was to want a woman."

"Then why are we here on the stairs and not in my bed?"

Turning again, she pulled his hand.

He should have been wiser. Yet he knew exactly how she felt. Daring, devil-may-care, angry at what had happened to them, saying to hell with whatever rules they'd been reared to believe.

No longer. Not one second more. No more time would elapse before they loved each other freely, completely, making their own rules and their own destiny.

How LONG HAD it been since he'd kissed her? Only weeks, but it felt like years. Longer than that, perhaps. An eon. How had she lived without him? She hadn't. She'd merely existed, breathing

in and out, eating when hunger compelled her to, sleeping to escape everything.

Their early lives had been spent together, but their upbringing had been so different. She'd been loved and cherished by not only her parents, but by Ellen. Gordon hadn't had any kind emotion from Sean or Betty.

Adulthood had equalized them. Or perhaps it was simply that Gordon had gone out into the world and demanded more, something better for himself.

She was doing the same thing right at this moment. She wouldn't allow anything to separate them any longer.

She didn't care if she shocked Ellen, or the entire staff. Or all of society, for that matter. It felt like the most natural thing in the world to take Gordon's hand and lead him up the stairs to her suite.

At the door, he hesitated.

She didn't give him a chance to speak, but placed her fingers against his lips.

"Five years ago, I was going to give myself to you. I couldn't wait to love you, but then you were gone. You wouldn't have been able to stop me then, and you won't be able to stop me now."

"I could always leave," he said. "Return in the morning when saner heads prevail."

"Do you truly wish to leave?"

His smile was her answer.

She grabbed his hand again and pulled him inside her sitting room, closing the door behind him.

"I love you. I love you." It was the only thing

she could think of to say and the perfect explanation for everything.

He pulled her forward, wrapping his arms around her as she rested her cheek against his chest. His heart was beating as fast as hers. His breath was coming as rapidly.

So many things had come between them. Now nothing would.

She stepped back, pushing his coat off his shoulders before folding it carefully and laying it across the back of the sitting room sofa.

He was here. He was real.

She placed her hands flat on his chest, feeling the contours of his body, marveling at it, as well as the heat beneath his shirt.

Part of her wanted to rush through this act of giving herself to him, but another wiser part dictated that she slow her movements, make note of everything that happened, to make this night as momentous as possible.

As a girl she had watched him mature from a boy to a man. Yet the past five years had brought even more changes. His shoulders were broader. The way he carried himself was different.

One by one, she began to unfasten the buttons of his shirt. He didn't say anything, trapped in silence. As if they were in a church, and even one word would be sacrilegious to this moment.

Her smile began deep inside. Or in her heart, where she'd always loved him.

She parted the shirt, her hands burrowing beneath the material to touch his bare skin. She kissed his chest, softly, sweetly, still smiling. Her tongue darted out and touched his nipple,

and that was all it took for him to pull her tight against him. She thought her feet were dangling in the air, but she didn't care.

Excitement raced through her, sparked by desire. She'd only felt that with Gordon. When she'd been a girl, a kiss had been enough. Now she needed more.

Chapter Forty-Two

She kissed his cheek, then the corner of his mouth. "Come to my bed, my darling Gordon. Please."

Suddenly, she was in midair, grabbing onto his shoulders for balance as he lifted her.

"Gordon!" Her laughter rang through the sitting room as he headed for her bed.

A moment later, she was bouncing in the middle of the mattress with Gordon looming over her, his grin matching her smile.

"Well, it's where you wanted to be."

She grabbed his shirt and pulled him to her. "You're talking too much."

Not a thought passed through her mind when he kissed her, only sensation. Excitement pooled in the bottom of her stomach, raced through her body as the kiss ended and he began to nuzzle her throat. One by one, he unfastened the buttons of her dress, exposing her bare skin before anointing each spot with a kiss.

She'd waited for this moment for years and years. She was thirteen when she realized that what she felt for Gordon was special, fifteen when she kissed him for the first time, eighteen when her thoughts turned to seduction.

They were both wearing too many clothes, and for the next several moments they were engaged in unfastening, opening, and hurriedly removing the garments that were in their way.

Finally, finally, they were skin to skin.

This was Gordon. She felt no shame or even embarrassment to be naked in front of him. She'd seen his chest before, but she spent a great deal of time now kissing her way from one side to the other, making certain that he hadn't changed in any way.

He did the same, spending delightful moments on her nipples and smiling when she moaned.

She felt strangely buoyant, almost as if there was air inside her, lifting her. Her fingertips and toes tingled, even as a sensation deepened in her core. She knew what it was; she'd felt desire whenever they'd begun kissing or his hand brushed against her breasts.

His hands explored her everywhere, but not in silence. He amused her with his comments, and more than once nearly brought her to tears.

"I've always thought your legs were beautiful. I'm glad to see I was right."

"I might've been knock-kneed. Would you have loved me then?"

He raised up over her and pretended to consider the matter. "Very knock-kneed?"

"Very."

He bent and kissed her mouth lightly. "I think it would probably be better than being pigeon-toed."

"While you're absolutely perfect." Her hands slid down his back to grip his buttocks. "Even there."

He grinned back at her.

"I have to admit that I think your breasts are magnificent." He bent and kissed one, then the other. "You have very demanding nipples, however. See how they're standing erect?"

"Demanding?"

He nodded. "Insisting on the touch of my lips and tongue."

He matched the action to his words, causing her to moan.

"Even your feet are beautiful."

"You've seen my feet before."

"Then I wasn't paying attention."

She put her hands on his shoulders and drew him down to her. "You're talking too much and not kissing enough."

"You always were bossy," he said.

Being with Gordon was the culmination of every dream she ever had, every thought, every occasion of wondering what loving him or making love might be like.

Her skin heated when he touched her, his fingertips stroking over her arms, legs, torso as if it was vitally necessary for him to learn everything about her.

She felt the same, exploring the whole of his magnificent body from his shoulders to his muscled legs. A moment later, she straddled him, bending down to kiss his chest.

"I saw you once, washing yourself at the river. I think it was the first time I realized how beautiful you were and how much I wanted you."

"Men aren't beautiful."

"You are."

"How old were you?"

How foolish of him to expect her to be able to speak, especially when his fingers were exploring her. He'd never touched her there before, but it was wondrous.

A moment later, she finally managed to say the words. "I think I was thirteen."

"Very precocious, then."

"Do you think so?"

"I do."

He bent his legs, then pushed her gently back onto his thighs. Now she was even more at the mercy of his fingers.

"Gordon."

"Am I hurting you?"

"No."

"I'm glad. It doesn't feel like I'm hurting you. You seem to like it."

She could only nod.

He was driving her mad, especially when he pulled her forward so that he could suck on her nipples.

A few moments later, he rolled to the side, placing her on her back. When he rose over her, she looked up at him, adrift in need.

"Gordon. My love."

EVERY SINGLE ONE of his dreams was coming true. Just holding Jennifer had been something forbidden to him for the past several weeks. Now it was as if Fate, Providence, or even God was smiling down on them.

She epitomized everything he wanted: love,

family, belonging, all those things that had been taken from him by an act of greed.

His fingers skimmed over her skin reverently. He wanted to know her everywhere, all those places that had been hidden from him. Those spots that he had dreamed about as a boy and fantasized over as a man. He placed his palm flat on her stomach, splaying his fingers.

He wanted everyone to know, just from looking in her eyes, that they belonged together. He wanted the world to understand that he was not complete without Jennifer, and that she felt the same about him.

He kissed the tip of her nose, smiling as he did so. He had flicked his finger at her nose once, and she had responded by balling up her fist and striking him on the chin.

They'd stared at each other in surprise, then began to laugh.

Now her lips curved in a smile as she looked up at him, then linked her fingers together behind his neck.

"This is what we should have done all those years ago."

"Then I really would have been drummed out of Adaire Hall. Your reputation would have been shredded."

"It would have been worth it, Gordon."

He heard the solemnity in her voice and knew that she would have been willing to give herself to him, regardless of what might have happened. Yet he wouldn't have done that to her.

He bent his head and kissed her, need thrumming through him.

She was his. No one else would ever be able to separate them. They would always be together.

Her mouth opened below his, her soft moan encouraging him to deepen the kiss. His hands speared through her hair, dislodging pins and tossing them to the floor.

He had never felt as he did right now, invincible, ready to face the world to protect her. He would do everything in his power to shield her from hurt or disappointment and create a perfect world for her.

He entered her slowly, giving her time to get used to him. Her quick intake of breath alerted him. He would have retreated had her hands not gripped his hips.

"No," she said. "Don't leave me. It doesn't hurt."

He stayed where he was for a moment, balanced on his forearms.

Her hands trailed up and down his sides, and then his back, as if she were trying to memorize him.

She didn't speak, but the upward thrust of her hips was encouragement for him to move. He slowly withdrew, then entered her again. She sighed her approval.

"Jennifer." Her name was an aphrodisiac. The soft stroke of her fingers where they joined pushed him even closer to completion.

He bent and kissed her again, lost in the maelstrom of sensation. Her breasts were so soft and round, tempting to kiss. He tongued one nipple, then another, doing it again when she loudly sighed.

He wanted her to remember this night for more than simply losing her virginity. He wanted to bring her pleasure, make her soar with him, make her scream her release.

He pulled back, out of her, and when she gripped his hips and would have demanded that he enter her again, he shook his head, bent and trailed a path from between her breasts down to her navel.

Her hands gripped his shoulders, trailed through his hair as he bent lower, licking his way.

He lifted her up to meet his mouth, hearing her indrawn gasp of surprise.

He took his time, slow and deliberate, teasing her. Her hands were now gripping his hair, her hips arching upward to meet his mouth.

He loved everything about her, from her response to the silky softness of her skin. This was the woman he would make love to for the rest of his life. Tonight would begin their lives together, and he wanted her to remember it just that way.

She was gasping now, saying his name.

When she exploded beneath him, he kissed his way back up her body, leaving tender kisses on her nipples.

Only then did he enter her again, feeling the rhythmic shudders still going through her.

He wanted to last, but as she gripped him, he realized that that was a fool's errand. He bent to kiss her breasts again, tongued one nipple after another, his hands at her back, gripping her shoulders. He pulled himself deeply into her as

she raised her hips again, her heels digging into the mattress.

She met him thrust for thrust, encouraging him with her soft cries of pleasure. His vision grayed and the room fell away. There was only Jennifer, his lodestone, his anchor, and his love.

Chapter Forty-Three

The moment she arrived home, Ellen was waylaid by Davis.

"We have had a caller, Mrs. Thornton. A Mr. Gordon McDonnell. However, I am currently unable to ascertain the whereabouts of this visitor."

Ellen bit back a sigh. Davis was the most obsequious majordomo in London. However, he was also the most starched. He had appointed himself guardian of her morals and those of her friends. More than once, she knew that she'd sorely disappointed him. She'd been left with no doubt of his disapproval, evident in the twitch of his nose and the stiffness of his bearing.

No one was more proper than Davis. No one.

She refrained from telling him that it was truly none of his business where Gordon was at the moment. Davis wouldn't see it that way. Her house was his domain and he ruled it well.

"I don't think we need to worry about it, Davis," she said. "I'm certain that all is well."

No doubt she should have been shocked or dismayed, but she was human. A trait that she wasn't entirely certain that Davis shared. Strangely enough, he and Abigail disliked each

other heartily. She would have thought, with both possessing such dour personalities, that they would be well suited for each other.

She knew exactly where Gordon was. And Jennifer, for that matter. She had no intention of disturbing either of them. In the morning was time enough to feign outrage. For now, the two of them deserved a little happiness after what they'd gone through.

JENNIFER RESTED HER head on Gordon's shoulder as he put his arm around her. She curled against him, her hand on his chest. His heart still beat thunderously. Held there within the shelter of his arms, she felt safe, loved, and cherished.

She wanted to smile and wondered if that was a normal reaction to lovemaking. She hadn't felt as much discomfort as she'd expected. Perhaps that came from climbing trees and hills or racing through the strath.

Or perhaps it was simply being with Gordon. He'd made everything magical and beautiful, a memory she'd never forget.

"I'm yours," she said. "Completely. And you're mine." She smoothed her hand over his chest, claiming him with the action.

"I always have been."

She looked at his face, his beautiful, beloved face. It had been in her mind ever since she was a little girl. Gordon had always been her North Star—and now? Now he was her love, her lover.

No one else would ever be able to separate them.

She never wanted to sleep unless it was next to him. When she said as much, he rolled over and rose above her.

"You'll never have to. I promise you that, Jennifer."

That necessitated a few kisses.

He lay beside her again, and she cuddled next to him.

That required a kiss or two, followed by a bit of nuzzling. He had the most beautiful body. She'd seen some of it when he was working for Sean, but she was even more delighted to be able to touch, stroke, and fondle it now.

He did the same, kissing his way over her shoulder to her arm, then hesitating at the juncture of her elbow.

"Have I told you how beautiful you are?"

"I believe it's been about five years."

"Then I'm certainly due."

She laughed. "I've been taught that it's excessively poor manners to solicit compliments."

"What a pity. I might have said what a beautiful smile you have."

"Thank you."

"I've always loved the color of your eyes."

"I've recently noticed that they're Ellen's color. Isn't it odd that I never saw that before?" She pulled back. "Did you see a resemblance between us the night Harrison came home?"

"A resemblance?" He shook his head. "No."

"Ellen thought you did."

"I think we see what we want. I never thought you were anything but an Adaire. Speaking of

which, it's recently been brought to my attention that I'm the mirror image of the Earl of Burfield."

"Are you?"

"Evidently, that will go far to establish my claim."

"I wish I could remember him more. Everyone always told me what a wonderful man he was. I doubt, however, that he was half as wonderful as you."

That required yet another kiss.

Loving Gordon was even more wondrous the second time.

Pleasure hit her like an explosion, tendrils of sensation skittering across her flesh. Deep in the core of her, where they were joined, it felt as if she were melting from the heat.

She felt limp, exhausted, and happy from her head to her toes.

Being with Gordon was the culmination of every dream, fantasy, or imagined moment.

She now knew all those secrets that had eluded her as a girl. She felt as if she'd been allowed into a privileged membership of women. She'd never realized that there was something as wondrous as this, where your soul soared and a cavern expanded in your chest, filled with lust and love, delight and desire.

Her fingertips felt every inch of his body, glided over soft hills and deep indentations, the hardness of his cock and the muscles defining his arms and chest and legs. There was a scar on his knee from where he'd fallen out of a tree when he was ten. She kissed it softly, then trailed her lips down

to his ankle, smiling when he pulled his foot out of range.

"You're afraid I'm going to tickle you," she said, a smile in her voice.

"Right now, I'm defenseless. You could do almost anything to me and I would let you."

She raised up and straddled him, her knees on the bed. There was no false modesty between them. They knew each other too well to hide anything, even their vulnerabilities.

"I want you to know me," she said. "Completely. How much I like your kisses. What the touch of your fingers on my skin does to me. To do that, you'll need to make love to me a great many times."

His hands reached up and stroked her breasts with talented fingers. He drew out the touch, circling her hard nipples.

"I have always been partial to academic instruction," he said. "I'd be more than happy to consent. Only as an educational experiment, you understand."

"Perhaps we should compare notes after a thousand nights," she said, finding it difficult to talk when he was paying such assiduous attention to her breasts.

"Only nights? You can make love during the day, you know."

"Really? People do that?"

"Indeed they do."

"I should very much like to do that, then. As often as possible, please."

"I will do my best to accommodate you."

"You're very kind."

He rolled her over, changing places with her until he was on top. He smiled down into her face.

"I think we've talked too much, don't you?"

She only smiled in response.

Her core was hot and wet and welcoming. She guided him into her and kept him there, her hips rocking on the mattress, the pleasure so sharp that it came within a hairbreadth of pain.

Just when she thought she couldn't feel any more, he showed her another dimension to bliss. When it was over, when she was spent, she found the strength to raise her hand and place it on his back, needing that connection.

Love for him flooded through her.

"If I'd only known, I would never have let you stay away five whole years, Gordon."

He raised up on his forearms and kissed her lightly before dropping his head back on the pillow. A moment later, he sat up on the edge of the bed and started to gather up his clothing.

"What are you doing?"

"I'm getting dressed. I need to find Ellen."

She frowned at him. "Why?"

"The Earl and Countess are dead. As your mother, Ellen is the one I need to see." He glanced at her. "To ask for your hand in marriage."

She couldn't help but smile.

"Shouldn't you ask me, first?"

He came around to her side of the bed and startled her by kneeling there naked. He grabbed her hands, placing a kiss on the back of each one.

"Lady Jennifer, Jennifer, my dearest love, will you marry me?"

"Of course I will. Hopefully, soon. You won't make me wait too long, will you?"

His answer was to kiss her soundly. Long moments later, he released her and stood. She noted that his breathing was as hard as hers. She also noted that he was remarkably recuperative. However, he retrieved the rest of his clothes and dressed, with her watching the whole time.

"Just think," she said, "I'll be able to do this every day."

He hesitated in the act of buttoning his shirt. "Only if I get to reciprocate."

"Of course."

Once he was ready, he bent and kissed her. That took a few minutes and would have taken longer if Jennifer had her way. Unfortunately, Gordon was determined to do the right thing and left the room, intent on finding Ellen.

ELLEN REALIZED THAT people still had the ability to surprise her, no matter how old she got.

Who would have believed that Gordon McDonnell—misnamed, but he would probably keep it—would find his way to Davis, who would knock on her door and inform her that she was needed? She certainly hadn't expected it. Perhaps that was her first mistake. Her second was underestimating the man who stood waiting in her sitting room.

"Mrs. Thornton."

Anyone with half a brain knew that he'd spent a considerable amount of time in Jennifer's room. Should she say something to that effect?

He took the decision out of her hands with his next words.

"Since you are, essentially, Jennifer's only relative, I thought it would be best to consult you."

She didn't get a chance to ask on what, when he spoke again.

"I'm asking your permission to marry Jennifer, Mrs. Thornton."

She had the decided feeling that Gordon truly didn't give a flying farthing if she approved or not. That fact made her like him a little more. Evidently, she gravitated to iconoclasts, witness her union with Colin and her growing affection for this man.

"Well, I know you already love her," she said, sitting on the end of the sofa. "Now is the time to ascertain whether or not you can support her."

"Would you like my financial statements?"

She couldn't help but smile. "Would you send them over?"

"Yes, if it meant that you'd approve of the marriage. I don't want Jennifer upset."

"I've heard good things about you from a number of people, Gordon, and I have made it my business to ask. However, I know that no one is perfect. Tell me your worst failing."

One of his eyebrows arched upward, but he didn't protest the question.

"I'm impatient. Idiots bore me. I haven't the tact I need occasionally."

He truly did remind her of Colin. And Alex, as well. His father had been exactly the same way, only perhaps not as aware of his drawbacks.

More than once, she and Mary had commiserated about Alex. When he thought someone was being foolish, he didn't hesitate to express his opinion. More than one person had left a gathering at Adaire Hall because of Alex's words.

"Will you be a good husband?"

"Yes."

"Will you tolerate my presence in your life?"

Now he smiled. He was a handsome man, but smiling gave his face another dimension. Perhaps it was charm overlaid on top of his good looks.

"I shall attempt to tolerate it, Mrs. Thornton."

"I think, in light of what's happened, that you should begin to call me Ellen, don't you?"

"Thank you, Ellen."

"There's only one thing that concerns me, Gordon. Although I visit London periodically, I prefer my home in Edinburgh. I would be remiss if I didn't urge you to return to Scotland."

"I completely agree, Ellen."

They smiled at each other.

"Good, now that's settled, go home before you scandalize Davis even further. Come back later today and we'll plan a wedding."

She watched him leave the room, feeling a warmth that came solely from happiness. Although she was not given to addressing Colin's ghost, she did so now, looking up at the ceiling as if he were floating in the corner.

"You would like him, my love. He's very like you. But Jennifer is woman enough for him. Just as I was in your case."

In her mind, he laughed in agreement.

Chapter Forty-Four

Winter, 1870
Edinburgh, Scotland

*W*hen Gordon was told a guest was waiting for him in Mrs. Thornton's study, he assumed it was one of the innumerable people Ellen had invited to their wedding.

To his surprise, however, it was Richard McBain who sat there. He hadn't seen the man since that night he'd been banished from Adaire Hall.

"Have you come to announce some impediment to this marriage, McBain? I assure you there is none. Nor will I tolerate any interference in my life."

The older man sat back in the chair and studied him.

"They tell me you're quite a success, McDonnell. I have to admit that I'm surprised, but pleasantly so. Evidently, you take after your father."

Gordon held himself still, watching McBain. He didn't trust the man, based on his past deeds, but sometimes such an attitude was unwise.

"Alex was a good friend of mine. I always thought you were his by-blow," McBain said.

He stared at the other man. "You thought I was the earl's bastard?"

"Actually, I did."

"And that Betty was my mother?"

"As impossible as it is to consider," McBain said, smiling slightly. "Yes. I've seen stranger pairings. You look like your father. What else was I to think? The only reason more people didn't remark on the resemblance was because the countess had become a recluse after the fire."

Gordon kept silent.

"I thought the countess left you a bequest because you were the illegitimate son of her dead husband. Frankly, I saw the gesture as an indication of her kindness. The countess had a great heart."

Gordon remained silent.

"Evidently, you've taken that bequest and done something good with it."

"So, this visit isn't to dispute my wedding?"

"Indeed, it isn't."

"Why?"

McBain smiled again. "If you're asking what I think you are, I knew about Jennifer. As I said, I was a good friend of your father's. He shared that information with me."

To his surprise, McBain stood and extended his hand. "I wish you the very best of luck in your challenge to Harrison. I believe that you would be a better earl than he has been."

"How did you know about the challenge?" Gordon asked.

"Alex's friends are also mine. When I heard

the story, I knew that I'd been in the wrong five years ago. I wanted to come and tell you that."

"I'm not sorry you did what you did," Gordon said. "If you hadn't sent me away, I would never have made my fortune."

"Oh," McBain said, "I think you would've found a way to make your mark on the world, one way or another."

He watched as the man stood and headed for the door. Before McBain left the room, Gordon said, "Stay for the wedding. There's a party afterward."

McBain's look of surprise was justification enough for the impromptu invitation.

"IT'S UNSEEMLY," ABIGAIL said as she made the finishing touches to Ellen's hair. "They're marrying barely after the banns were read. The world will think they're trittle-trattle."

Abigail handed Ellen a mirror so that she could see the back of her hair. Once again, she'd performed miracles. Ellen decided that she looked quite nice, barely old enough to be the mother of the bride.

"They love each other, Abigail."

"Still, it doesn't look right. People are going to wonder at the haste."

She smiled absently, blocked out Abigail's comments, and moved to the window. The day was beautiful for a wedding. Cold, wintry, but with a clear blue sky.

Everyone knew not to marry in May, but January was also considered unfortunate. However,

both Gordon and Jennifer had refused to settle for a date further out than January. Therefore, she'd been pressed to arrange everything in four weeks. The only nagging detail—which was a formality only—was the marriage contract. That should have been done last night, but due to inclement weather, the legal parties couldn't get here. Therefore, the final details were taking place now.

Everything had been done to make the wedding perfect. She'd put on more staff to help the cook in the preparation of all the food. The maids had dusted and polished and cleared out the furniture from the ballroom, since it was rarely used except for storage. An orchestra had been hired for the reception. She'd purchased crates of whiskey and wine.

Ellen had freely admitted, both to Gordon and Jennifer, that she had a somewhat jaundiced view of religion ever since her parents had dived headfirst into it. Consequently, would they consider being married in the ballroom with the minister of the Free Church officiating? As she suspected, they didn't care, as long as the ceremony was legal and valid. She assured them it was, so the space was prepared for the saying of the vows—in less than an hour.

She and Jennifer had returned to Edinburgh within a week, accompanied by Gordon. In the intervening days he'd made arrangements to sell the Mayfair Club but keep the ownership of his three music halls. He was planning to branch out in Scotland. First, Edinburgh, and then Glasgow. To everyone's surprise, Mr. Campbell had ex-

pressed an interest in being Gordon's minority share partner. She wasn't certain if Gordon had agreed.

As soon as the wedding was over, Gordon and Jennifer would go off to live in the house he'd found for them. The two of them would be under one roof, unlike the arrangements that had been in effect for the past month. Gordon had been staying with Hamish and Lauren, to Jennifer's irritation.

Ellen had gone to some considerable expense decorating her home for the occasion, not to mention inviting everyone in Edinburgh. Or nearly everyone. Gordon's Scottish advocates were here as well as his London solicitor, not to mention a goodly number of his London employees.

There were only two notable exceptions to the guest list. Maggie hadn't been invited. Nor had Harrison.

When Abigail began to complain again, Ellen looked at her. "Thank you, Abigail. I won't need you anymore. Perhaps you can go and see if you could assist the housekeeper with any tasks."

Abigail frowned at her, which was a clear indication that she didn't want to be banished. Either that, or she didn't want to assist the housekeeper in any way. That was another difficult relationship for Abigail.

In a few moments, Ellen would go and help Jennifer don her wedding dress.

Right at the moment, however, she wanted to spend a few moments thinking of Mary. She would forever be grateful to the Countess of Burfield for her love, kindness, and generosity.

If there was such a thing as angels, then Mary Adaire was one. Perhaps she would be a witness to this wedding and the happiness of her son and Ellen's daughter.

JENNIFER STARED AT Gordon, unable to speak.

"You can't be serious," she finally said.

"I've never been more serious, Jennifer."

He was fully dressed for the ceremony, in a kilt and formal jacket. He'd never looked more handsome.

She, on the other hand, was only wearing a wrapper. She'd been waiting for Ellen to help her with the French confection she would wear for the ceremony when Gordon had knocked on the door to her sitting room.

"You can't do that, Gordon. I won't let you."

He'd delivered the most astounding news. How could she possibly allow him to do what he'd suggested?

She sat on the ottoman in front of her reading chair. He stood in front of her, a half smile on his face.

They both turned when the door opened to reveal Ellen.

"Is it a bit late for me to comment about the shocking nature of your undress, Jennifer? You're not married yet."

"I doubt I shall be," Jennifer said, frowning up at Gordon. "You'll never believe what he's done, Ellen. He's giving up his claim to the earldom. He's just going to hand it over to Harrison."

"Whatever do you mean?" Ellen asked.

"He's no longer going to contest the earldom."

Jennifer looked up at Gordon again. "It's your family, Gordon. Your heritage."

"With you at my side, Jennifer, I can start my own heritage."

"I can't let you do it."

Ellen glanced at Gordon. "Why are you giving up your claim?"

"The moment we're married, people will speculate as to Jennifer's relationship to me. They'll either think she's my sister or they'll figure out the truth."

"Then we simply won't marry," Jennifer said.

He folded his arms and stared at her. "That's not an acceptable alternative."

She continued to shake her head. "I can't let you do this. Not for me. I don't care what people say about me, Gordon."

"Gordon's right, of course," Ellen said. "People enjoy a scandalous story, and this is one that only comes along once in a lifetime. The girl who was brought up as Lady Jennifer and the man who would be earl. They won't be shy about the names they'll call you: *merry-begotten*, for conceived out of wedlock. Or being a *cludfawer*, an illegitimate child."

"I don't mind the world knowing I'm illegitimate."

Ellen frowned at her. "I do. Why do you think I went to such an effort to ensure that Mary and Alex raised you? It wasn't only for myself, but for you. There's a stigma attached to being illegitimate, Jennifer, even as an adult. To Gordon, it's simply not worth it. I think being willing to give up the title is a magnanimous gift. A gift of love."

"I can't let you do it," Jennifer said, looking at Gordon. "It's too much."

Ellen smiled at both of them. "Love is never too much, my darling child. Whatever sacrifice it requires, whatever you give up, it's never too much. Besides, Gordon isn't giving up his heritage, Jennifer. He's simply choosing you."

When Jennifer looked at her, Ellen continued. "Don't you see? He wasn't raised to be an Adaire. The heritage, the legacy doesn't mean as much to him as you do."

Ellen glanced at Gordon. "From what I've come to know of you, you thought about this decision at great length."

"I have," he said. "The title's not as important as Jennifer."

"But you're an Adaire. The world should see you as one," Jennifer said.

"I'm myself. That counts as more."

Ellen walked up to Gordon and kissed him on the cheek. "Indeed, it does. The only bad thing about your decision is allowing Harrison to remain the Earl of Burfield. He doesn't deserve the title. Nor will he do it any good."

"He's out of money," Gordon said. "He owes me a fortune. I've given his markers to Jennifer as a wedding gift. Perhaps she can use them as leverage over his behavior."

Ellen laughed. "You're very like your father, you know. Title or not."

Jennifer looked up at Gordon. "You're going to do this, aren't you?"

"Yes."

She sighed. A moment later, she stood and

walked to the window. The carriages were still arriving, hundreds of people invited to witness their marriage.

A surprise guest was Mrs. Farmer, who looked splendid in her finery. Lauren and her father had already arrived, but Ellen had deliberately not invited Harrison. No one had heard from him in weeks. Mrs. Thompson was here from Adaire Hall, along with a great many of the staff. She was going to have to be honest with them about Adaire Hall's finances if Harrison didn't face his responsibilities. Perhaps they would like to move to Edinburgh and come to work for Gordon and her.

How could she allow him to give up so much for her? The extent of Gordon's sacrifice humbled her.

He's making his own heritage. The thought was so much like Gordon. Very well, together they would create a future for themselves. She'd be beside him every step of the way.

All that truly mattered was that they were free to love each other.

She turned, finally, looking at Gordon. "I love you," she said. "I'd do anything for you."

"I know that," Gordon said. "I feel the same."

"How can I possibly equal what you've done?"

"It isn't a race, Jennifer. It's our life. Our life together."

Gordon pulled Jennifer into his embrace. A second later they were kissing.

Ellen sighed. "Do you want to get married? Today?"

They separated and looked at her.

"Go and let her get dressed," Ellen said. "You'll have plenty of time together as soon as you're married."

"Don't take too long," Gordon said, smiling. "I've been waiting too many years as it is."

That necessitated another kiss.

Author's Notes

The Alhambra was a famous music hall in Victorian London.

An attorney in Scotland is called an advocate.

Queen Victoria was administered chloroform during the birth of her eighth child, Prince Leopold, in April 1853 by Dr. James Snow. After the birth, Dr. Snow became the darling of the elite of London.

It was considered bad luck to give compliments to a newborn or to put him in a new cradle. Similarly, it was considered bad luck to have water touch his palms for fear that it would affect his ability to acquire worldly goods later in life.

It was customary to put a bit of silver in a new baby's cradle. Women were encouraged to stay in bed for at least two weeks following childbirth, at least those who didn't have to work for a living. A midwife was normally called a *howdie*, or a handy woman. A doctor was rarely called in the case of a birth.

In Scotland, it was considered a mark of disrespect if a funeral took place before a set number of days elapsed. The timing differed depending on where you lived in Scotland, but it varied anywhere from three to nine days. Most of the funerals in this time period were held at home and then the body taken to be buried. Women did not go to the churchyard for the burials.

The body was placed in the best room in the house/cottage and wrapped in a winding cloth. Women often made their own winding cloths. It was common for a married woman to make her husband's winding cloth as well. They were stored in chests with the best linen for when they were eventually needed.

Adaire Hall was modeled after several great houses of Scotland.

Scottish terms:
Trittle-trattle - trash
Cludfawer - an illegitimate child
Merry-begotten - illegitimate
Dreich - gray, rainy, drizzling weather

And don't miss the next stunning romance
in Karen Ranney's Highland Fling series

Her Highland Hero

On sale June 2020
from Avon Books